DICKENS STUDIES ANNUAL
Essays on Victorian Fiction

DICKENS STUDIES ANNUAL

Essays on Victorian Fiction

DICKENS STUDIES ANNUAL

Essays on Victorian Fiction

VOLUME
36

Edited by
Stanley Friedman, Edward Guiliano,
Anne Humpherys, and Michael Timko

AMS PRESS
New York

Dickens Studies Annual: Essays on Victorian Fiction is published in cooperation with Queens College and The Graduate Center, CUNY.

International Standard Book Number
Series: 0-404-18520-7
Vol. 36: 0-404-18936-9

Dickens Studies Annual: Essays on Victorian Fiction welcomes essay- and monograph-length contributions on Dickens and other Victorian novelists and on the history of aesthetics of Victorian fiction. All manuscripts should be double-spaced and should follow the documentation format described in the most recent *MLA Style Manual*. The author's name should appear only on a cover-page, not elsewhere in the essay. An editorial decision can usually be reached more quickly if two copies of the article are submitted, since outside readers are asked to evaluate each submission. If a manuscript is accepted for publication, the author will be asked to provide a 100- to 200-word abstract and also a disk containing the final version of the essay; providing an e-mail address facilitates communication. The preferred editions for citations from Dickens's works are the Clarendon and the Norton Critical when available, otherwise the Oxford Illustrated or the Penguin.

Please send submissions to The Editors, *Dickens Studies Annual*, Ph.D. Program in English, The Graduate Center, CUNY, 365 Fifth Avenue, New York, NY 10016–4309. Please send inquiries concerning subscriptions and/or the availability of earlier volumes to AMS Press, Inc., Brooklyn Navy Yard—Unit #221, 63 Flushing Ave., Building 292, Suite 417, Brooklyn, NY 11205–1005.

Manufactured in the United States of America

All AMS books are printed on acid-free paper that meets the guidelines for performance and durability of the Committee on Production Guidelines for Book Longevity of the Council on Library Resources.

Contents

Illustrations

Preface

Since this is an extra issue, it does not include a survey of a recent year's work in Dickens studies. We are pleased, however, to offer a wide range of essays employing distinctive approaches to writings by Dickens and two major contemporaries.

In addition, a special section in this volume, "Dickens in Latin America: Perspectives from Montevideo," presents an introduction and nine essays developed from some of the papers offered at a Dickens conference in Uruguay from June 23–25, 2003, an event attended by one of the editors of *Dickens Studies Annual,* Professor Michael Timko, whose participation was sponsored by the United States Embassy to Uruguay. We are especially in debted to Professor Beatriz Vegh for gathering these nine articles and for preparing the introduction. In a new century when the word "globalization" seems ubiquitous, these papers remind us that Dickens has long been an international author, and they provide stimulation and insight by offering unusual perspectives of some readers in "Southern South America." (Because Professor Vegh's introduction briefly describes each of the nine articles, abstracts are not provided for the other individual essays.)

We extend thanks to the authors of essays submitted to us, and we also thank our many outside reviewers, readers who generously provide informed, detailed responses that are extremely valuable to the editors and also to the contributors.

For valuable practical help, we express our appreciation to the following administrators: President William P. Kelly; Acting Provost Linda N. Edwards; Ph. D. Program in English Executive Officer Steven F. Kruger; Marilyn Weber, Assistant Program Officer, Ph. D. Program in English; and Meghan Mehta, Assistant Program Officer, Ph. D. Program in English, all of The Graduate Center, CUNY; and President James L. Muyskens; Dean of Arts and Humanities Tamara S. Evans; and Department of English Chair Nancy R. Comley, all of Queens College, CUNY.

We thank, too, Professor John O. Jordan, Director of The Dickens Project at the University of California, Santa Cruz; JoAnna Rottke, Project Coordinator for The Dickens Project; and Jon Michael Varese, the Project's Research Assistant and Web Administrator, for placing on the Project's website the tables of contents for volumes 1–27 of *DSA*, as well as abstracts for subsequent volumes. (These materials are included in the Project's Dickens Electronic Archive; the Dickens Project can be reached at http://humwww.ucsc.edu/dickens/index.html).

We are grateful to Gabriel Hornstein, President of AMS Press, for his consistent interest and generous help; to Jack Hopper, who, although retired as Editor-in-Chief at AMS Press, continues to provide resourceful and intelligent assistance to *DSA*; and to Ashlie K. Sponenberg, now Editor-in-Chief at AMS Press, who has cheerfully given prompt, effective support. Finally, we take great pleasure in thanking our editorial assistant for this volume, Marta Bladek, for her skill and reliability.

—The Editors

Notes on Contributors

PHILIP V. ALLINGHAM is currently Associate Professor, Faculty of Education, Lakehead University, Thunder Bay, Ontario, Canada. Readers of such publications as *The Dickensian, Dickens Quarterly,* and *The Hardy Review* will be aware of his work on Victorian illustration. He is a Contributing Editor to George Landow's Victorian Web (http://www.victorianweb.org). In Vol. 33 of *Dickens Studies Annual* he complemented Michael Steig's groundbreaking work on Dickens and Phiz with a thorough discussion of the plates for their last collaboration, *A Tale of Two Cities.*

JEAN-PHILIPPE BARNABÉ is Professor of Latin American Literature in the Spanish Department of the University of Picardie in France. Recently, he has worked in the field of textual genetics and critical editions. His most recent publications include articles on Rio de la Plate literary authors such as Felisberto Hernández and Jorge Luis Borges. He is currently working on a new edition of W. H. Hudson's *The Purple Land.*

MIGUEL ANGEL BATTEGAZZORE graduated from the National School of Fine Arts in Montevideo and is now Professor of History of Art at the Faculty of Humanities, University of the Republic, Montevideo, Uruguay. A member of the National Commission of Plastic Arts, he has exhibited his work (painting, drawing, graphic arts) individually and collectively in his country and in other nations all over the world. In 2000 the Ministry of Education and Culture of Uruguay awarded his book *Joaquin Torres Garcia. La trama y los signos* the National Literature Prize as the best art essay that year.

ROSEMARY COLEMAN received her Ph.D. in English Literature from Rice University. She is currently working on an article on the multiple endings of *Dombey and Son.*

GARY COLLEDGE was a postgraduate student, St. Mary's College, Divinity at the University of St. Andrews, Scotland, at the time of writing this article. Prior to this, he has published a few brief articles in the *New Interpreter's Dictionary of the Bible.* He hopes to write further on Dickens and Christianity, and on the impact of nineteenth-century Anglicanism in England on conservative evangelicalism in twentieth-century America.

LINDSEY CORDERY is Assistant Professor of English Cultural Studies in the School of Translation and Assistant Professor of English Literature at the Faculty of Humanities, University of the Republic, Montevideo, Uruguay. She is also Head of Literature, Anglo-Uruguayan Cultural Institute, Montevideo, Uruguay.

MARÍA CRISTINA DALMAGRO is Assistant Professor of Spanish at the National University of Córdoba in Argentina. She has published several articles on Latin American writers as well as on other literary and linguistic issues in academic journals. She is currently writing her doctoral thesis on Armonia Somers.

VERÓNICA D'AURIA is a B.A. graduate in Classical Philology from the Faculty of Humanities, University of the Republic, Montevideo, Uruguay, and has done postgraduate work in Shakespeare Studies at The Shakespeare Institute, Stratford-on-Avon, of the University of Birmingham. Her publications include two books of narrative and poetry as well as a series of interviews entitled *Oblique Conversations between Culture and Power*.

LETICIA EYHERAGARAY is a recent B.A. graduate from the School of Humanities, University of the Republic, Montevideo, Uruguay. She has done research on Uruguayan theater and is currently working as a lecturer in Spanish at the University of St. Andrews in Scotland.

MICHAEL J. FLYNN is a Ph.D. candidate at Washington University in St. Louis. He is currently finishing work on his dissertation, which examines the strained relationship of Thackeray and Dickens and considers issues of intertextuality, fictional form, and the dignity of literature in early Victorian England. Another part of this study has previously appeared in *Notes and Queries*.

MICHAL PELED GINSBURG is a Professor of French and Comparative Literature at Northwestern University. She is a specialist in the nineteenth-century novel (primarily British and French). Her publications include *Economies of Change: Form and Transformation in the Nineteenth-Century Novel* (Stanford UP, 1996) and essays published in *Dickens Studies Annual, Novel,* and *ELH*. She has recently published an essay on "Dickens and the Scene of Recognition" in *Partial Answers,* 3 (2005).

SHARI HODGES HOLT is an Instructor of English at the University of Mississippi and has authored papers on Gothic fiction and film adaptations of literature. Her present research examines cinematic adaptations of Dickens's novels as critical interpretations of their literary originals that demonstrate how Dickens is "read" under varying cultural and historical circumstances. She is also co-authoring a critical study of the works of nineteenth-century novelist Ouida (Marie Louise Rame).

TOMÁS DE MATTOS, a Uruguayan lawyer and writer of fiction, lives in Tacuarembó, a small town near the Brazilian border, and has published three short story collections (*Sons and Dogs* [1975], *Muddy Traps* [1983], *The Big Drought* [1984]); four novels (*Bernabé, Bernabé!* [1988], *The Frigate of the Masks* [a retelling of Melville's *Benito Cereno*: 1996], *In the Shade of the Paradise Tree* [2000], *The Gate of Mercy* [2003]); and two novellas ("God Forbid!" [2001], "Baghdad Sky" [2001]).

JOHN R. REED is Distinguished Professor of English at Wayne State University in Detroit, Michigan. He has published widely on nineteenth- and twentieth-century British literature. His most recent book is *Dickens and Thackeray: Punishment and Forgiveness*. He is currently at work on two book-length projects, the first a study of the armed forces in British literature of the nineteenth century, the second a study of Dickens in relation to realism.

NATALIE SCHROEDER is an Associate Professor of English at the University of Mississippi. She has had a number of articles published on Roche, Dickens, Collins, Braddon, and Ouida. Her Broadview edition of Ouida's *Moths* was published August 2005. She is currently completing a manuscript on Ouida's fiction and editing an edition of Regina Maria Roche's *Clermont* for Valancourt Books.

ALICIA TORRES, who holds an M.A. in Latin American Literature from the University of the Republic, Montevideo, Uruguay, works as a literary researcher for the weekly *Brecha* in Montevideo and is Assistant Professor of Spanish Literature at the University of the Republic. Her publications include mainly articles on Latin American writers.

BEATRIZ VEGH is a Ph.D. graduate in General and Comparative Literature from the University of Paris III, Sorbonne. She is Professor of Modern Literatures at the University of the Republic, Montevideo, Uruguay, and has published articles on Dickens in relation to the illustrations for a 1921 edition of *Hard Times* by the artist Rafael Barradas and on Dickens in relation to the Argentine writer D. F. Sarmiento, both in *Dickens Quarterly*.

DAVID M. WILKES, an English professor and the Dean of Arts and Humanities at Mount Vernon Nazarene University, has published articles in *Dickens*

Studies Annual and *Dickens Quarterly*. He is currently finishing a novel on the New England fishing industry.

JOLENE ZIGAROVICH is a Visiting Lecturer at Scripps College, finishing work on the book project *Missing Bodies and Embodied Narratives: The Implications of Death and Absence in the Victorian Novel,* of which this essay forms a part. She has also published in *Studies in the Novel.*

The Gin Epidemic: Gin Distribution as a Means of Control and Profit in Dickens's Early Nonfiction and *Oliver Twist*

Natalie Schroeder and Shari Hodges Holt

Although a complex variety of factors promoted a culture of alcohol consumption in pre-industrial England, the dramatic increase in gin consumption among England's poor during the Industrial Age was strongly associated with industrial class conflicts. Middle-class attempts to regulate working-class gin consumption suggested that control of gin consumption correlated with control of a vastly productive proletariat. Charles Dickens portrayed the "gin epidemic" as resulting from a consumerist ideology of class exploitation that perpetuated working-class poverty, ignorance, and crime. Beginning with Dickens's assessment of works by William Hogarth and George Cruikshank, this essay explores references to the gin epidemic in Dickens's personal correspondence, early journalism, and Oliver Twist, *a novel in which characters consume gin to deaden poverty's horrors, distribute gin to manipulate others for personal profit, and rely on gin to facilitate business transactions in human commodities. Dickens uses gin distribution throughout the novel to unite criminal enterprise with commercial exploitation of individuals, thereby implying the inherently criminal nature of early capitalism's materialistic ethic. Gin abuse in Dickens's early works thus emblemizes a phenomenon central to Dickens's critique of Victorian bourgeois ideology—the individual's commodification and control by a consumer culture that valued human life primarily in materialistic and utilitarian terms.*

Class Conflict and the "Gin Epidemic"

Although a complex variety of factors promoted a culture of alcohol consumption in pre-industrial England, the gin epidemic of the eighteenth and nineteenth centuries was strongly associated with the class conflicts accompanying the Industrial Revolution. Charles Dickens's criticism of nineteenth-century temperance movements and his use of gin distribution as a metaphor for social control in novels such as *Oliver Twist* suggest that he viewed the "general epidemic" of gin consumption among England's poor (*Sketches* 182; ch. 22) as a symbol of a greater national disease—the abuse of the impoverished working classes by an increasingly callous, materialistic society.[1]

In their study of drinking in Dickens's novels, Edward Hewett and W. F. Axton note that the industrialization of England in the eighteenth and nineteenth centuries was accompanied by the onset of mass alcoholism among the working classes, particularly in the consumption of gin (89). The "gin epidemic" or "gin craze" arose in England between 1720 and 1770 when overproduction of corn led to the distillation of gin in great quantities (Nicholls 127). According to Jessica Warner, when distilled spirits such as gin became cheap and easily obtainable, they "very quickly emerged as the drug of choice among the nation's urban poor" (*Craze* 2). James C. Nicholls agrees and states that "gin was not simply about drunkenness; it was about the drunkenness of the lower classes. The anxieties expressed over this new drunkenness were not just about health or self control . . . . The consumers of this cheap, potent and often deadly drink were, by and large, the poor; and the drunken poor were the dangerous poor, the violent poor, and the economically useless poor" (129).

As the newly developing urban proletariat turned to this inexpensive and readily available panacea for the working-class miseries of the Industrial Revolution, gin consumption furthered the dehumanizing commodification of the individual worker by bourgeois ideology. Hewett and Axton point out that "gin-shops often served as hiring-halls, pay-offices, and loan-shops" where "unscrupulous employers and publicans conspired to enforce a kind of wage-slavery based on gin" (92). Landowners who grew the grain for domestic distilleries also encouraged the "gin epidemic" among poor and working-class consumers. Similarly, Parliament welcomed gin consumption as a valuable revenue source, while introducing legislation for its control based on "the belief that the excesses of the working poor posed a particular threat to the nation, threatening to deprive it of both workers and soldiers" (Warner, "Mother Gin").[2]

In her study of the eight "gin acts" Parliament passed between 1729 and 1751 (*Craze* 221), Warner has shown that such legislation was motivated by a desire to obtain revenue from working-class excesses in times of war and to control such excesses in times of peace to secure a compliant working populace (*Craze* 4–5). She attests that the agenda behind the gin laws was "unabashedly elitist, taking its cue from an essentially hierarchical vision of the social order in which rich and poor were governed by two very different sets of rules" (*Craze* 11).

Brian Harrison identifies a similar subtext in the nineteenth-century temperance movement, a primarily middle-class reform campaign which developed in response to the continuing predominance of drunkenness among the working classes. He points out that, while the temperance movement fostered social awareness across class lines and promoted a "*growth* of working-class consciousness" (366–67), it also functioned as a tool of bourgeois ideology that accentuated class divisions and reinforced middle-class respectability (356–57).[3] By discouraging working-class alcohol consumption (particularly gin consumption), the temperance movement attempted to encourage "respectable" behavior, curb working-class drunkenness, and address "the industrialist's increasing need for punctuality and regularity in his employees" (Harrison 62). But in attacking "the bonds between drink and every aspect of life" that had established drinking in pre-industrial England as a symbol of community between the classes, the nineteenth-century anti-spirits campaigns, like the eighteenth-century gin laws, signified the "impending fragmentation of traditional social relations" that accompanied England's transformation to a capitalist culture (Harrison 44). Such attempts to reshape working-class drinking habits to meet the needs of industrial society indicated the new consumerism dominating social relations and suggested that, in the perception of those who reaped the benefits of industrialization, control of gin consumption correlated with control of a vastly productive proletariat.

In the 1830s, in an attempt to reduce gin drinking, the legislature passed the Beerhouse Act, which removed taxes from beer. Gareth Cordery points out that to compete with the resulting increase in beer-selling establishments, gin-shops "went upmarket and turned themselves into so-called gin palaces" ("Public Houses" 1: 4), the most ornamental of the nineteenth-century taverns. Cordery states that these bars, with separate entrances and drinking rooms that "enabled the segregation of customers on the basis of wealth and social position," represented a form of social control linked to the rise of capitalism ("Public Houses" 1: 6). As the development of the new gin palaces demonstrated, the gin market of the early 1800s in England exemplified the commodification and control of the individual by a consumer culture that valued human life primarily in materialistic and utilitarian terms.

The "Gin Epidemic" in Dickens's Early Journalism, Correspondence,
and Short Works

Dickens interpreted working-class gin consumption in this manner throughout
his journalism and fiction of the 1830s. In the following passage from "Gin-
Shops," a piece from *Sketches by Boz* (1836), he vividly contrasts the squalor
of the Seven Dials slum with the lurid splendor of a typical "gin palace."

> The filthy and miserable appearance of [the slums] . . . can hardly be imag-
> ined . . . . Wretched houses with broken windows patched with rags and pa-
> per . . . filth everywhere . . . clothes drying and slops emptying, from the
> windows; . . men and women in every variety of scanty and dirty apparel,
> lounging, scolding, drinking, smoking, squabbling, fighting, and swearing.
>   You turn the corner. What a change! All is light and brilliancy. The hum of
> many voices issues from the splendid gin-shop . . . and the gay building with
> the fantastically-ornamented parapet, the illuminated clock, the plate-glass win-
> dows surrounded by stucco rosettes, and its profusion of gas-lights in richly-
> gilt burners, is perfectly dazzling when contrasted with the darkness and dirt
> we have just left. The interior is even gayer than the exterior. A bar of French-
> polished mahogany, elegantly carved, extends the whole width of the place,
> and there are two aisles of great casks, painted green and gold . . . and bearing
> such inscriptions as "Old Tom, 549"; "Young Tom, 360"; "Samson,
> 1421"—the figures agreeing, we presume, with "gallons," understood.
>
>   (184–85; ch. 22)

The contrast suggests that the gin palace served as a dazzling panacea for
poverty, one of the few places of entertainment for the working classes where
they could escape a miserable existence in a fantasy of finery and brilliance.
George Cruikshank's accompanying illustration for this passage emphasizes
the fanciful nature of this working-class retreat by depicting the festive scene
dominated by the palace lights, ornamental columns and ceiling, and the
oversized casks of gin that seem to offer the escape of perpetual intoxication
in their prominently displayed gallons (fig. 1). The scene's convivial nature
is enhanced by such images as a gentleman flirting with a barmaid in the
foreground and a man and woman drinking together in the corner. But a
crippled man and ragged child in the center ordering drinks at the bar suggest
a more disturbing correlation between poverty and gin consumption. Cordery
notes that the bar, a nineteenth-century addition to public-house architecture
that accentuated the mercenary rather than communal character of tavern
drinking by separating the drink-seller from the customers, was "a structure
central to making money, maintaining control and at the heart of a panoptical
public house in an age of capitalism" ("Public Houses" 1: 10). In Dickens's
and Cruikshank's portrayals, the striking contrast with the impoverished consumers, "cold, wretched-looking creatures, in the last stage of emaciation

Fig. 1. Cruikshank's illustration *The Gin Shop* from *Sketches by Boz*. Note how the scene's conviviality is undercut by the improverished customers, a cripple and a ragged child, in the center. *Source:* Charles Dickens. *Sketches by Boz.* London: Oxford UP, 1973. p. 184.

and disease'' (*Sketches* 186; ch. 22), separated by the bar from the portly, well-dressed publican, who surveys his clientele from an elevated station, effectively visualizes the mercenary class relations that perpetuated poverty and the gin epidemic.

Dickens's emphasis on the powerful allure of the gin shop suggests his attitude toward England's gin epidemic, as more directly expressed in a later passage from ''Gin-Shops'': ''Gin-drinking is a great vice in England, but wretchedness and dirt are a greater; and until you improve the homes of the poor, or persuade a half-famished wretch not to seek relief in . . . temporary oblivion . . . gin-shops will increase in number and splendor'' (*Sketches* 187; ch. 22).

Dickens further supported the notion of alcoholism as primarily a result rather than a cause of industrial poverty in his 1836 attack on the Sabbath Bills, legislation which proposed honoring the Sabbath by closing all work places on Sundays, the single holiday of the working-class week. The bill instituted heavy penalties for public assemblies (excluding church services), public drunkenness, or any form of work (''Sunday''). In his pamphlet ''Sunday Under Three Heads,'' Dickens admits that in some working-class English neighborhoods, ''drunkenness and profligacy in their utmost disgusting forms, exhibit in the open streets on Sunday, a sad and a degrading spectacle.''

Although not composed for Dickens's text, another of George Cruikshank's engravings, ''Low Sunday,'' which depicts a working-class crowd at the exterior of a gin palace on Sunday, effectively illustrates Dickens's description of such Sunday spectacles: ''Women . . . rendered hideous by habitual drunkenness—men reeling and staggering along—children in rags and filth—whole streets of squalid and miserable appearance, whose inhabitants are lounging in the public road, fighting, screaming, and swearing'' (''Sunday''). Cruikshank's illustration abounds in images of drunken brawling but likewise depicts impoverished vendors who instead of taking a holiday must take advantage of the Sunday crowds to sell their goods on the street (fig. 2).

Dickens claims that poverty and the government's indifference to the horrors of poverty are responsible for such scenes. While admitting that the poor ''spend in liquor, money with which they might purchase necessaries,'' he argues that ''even if they applied every farthing of their earnings in the best possible way, they would still be very—very poor'' and remain in barbarous living conditions that naturally encourage escape to the gin-shops as their ''only resource'' (''Sunday''). Dickens also attests that the Sabbath bills, by adding further restrictions to an already remarkably oppressive lifestyle, would incite resentment among the poor and actually promote private drunkenness by depriving the working classes of any form of recreation on their sole holiday. He proposes that instead of enacting Sunday Closing laws, the government should work to eliminate the root cause of the gin epidemic by

Fig. 2. George Cruikshank's *Low Sunday*. Cruikshank's engraving dramatically illustrates the spectacle of working-class drunkenness which Dickens addresses in his attack on the Sabbath Bills. *Source:* Edward Hewett, and W. F. Axton. *Convivial Dickens: The Drinks of Dickens and His Times.* Athens: Ohio UP, 1983. p. 92.

improving the urban proletariat's standard of living and providing alternative forms of recreation, arguing that "the labourers who now lounge away the day in idleness and intoxication" would no longer need the escape offered by gin ("Sunday").

Dickens saw the same mistaken philosophy motivating the teetotaling temperance societies of the 1830s and 1840s. When his friend and illustrator George Cruikshank joined the temperance movement in the late 1840s, Dickens came to see Cruikshank's extravagant advocacy of abstinence not only as a fanatical attitude that punished moderate and immoderate drinkers alike, but also as an example of extremist reform movements that diverted attention and vital resources from alleviating the fundamental social ills of poverty and ignorance (see Cordery, "Drink" 60–61). In 1847, when Cruikshank published his first great temperance propaganda piece *The Bottle*, a series of eight etchings depicting the destructive effects of alcoholism on a family, Dickens objected to the social criticism inherent in the work, writing in a letter to his friend and biographer John Forster, "The philosophy of the thing, as a great lesson, I think all wrong; because to be striking and original too, the drinking should have begun in sorrow, or poverty, or ignorance—the three things in which, in its awful aspect, it *does* begin" (*Letters* 5: 156).

8 DICKENS STUDIES ANNUAL

Fig. 3. The opening plate of Cruikshank's series *The Bottle* presents a comfortable working class family unknowingly on the verge of descent into ruin through the father's fondness for gin. *Source:* Robert L. Patten, Ed. *George Cruikshank: A Revaluation*. Princeton: Princeton UP, 1974. (no page number). Also found in Hilary and Mary Evans. *The Man Who Drew the Drunkard's Daughter: The Life and Art of George Cruikshank 1792–1878*. London: Frederick Muller, 1978. p. 128.

The opening etching of *The Bottle* depicts a family party in a working-class home that exhibits numerous signs of prosperity and comfort (fig. 3). The husband entices his wife to share a drink, but the bottle leads them to destitution in the remaining illustrations (e.g., see fig. 4). In *The Drunkard's Children*, Cruikshank's 1848 sequel to *The Bottle*, he depicts gin consumption as the direct and primary cause of poverty and crime, as the alcoholic's son becomes a thief who dies of alcohol-related illness aboard a prison ship, and his daughter becomes a prostitute whose "gin mad" state prompts her to commit suicide (caption to Plate 8 of *The Drunkard's Children*, qtd. in Evans 137). But this time Dickens responded publicly with a review of the work in *The Examiner* in which he expanded on his earlier complaint that the artist should have depicted gin consumption as a result of impoverished living conditions (Dickens, *Letters* 5: 156, n. 7). Dickens thus implied that temperance propaganda was dangerously misdirecting the impulse for social reform away from root causes.[4]

Fig. 4. A later plate from *the Bottle* series suggests the destitution Cruikshank attributed to alcohol abuse. The baby from the earlier plate of the series now lies dead from neglect encased in a coffin in the background. *Source:* Robert L. Patten, Ed. *George Cruikshank: A Revaluation*. Princeton: Princeton UP, 1974. (no page number). Also found in Hilary and Mary Evans. *The Man Who Drew the Drunkard's Daughter: The Life and Art of George Cruikshank 1792–1878*. London: Frederick Muller, 1978. p. 130

Gin Consumption in *Oliver Twist*

In his novels, Dickens likewise portrays alcoholism as a result rather than a source of working-class misery, which leads in many cases to crime. While Dickens typically uses convivial drinking to symbolize benevolent social relations, gin-drinking scenes in Dickens's works frequently involve the abuse of drinking's communal significance. The distribution of gin in Dickens's fiction often serves as an agent for mercenary manipulation of individuals, making gin consumption a metaphor for the materialistic social attitudes behind working-class ills.[5] The motif of "feeding" gin as a means of commodification and control of characters is particularly significant in *Oliver Twist* (1837–39), a novel awash in references to the popular working-class beverage. From the poorhouses to the criminal dens, characters throughout the novel imbibe gin as an escape from poverty and squalor, distribute gin as a means of manipulating others for personal profit, and rely on gin as a catalyst for business transactions dealing in human commodities.

In his "Preface" to *Oliver Twist*, Dickens writes that he wanted to show in the character of Oliver "the principle of Good surviving through every adverse circumstance" (33). He says that he

> had read of thieves by the score; .... But I had never met (except in HO-GARTH) with the miserable reality. It appeared to me that to draw a knot of such associates in crime as really did exist; to paint them in all their deformity, in all their wretchedness, in all the squalid reality of their lives; to show them as they really are, for ever skulking uneasily through the dirtiest paths of life, with the great black ghastly gallows closing up their prospect . . . would be a service to society.   (33–34)

William Hogarth, whose realistic depictions of criminals Dickens so admired, shared his friend Henry Fielding's belief that lower-class crime was exacerbated by gin drinking among the poor. To address this social problem, Hogarth created his famous prints, "Beer Street" and "Gin Lane," and made them affordable for the working-classes (figs. 5 and 6). He wanted to emphasize that on beer-street, "all is joyous and thriving. Industry and Jollity go hand in hand." In gin-lane, on the other hand, "idleness, poverty, misery, and distress, which drives even to madness and death, are the only objects to be seen; and not a house in tolerable condition but Pawnbrokers and Gin-shops" (Hogarth qtd. in Warner, *Craze* 195, 199). Nicholls points out that in "*Beer Street* and *Gin Lane* drink and drunkenness reflect both the utopian conception of the city as the convivial hub of social and commercial life, and the dystopian vision of it as the irrational site of swarming humanity at its most excessive and degraded" (134).

A passage accompanying "Gin Lane" in an early edition of Hogarth's complete works expostulates that poverty "is the usual attendant on gin-drinking, and . . . where this vice prevails, none are known to thrive, but such as feed upon the property of others. This abominable liquor [gin] is . . . found to waste the substance of those poor wretches that accustom themselves to the drinking it, by a continual drain, not leaving them at the last the bare necessaries of life" (Hogarth n. p.). James Towley's 1751 poem serves as the caption to "Gin Lane":

> Gin, cursed fiend! With fury fraught,
> Makes human race a Prey;
> It enters by a deadly Draught,
>   And steals our Life away.
>
> Virtue and Truth driv'n to Despair,
>   Its Rage compels to fly,
> But cherishes, with hellish Care,
>   Theft, Murder, Perjury

Fig. 5. Hogarth's print *Beer Street* shows a thriving, jovial community enjoying beer. The contrast between this print and "Gin Lane" (fig. 6) demonstrates that Hogarth did not ascribe poverty and crime to alcohol consumption, but instead interpreted gin addiction as a major symptom of poverty that exacerbated its negative effects. *Source:* "Haley and Steele Presents William Hogarth (1697–1794) Beer Street," 30 June 2004. <http://www.haleysteele. com/hogarth/plates/beerst.html>.

Fig. 6. Hogarth's *Gin Lane* envisions the horrific living conditions for the poor that gave rise to the gin epidemic. *Source:* Elizabeth Kathleen Mitchell. *Death by Hogarth.* Cambridge: Harvard UP, 1999, p. 62.

Damn'd Cup! that on the Vitals preys,
    That liquid Fire contains;
Which Madness to the Heart conveys,
And rolls it thro' the Veins.

(qtd. in Paulson 210)

Dickens was a great fan of Hogarth because he showed both the causes and effects of gin drinking in his art. Dickens told his friend John Forster that

> I find it a remarkable trait of Hogarth's picture ["Gin Lane"], that, while it exhibits drunkenness in the most appalling forms, it also forces on our attention a most neglected wretched neighborhood, and an unwholesome, indecent abject condition of life that might be put as a frontispiece to our sanitary report of a hundred years later date . . . . [B]eside that wonderful picture of what follows intoxication, we have indication quite as powerful of what leads to it among the neglected classes. There is no evidence that any of the actors in the dreary scene have ever been much better than we see them there. (qtd. in 2: 42)

Hogarth's art affirms Dickens's belief that the gin epidemic is a result rather than a cause of poverty.

"Gin Lane" is set in the slum called the Ruins of St. Giles (fig. 6). The pawnbroker S. Gripe, the gin houses, and the undertaker are the only successful businesses in this neighborhood, but even their buildings are threatening to topple over. On the left, the pawnbroker is taking a carpenter's coat and saw and a ragged woman's pot and saucepan in exchange for money to consume gin. By the wall, a man and a dog are fighting for a bone beside a stupefied woman who is leaning on the parapet.

The most eye-catching image, however, is the bare-breasted drunken woman in the foreground sprawled on the steps of the gin-house ("GIN ROYAL" is on the flagon). As she takes a pinch of snuff, her baby falls to certain death. Below the woman, a skeletal ballad-seller is either dead or dying with an empty gin glass in one hand. His cry is, " 'Buy my ballads, and I'll give you a glass of gin for nothing.' . . . The ballad in the basket is *The downfall of Mdm Gin*'; he has sold most of his clothes to buy gin—which was popularly called 'Strip Me Naked' " (Paulson 210).

The building on the right is marked *KILMAN* DISTILLERY (emphasis ours). A woman is pouring spirits into the mouth of a drunken man in a wheelbarrow. A woman near the wall is feeding her baby gin, and behind her two young orphans are toasting one another with gin. The other two houses on the street are an undertaker's and a barber's. The barber has hanged himself; a drunken cook is waving an impaled baby; and a beadle looks on as a naked woman is placed into a coffin, her baby on the ground beside it. Finally, the church spire in the background is seemingly barred by the ruins of the neighborhood. Dickens has pointed out that, besides the pawnbroker, the only other sober person in the print is the beadle, " 'and he is mightily indifferent to the orphan-child beside its parent's coffin . . . . The church indeed is very prominent and handsome; but . . . quite passive in the picture, it coldly surveys these things in progress under the shadow of the tower' " (qtd. in Forster 2: 42). It is not surprising then that many of these Hogarthian images reappear in *Oliver Twist*: the dead mother, the orphaned baby, the undertaker, the coffin, the beadle, the drinking children, the man-dog fight, the pawnbroker, the hanged man, and, of course, the ruins.

As previously noted, Cruikshank's failure to treat the roots of the gin craze caused Dickens to become increasingly disappointed with the illustrator. Dickens's differing assessments of Cruikshank's and Hogarth's gin-related works suggest that the approach Dickens takes to gin consumption in *Oliver Twist* has more in common with the complexity of Hogarth's work (although, ironically, Cruikshank was the illustrator for *Oliver Twist*). Like Hogarth's narrative prints, Dickens's narrative fiction treats the gin epidemic as a result of profound social dilemmas that England consistently failed to address.

Although Hewlett and Axton discount gin's role in the criminality of the characters in *Oliver Twist*, claiming in particular that Fagin's "evil doing owes nothing to drink" (99), gin does serve as an agent (rather than a cause) of dehumanizing and criminal activities throughout the novel. Both parish authorities, referred to as "sage, deep philosophical men" (*OT* 55; ch. 2), and thieves preserve their self-interest by commodifying their victims through gin distribution. They learned their dehumanizing ethic from nineteenth-century Utilitarians—or Benthamites—middle-class philosophers and reformers who preached the "greatest happiness for the greatest number." That is, one could "obtain the greatest amount of necessaries, conveniences and luxuries, with the smallest amount of labour and physical self-denial" (Altick 117). It became a "wholly hedonistic" ideology; for Utilitarians, self-interest was "the prime, in fact the only, motivation behind human conduct, and . . . achievement of pleasure and the avoidance of pain alone constitute that self-interest" (Altick 117). It is no wonder that "philosophers" like the parish board and Fagin embrace the ideology of the age. Fagin, for example, teaches the children he corrupts that "self preservation is the first law of nature" (116; ch. 10). But preservation of Fagin is what he really means. For him "number one" (himself) is the most important number.

Throughout *Oliver Twist*, Dickens uses gin distribution and consumption to dramatize the more insidious social problem perpetuated by Victorian Utilitarianism—the inhumane, commercial exploitation of individuals. Steven Marcus summarizes the effects of Utilitarian ideology on human relations in the novel:

> In the society of *Oliver Twist*, relations between men have been reduced to abstract calculations, and men themselves have been transformed into isolated and dehumanized objects. Oliver, a nameless orphan, "outcast . . . desolate and deserted" (ch. 20), is himself a model of the mechanical, disinherited, relationless being of classical economic doctrine. He is converted into a piece of property and put out "To let . . . five pounds would be paid to anybody who would take possession of him" (ch. 3). At birth he is "badged and ticketed" (ch. 1) like an article of merchandise. (64–65)

Even before Oliver falls into Fagin's clutches, as an orphaned child, he suffers under the Utilitarian philosophical system which "farms" indigent children under nine to branch-workhouses.

Mrs. Mann, "a very great experimental philosopher" (48; ch. 2), receives a weekly allowance to feed and clothe her charges at the "baby farm," but the children receive only small portions of unsubstantial food: "she appropriated the greater part of the weekly stipend to her own use" (48; ch. 2). As a result, most of the orphans die before they reach the age where they can be apprenticed. Mrs. Mann apparently uses her parochial stipend to buy gin for her own consumption and to dispense to "sick" children to control them.[6] To placate the beadle when he comes to examine the branch-workhouse for the board, Mrs. Mann offers Mr. Bumble gin and water. She explains that she has gin "in the house to put into the blessed infants' Daffy [the name of a medicine that became a slang term for gin], when they ain't well." The matron, who also beats the children, goes on to say that she "couldn't see them suffer before my own eyes, you know, sir" (51; ch. 2). The children, in fact, die before her eyes. When Oliver, for example, stops at the baby farm to say goodbye to Dick, his former playmate, the child, who repeatedly "had been beaten and starved" and "shut up," is now dying, dreaming of "Heaven, and Angels" (96; ch.7). Ironically, when Mr. Bumble feels the "temporary blandness which gin-and-water awakens" (53; ch. 2), he praises the matron for her "humane" and motherly nature and promises to mention it to the board. Because the Victorian female caregiver was expected to be angelic, Dickens undercuts the ideology of the age by making the woman the perpetrator and the children her victims.

Dickens makes several other pointed references to gin in the parish setting. Mrs. Thingummy, the workhouse hag who helped deliver Oliver, is another nurse who uses spirits to cope with her miserable life. She keeps hidden in her pocket "a green glass bottle, the contents of which she had been tasting in the corner with evident satisfaction" while attending Oliver's mother (46; ch. 1). She sets in motion the cruel cycle of commodifying the orphaned baby. Made bold by gin, Mrs. Thingummy steals the gold locket from Oliver's mother's corpse (46; ch. 1); and the funds she gains by pawning Oliver's future will support the alcoholism that acts as her buffer against workhouse horrors.[7] When she later lies dying in a reversal of the death scene at which she had earlier officiated, attending old crones give Mrs. Thingummy gin and water with opium in "the openness of their hearts," hoping that she will confess a secret that would be profitable to them (227; ch. 24).

But the workhouse matron Mrs. Corney, rather than the "nurses," profits from the drink-induced confession about pawning the locket and takes the pawnbroker's ticket from the dead hag. Seemingly agitated by the death, Mrs. Corney returns to her home, where Mr. Bumble is waiting to propose. Her gallant suitor suggests she sip some wine to recover, but she asks for stronger medicine from the green-glass bottle in her closet. After Mr. Bumble pours her a cup of peppermint "with a little—a little something else in it" (248; ch. 27), she offers the "medicine" to Bumble. He is "doubtful," but upon tasting it, he drinks it all down. Both of them are "comforted" by the liquid (248; ch. 27). The juxtaposition of robbing the dead and proposing marriage for silver teaspoons, sugar tongs, and a silver milk-pot emphasizes that the union of Mr. Bumble and Mrs. Corney will be one based purely on economic interests, interests that each of them furthers by manipulating others. Thus, the "domino effect" of gin distribution among the parish workers effectively dramatizes the dehumanizing cycle of Victorian materialism.

The "romantic" union of Mr. Bumble and Mrs. Corney evolves into a business partnership in which the two parish officials collude with the criminal world in a scheme to steal Oliver's birthright. The scheme begins with a "business meeting" conducted through the manipulative use of gin. The villainous Monks exploits Bumble as he sits in a public-house drinking gin and water. Monks asks the former Beadle if he still has " 'the same eye to your own interest,' " and tells the landlord to refill Bumble's glass. Monks's intent is to manipulate him to "sell" Oliver's history. When Monks orders the gin " 'strong and hot,' " Bumble says, " 'Not too strong' . . . with a delicate cough." Monks dryly tells the landlord, " 'You understand what that [the cough] means.' " The drink the landlord serves is so strong that the "first gulp brought the water into Mr. Bumble's eyes" (330–31; ch. 37). Although Bumble makes it clear that he will not " 'refuse any little fee, when it comes to them [him and his wife] in a civil and proper manner' " (330; ch. 37), the intoxicating brew is his first payment. This is another case in which gin consumption denotes commodifying a victim for personal profit; the alcohol and the child become objects of consumption as the parish authorities and the criminal unite in a gin-ratified contract to "consume" Oliver's birthright.

After Oliver journeys from country to city, he finds himself thrust into a Hogarthian world in which drunkenness emblemizes poverty's depreciation of human life. As the Artful Dodger (Jack Dawkins) leads Oliver to Fagin's lair, they pass Saffron Hill, where

> There were a good many shops; but the only stock in trade appeared to be heaps of children, who, even at that time of night, were crawling in and out at the doors, or screaming from the inside. The sole places that seemed to prosper amid the general blight of the place, were the public-houses; and in them, the lowest orders of Irish were wrangling with might and main. Covered ways and yards, which here and there diverged from the main street, disclosed little knots of houses, where drunken men and women were positively wallowing in filth.
>
> (103; ch. 8)

Cordery points out that the proximity of the pubs, streets, and houses

> undermines the middle-class ideology of the separation of public and private space. Houses, pubs, shops, streets covered ways and yards, are heaped together in an inextricable jumble; walls and thresholds are breached by ill-looking fellows and children, the latter, indistinguishable, in fact, from what the shops sell: if children are their "stock in trade" then business and family are truly identical. ("Public Houses" 2: 82)

The public houses of *Oliver Twist* therefore visualize bourgeois ideology's contradictions. Its consumerist ethic profanes and commercializes the home and family which nineteenth-century middle-class culture had sanctified as a symbol of humane principles.

The Three Cripples, the public-house where Fagin does his business receiving stolen goods to fence and hiring criminals from the drunken clients, is in the filthiest part of the slum. It presents another mercenary twist on the sacred values the Victorians associated with the domestic sphere. The bar is filled with smoke and the smell of liquor, and the Hogarthian faces of the inhabitants,

> [which were] expressive of almost every vice in almost every grade, irresistibly attracted the attention, by their very repulsiveness. Cunning, ferocity, and drunkenness in all its stages, were there, in their strongest aspects; and women: some with the last lingering tinge of their early freshness almost fading as you looked: others with every mark and stamp of their sex utterly beaten out, and presenting but one loathsome blank of profligacy and crime; some mere girls, others but young women, and none past the prime of life; formed the darkest and saddest portion of this dreary picture. (237; ch. 26)

These women have been commodified (prostituted) with the aid of gin. As in the cases of Mrs. Mann, Mrs. Thingummy, and Mrs. Corney, alcoholism's perversion of the nineteenth-century womanly ideal in this passage typifies poverty's detrimental effect on treasured human values. Warner notes, "Literary images of Mother Gin . . . are strongly suggestive of age without dignity" and tend to be associated with the figure of the decrepit woman no longer able to fulfill the ideal of motherhood (*Craze* 74). The appearance of such degraded, prematurely aged women in the public house foreshadows that Oliver will find no nurturing protector from the dehumanizing forces of commodification and consumption. Nancy, Oliver's one female defender in Fagin's world, has herself been commodified by Fagin and is ultimately ineffectual in shielding Oliver from the dangers of poverty and crime.

When they arrive at Fagin's den, Oliver meets "the villainous looking" old Jew and his "pupils," four or five young boys "smoking long clay pipes, and drinking spirits with the air of middle-aged men" (105; ch. 8). Under the pretense of providing sustenance and lodging for them, Fagin has for years enmeshed children into a life of thievery and prostitution by feeding them gin and encouraging, rather than cautioning, them to drink to excess (241; ch. 26). Enacting his Utilitarian philosophy of self-interest, Fagin uses gin to facilitate his traffic in human lives. His business, Cordery states, is "a parody of and thus a challenge to bourgeois capitalism" ("Public Houses" 2: 82).

Like the public houses, Fagin's den links business to the home, implying the age's commercialization of the home. Dickens continues his materialistic perversion of the Victorian motherly ideal by portraying Fagin as a demonic mother figure, toasting sausages over the blazing fire, providing gin as "mother's milk," and feeding his "dears," like the witches of fairy tales, with the true intent of consuming them himself (see fig. 7). Towards the end of the novel, Nancy lashes out at Fagin (probably the only "mother" she has ever known) for corrupting and commodifying her in this manner: " 'I thieved for you when I was a child not half as old as this! . . . I have been in the same trade and in the same service, for twelve years since . . . . It is my living; and the cold, wet, dirty streets are my home; and you're the wretch that drove me to them long ago, and that'll keep me there, day and night, day and night, till I die!' " (167; ch. 16).

But to lure children into his family of thieves, Fagin initially creates an illusion of middle-class comfort. He offers a new recruit, for example, the opportunity to " 'live like a gentleman—board and lodging, pipes and spirits free—half of all you earn' " (385; ch. 42). And, indeed, the youths imitate middle-class gentlemen in their dress, their names, and their affected mannerisms. Like gentlemen, the boys have access to seemingly unlimited amounts of alcohol, which they use to perpetuate Fagin's materialistic principles. For instance, as Mr. Jack Dawkins, Master Charles Bates, and Mr. Chitling play a game of whist, "for the accommodation of the company . . . a quart pot [sat] on the table, which stood ready filled with gin-and-water" (229; ch. 25). When Master Bates becomes inebriated and falls off his chair, Fagin tells the other boys: " 'Never mind him, my dear,' . . . winking at Mr. Dawkins, and giving Master Bates a reproving tap with the nozzle of the bellows" (231; ch. 25). Jack Dawkins or the Dodger, Fagin's most accomplished pupil, then uses Charley's drunken state to win money from him in the card game in which he is also cheating. As Dickens describes Fagin and the Dodger's crafty calculations and the other players' crude, drunken behavior in a tone typical of polite society, gin, the drink of the lower classes, facilitates a criminal parody of middle-class behavior that emphasizes its underlying criminality.

Upon Oliver's arrival at Fagin's hide-out, the Jew immediately starts to "recruit" Oliver. First he provides him with food and lodging. But, before

Oliver introduced to the Respectable Old Gentleman

Fig. 7. Cruikshank's illustration for Oliver's introduction to Fagin. Notice the bottle on the mantle and the tankard of gin the children at the table are consuming. *Source:* Charles Dickens. *Oliver Twist.* Ed. Peter Fairclough. Harmondsworth: Penguin, 1984. p. 104.

Oliver goes to sleep, the old man gives the boy a glass of hot gin and water and insists that he drink it immediately because someone else needs the tumbler. Oliver obeys, and later awakening from a deep (gin-induced) sleep to a dreamlike state "between sleeping and waking . . . half conscious of everything that is passing around [him]," he witnesses Fagin fondling his treasures and muttering how he has used other thieves for his own profit—men who went to the gallows in his place (106; ch. 9). The gin-induced "dream" reveals the truth behind Fagin's pretense of motherly nurturing. He is sheltering Oliver and feeding him gin to manipulate him into becoming a thief who will be willing to go to the gallows for Fagin. Thus, the dream becomes a conduit for "subconscious" truths from the dark underside of the Victorian social consciousness. The reality of Fagin's selfishness exposed in Oliver's "vision" dramatizes the reality Dickens saw underlying the Utilitarian philosophy. Despite this philosophy's pretense of compassion (achieving the "greatest good for the greatest number"), it actually encourages the exploitation of others for self-interest. Oliver's yearning to be valued, loved, and nurtured degenerates into a nightmare of abuse and exploitation when Fagin catches him watching and furiously threatens Oliver with a knife, demanding to know what he saw. That same day Fagin begins Oliver's thief training.

Although Monks, in offering Fagin a substantial monetary reward for corrupting Oliver, provides Fagin with an ulterior motive for making Oliver a thief, "the merry old gentleman" wants to objectify the innocent boy—he wants Oliver to be his "for life," and he uses his instrument, the housebreaker Bill Sikes, to help him by giving him Oliver as an accomplice in a robbery (192; ch. 19). Sikes likewise furthers his own material interests by employing alcohol to control Oliver. The night before the burglary, Sikes and Toby Crackit force Oliver to drink a glass of gin. Toby toasts to success with the robbery and to Oliver's pending corruption: " 'Down with it, innocence!' " (209; ch. 22). When the two men badger Oliver into drinking despite his protests, Oliver's second draught of gin and his exhaustion induce another nightmarish dream-like state that foreshadows the fatal consequences of such manipulation: "He fell into a heavy doze: imagining himself straying along the gloomy lanes, or wandering about the dark churchyard" (210; ch. 22). The nightmare becomes reality when Oliver is forced to participate in the housebreaking. When he realizes what they want him to do, he is mad with grief and terror: "He clasped his hands together, and involuntarily uttered a subdued exclamation of horror. A mist came before his eyes; the cold sweat stood upon his ashy face; his limbs failed him; and he sank upon his knees" (211–12; ch. 22). Oliver's reaction resembles symptoms of delirium tremens from which Sikes suffers later in the novel, reinforcing the cyclical nature of gin-facilitated exploitation in the narrative.

In another dream sequence that has evoked much critical commentary, Oliver stirs from a doze in the safe haven of the Maylie house to see Fagin and Monks leering at him through the window; but when the two villains disappear, no evidence can be found that they were ever there (chs. 34–35). Although Oliver has not been consuming alcohol, this "vision" coincides with the novel's emblematic use of intoxicated trances and dreamlike states to reveal the horrors of exploitation and control:

> There is a kind of sleep that steals upon us sometimes, which, *while it holds the body prisoner, does not free the mind from a sense of things about it, and enable it to ramble at its pleasure. So far as an overpowering heaviness, a prostration of strength, and an utter inability to control our thoughts or power of motion can be called sleep, this is it;* and yet, we have a consciousness of all that is going on about us, and, if we dream at such a time, words which are really spoken, or sounds which really exist at the moment, accommodate themselves with surprising readiness to our visions, until reality and imagination become so strangely blended that it is afterwards almost a matter of impossibility to separate the two.   (309; ch. 34, emphasis ours)[8]

Imprisoned by this vision, Oliver sees united two characters whose earlier use of gin illustrated their mesmeric powers in manipulating others for personal gain. Again the dream reveals a dark truth: the union of the confirmed criminal (Fagin) with the would-be gentleman who is a criminal at heart (Monks) suggests the true criminality underlying Victorian middle-class ideologies that manipulated the poor. That this apparently supernatural visitation occurs when Oliver has finally left his lower-class existence behind and achieved bourgeois security is significant. The preternatural presence of villains who are still attempting to control Oliver for profit suggests the insidious power of commodification lurking behind Victorian bourgeois complacency.

Although Fagin ultimately fails to make Oliver his own, he is for awhile more successful in using alcohol to make Noah Claypole his instrument (see fig. 8). Fagin first spots Noah at The Three Cripples in a back-room behind the bar, where the Landlord, or regulars like Fagin, can spy on customers.[9] After eavesdropping on Noah and his paramour Charlotte while they discuss robbing their former employer, Fagin easily ensnares Oliver's former tormenter by offering him liquor "in a very friendly manner" (382; ch. 42). When Noah remarks, " 'Good stuff that,' " Fagin replies that it's " 'dear' " and that if a man wants to drink it regularly, he " 'need be always emptying a till, or a pocket, or a woman's reticule, or a house, or a mail-coach, or a bank,' " thus revealing that he has overheard the discussion of their thievery and has them in his power (382; ch. 42). As noted earlier, because gin-shops were often used as employment offices, employers, by administering gin, were able to enforce slave-labor. Cordery states that such "scenes at the Three Cripples are, like those at Fagin's den, parodies of capitalist enterprise" ("Public Houses" 2: 85).

The Jew and Morris both begin to understand Each Other

Fig. 8. Fagin's mode of recruiting thieves: Fagin engages Noah Claypole and his mistress by sharing a "friendly drink." *Source:* Charles Dickens. *Oliver Twist.* Ed. Peter Fairclough. Harmondsworth: Penguin, 1984. p. 383.

Fagin trains his new employee to be an informer, but ultimately it backfires on Fagin when Noah decides to take care of himself "number one" rather than taking care of Fagin "number one" (388; ch. 43).[10] After he "peaches" on Fagin, sending him to the gallows, Noah becomes an informer against "charitable publicans" who sell liquor on Sundays. He walks out with Charlotte, who pretends to faint in front of the public-house door, and when the owner sells brandy as a restorative, Noah informs against him (477; ch. 53; see also Cordery "Public Houses" 2: 284–85).

Finally, Fagin has used gin to commodify both Nancy and her lover, the brutal robber Bill Sikes. When Oliver first meets the "nice" young ladies Bet and Nancy, he thinks them "remarkably free and agreeable in their manners" (111; ch. 9). Because one of the female visitors complained of a "coldness in her inside, . . . Spirits were produced" (111; ch. 9). Nancy has apparently been drinking gin for twelve years, ever since Fagin first took her in. "Nancy . . . was not exempt from a failing which was very common among the Jew's female pupils; and in which, in their tenderer years, they were rather encouraged than checked" (241; ch. 26). And when she first meets Rose Maylie, Nancy tells Oliver's benefactor that she grew up " 'in the midst of cold and hunger, riot and drunkenness' " (362; ch. 40). According to Warner, gin-drinking was a typical escapist activity for eighteenth and nineteenth-century working-class women: "Gin was commonly known as 'the ladies' delight' . . . . [Women drank] vast quantities of cheap gin, sometimes on their own, sometimes with other women, and sometimes with men whom they had just met" (*Craze* 65–66).

Nancy initially participates in Fagin's commodification of Oliver by stealing him away from Mr. Brownlow (see fig. 9) in a scene in which the public-house again contributes to the text's subversion of middle-class values. Oliver's kidnapping, which takes place significantly in front of a beer-shop rather than a gin-shop, blurs the boundaries between middle-class respectability and lower-class criminality. The scene features lower-class characters and establishments engaged in a bourgeois ruse. Pretending to be Oliver's sister and disguised as a servant or housekeeper in attire Fagin chose to make her appear "respectable" (139; ch. 13), Nancy lays claim to Oliver with a speech that embodies the simplistic class distinctions the text undermines: "He [Oliver] ran away, near a month ago, from his parents, who are hard-working and respectable people; and went and joined a set of thieves and bad characters; and almost broke his mother's heart" (157; ch. 15). While Nancy's appearance and speech identify her with those "decent" members of the working classes who aspire to the bourgeois ideals of family, property, and respectable behavior, her criminal and commercial intentions reveal the facile nature of distinctions between the criminal and the bourgeois.[11] Oliver, the former pauper/potential thief now attired as a young gentleman and carrying

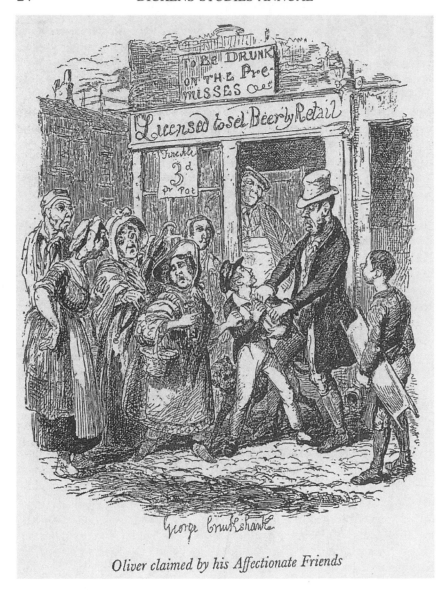

Oliver claimed by his Affectionate Friends

Fig. 9. Oliver is commodified as Nancy and Bill Sikes steal him away to Fagin's hideout to be ''sold'' to the criminals Fagin and Monks. Cruikshank's illustration sets the kidnapping at the exterior of a public house. *Source:* Charles Dickens. *Oliver Twist.* Ed. Peter Fairclough. Harmondsworth: Penguin, 1984. Cover page.

expensive books (commodities that symbolize middle-class empowerment), likewise suggests the contravention of class restrictions.

The parody of middle-class ideology continues when Sikes, pretending to be Oliver's father, takes from Oliver the books he is delivering for Brownlow, accuses Oliver of stealing them (while Sikes himself will profit by selling them to Fagin), and gives the child a brutal beating that the onlookers witness with approval, assuming that the blows come from a "hard-working and respectable" parent. Sikes rushes from the beer-shop to attack Oliver, and Cruikshank's accompanying illustration calls attention to the scene's commercial nature with a sign displaying the price of beer and the shop's boast, "Licensed to sel [sic] Beer by Retail," prominently posted above the criminals as they struggle to reclaim Oliver for their own profit (see fig. 9). The fat publican apparently looking down on the proceedings from just inside the beer-shop's threshold recalls the mercenary image of the publican observing his clientele in Cruikshank's earlier etching "The Gin Shop" (see fig. 1). Cordery notes that when this "family reconciliation" takes place, the beer-shop becomes "the mediating space where the barrier between home and street collapses" ("Public House" 2: 84). The union of middle-class family values, bourgeois commercialism, and criminal machinations in the scene intimates the criminal materialism inherent in bourgeois ideology.

The choice of a beer-shop rather than a gin-shop for the setting of the kidnapping also contributes to the novel's indictment of middle-class materialism. The beer-shop, an establishment sanctioned by the 1830 Beerhouse Act as a respectable alternative to gin-shops, represented in part a middle-class attempt to reinforce bourgeois power and secure a more compliant proletariat by encouraging the more "respectable" behavior associated with beer drinking as opposed to consumption of more intoxicating liquors such as gin. As evidenced by Hogarth's "Beer Street" print (see fig. 5), the middle classes promoted beer drinking for those "decent" members of the working classes who embraced middle-class attitudes and thus reinforced the dominant ideology. Therefore, the beer-shop, a working-class establishment founded on a pretense of middle-class respectability, is an ideal location for the criminals to stage their bourgeois masquerade.

After the kidnapping, however, Nancy begins to reassess her cohorts' materialistic attitudes in light of Oliver's innocence. The narrative expresses Nancy's transformation by giving new meaning to language and behavior previously associated with her episodes of inebriation. When Bill's dog threatens Oliver with violence, for example, she stands up to Bill and then to Fagin after he hits the boy with a club. Her passion aroused at the prospect of their making Oliver a thief, she cries out,

> "Let him be—let him be—or I shall put that mark on some of you, that will bring me to the gallows before my time."

> The girl stamped her foot violently on the floor as she vented this threat: and with her lips compressed, and her hands clenched, looked alternately at the Jew and the other robber: her face quite colourless from the passion of rage into which she had gradually worked herself. (165; ch. 16)

Here the passion of inebriation is replaced by the rage of indignation against the commodification of a child. As Nancy's behavior escalates to the uninhibited ferocity of a drunken brawl (but a ferocity inspired in this case by outrage rather than drink), she rushes violently at Fagin, exclaiming, " 'I wish I had been struck dead . . . before I had lent a hand in bringing him here . . . . He's a thief, a liar, a devil, all that's bad, from this night forth' " (167; ch. 16). Seeing her own history of abuse by Fagin repeated in Oliver's plight, Nancy no longer views the boy as a means of profit but as a fellow sufferer in a brutal cycle of exploitation and degradation. And she determines to attempt breaking the cycle.

All this leads to Nancy's subsequent rebellion in which she uses Fagin's tools of exploitation against him. Recognizing Fagin's manipulative use of gin (she tells him, " 'You'd never have me anything else [but drunk], if you had your will' " [240; ch. 26]), she weans herself from spirits and uses liquor to gain power over both Sikes and Fagin. When Fagin momentarily loses control and reveals that Oliver is worth one hundred pounds to him (due to the reward Monks has offered Fagin for corrupting Oliver), Nancy feigns drunkenness to learn more: "she subsided, first into dullness, and afterwards into a compound of feelings, under the influence of which she shed tears one minute, and in the next gave utterance to various exclamations of 'Never say die!' " Because Fagin "has had considerable experience of such matters in his time," he believes that she is "very far gone indeed" (241; ch. 26). Nancy is then able to follow him, and she learns about Monks's and Fagin's plot against Oliver.

Although Bill Sikes is overpowering and abusive to both his lover and his dog, he remains Fagin's for life, and it is gin that allows the old man to control him. In virtually every scene in which he appears, Bill is either drinking, drunk, or passing out (see, for example, 137, 140, 152, 155, 187, 201, 209, 350, 356). Bill first appears after Oliver has been arrested. He is in a foul temper because Fagin tosses at the Dodger a pot of beer that accidentally hits Sikes, and he accuses Fagin of mistreating the boys: " 'I wonder why they don't murder you; *I* would if I was them. If I'd been your 'prentice, I'd have done it long ago' " (136; ch. 13). But "after swallowing two or three glasses of spirits," Bill calms down (137; ch. 13). Later, after they agree that Oliver will assist at the robbery, Bill, who has been drinking all evening, continues to drink

> at a furious rate, and to flourish the crowbar in alarming manner; yelling forth, at the same time, most unmusical snatches of song, mingled with wild execrations. At length, in a fit of professional enthusiasm, he insisted upon producing

his box of housebreaking tools: which he had no sooner stumbled in with, and opened for the purpose of explaining the nature and properties of the various implements, than he fell over the box upon the floor, and went to sleep where he fell. (193; ch. 19)

It is clear that Sikes is addicted to alcohol.

Both Fagin and Nancy utilize gin to manipulate Sikes (and each other) in their ongoing contest to control Oliver's fate. Following the robbery attempt in which Oliver is rescued from the criminals, Fagin employs gin to regain command of Bill and plots to use Bill to thwart Nancy's machinations. Bringing a conciliatory offering of food and drink to Bill's lodging, Fagin finds Nancy, who has nursed Bill through a long illness, overcome with hunger and exhaustion. When she faints, Fagin and the Dodger revive her by pouring spirits down her throat. Afterwards Fagin gives a "sly wink" to the Dodger and Charley, who begin "to ply her [Nancy] with liquor: of which, however, she took very sparingly; while Fagin, assuming an unusual flow of spirits, gradually brought Mr. Sikes into a better temper." When Bill begins to make "rough jokes . . . after repeated application to the spirit bottle," Fagin laughs "very heartily" (351; ch. 39). Similarly, Nancy exploits Bill's weakness for liquor in her attempts to protect Oliver from Fagin. In order to meet Rose Maylie and Mr. Brownlow on the bridge, she replenishes Bill's glass of hot water and gin three or four times, hoping he will "drink himself asleep" (356; ch. 39), and then she laces his drink with laudanum, sending him into "a profound trance" (357; ch. 39).

But Nancy's attempt to govern Bill recoils upon her. Because Fagin has controlled the robber for so long, it is very easy for him to manipulate Sikes to kill his lover, especially since his system still contains the alcohol and laudanum that Nancy administered. Learning that Nancy talked to Rose Maylie, Fagin forces Noah to describe the meeting to provoke the "wild beast" into a murderous frenzy. Slyly playing on the inebriated Bill's lack of inhibition, Fagin pronounces Nancy's death sentence, prompting, " 'You won't be—too—violent, Bill?' " and " 'Be crafty, Bill, and not too bold' " (421; ch. 47).

The aftermath of the murder brings the novel's metaphorical use of gin distribution full-circle. Bill's behavior is symptomatic of an alcoholic in detoxification: believing that a phantom is following him, he wanders irrationally like "some drunken sullen fellow" (427; ch. 48). He has hallucinations, and he fears all objects before him. What's more, his reaction to the apparition of Nancy's accusing eyes manifests physical symptoms of detoxification (or delirium tremens):

A vision came before him, as constant and more terrible than that from which he had escaped. Those widely staring eyes, so lusterless and so glassy, that he

had better borne to see them than think upon them, appeared in the midst of
the darkness; light in themselves, but giving light to nothing. There were but
two, but they were everywhere. If he shut out the sight, there came the room
with every well-known object . . . each in its accustomed place. The body was
in *its* place, and its eyes were as he saw them when he stole away. He got up,
and rushed into the field without. The figure was behind him . . . . The eyes
were there . . . . And here he remained in such terror as none but he can know,
trembling in every limb, and the cold sweat starting from every pore

(429; ch. 48).[12]

This controlling vision, like Oliver's previous "dreams" and intoxicated
trances, suggests the fatal consequences of the self-centered, materialistic
ethic that the novel embodies in gin consumption. Bill's manipulation of
others for profit brings about his own entrapment.

Ultimately, precipitated by a final terrifying hallucination, Bill loses his
balance and falls from the roof with the noose around his neck—an accident
that is strongly suggestive of both suicide and Fagin's forthcoming criminal
punishment. Thus we return to the hanging figure in Hogarth's print who
apparently was "driven suicidal by gin madness. This visual link between
hanging and alcohol registers drunkenness both as a vice and as its own
punishment for vice" (Mitchell 62). The image of the hanged alcoholic criminal, both victim and perpetrator in the dehumanizing enterprises of a commercial culture, unites the themes of poverty, criminality, and materialism.

Thus, gin-drinking becomes a conduit into the criminal world of *Oliver
Twist*, a subtle agent for the commercial manipulation of the characters, and
a metaphor for the inherently criminal nature of early capitalism's materialistic ethic. Both the parish system and London's criminal underground were
natural results of nineteenth-century capitalist and utilitarian ideologies and
exemplify society's mercenary treatment of the working class, a treatment
reflected in the gin metaphor that permeates the novel. Hence *Oliver Twist*
epitomizes the inclination of Dickens's early writings to portray gin abuse in
the nineteenth century as symptomatic of a greater social problem, a philosophy that perpetuated poverty, ignorance, and crime.

NOTES

1. In his essay "Drink in *David Copperfield*," Gareth Cordery notes that "there
   have been few attempts to view drink as part of the symbolic economy of Dickens's fiction" (59). He goes on to discuss drinking in *David Copperfield* (oddly
   enough never making reference to Mr. Micawber) as "a mark of a society in
   transition and an index for Dickens's own uneasiness about class" (59).
2. Of course, working-class gin consumption was not solely due to the governing
   classes's mercenary manipulations. Brian Harrison studies a variety of cultural

factors that contributed to alcohol consumption and intoxication in pre-industrial England, including poor water quality and high costs of non-intoxicating beverages, climatic conditions that prompted resort to the comforts of alcohol, widespread belief in alcohol's medicinal qualities, the numerous social and recreational functions provided by drink-sellers, and the complex role of drinking as a social/cultural signifier. But Harrison points out that the rise of capitalist culture prompted significant changes in attitudes toward alcohol consumption. The need of industrial capitalists for a reliable work force was at odds with the drinking habits encouraged by a culture steeped in alcohol (62). And since distilled spirits (particularly gin) dominated working-class alcohol consumption, attempts to control the gin market were a natural product of the era's class politics.

3. Despite the temperance movement's failure to address the social causes of working-class alcoholism, Harrison credits "the social conscience of temperance reformers and others" with averting "the polarization of English society which Marx in the 1840s forecast" (25). While propagating the dominant bourgeois ideology of respectability, anti-spirits and teetotal campaigns likewise contributed to a growing humanitarian awareness of lower-class dilemmas. According to Harrison, "the temperance and prohibitionist movements were two of several nineteenth-century campaigns helping to ensure that a more equitable social order would be realized through guilt in a minority of the wealthy, not through anger in the majority of the oppressed" (366).

4. In *The Pickwick Papers* (1836–37), Dickens humorously portrays the failures of the temperance movement in his satirical account of a temperance society meeting at which mass consumption of tea replaces gin drinking. The society patrons "drank tea to a most alarming extent," prompting Tony Weller's observation that some of the attendees are "a-swellin' wisibly before my wery eyes" and will "want tappin' to-morrow mornin' " (503–504; ch. 33). After a series of ridiculous testimonials in which various society members blame drink for everything from unrelated industrial accidents to faulty wooden legs, the meeting is disrupted by an intoxicated visitor from a branch society who attacks the patrons claiming that they are drunk.

5. *Oliver Twist* is unique in that there are actually no scenes in which Dickens uses alcohol as a symbol of communion and conviviality, which is illustrated repeatedly in other works by such examples as Mr. Micawber's punch and Dickens's many Christmas celebrations. In *Nicholas Nickleby* (1838–39), however, which he wrote while completing *Oliver Twist*, Dickens uses both convivial and destructive drinking to signify a variety of human relations. For instance, while ruined gentleman Newman Noggs's addiction to gin and water allows Ralph Nickleby to control him for years, Noggs offers gin to both Nicholas and Smike as a communal gesture. Mr. Squeers, who likes to consider himself a "gentleman," drinks brandy but manipulates Peg Sliderskew for his own profit by feeding her gin. The Crummles use gin to stunt the Infant Phenomenon's growth and ensure her marketability, but their meals, like the gatherings of the Kenwigs and the Cheerybles, are all celebrations where imbibing spirits and punch signify friendship and love. Finally, Sir Mulberry Hawk's villainy is expressed in a wine-induced drunken riot caused by his rejection of Lord Frederick's request that he

not seek violent revenge against Nicholas. The participants's wild behavior—"glasses were dashed upon the floor by hands that could not carry them to
lips, oaths were shouted out by lips which could scarcely form the words to vent
them in; Tumult and frenzy reigned supreme . . . " (757; ch. 50)—illustrates
uninhibited aristocratic arrogance. In his study of drinking in *The Pickwick Papers*, David J. Greenman likewise notes a contrast between convivial and destructive alcohol consumption. Greenman's observation that most episodes of
convivial drunkenness are set in a nostalgic, pre-industrial past while scenes of
destructive and debilitating drunkenness tend to have contemporary settings (11)
suggests that *Pickwick* is an early step in Dickens's movement towards using
drink as a vehicle of contemporary social criticism.

6. Nurses like Mrs. Mann often neglected their duties and sedated children in their
care. An eighteenth-century pamphlet characterized such nurses: "The suckling
Brat declines her shrivl'd Pap, / The cordial Bev'rage sips, and takes a Nap. /
Hush'd with few Drops he holds his Infant cries, /And spares the maudlin Nurse
her Lullabies" (qtd. in Warner, *Craze* 70). One nurse returned to her charge one
afternoon drunk with gin. While she slept, the child caught on fire, and a coroner's
inquest ruled the death accidental because "the Woman always used the Child
with great Tenderness and Humanity at other Times, and never committed any
Act of Cruelty; so that all was owing to that pernicious Liquor" (qtd. in Warner,
Craze 69).

7. Mrs. Mann and Mrs. Thingummy are the precursors of Dickens's later satirical
creations, drunken nurses such as Sarah Gamp and Little Dorrit's nurse, Mrs.
Bangham. By perverting the maternal image in such characters, Dickens suggests
how his society's most cherished ideals were corrupted by a materialistic ethic.
The self-denying, life-affirming mother-figure that was the repository of spiritual
values for the Victorian middle-class is twisted by nineteenth-century materialism
into a selfish harpy that takes advantage of the charges she is meant to protect.
Warner attests that "Mother Gin" was frequently personified in "hags" and
other images of "older women . . . that best symbolized the moral and physical
decay that contemporary reformers associated with gin" (*Craze* 73–74).

8. The description of the sleeping Oliver resembles John Jasper's opium-induced
sleep at the beginning of *The Mystery of Edwin Drood*. Jasper is another master
manipulator who uses alcohol to control others, although he employs wine (more
appropriate to the middle-class gentleman) apparently laced with opium (intimating a connection with crime and the lower-classes) (see *Drood* ch. 8).

9. Cordery says that rooms like this one functioned in pubs and gin houses as means
of maintaining social control, which was "central to making money" ("Public
Houses" 1: 9, 10).

10. Another example of the boys's absorption of Fagin's philosophy occurs earlier
when Oliver is caught supposedly picking Mr. Brownlow's pocket. The other
boys, concerned only with self-preservation, abandon Oliver to be their scapegoat. They act "philosophically":

> It is the invariable practice of many mighty philosophers in car-
> rying out their theories, to evince great wisdom and foresight in

providing against every possible contingency which can be supposed at all likely to affect themselves. Thus, to do a great right,
you may do a little wrong: and you may take any means which
the end to be attained will justify; the amount of the right, or the
amount of the wrong, or indeed the distinction between the two,
being left entirely to the philosopher concerned, to be settled by
his clear, comprehensive, and impartial view of his own particular
case.   (133; ch. 13)

11. Cordery's description of Nancy's attire as that of a "middle-class housekeeper"
("Public Houses" 2: 84) misses a more subtle level of complexity in the class
relations this scene expresses. Actually lower-class criminals (and confirmed gin-
drinkers), Nancy and Sikes masquerade not as middle-class citizens but as members of that working-class elite (Nancy's attire suggests the mid- to upper-levels
of domestic service) which strove for middle-class respectability. The criminals's
patronage of the shop that sells the more "respectable" liquor (beer rather than
gin) adds to the complex ruse and further emphasizes their insidious manipulation
of class boundaries.
12. Sikes's symptoms anticipate those of Mr. Dolls in *Our Mutual Friend*, who has
a series of attacks of the horrors and the trembles before he dies.

WORKS CITED

Altick, Richard D. *Victorian People and Ideas.* New York: Norton, 1973.

Cordery, Gareth. "Drink in *David Copperfield.*" *Redefining the Modern: Essays on Literature and Society in Honor of Joseph Weisenfarth.* Ed. William Baker and Ira B. Nadel. Madison and Teaneck, NJ: Fairleigh Dickinson UP, 2004.

———. "Public Houses: Spatial Instabilities in *Sketches by Boz* and *Oliver Twist* (Part One)." *Dickens Quarterly* 20 (March 2003): 3–13.

———. "Public Houses: Spatial Instabilities in *Sketches by Boz* and *Oliver Twist* (Part Two)." *Dickens Quarterly* 20 (June 2003): 81–92.

Dickens, Charles. *Oliver Twist.* New York: Penguin, 1982.

———. *The Letters of Charles Dickens.* Vol. 5. Ed. Graham Storey and K.J. Fielding. Oxford: Clarendon, 1981.

———. *The Mystery of Edwin Drood.* Oxford: Oxford UP, 1987.

———. *Nicholas Nickleby.* Oxford: Oxford UP, 1987.

———. *Our Mutual Friend.* Oxford: Oxford UP, 1987.

———. *The Pickwick Papers.* Oxford: Clarendon, 1986.

————. *Sketches by Boz*. London: Oxford UP, 1973.

————. "Sunday Under Three Heads." *Victorian London*. Ed. Lee Jackson. 1 Feb. 2003 http://www.victorianlondon.org/entertainment/sundays.htm.

Evans, Hilary and Mary. *The Man Who Drew the Drunkard's Daughter: The Life and Art of George Cruikshank 1792–1878*. London: Frederick Muller, 1978.

Forster, John. *The Life of Charles Dickens*. Vol. 2. London: Dent, 1966.

Greenman, David J. "Alcohol, Comedy, and Ghosts in Dickens's Early Short Fiction." Dickens Quarterly 17 (March 2000): 3–13.

Harrison, Brian. *Drink and the Victorians: The Temperance Question in England: 1815–1872*. Pittsburgh: U of Pittsburgh P, 1971.

Hewett, Edward, and W. F. Axton. *Convivial Dickens: The Drinks of Dickens and His Times*. Athens: Ohio UP, 1983.

Hogarth, William. *Marriage A La Mode and Other Engravings*. New York: Lear, 1947.

Marcus, Steven. *Dickens from Pickwick to Dombey*. New York: Simon and Schuster, 1965.

Mitchell, Elizabeth Kathleen. *Death By Hogarth*. Cambridge: Harvard UP, 1999.

Nicholls, James C. "Gin Lane Revisited: Intoxication and Society in the Gin Epidemic." *Journal for Cultural Research* 7 (2003): 125–46.

Patten, Robert L., ed. *George Cruikshank: A Revaluation*. Princeton: Princeton UP, 1974.

Paulson, Ronald, ed. *Hogarth's Graphic Works*. Vol. 1. Rev. ed. New Haven: Yale UP, 1970.

Warner, Jessica, Minghao Her, Gerhard Gruel, and Jurgen Rehm. "Can Legislation Prevent Debauchery? Mother Gin and Public Health in 18th-Century England." *American Journal of Public Health* 91.3 (March 2001). EbscoHost. 00900036.

Warner, Jessica. *Craze: Gin and Debauchery in an Age of Reason*. New York: Four Walls Eight Windows, 2002.

Nell and Sophronia—Catherine, Mary, and Georgina: Solving the Female Puzzle and the Gender Conundrum in *The Old Curiosity Shop*

Rosemary Coleman

In exploring early Victorian constructions of masculinity, Herbert Suss-man has observed that the regulation of male aggression and sexual energy was the central problem in the Victorian practice of masculinity. The same observation can be applied to the central problem of The Old Curiosity Shop, *as the text enacts physical punishments on its males' bodies, and performs radical, reconstructive surgeries on the bodies of its two principal female characters. The surgical transformations of the two young women are presented as socially and morally proper re-sponses to a gender conundrum compounded of male needs, female threats, and Dickens's own need for compartmentalization among the spiritual, domestic, and sexual qualities in his women. In defining female bodies as mutable, malleable, and tractable, and then pointing to them as responsible for the control of male transgressions, the* Shop *simulta-neously reflects and shapes the convictions of the larger culture. The metaphoric surgeries performed on Nell and the Marchioness create a peculiar configuration of female types, a pattern of women, which in turn gestures toward the arrangement of females with which Dickens would surround himself in the early years of his marriage. That is, he serially acquired the three Hogarth sisters, thus creating a web of women who would provide the domestic solution to his female puzzle.*

Dickens Studies Annual, Volume 36, Copyright © 2005 by AMS Press, Inc. All rights reserved.

In the late summer of 1840 Charles Dickens moved his family to Broadstairs, and invited assorted relatives and friends to join him there. It was to be a working vacation for him, as he continued to write those chapters of *The Old Curiosity Shop* in which Nell's illness of body and sickness of heart become so extreme that she collapses senseless at the feet of the schoolmaster. Already celebrated in both England and America at only 28, Dickens had been married for four years, had fathered three children (the fourth would be born in four months), and written three best-selling novels. The editors of his *Letters* for 1840 describe his state of mind during the writing of the *Shop* as "buoyant and cheerful" (2: xii). His biographers, however, paint a more complex picture. Peter Ackroyd believes he was "chafing against the strains of domesticity" as early as 1838 (271), and Edgar Johnson also marks 1838 and 1839 as the beginning of domestic "rifts" between himself and Catherine, and of his impatience with a wife who "could not sustain a role in society" (1: 266, 267).[1] Ackroyd further calls him "Odd. Mercurial. Unpredictable." (315) during this period, while Fred Kaplan characterizes him as restless and unstable (116). Perhaps Ackroyd comes closest to grasping the young novelist's contradictions when he describes a deep division between the outer and inner man: "His habitual external response to the world is one of quickness and vivacity, his habitual interior temperament one of loss and anxiety; it is in the revolution of these two spheres around each other that we begin to understand why he seemed so odd and so mercurial, even to those who knew him best" (319).

During these weeks of September at the seaside resort, Dickens was at the center of a group which included the principal female figures in his life—those who had been, and would be again, mythicized in his fiction: his mother, Elizabeth; his beloved sister, Fanny; his yet-again pregnant wife, Catherine; and the constant memory of his late, much lamented sister-in-law, Mary Hogarth. In addition, blonde, nineteen-year-old Emma Picken—the houseguest of neighbors—was included in the amusements of the Dickens group, participating in the charades, *tableaux vivants,* and other diversions of which they were so fond. During the course of the vacation, Dickens "pretended to be engaged in a semi-sentimental, semi-jocular, and wholly nonsensical flirtation" with the pretty Emma (Christian rptd. in Collins 35). Both nonsense and flirtation got out of hand on several occasions, during one of which Dickens seized the girl and ran her down a jetty until they were both knee-deep in salt water, holding her there as the waves broke over her only silk dress. He proclaimed in mock romance cadences that he would restrain the screaming Emma until the tide submerged them both, and he did keep her there, pressed against his body, while the water stained her dress, and she pleaded with the watching Catherine Dickens to make him stop. The moment is suggestive. Dickens's desire to embrace and stain the girl before the eyes of the thickening, fecund Catherine presents a powerful and Quilpish metaphor for the conflicting emotions and disruptive energies within him which contributed so much tension to his creation of Nell Trent and her counterpart, the Marchioness.

In exploring early Victorian constructions of masculinity, Herbert Sussman has observed that the regulation of male "energy," characterized as both potent and dangerous, was the "central problematic in the Victorian practice of masculinity" (3). I think the same observation can be made about the central problematic of the *Shop*, as we witness the text's efforts to regulate its male characters' aggressions—most obviously by physical punishments enacted on their bodies. Dick Swiveller undergoes a major illness which transforms him from sexual predator (in partnership with Fred Trent) to domesticated husband. The outrageous Quilp suffers a ghastly death, and grandfather dies of his vices and a broken heart. Even more interesting, however, if less transparently displayed, is the text's second solution to its males' excesses—that is, the radical, reconstructive surgeries performed on the bodies of the two principal female characters. In defining female bodies as mutable, malleable, and tractable, and then pointing to those same bodies as somehow responsible for the control of male transgressions, the *Shop* simultaneously reflects and shapes the convictions of its larger culture.

Sussman contends that "[f]rom Carlyle through Pater the practice of masculine art is consistently theorized as being grounded in the regulation of male sexual energy" (4). Victorian writers sought ways to resolve or escape the tensions between their desire for a homosocial "world of chaste masculine bonding," and the more normative world of heterosexual marriage and domesticity; between, that is, what Sussman denominates as the "masculine plot" and the "marriage plot." Moreover, according to Sussman, the writers' desire for a chaste, homosocial world "clearly resonated with the longings of their middle-class readers" (5). Carlyle, for example, looked to the past—to the world of the cloistered monk in which the dangerous female has been "magically eliminated" (5). In the monastery's masculine plot, male restraint is achieved by the excision of female temptation. As a result, the marriage plot is simply a non-starter, and male creative energies remain unimpaired and undiluted by female-inspired male sexuality. Thus Carlyle posits an all-male ideal—a utopia to be attained through the performance of that most radical of surgeries, the erasure of the female body.

In the world of the *Shop* the central problem is the same—how to contain and regulate male aggression and sexuality. Certainly the novel's proffered solution is not the same as Carlyle's; nonetheless it plays a variation on the same theme. Dickens does not construct a closure in which he eliminates the female, nor does he choose the masculine plot to the exclusion of the marriage plot. Rather, he deals with the male problematic in three ways. As we have seen, he punishes and/or restrains the *Shop's* male bodies. Secondly, he performs radical surgeries on the two principal female bodies in order to fit them to his ideological template. Finally, in the text's happy ending, he evenhandedly constructs both a masculine plot and a marriage plot as twin entities in which Dick Swiveller can thrive and prosper.

The separate destinies of Nell and the Marchioness proffer two very different solutions to the problems posed by excessive male "energies," and their presumed cause—excessive female temptation. The *Shop* does not overtly punish or humiliate its female bodies as it does its males. Rather, the surgeries performed on the two young women are presented as socially and morally proper responses to a gender conundrum compounded of male needs, female threats, and Dickens's need for compartmentalization in his women. In addition, the ultimate fates of the *Shop's* female bodies speak obliquely to Dickens's own excess of dangerous energy—his Quilpishness—as emblematized in the real-life temptation embodied by Emma Picken. In the *Shop*, Dickens sought to solve his, and his culture's gender conundrum through radical reconstruction of his heroines. To match that achievement in his life, he serially acquired the three Hogarth sisters.

Dickens has often been excoriated for his vapid little heroines, and accused of lacking an understanding of women. One of his friends complained: "I'm never up to his young girls—he is so very fond of the age of 'Nell' when they are most insipid" (qtd. in Slater 358). And after his death, Dickens's daughter, Kate, would comment: "My father did not understand women" (Ackroyd 823). But what he did thoroughly understand, on whatever level of consciousness, were his own requirements for a compartmentalization of roles in both his fictional female characters and the real women in his life. The *Shop* thus creates a peculiar configuration of female types, a pattern of women, which in turn gestures toward the arrangement of actual females with which Dickens would surround himself in the early years of his marriage. Death, and a belated education a la Mrs. Ellis, are the metaphoric surgeons which, in effect, quadruple the *Shop's* female types, and produce a satisfactory and safe female configuration at closure. The need for this pattern of multiple females illustrates what Slater has termed "Dickens's extreme difficulty in reconciling the sexual with the domestic ideal" (311). Erotic sexuality, companionate domesticity, and idealized spirituality are mutually exclusive categories in the *Shop's* females.

*

Nell has her origins in what Dickens called "the little child story" (Forster 1: 117), but even in what was initially intended to be only a short segment of *Master Humphrey's Clock,* her contradictions and mysteries exceed the terms of this originating phrase.[2] The "little child" is almost fourteen years old (well past the then-current age of consent), the time of pubescence when the female body has acquired flesh, curve, and bloom. Dickens intends a myth of idealized, childlike purity and innocence, but the integrity of the myth is sabotaged by tempting female flesh and the contradictions of a cultural binary: the child/woman is innocent; the child/woman is erotic. As James Kincaid has observed, the child is a cultural construct (*Child-Loving* 72), and "the way in which we have constructed the child, the way in which it has been constructed historically, makes its desirability inevitable" (198). According to Kincaid, the early Victorian construct of the child was never one of total innocence anyway, but always a more complicated model composed of contradictory images: a being inflected with "evil impulses," "in touch with primal feelings," "difficult to control" (74). Moreover, "[t]he child's innocence . . . becomes a vulnerability" (73), all too easily defiled and victimized. There is no better definition of Nell, her contradictions a perfect reflection of her creator's, and his culture's fears, desires, and anxieties. Dickens's little child, his allegory of innocence, holding her solitary way among a crowd of wild grotesques, is endangered and dangerous from the start. Her innocence is so commingled with infusions of culturally determined eroticism and tempting vulnerability, both in her author's mind, and in the minds of his readers, that she must die in order to save herself—and all of us.

Robert Polhemus's essay on Millais and his painting, *The Woodman's Daughter,* shows how culturally widespread was the commingling of innocence and eroticism in renderings of the child. For Polhemus, *The Woodsman's Daughter,* featuring a male and female child of different classes, honors "childhood as a center of innocence and potential virtue, but it also can be seen to eroticize childhood" (435). Millais makes of both children "dramatic, seductive, libidinous subjects," as well as objects of "an appropriating gaze" (439). Polhemus's point is much more complex than these brief citations can indicate, but his essay illustrates how the child, even in the midst of its innocence, can be, and was, both rendered and viewed as "a popular object of libido and narcissism" (446)—a practice as prevalent in Victorian painting as it is in the *Shop.* But where Millais succeeds (at least in this painting) in making the children libidinous subjects as well as objects, the *Shop* dedicates itself to making sure that neither Nell nor the Marchioness will become subjects, libidinous or otherwise. Polhemus remarks that "[w]hat we value as pure and loving can quickly change to what is impure, impious, and fallen" (439). His statement could serve as a very succinct summary of the *Shop*'s subtextual fears about Nell.

Leonore Davidoff and Catherine Hall, in discussing the ambiguous relationships between Victorian fathers and daughters, as well as between brothers and sisters, note that the young female's combination of childishness and womanliness, coupled with implicit erotic overtones, "seems to have been a powerful, even titillating image" to many early Victorian readers (348). Not surprisingly, they cite Dickens's novels as their literary examples wherein contradictory innocence and eroticism are combined, as Dickens and his readers, on whatever level of consciousness, fantasize a "sexual attraction to young girls" (351). As Malcolm Andrews has also pointed out, the "idea of the adorable vulnerability of children was deeply rooted in the popular imagination" (75).[3] The boundary between female innocence and female eroticism, between child and woman, is deliberately blurred in the *Shop*. Nell, her personality a near blank, occupies a permeable space easily penetrated, an ill-defined category easily modified. And that is where and how Dickens, and his readers, wanted her to be, an emptiness capable of being occupied, capable of containing all the possibilities posed by the cultural binary.[4]

The *Shop*'s opening scene immediately echoes the culture's disjunctive attitude toward the "child"—Nell Trent. The elderly Master Humphrey rescues the girl, who has lost her way on the dark streets of London. He refers to her always as "the child" (although we will shortly discover that she is almost fourteen), and describes her as "fresh from God" (46), and as "pure, fresh, youthful" (56).[5] At the same time, he carefully marks her scantily-clad body, her need for male assistance, and her exposure to the dangers of the public street, all of which gesture toward a potentially dangerous sexuality. Already the boundary between childish innocence and pubescent titillation is blurred. When he returns to his rooms, he continues to obsess about Nell, fixating particularly on the child "in her bed" (55). His fantasies verge on the sadistic, so that when the girl's budding body is juxtaposed with his ruminations on "all possible harm that might happen" (54), "villainy of the worst kind," and "dark and secret deeds" (55), she becomes a signifier of meanings very different from those of the child "fresh from God." In fact, Nell's fate is sealed from the outset precisely because she fascinates as both child and woman, her innocent face and her vulnerable, budding body sending mixed signals which the observer (reader) may interpret at will. Alone and unprotected, she freely wanders the city—a street-walker, and marked as such by Master Humphrey's feverish fantasies of danger.

Even when at home in the Shop, Nell's circumstances deprive her of the conventional protections of the domestic sphere, and warn of her peril. No fence, garden, or locked front door marks the boundary between public and private sphere for her. She lives in a public place, amidst bizarre commodities displayed for sale, where men like Quilp and Fred Trent are free to enter, leer, and handle the merchandise at will. As Judith Flanders has remarked, a Victorian house and its decoration is "an expression of the morality that reside[s] within" (18), and the Shop offers, at best, a morally ambiguous environment. Possessing neither a conventional domestic framework nor familial protection, Nell is both physically and morally out-of-place. Through no fault of her own, she poses a threat to herself; to the social order; and, ultimately, to Dickens's impossible originating construct—a construct in which childlike innocence, safe and intact, resides within an erotic female body.

The *Shop* repeatedly casts Nell as the passive leading lady of male plots and gazes, as her very purity continues to excite the imagination of all who see her. Already the heroine of Master Humphrey's over-heated reveries, Nell also stars in grandfather's gambling fantasies in which she is simultaneously the excuse for, and victim of his addiction.[6] Quilp, his lust overt and undisplaced, propositions her in the most lewd manner to be his "number two," his "rosy, cosy little Nell," his "little bud" (93, 125). Meanwhile, the girl's own brother and Dick Swiveller plot to marry her off to Dick in order to obtain the grandfather's putative fortune. For them, she is a sexual and monetary opportunity—a pretty face and available maidenhead attached to an inheritance. She is also, according to Fred Trent, an easy target, a malleable cipher with "strong affections," "easily influenced and persuaded" (103). Quilp himself could hardly have been more candid in pointing to the girl's potential for victimization. Even humble Kit Nubbles obsessively watches her window every night. Clearly Nell is what men want to make of her and, from the beginning, what they make of her is far too much.

As grandfather's gambling obsession worsens, Nell decides they must escape to the countryside, in a journey that soon becomes a Pilgrim's Regress. Ominous signs appear almost immediately. Nell's suffering is objectified in her bleeding feet, the only parts of her body which seem to belong fully to her. Pure as she may be, she is ever more compromised by her erotic charisma, her dangerous freedom, and the spectacle her life on the road makes of her.[7] When she and grandfather enter a town where races are being held, the girl tries to sell homemade nosegays in the drunken crowds, but her tempting body and winning ways are her only marketable commodities. Once again forced to flee, Nell and grandfather encounter Mrs. Jarley who offers Nell a job as guide to her traveling Wax-Work. As before, Nell's attractions exceed the restraints of propriety. Inside and outside the Wax-Work, she metamorphoses into a local celebrity, the object of the public's gaze and adulation. Sent out on a cart to display a sample of the wax figures, Nell displays herself as well, her fascinations far eclipsing the novelty of the wax Brigand. The perceptive Mrs. Jarley soon concludes that she must keep the girl off the street, and inside the exhibition hall, "lest Nell should become too cheap" (286). But Nell has already become a public spectacle, with an involuntary talent for unleashing masculine energies and attracting male voyeurs of all ages. Compounding her impropriety, she roams the town at night by herself. During the course of her wanderings she secretly observes the monstrous Quilp in the street, almost as if her pubescent vulnerability, in and of itself, conjures his sexually threatening presence.

Grandfather's misdeeds dictate that Nell must again escape with the old man. Now she is "torn and bleeding from the wounds of thorns and briars," these stigmata mute testimony to both her agony of mind and violation of body (404). As drunken bargemen make her the object of their lewd attentions and crude compliments, she continues to be out-of-place, and to transgress conventional mores.[8] The nightmarish journey continues, and all the girls's symptoms speak of imminent collapse. Made cheap by what John Forster early on perceived as her "sad maturity of experience" (1: 124), Nell is very nearly a fallen woman. At this juncture, she loses consciousness in a literal fall. It is a fortunate fall as well, however, for she faints at the feet of her old friend, the schoolmaster, who provides the girl and her grandfather with help and shelter. Her new home is a dilapidated building near an old, ghostly church, crumbling ruins, and a graveyard. At last given an opportunity for domesticity, however aberrant, she gardens in a graveyard, and keeps house in a mausoleum, a fitting setting for the beautiful death to come.

In the schoolmaster's new village, as Nell prepares to waste and die, she again undertakes a public role. Like Ruth Pinch and Esther Summerson after her, she is invested with a set of keys, but these keys open neither cunning larders nor charming triangular rooms. Rather, they unlock the doors to a world of death in which the very air seems laden with decay. As she had formerly exhibited the Wax-Work, now she exhibits the features of the local church. And as before, people come to gaze at Nell rather than the religious objects. Tourists who visit the village "speaking to others of the child, sent more; so that even at that season of the year they had visitors almost daily" (508). On Sundays, the country folk come from three or four miles around to look at her, and to bring her presents (509). The public scrutiny of Nell has an added dimension now; what were heretofore merely obsessively admiring stares are now also reverential. Her body is no less physically attractive than before, but the very fact that the too-fascinating and thus dangerous body is approaching death renders it less threatening.

Once again it proves impossible to contain the girl's attractions this side of the grave. Her fascinations lead men either to worship (the common talk is that she "will be an angel" [509]) or lust, or some curious commingling of the two. Death adds a final frisson; she continues to be irresistible on her deathbed as Eros and Thanatos melt sweetly into one another.[9] And now the narrator takes his pleasure with the never-lovelier body, his desire displaced in sentimental blank verse, his temptation sublimated in grief. Now he can gaze to his heart's content, safely protected from physical connection. Nell will remain chaste forever; her slow decline, marred by neither illness nor struggle, ensures that her body is simultaneously ethereal, desirable, and unavailable. A beautiful death is the perfect solution to the problems posed by Nell's contradictions. The magnetic female has achieved her final transformation, perpetually virginal and impermeable—if not to the worm, at least to man.

The narrator's (and Dickens's) obsessive concern with the young female's beautiful death reflects a larger preoccupation of the culture. As Sylvia Manning has noted, Tennyson's poems present "a range of female figures in whom sex and their own deaths are conjoined," and in which the deaths are marked by "a strange beauty" (206). She particularly cites "The Lady of Shalott" in which "death is fulfillment, completion, climax" (202), and concludes that "the eagerly dying or eager to die female is a literary trope of high frequency in the period" (210). In her study of paintings and photographs of children, Anne Higonnet also remarks that "[t]he beautiful child corpse is one morbidly logical conclusion of the Romantic child image . . . . The dead child's body is one that never did and never will know desire, that allows adults to project the full measure of their longing" (29–30). And, finally, James Kincaid notes that "[t]he particular attractions of the sick or dying child seem to have figured importantly for the [Victorian] culture generally" (*Child-Loving* 199).

Like her death, Nell's burial is near-orgasmic. The interment takes place only after three days of intense visual homage rendered to the beautiful body, "unaltered in this change" (654). Even after the corpse is lowered into the ground, "the villagers closed round to look into the grave" (658).[10] An aura of the Sleeping Beauty surrounds Nell's body, but this Beauty will never be awakened by a kiss. Rather, she will be eternally available as a fantasy of female perfection—a pure and flawless soulmate—for both narrator and reader.[11] In a revelatory metaphor, the narrator equates Nell with Eve at the creation: "She seemed a creature fresh from the hand of God, and waiting for the breath of life; not one who had lived and suffered death" (652). She is Eve, fresh and beautiful, but death prevents her body from re-enacting the treason of the temptation and man's first fall. Like the dead Mary Hogarth, Nell is associated with temptation removed, and perfection forever inviolable. Death has performed the necessary surgery guaranteeing the separation of sexuality and spirituality, and one piece of the female puzzle has been fitted to the required pattern of females.[12]

Almost as soon as he realized that Nell must die in order to be saved, Dickens began to create a second female curiosity for his *Shop*—the comic Marchioness. Her creation and subsequent transformation offer an opportunity for the fulfillment of the marriage plot denied to Nell. Even as Nell trudges toward her beautiful death, the Marchioness arrives on the scene in a comic burst of common sense and sturdy independence unknown to her pathetic counterpart. Dickens's second heroine, the "small, slipshod girl"

(333), seems designed, from her inception, to be a less troubled and trouble-some alternative to Nell. In the course of the ensuing chapters, the Marchio-ness is changed from comic grotesque to provident wife, from starved servant to lovely homemaker. Her construction and subsequent reconstruction gloss Nell's story, and afford further insight into Dickens's conception of the safely compartmentalized female.

We first encounter the Marchioness as a nameless, diminutive scullery maid by day, a prisoner in the Brass's dank basement by night. She is compounded of one part dirty, coarse apron, and one part perpetual head cold from damp living. Like Nell's, the house she occupies is a public place, in her case both home and law office. Like Nell's, it is inhabited by grotesques: the masculine and dragon-like Sally Brass and her brother, the androgynous Sampson. But unlike Nell, the stunted and starved Marchioness possesses neither freedom nor beauty, nor has she any opportunity to make a spectacle or a temptation of herself. In addition, what the small servant makes of her restrictive and abusive environment differs entirely from Nell's sad struggles. Even impris-oned in the bowels of the earth beneath Bevis Marks, the girl remains bold of temperament, eager for experience, and quick of perception, adroitly ex-plaining to Dick Swiveller the strategies required to snare a lodger, and dis-closing the secrets of the household. The Marchioness takes advantage, with gusto, of the scanty opportunities life offers her, and shrewdly observes all that goes on around her. Her energy and enterprise are a counterweight to Nell's despair, her strength and independence a contrast to Nell's resignation.

The servant knows neither her name nor her age. Repeatedly and savagely beaten by her sadistic employer, she nonetheless possesses comic abilities and a lively imagination which ensure both her appeal and her survival. Sally Brass locks her in the dark kitchen each night, but the girl has cleverly searched out a duplicate key which allows her the freedom of the house. Listening at and looking through keyholes, she notes the plots and eccentricit-ies of the members of the household. Just as she supplements her starvation diet with found bits of discarded "sangwitches" and orange peel, so she supplements the male gaze, omnipresent in this text, with her own female curiosity and observation. In a textual world in which Nell passively endures the obsessive stares of every man she encounters, the Marchioness contrives a notable reversal of roles. She replaces the male voyeur, her eye "gleaming and glistening at the keyhole" as she zestfully gathers all the information available in her small world (526). Unlike Nell, the Marchioness eats and drinks with appetite when Dick supplies her with beer and purl, refusing the role of either victim or anorexic. When he teaches her to play cribbage she not only enjoys it, she wins (528).

The Marchioness shows her true mettle when Dick falls ill. Single-handedly escaping from Bevis Marks, she nurses him through three weeks of fever and delirium, cleverly supporting both of them by selling his clothes to buy food and medicine.[13] He is embarrassed at his nakedness ("even an umbrella would be something," he remarks [589]), but she remains matter of fact. Personifying the comforts of female nurture and nursing, she sets up housekeeping in Dick's squalid room, and shows herself a true mistress of the cult of domesticity, of hot tea and crisp toast, medicines and mopping. However, the Marchioness's independence and unconventionality, as well as her lack of education and gentility, mark her as incompatible with the Dickensian female paradigm, thus creating the need for her transfiguration. Just as Nell required a kind of surgery in order to guarantee her idealization, so the Marchioness must undergo a transformational operation of a different sort in order to become the perfect domestic companion. As a result, the crisis of Dick's illness signals not only the beginning of his moral transformation; it also marks the onset of the Marchioness's change from illiterate comic servant to young and lovely girl exhibiting all the proper female virtues. But before her final reconstruction, the Marchioness has one more opportunity to demonstrate her courage and enterprise.

Kit Nubbles requires rescue, and it is the small servant who risks her own safety, plunging into the chaos of London's dark alleys to fetch help. No other Dickens heroine is allowed to be so athletic and aggressive until Lizzie Hexam (also a member of the lower orders) saves her man from drowning. On the morning after the Marchioness's adventure, the male world of middle-class authority intrudes itself into the hitherto female-dominated world of nurse and patient. The men try to approach Dick's bed, but "his little nurse, pushing the visitors aside and pressing up to his pillow as if in jealousy of their interference, set his breakfast before him, and insisted on his taking it before he underwent the fatigue of speaking or being spoken to" (596). Thus the Marchioness remains in charge for a few more minutes, able to create a final moment of female authority by sheer exertion of will—a moment in which she challenges conventional gender and class hierarchies. At this climactic moment, the female is potent and strong, Dick passive and dependent, the male visitors mere marginal presences. The meaning of Dick's illness, recovery, and relationship with the Marchioness are generally presented somewhat differently than I do here, with Dick cast in the starring role, and the Marchioness appearing merely as a bit player. For example, James Kincaid views the pair as a triumph of love and humor, "a very movingly realized alternative" to the pessimism of the *Shop* (*Rhetoric* 99). Steven Marcus suggests that Dick is reborn "into authentically heroic circumstances" as a result of his illness, and that his "rescue" of the Marchioness is his "heroic ordeal" (165–68). Both interpretations may be legitimate in terms of a male-hero myth, but Kincaid doesn't take into account the price that the Marchioness will pay for this triumph of love and humor, while Marcus ignores the fact that it is the Marchioness who first rescues Dick, and then rescues Kit as well.

The girl's bold actions, and her ability to hold the center of the stage, though momentarily allowable in a comic servant, cannot be permitted to continue if she is to become a suitable Dickensian wife. Almost immediately after her defiance of convention, the Marchioness's circumstances, character, and body are forced to undergo drastic change. As if text and narrator suddenly recall their ideological responsibilities, as if both realize that male authority must be exerted, Dick's male visitors are finally allowed to intervene. The Marchioness, having already undergone a sea change from starved grotesque to authoritative nurse, now embarks on the third and final stage of her transformative surgery. A huge hamper of food and drink is delivered to Dick's sickroom, accompanied by the respectable, middle-aged Mrs. Garland who displaces the young girl from her position of raffish authority. When the Marchioness sees the treasures of the hamper, opulent commodities of a middle-class, male world of business and luxury, "the small servant, who had never thought it possible that such things could be, except in shops, stood rooted to the spot in her one shoe, with her mouth and eyes watering in unison, and her power of speech quite gone" (601).

The Marchioness never speaks again. The resourceful girl who has taken charge of both Dick and events is about to be recast in order to conform to Dick and Dickens's ideological requirements. Having conveniently inherited an annuity from an aunt, the now-recovered Dick buys the Marchioness handsome clothes, and sends her off to "the school of his selection" (667). There the shrewd, daring girl is transformed into an efficient and domesticated Angel-in-the-House, as if she had digested (or been digested by) the entirety of Mrs. Ellis's advice book for young ladies, *The Daughters of England*. Education reconstructs and re-embodies the lower-class servant, making of her a respectable, middle-class young woman who will be both a competent homemaker and a charming companion. Dick once named her the Marchioness; now, marking the completion of her transformation, he renames her Sophronia Sphynx. And indeed she is as silent as the sphinx for the remainder of the narrative. In exchange for her lost voice and unconventionality, for the loss of her autonomous gaze, she acquires good taste, gentility, and tact, learning to be a credit both to Dick and the cult of the feminine. When the educational surgery is completed, when she can be certified as "good-looking, clever, and good-humored" (668), Dick marries her, and they repair to the little cottage at Hampstead. Just as Nell's actual death takes place between chapters, so does the Marchioness's sanitization and transformation occur in the gaps between paragraphs. Her courtship is nonexistent, her maturity and marriage hastily summed up in a very few words. Her evolution to wife is rendered comic even in its brevity, thus further diluting any dangers which might be posed by her now mature and healed body. Hers is hardly a calamitous fate; after all, she is rescued from brutal beatings, starvation, and grinding toil. But there will be no more adventures in London, no more bold gazes, no more shrewd improvisations, no more taking charge.

The Swivellers' domestic menage is not entirely conventional, and its departures from the norm deserve attention. Because Dick has inherited money, he and Sophronia never occupy separate spheres. John Tosh has posited a "polarization of breadwinner and homemaker" in the Victorian era, which "loaded the odds against fulfilling marriages" (26). But the *Shop* is very careful to construct for the Swivellers a comfortable and companionate marriage—he an "attached and domesticated husband," she "a cheerful, affectionate, and provident wife" (669)—without polarization. In addition, Dick and Mr. Chuckster spend each Sunday together in Dick's smoking-box. This male companionship seems to obviate any need for further homosociality or adventure outside the home, and Dick is fully content with his domesticated life in the private sphere. Mrs. Ellis enjoined the wives of England to learn to manage their husbands so that the latter do not know it (41). In apparent agreement, the *Shop*'s creator has gifted Sophronia with the cleverness and calculation to tolerate and even encourage Mr. Chuckster and Dick in their "occasional outbreak" (669). Thus the *Shop* has not only constructed a paragon of companionate marriage, it has also negotiated the tensions between Sussman's "masculine plot" and "marriage plot" (64): here the former is a happy combination of cigars and Mr. Chuckster, the latter carefully circumscribed to include only a comic fantasy of ordered domesticity and asexual companionship. The reader has every reason to believe that Sophronia (even or perhaps because), silent and sphinx-like, will keep Dick well-entertained and content with those "many hundred thousand games of cribbage" (669). The narrator does not tell us if she ever wins.

Perhaps the most noteworthy aspect of the Swivellers' marriage is the fact that, unlike so many other Dickensian couples at closure, they do not reproduce themselves. It is possible that their lack of progeny is the result of Sophronia's grisly antecedents (the monstrous Quilp and the dreadful Sally Brass are her parents). I think it more likely, however, that their creator, on some level, deemed it desirable that the newly-created Sophronia should remain efficient, slim, and focused solely on her husband and his domestic environment. The Swivellers' childlessness further italicizes the companionate aspect of their marriage, and minimizes the sexual side. Having erased Nell's tempting body in the course of the narrative, the text then elides the Marchioness's voice, energy, and cunning. Finally, it eliminates Sophronia's reproductive capacity at closure, happily making of her as much sister as wife. Indeed, the *Shop* has enacted an elaborate makeover of its second female curiosity, has then sold her into respectable domesticity, and thus fitted another piece of the female puzzle to the required pattern of women.

**

Garrett Stewart has contended that the *Shop* is structured by Quilp and Nell's polar opposition (*Trials* 91), as has Steven Marcus (151). But the doubling, and subsequent redoubling, of the female heroines structure this text in equally important ways. Chronologically analyzed, the sequence of events within the novel confirms the connection between the two heroines. On one day, the Marchioness is displaced and silenced by the arrival of the male authorities in Dick's sickroom, thus beginning her metamorphosis. The very next day Nell dies, to be replaced by the soon-to-be genteel Sophronia.[14] Nell and the Marchioness are carefully isolated one from the other textually so that death can cancel sexuality, and rebirth by metamorphosis can balance death. The two heroines in their original forms are puzzle pieces that must be fit to a pattern; their transformations then become partial answers to the ultimate gender conundrum posed by male energies, male needs, and female threats. The two Nells, the Marchioness, and Sophronia gloss, contradict, and fulfill each other in the world of the *Shop*, as well as in the sexual and ideological fantasies of their creator. The list of oppositions and contradictions among the heroines is revealing.

Nell's fascinating, tempting body is opposed to the stunted, starved body of the lower-class servant—and neither body will prove satisfactory to its creator. Nell is burdened with a dangerous, erotic magnetism; the small servant, neither erotic nor magnetic, possesses more useful, though less romantic and genteel skills. Her chaste life entangled in male plots to use and abuse her, and her essential nullity of character complicated by her curious blend of spiritual and erotic attraction, Nell is an allegory gone out of control, a failed myth. Neither allegoric nor mythic, the Marchioness proves herself a practical, serviceable female—ready to clean a house, play a game of cribbage, or take charge of a sick man. It is as impossible to imagine poor, noble Nell at the cribbage board as it is to imagine the Marchioness voluntarily wasting away. Nell's natural and inevitable habitat lies in that indeterminate upper air through which the angels in the novel's last illustration bear her. The Marchioness, by contrast, appears "mysteriously from under ground," firmly bound to sloppy floors, dirty kitchens, and human service (334). Nell's speech and demeanor are naturally upper-class, those of the Marchioness as coarse as her apron. The Marchioness's enterprise and sturdy will to survive, enjoy, and flourish create a stark contrast with Nell's resolute death march. Nell, tending graves, preoccupies herself with a beautiful death; her counterpart, tending Dick, occupies herself with a useful life. Nell loses her way in the streets of London, and allows herself to be picked up by a strange man, requiring male guidance to get back home. The servant, at the same age, loses herself in the streets of London, inquires her way of apple-women until she finds her own direction, and single-handedly accomplishes her mission. While Nell is perpetually victimized by her grandfather, the Marchioness has the enterprise to make an escape from wicked Sally Brass, thus displacing the power of the mother through her own initiative.

And yet, neither of these heroines, neither body, neither temperament, can supply a satisfactory answer to the novel's female puzzle. Tempting, wandering Nell is a Victorian nightmare from which men must be awakened and protected. The Marchioness is a Victorian fairytale, a lower-class Cinderella —unacculturated, unconventional, and unable to transcend her limitations without a Fairy Godfather. But Sophronia, in sharp contradistinction to both of them, is a Victorian success story—reassuringly asexual, respectably middle-class, and efficiently domestic. Nell's body, in order to remain pure, must be reconstructed as ethereal memory. The Marchioness's body—brutalized, damaged, and half-starved—must be healed and reconstructed so that the newly-minted Sophronia can be born. Quite literally a class act, she emerges from the educational womb as the perfect sister-wife. By thus operating on his heroines, Dickens ensures that female sexuality remains safely separated from both Dick and domesticity, while simultaneously ensuring that disembodied Nell remains virginal and perfect. It is these two recreations which structure the gender ideology of the novel, making complete the critical compartmentalizations so necessary to the successful Dickensian female pattern, and so necessary to the safety and happiness of the *Shop*'s hero.

With all their differences, Nell and the Marchioness, in their original incarnations so dissimilar in class, temperament, and magnetism, share one characteristic. Both are too unconventional and too excessive to remain intact. Both must be diluted, disciplined, reimagined, and fitted to the narrative's twin Procrustean beds: the first a grave; the second an orderly, domestic bed from which the stains of sexuality and birth are excluded, but on which there are undoubtedly always clean linens. In the end, only death and a uniquely Dickensian/Sophronian domesticity—both suitably sanitized and idealized—provide safe and satisfactory answers to the problems posed by an erotic female body and an unconventional lower-class female servant.[15] In the *Shop*, death has its own charms, while Dickensian domesticity serves as a kind of magical garment capable of transformation at need. On the one hand it is a translucent gossamer of effortless comfort and service; on the other, an opaque cloak to be thrown over a sexual female body.

John Kucich has observed that ''Nell comes to stand for values and principles of extreme selflessness that revitalize the notion of community for the good characters who try to save her'' (218). While certainly true of the *Shop*'s textual intentions, Kucich's statement does not sufficiently allow for the meanings of the narrative's subtext. The novel, despite its abundance of humor and its theoretically happy endings, is not a novel of revitalization or conventional affirmation. The narrative ends with a vignette in which Kit Nubbles's children (none of them named for Nell) beg him to "tell again that story of good Miss Nell who died" (671). But Kit's account consists less of Nell's story than of homilies about death and heaven, and ends in a narrative of his own needy youth. He takes the children to the street where the Shop once stood, but finds that the neighborhood has changed so much that he becomes "uncertain of the spot, and could only say it was thereabouts, he thought, and that these alterations were confusing" (672). To Kit's failure of memory the narrator adds a cursory dismissal: "so do things pass away, like a tale that is told" (672). In the final words of the novel, then, both death and forgetfulness mitigate affirmation.[16] Further, the *Shop*'s harsh punishments exacted on its male bodies (even the good males of the Garland family are genetically club-footed), and radical surgeries inflicted on its female bodies, dilute any sense that a community has been revitalized.

Jeff Nunokawa finds that the pattern of the Victorian novel "ensures that all passion leads either to the altar . . . or to the graveyard" (137). Grandfather and Quilp, victims of their uncontrolled passions, are led to the graveyard. Beautiful, virtuous Nell ends there as well, also the victim of uncontrolled male passions (including those of the narrator). Dick and the now-genteel Sophronia, neither of them passionate nor aggressive, are the domesticated beneficiaries of the altar. Thus is the Victorian concern with the control of male energy seemingly brought to a satisfactory conclusion in the *Shop*: either in the grave or at the altar; either through the punishment of male bodies, or through the manipulation of the female body. And yet there remains one body among the female curiosities of the *Shop* which survives unaltered, threatening the novel's stability and its carefully constructed limitations of male and female characters. Sally Brass continues to wander the streets of London.

Miss Brass cannot be dismissed as merely a comic grotesque. Troped variously as female vampire, Medusa, and amazon, she is also one of fiction's most abusive mothers—thus, both a mythic and a domestic monster. A sexually desirous female imprisoned in an ugly, masculinized body, she dominates the Brass law business as well as her brother, Sampson, who fears her. Dick Swiveller can't take his eyes off her, likening her to a "strange monster" who renders him "powerless" (327, 328). Clearly Miss Brass, ugly and charmless as she may be, is potent and mesmerizing as well. Sally and Sampson Brass are the only brother/sister pair in the Dickens canon who hate each other, their vitriolic relationship a marker for their aberrant gender identities. Sally is a daughter who has been reared as a son, a macabre sexual partner who can match the monstrous Quilp, and a mother who is an abusive fiend. But it is her final role, as femme fatale, that reveals her uncontrolled and uncontrollable female potency. Sally seems at first an unlikely femme fatale, but the text posits a sexual past for her, as well as a desire for an erotic present. The former is suggested when Quilp visits Bevis Marks, and says of Sally, "There she is . . . there is the woman I ought to have married . . . Oh Sally, Sally!" (325). Quilp exhibits respect for her abilities—sexual as well as business—even as he satirized her "charms." Moreover, Sally is not yet finished with the erotic potential of the male. She is attracted to Dick, so much so that she is willing to "undertake his share of writing in addition to her own" (349). Sally, like Barkis, is willing.

That Sally's power exceeds that of the conventional male world of authority is clearly demonstrated when she defeats the ineffectual attempts of the single gentleman, the Notary, and Mr. Garland to imprison her for her crimes. Escaping their custody, the wily female slips away unobserved. Her last appearance in the narrative marks her as literally a fatal woman. The narrator tells us that "conflicting rumors went abroad" about Sally—that she had been seen on the docks in male attire, or in a sentry-box in St. James's Park leaning on a musket. He then engages to tell us what "the truth appears to be": Sally haunts the night streets and "the obscene hiding-places of London." She and her brother are the embodied spirits of Disease and Vice, and to this day they pass "close at the elbow of the shrinking passenger" (665). This powerful female, this femme fatale, is intimately associated with the sexual tropes of the diseased prostitute. She is a mythic presence, her carnal, potent femaleness embodying that age-old threat to the social order posed by the wandering sexual woman. Like Nell, she is a streetwalker—that which Nell might have been forced to become had her creator not intervened. But unlike Nell, this streetwalker's body lingers intact and unchanged. She endures despite the text's evident desire to create and countenance only certain kinds of circumscribed female bodies and psyches. Sally survives and continues to pose a threat—temporarily marginalized, but not diminished.

***

A sexually enticing Nell, alive; an idealized, romanticized Nell in heaven; a sororal, domestic, companionate Sophronia. The fictional triad gestures toward the Hogarth sisters, the three women involved in a lifelong collaboration to satisfy the complex, antithetic needs of one man. Dickens married the sexually available Catherine Hogarth in April, 1836, and kept her pregnant for the next sixteen years. Catherine's pretty, vivacious younger sister, Mary, lived with the newlyweds off and on from the time of their marriage until her shockingly sudden death in May of 1837. "[S]he had not a single fault," Dickens would write after her death (*Letters* 1: 263). He was still mourning and idealizing the sixteen-year-old years later, when she appeared to him in a dream as a Madonna figure, filled with "the greatest compassion for me," and "heavenly tenderness for me" (*Letters* 4: 196). Georgina, the third and youngest sister, was the same age as Nell and the Marchioness when Dickens was writing the *Shop* in 1840–41. She came to live with Catherine and Charles in the fall of 1842, when she was approximately the same age as Mary had been at her death. Intelligent, cheerful, and devoted, Georgina took charge of the children, and helped to run what was a very complicated household.

The psychodrama of relationships in the Dickens menage-à-quatre is repeated in the inadequacies and excesses of the females in the *Shop*. The fecund and sexualized Catherine clearly could not fulfill the role of pure, perfect young virgin, nor did her near-constant pregnancies and frequent depressions allow her to be either a lively companion or efficient domestic manager. The idealized and perfect Mary of Dickens's memories, on the other hand, would always be both virginally fresh and safely unavailable—like the dead Nell, neither a temptation nor a disappointment. Georgina was what Albert Guerard characterizes as "the reliable, self-effacing housewife" (72)—like Sophronia, safely asexual, while cheerfully (and apparently flawlessly) performing domestic and companionate duties, making home life comfortable and happy.[17] Having re-configured his novel's heroines, Dickens echoed that achievement in his life by means of serial, sororal accretion. Michael Slater has remarked Dickens's lifelong need for "the 'other woman' sister-figure so necessary for a happy Dickens menage whether in life or literature" (25). When we consider the extent of Dickens's energies, and the complexity of his domestic and emotional requirements, it is hardly surprising that the necessary number of sister-figures in his life turns out to be three rather than two. In life and in the *Shop*, Dickens created a pattern of females, each one carefully circumscribed and bounded.[18] He made use of this web of female variations to negotiate the tensions between his own desires and the requirements of Victorian domesticity; between his gargantuan energies and his need for control of self and others; and between his demands of the females in his life and their abilities to respond to those demands. I do not mean to assert a one-for-one association or identity between the heroines of the *Shop* and the women in Dickens's life, but merely to point toward his always complicated organization of female possibilities—his web of women—which far exceeds the conventional cliche of the Angel/Whore bifurcation.

In one of those strangely apposite historical coincidences, 1842—the very year Georgina became a part of the Dickensian female pattern/household—was the year of the first attempt to overturn the "Deceased Wife's Sister Bill" of 1835. The original bill prohibited a man from marrying the sister of his dead wife, and it remained in force until 1907, despite lengthy debates and repeated attempts to repeal it. Leila May states that the prohibition endured so long because Victorian culture was "permeated by a denial of the potential for incest and a deeply entrenched anxiety about its possibility" (22). I speculate, however, that Dickens's genius for compartmentalizing the female would allow him to suppress anxiety about any Hogarthian incestuous possibilities. After all, in his understanding of his own life's story, as he might narrate it to himself in 1842, the first sister is alive, legal, and available; the second both unavailable and idealized; and the third an asexual, domestic companion.

The *Shop* has provided one kind of answer to its female puzzle—the problem of untidy fusions of sexuality and domesticity, of innocence and eroticism, in one female body. It has also offered one kind of solution to the culture's gender conundrum—the problem posed by excessive male "energies" confronted by excessive female erotic attraction. It has contained and controlled those excesses by means of the deaths of its most threatening male bodies, and manipulations of, and restraints on its female bodies. As a result, Dick (and Dickens) will not succumb to Quilpishness this time, and neither Nell nor Sophronia will become a Catherine Dickens, a Mrs. Quilp, or a Sally Brass. The magic cloak of domesticity guarantees that most anomalous of domestic outcomes, a safely asexual marriage plot in which erotic temptation and reproduction are elided altogether at closure. Dick and Sophronia—and Dickens and Catherine, Mary, and Georgina—abide. Happy endings indeed—although Sally Brass remains at large, while Ellen Ternan awaits in the future: "a young and lovely girl" growing into a woman expressly on Dickens's account.

NOTES

1. Michael Slater has criticized Johnson's assessment of the rifts in the Dickens marriage, concluding that Johnson "accept[s] without reserve Dickens's own 'plot' for the story of his marriage," without offering evidence "apart from Dickens own later words" (114). Ackroyd strikes a middle course, citing "a sense in his life of his wishing to break away from bonds even as he was tying them for himself" (271).

2. For a detailed account of the evolution of the *Shop*, as it grew from a vignette to a full-length novel, see Patten 44–64.

3. Andrews describes *Martin Chuzzlewit*'s Infant Phenomenon as representing "the commercialism of the cult of childhood" (74), during a time of mass theatrical obsession with child actors. It is possible to see the stunted Phenomenon as a comic-grotesque version of Nell's objectification in the eyes of the world.

4. For a fascinating conversation about the meanings of the child's body in Millais's *Cherry Ripe*, see the articles in *Victorian Studies* by Bradley, Reis, and Polhemus.

Bradley sees the little girl as a glorification of purity and innocence. A year later, Reis responds with her own interpretation of the child's image as sexually aggressive and erotic. Two years later Polhemus comments on Millais, Bradley, Reis, and *Cherry Ripe* in an essay which attempts to make some sense of why we see what we do, and tries to avoid "projections of reductive cultural and political ideologies" (449).

5. All page references are to the Penguin edition of *The Old Curiosity Shop*.

6. Albert Guerard has pointed out that it is grandfather who represents the greatest threat to Nell, inspiring the most intense moments of her terror (83). It is certainly possible to read the scene in which he steals her gold pieces as a rape.

7. Laurie Langbauer alludes to Dickens's "restless, errant women," and their "wayward roving" (131).

8. Davidoff and Hall remark the increasingly stringent confinement of the female in the Victorian era: "Growing restraints on the physical and social mobility of women, especially young girls, is a motif across a range of activities" (403). "But solitary ramblings, much less longer journeys, came to be out of the question and girls were increasingly closely guarded" (405). Her very freedom victimizes Nell, as she wanders outside society's rules.

9. In a most appropriate coupling of novel and reviewer, Edgar Allen Poe was assigned to review the *Shop* in America. He concludes that the scenes of Nell's death "are so drawn that human language, urged by human thought, could go no further in the excitement of human feelings" (24).

10. Garrett Stewart, in analyzing Victorian novelists' renditions of death scenes, has noted that the description of the death of a character can often epitomize that character's life, organizing "the finished life toward compressed biography" (*Death Sentences* 16). And so it is that Nell's body, in death as in life, continues to be a magnet for the public gaze.

11. Susan Sontag's analysis of the use of tuberculosis as a metaphor is illuminating here. She notes that tuberculosis provided two contradictory applications for Victorian novelists: "It described the death of someone (like a child) thought to be too 'good' to be sexual: the assertion of an angelic psychology. It was also a way of describing sexual feelings . . . It was both a way of describing sensuality and promoting the claims of sublimation . . . " (25–26). Sontag's analysis is perfectly applicable to the narrator's description of Nell's body.

12. Dickens's comments in his letters reflect the narrator's preoccupation with Nell's death. To George Cattermole he wrote: "I am breaking my heart over this story, and cannot bear to finish it" (December 22, 1840). And to Forster: "this part of the story is not to be galloped over" (January 8, 1841). He then goes on to associate Nell's death with that of Mary Hogarth: "Dear Mary died yesterday, when I think of this sad story" (*Letters* 2: 172, 181–182).

13. Dick's illness, unlike Nell's, is neither erotic nor ambiguous. His fever is a sign of his moral transformation, but I think it is convenient as well. Since he is too ill to take action himself, others must save Kit and punish the Brasses. As James Eli Adams has noted, there are "many ritual humiliations of male characters in Victorian fiction." They "enjoy moral redemption, and the love of the heroine, only after their aggression has been thoroughly disarmed, even to the extent of

physical incapacitation'' (130). Dick is another in a long line of Dickens's male protagonists who are known by their passivity. Dick, however, is funnier than most.

14. Garrett Stewart has pointed out that Nell and Quilp die on the same day (*Trials* 98).

15. Not until wicked little Ruth Pinch puts that beefsteak pudding together, while Tom and the narrator salivate, does a Dickens heroine combine domesticity with sex appeal. And even in that case, the combination is temporary, and performed for a brother. There is no indication that Ruth is sexily domestic or domestically sexy after her marriage to John Westlock.

16. For a more optimistic interpretation of Kit as a storyteller, see Jaffe. She treats Kit's subordination of Nell's story to his own as conveying ''a sense that present and continuing life outweighs past sorrows'' (70).

17. Slater calls the lively, good-looking Georgina a ''companion'' for Dickens, and notes that he ''had a very high regard for her mental capacities'' (163, 174). By all accounts, she adored him, often accompanied him on his marathon walks, organized and executed the family's frequent travel arrangements, and became generally indispensable. She remained with Dickens until his death in 1870.

18. Dickens would also supplement the three sisters in his life with a series of flirtations and infatuations, of varying degree of seriousness, with other young women. But the Hogarth sisters would continue to embody the female pattern of his psychodrama until he met Ellen Ternan and found Catherine no longer useful or bearable.

WORKS CITED

Ackroyd, Peter. *Dickens.* New York: HarperCollins, 1990.

Adams, James Eli. ''Victorian Sexualities.'' *A Companion to Victorian Literature & Culture.* Ed. Herbert F. Tucker. Malden, Mass.: Blackwell, 1999.

Andrews, Malcolm. *Dickens and the Grown-up Child.* Iowa City: U of Iowa P, 1994.

Bradley, Laurel. ''From Eden to Empire: John Everett Millais's *Cherry Ripe.*'' *Victorian Studies* 34 (1991): 179–203.

Christian, Mrs. Eleanor. ''Dickens on Holiday (1840) and Afterwards.'' *Charles Dickens: Interviews and Recollections.* Ed. Philip Collins. Vol. 1. Totowa, N.J.: Barnes and Noble, 1981. 33–41.

Davidoff, Leonore, and Catherine Hall. *Family Fortunes: Men and Women of the English Middle Class 1780–1850.* Chicago: U of Chicago P, 1987.

Dickens, Charles. *The Letters of Charles Dickens.* The Pilgrim Edition. Ed. Madeline House, Graham Storey, Kathleen Tillotson, et al. Vol. 2. Oxford: Clarendon, 1969.

————. *The Old Curiosity Shop.* Harmondsworth: Penguin, 1972.

Ellis, Sarah Stickney. *The Wives of England: Their Relative Duties, Domestic Influence, and Social Obligations.* New York, 1843.

Flanders, Judith. *Inside the Victorian Home: A Portrait of Domestic Life in Victorian England.* New York: Norton, 2004.

Forster, John. *The Life of Charles Dickens.* 2 vols. London: Dent, 1927.

Guerard, Albert J. *The Triumph of the Novel: Dickens, Dostoevsky, Faulkner.* Chicago: U of Chicago P, 1976.

Jaffe, Audrey. *Vanishing Points: Dickens, Narrative, and the Subject of Omniscience.* Berkeley: U of California P, 1991.

Johnson, Edgar. *Charles Dickens: His Tragedy and Triumph.* 2 vols. New York: Simon and Schuster, 1952.

Higonnet, Anne. *Pictures of Innocence: The History and Crisis of Ideal Childhood.* New York: Thames and Hudson, Ltd., 1998.

Kaplan, Fred. *Dickens: A Biography.* New York: William Morrow, 1988.

Kincaid, James R. *Child-Loving: The Erotic Child and Victorian Culture.* New York: Routledge, 1992.

————. *Dickens and the Rhetoric of Laughter.* Oxford: Oxford UP, 1971.

Kucich, John. *Repression in Victorian Fiction: Charlotte Bronte, George Eliot, and Charles Dickens.* Berkeley: U of California P, 1987.

Langbauer, Laurie. *Women and Romance: The Consolations of Gender in the English Novel.* Ithaca: Cornell UP, 1990.

Manning, Sylvia. "Death and Sex from Tennyson's Early Poetry to 'In Memoriam'." *Sex and Death in Victorian Literature.* Ed. Regina Barreca. Bloomington: Indiana UP, 1990.

Marcus, Steven. *Dickens From Pickwick to Dombey.* London: Chatto and Windus, 1965.

May, Leila Silvana. *Disorderly Sisters: Sibling Relations and Sororal Resistance in Nineteenth-Century British Literature.* Lewisburg, PA: Bucknell UP, 2001.

Nunokawa, Jeff. "Sexuality in the Victorian Novel." *The Cambridge Companion to the Victorian Novel.* Ed. Deirdre David. Cambridge, UK: Cambridge UP, 2001. 125–48.

Patten, Robert. "The Story-Weaver at His Loom." *Dickens the Craftsman: Strategies of Presentation.* Ed. Robert B. Partlow, Jr. Carbondale: Southern Illinois UP, 1970. 44–64.

Poe, Edgar Allen. *"The Old Curiosity Shop."* *The Dickens Critics.* Ed. George Ford and Lauriat Lane, Jr. Ithaca: Cornell UP, 1961.

Polhemus, Robert M. "John Millais's Children: Faith, Erotics, and *The Woodsman's Daughter." Victorian Studies* 37 (1994): 433–50.

Reis, Pamela Tamarkin. "Victorian Centerfold: Another Look at Millais's *Cherry Ripe." Victorian Studies* 35 (1992): 201–05.

Slater, Michael. *Dickens and Women.* London: Dent, 1983.

Sontag, Susan. *Illness as Metaphor and Aids and Its Metaphors.* New York: Anchor, 1990.

Stewart, Garrett. *Death Sentences: Styles of Dying in British Fiction.* Cambridge: Harvard UP, 1984.

———. *Dickens and the Trials of the Imagination.* Cambridge: Harvard UP, 1974.

Sussman, Herbert. *Victorian Masculinities: Manhood and Masculine Poetics in Early Victorian Literature and Art.* Cambridge, UK: Cambridge UP, 1995.

Tosh, John. *A Man's Place: Masculinity and the Middle-Class Home in Victorian England.* New Haven: Yale UP, 1999.

House and Home in *Dombey and Son*

Michal Peled Ginsburg

In Dombey and Son *the narrator debunks Dombey's view of the home
as but a material sign of his name and firm. In so doing, the narrator
shows the house/home as subject to time and suggests that it needs
repeated acts of care to be maintained and reproduced. Thus the house/
home gradually becomes incompatible with the notion of family love
portrayed as spontaneous and independent of particular acts and circumstances for its reproduction. This notion of love, which allows the
novel to reach closure, resembles Dombey's old view of his name/firm
as reproducing themselves without labor. The narrator who started by
critiquing Dombey ends up being like Dombey (who himself does not
really change).*

It is a commonplace of Dickens criticism that his novels promote, perhaps
more than those of any other nineteenth-century novelist, middle-class idealization of family and home. This idealization means primarily that domestic
happiness is seen as static and stable, as what lies beyond time and change.
One consequence of such an understanding of domestic happiness is that the
labor of maintaining the home, in the double sense of continuously recreating
affective family bonds and of keeping house, either becomes unrepresentable
or is presented as mere reproduction of the same which, moreover, is most
effective when kept invisible. Thus, the first-person narrator of *David Copperfield* praises Agnes for perfectly maintaining the home: "The staid old
house was, as to its cleanliness and order, still just as it had been when I
first saw it ... even the old flowers [were] here" because Agnes "found a

---

Dickens Studies Annual, Volume 36, Copyright © 2005 by AMS Press, Inc. All
rights reserved.

pleasure . . . in keeping everything as it used to be.'' And elsewhere he comments: ''I knew who had done all this, by its seeming to have quietly done itself.''[1] By presenting the work of maintenance as a reproduction of the same, the creation of an eternal present, and by rendering this work doubly invisible (it is invisible both in the representation and in the represented world), the novel creates the illusion of the home as both natural (rather than produced by labor) and stable (its reproduction does not involve transformation, it is a reproduction of the same).[2] This makes functional domesticity the perfect closure for novels (while only dysfunctional domesticity can provide its plot) and this, in turn, further contributes to the erasure of the labor of reproduction—of maintenance—it requires.

Dombey and Son is similar to other Dickens novels in that its plot deals with dysfunctional domesticity—an emotionally abusive parent and a child, Florence, who for all practical purposes is an orphan. But its resolution and closure, while describing the reconstitution of a happy family out of the ashes of the unhappy one, has one curious note to it: this happy family does not seem to have a home.

The cause for the unhappiness described by the novel's plot, Dombey's main failing, is, as many critics have pointed out, his view of family relations as subordinate to and in service of his business interests.[3] In considering his home as nothing but ''the home department'' (as the title to chapter 3 puts it) of his firm, Dombey fails to appreciate the home as a site of affection and intimacy; in concentrating all his attention on Paul, his future business partner, the son of ''Dombey and Son,'' he fails to see the ''spirit of the home,'' his wife Fanny, and later on, his daughter Florence. By the novel's resolution Dombey has learnt how to feel tenderness and express it and he finds his place in the midst of Florence's family as well as in the company of other men of feelings, such as Uncle Sol, Captain Cuttle, and Mr. Toots. But of a home we hear not a word. The old house, now described as a ''desirable Family Mansion,''[4] is to be let and no new house is described or even mentioned. Our last vision of Florence, with her father and children, is on the seashore.[5]

This omission is all the more curious since the family home has been the object of much attention in the novel. Descriptions of the old house punctuate the narrative, appearing at each major turn of the plot of the novel: after the birth of young Paul and the death of the first Mrs. Dombey, after the death of Paul and the departure of Mr. Dombey in the company of Major Bagstock, after Mr. Dombey's engagement and marriage to Edith, and, finally, after the bankruptcy of the firm following the flight of Edith and Carker. One would have thought, therefore, that the vicissitudes of the house constitute a parallel narrative where physical changes reflect, objectify, or complement the changes in the characters and their feelings. If that were the case, the newly constituted happy family would have had a new or renewed home to dwell in. This, however, is not the case. In what follows I will argue, through a close reading of key passages, that the representation of the home/house as subject to time and therefore in need of care becomes gradually incompatible with the creed that family feelings do not depend on any labor for their reproduction since they are spontaneous and indestructible. As a result, by the end of the novel the house/home can no longer be a symbol, nor even the container, for home/family.

The first chapter of the novel, opposing father and son against the background of their similarity, introduces a notion of time that is repetitive rather than linear: time, which set marks on Dombey Sr.'s face, would smooth out the wrinkles on Dombey Jr.'s face, "as a preparation of the surface for his deeper operations" (1).[6] Hence, the operation of time consists in the repetitive and self-canceling actions of marking and wiping; any notion that a blank surface is the beginning of a linear process that leads to a marked surface at its end (or the other way around)—any notion that we move, for example, from innocence to experience or from suffering to tranquility (as the end of the novel seems to suggest)—is, according to this view, illusory because blank surface and marked surface alternate endlessly. The process of marking and wiping, the work of "Time and his brother Care," is a constant, repetitive one, without beginning or end.

This impersonal view of time as repetitive is not opposed but rather embraced by Mr. Dombey who, placing Dombey and Son at the center of the universe, sees history as a repetitive process by which a son joins and then replaces his father, to be then joined and replaced by his own son, to the end of time. Part of Mr. Dombey's "impersonality" has to be attributed not to psychological features (such as pride, or the inability to express emotions) but to this impersonal view he has of himself as but the temporary bearer of a name and a destiny (or the name as destiny); as he tells Major Bagstock: "I am the present unworthy representative of that name" (135). Thus, his self-importance is of a curious kind since it is not primarily attached to his own personal qualities but to a name he temporarily represents.

Dombey's view of repetition tends, however, to negate the effects of time and care. Eager to see Paul as his partner, he sees the interval that separates Paul from that destination as empty. Thus he tells Mrs. Pipchin that Paul is "getting on": he is now six, and "six will be changed to sixteen, before we have time to look about us" (148). His confidence in this smooth arrival has to do with the fact that Paul's trajectory is actually a repetition: "There is nothing of chance or doubt in the course before my son. His way in life was clear and prepared, and marked out before he existed" (148). Paul's course is already marked out because it is not quite his own; it is the course of the

firm which he, like Dombey Sr., represents. By fully identifying himself and
Paul with the firm that has existed before either of them, and will, he believes,
exist long after they are both gone, Dombey presents the continuity of the
firm as occurring almost by itself, not only without support from others, but
without any effort on the part of the principals: "Paul and myself," he tells
his sister, "will be able, when the time comes, to hold our own—the House,
in other words, will be able to hold its own, and maintain its own, and hand
down its own of itself" (50).

This striking pronouncement should not be attributed simply to irrational
pride. Rather, it is the result of the convergence of two related assumptions.
First: since the firm is seen as a name and since Dombey (and Son) are
seen as just the temporary bearers of this name, the firm appears to lack all
materiality.[7] Second: Dombey is not primarily interested in change (which
he may or may not understand requires effort and labor). Rather, he is mostly
interested in the maintenance and reproduction of the same which, in his
view, does not require labor or care. Since what Dombey desires is that
there should always be Dombey and Son, that the same/the name should be
maintained and repeated for ever, he seems to bracket time (which he believes
can be skipped over or arrested) and thus to disregard both the ravages of
time and care and the need for restorative care.

In his view of "Time and his brother Care" the narrator understands Care
solely as worry and trouble and does not seem interested in considering the
power of "care" in the positive sense (of taking care, guarding, and protecting) to attenuate the effects of "time and care." Though this might seem
a particularly pessimistic view of human destiny, as opposed to Dombey's
complacent view of his own destiny, one of its effects is that once the novel
works its way through the plot of feelings and reaches its predestined closure
in happy family and home, protected from "care" (in the sense of trouble
and worry), it does not have to concern itself with the work and care that are
necessary to maintain the home and the family in this happy state. We can
already see why finding a house for this home may present a problem; we
can see also that the narrator responsible for the novel's closure may be
closer to Dombey of the novel's beginning than we might have thought.

In the first chapters of the novel the main emphasis is on the house as the
firm. " 'The house will once again, Mrs. Dombey,' said Mr. Dombey, 'be
not only in name but in fact Dombey and Son' " (1). Some mention of the
house as home occurs when Dombey thinks of his wife who has "done the
honours of his house in a remarkably lady-like and becoming manner" (2).
As will become even clearer in his marriage to Edith, Dombey sees the role
of his wife in doing the honors of his house as representing him (and his
other house, Dombey and Son) to the outside world rather than creating an
intimate private space. This is why Dombey thinks of his wife as similar to

"his plate and furniture," objects that function as tokens of his status. Informed by the doctors that Fanny is rather sick after having given birth to his son and heir, the idea of her possible loss presents itself to him not as "death"—what may befall only the living—but rather as decay (5)—the fate of all material objects (including living things). This objectification of Fanny is also, necessarily, a materialization. If the house/firm is but a name, the house/home and all its furniture (human and non-human) are material tokens of it.

Once Fanny is dead and can no longer preside over the spectacle of Dombey's grandeur, the house has no function and can be shut down. Indeed, following the funeral, Dombey's house takes on the appearance of an unoccupied house, its furniture all covered up, the way it is when the family goes away, in order to minimize wear and tear in the absence of domestic care. But in this case the family has not left and "the various members of Mr. Dombey's household" all occupy their "places in the domestic system" (23). Since the only one departed is Fanny, this may suggest that she did have a hidden role that cannot be revealed except through her absence: the function of "care," the labor that through an endless number of repetitive acts counters the effects of time, protects against its destruction, and thus produces the appearance of sameness, of absence of change, and of an eternal present. The need for care can only be deduced here through negation: in Fanny's absence, apparently some measures have to be taken to fight against decay and, thus, artificially preserve what formerly was constantly (if invisibly) reproduced. Closing up the house and covering the furniture will also "preserve" it for a future moment when Son will become Dombey, with a wife of his own to do the honors of his house in a becoming manner.

The family house's function is to impress the world with the greatness of Dombey and Son and the house resembles Dombey in the sense that this representation is far from flamboyant. If Dombey is described as "cool" and "rigid," the house is of "dismal state" "on the shady side of a tall, dark, dreadfully genteel street" (23) with "dreary rooms of state" inside (25). The darkness and grimness of the inside, the lack of sun and the gaunt trees outside, suggest that the house lacks warmth but that this is rather congruent with Dombey's own idea of himself and of greatness. It is as if the lack of warmth—of life—of the house, like Dombey's "coolness" and "rigidity," is designed to freeze Dombey and the house, and thus perpetuate his greatness without "care," only by passive preservation of energy.

We can already tell that this process will not be entirely successful: the newspapers used to cover the furniture tell of "deaths and dreadful murders" and, in spite of all the attempts at preservation, odors—what cannot be contained—come "as from vaults and damp places . . . out of the chimneys" (24). The coolness of the house/vault cannot protect the possessions within it and the odors suggest the onset of decay. The attempt at preservation is also belied by the affinity the narrator observes between Dombey's house and the "dirty house to let immediately opposite" (24). Houses oscillate between being occupied and vacant—alive and dead; as we know from subsequent chapters, the house across the street, empty while the Dombeys's house is inhabited, will be "repaired and newly painted" (262) and occupied by a family of an affectionate widower and his daughters, while Dombey's house, in his absence, will become dirty as if it were entirely unoccupied and at the end of the novel will be deserted and about to be let. Thus, the house across the street addresses "a dismal eloquence to Mr. Dombey's windows" (24). The juxtaposition of the two houses, like that of Dombey Sr. and Jr. on the first page of the novel, shows a process of marking and wiping of marks in preparation for future marking: the work of time and care.

The withdrawal of life from the house could also be interpreted as a sign of mourning for the dead Fanny if Dombey's "cool regret" at the loss of his wife had not precluded the possibility of such an extravagant show of feeling. But mourning is not entirely absent from the scene: "Every chandelier or lustre, muffled in holland, looked like a monstrous tear depending from the ceiling's eye" (24). By comparing the ceiling to a crying eye, with its tears never falling but remaining suspended for ever, the narrator suggests that mourning itself is frozen or preserved. Either Dombey's cold nature does not allow him to show his sorrow by shedding tears, or he reserves and preserves his tears, the way he preserves his furnishings, "for the son with whom his plans were all associated" (24). Thus the image of Mr. Dombey watching his son from the "dark distance" of his room, at the beginning of the novel, already anticipates Mr. Dombey at the end of the novel in as much as he is already the "lone prisoner in a cell, or a strange apparition" (25) he will become. The "preservation" of time is more like a "bracketing" of duration that allows the present to precipitate into the future.

When young Paul dies, Dombey goes into full-scale mourning and subsequently goes away with Major Bagstock, leaving Florence "alone in the great dreary house" (337). The long description of the house in chapter 23 has as its major conceit the fairy tale motif of the king's daughter imprisoned or under a spell in an isolated dwelling place, as in "Sleeping Beauty" or "Beauty and the Beast."[8] But Florence is not only *imprisoned in* the house, like "the king's fair daughter in the story" (339); she is also *like* the house. Deserted by her father, she is "solitary" (as the first half of the chapter's title puts it), and so is the house: "No magic dwelling-place in magic story, shut up in the heart of a thick wood, was ever more solitary . . . than was her father's house in its grim reality" (337). In Dombey's absence the house is "deserted to the fancy," and so is Florence:

Shadowy company attended Florence up and down the echoing house, and sat
with her in the dismantled rooms. As if her life were an enchanted vision, there
arose out of her solitude ministering thoughts, that made it fanciful and unreal.
She imagined so often what her life would have been if her father could have
loved her and she had been a favourite child, that sometimes, for the moment,
she almost believed it was so.   (340)

Deserted by her father and "deserted to the fancy," Florence fancies not
being deserted by her father. This fancy, however, comes to an end when she
awakes to the "desolation of the solitary house ... with evening coming
on, and no one there!" (340). Thus the initial analogy between Florence and
the house (solitary, deserted to the fancy) develops gradually into a difference:
the house in its "grim reality" is seen more and more as the opposite of the
abode in the legend, and Florence, seen as the princess in the fairy tale,
becomes more and more unlike the house.

Thus, the narrator tells us,

There were not two dragon sentries keeping ward before the gate of this abode,
as in magic legend are usually found on duty over the wronged innocence
imprisoned; but besides a glowering visage ... there was a monstrous fantasy
of rusty iron curling and twisting like a petrifaction of an arbour over the
threshold ... There were no talismanic characters engraven on the portal, but
the house was now so neglected in appearance, that boys chalked the railings
and the pavement ... and drew ghosts on the stable door.   (337)

Instead of dragon sentries we have the "glowering visage" of the stone
gargoyle; instead of an arbor we have "rusty iron curling and twisting."
What was alive in the legend is here both decayed and petrified: the "*rusty
iron*" is like a "*petrifaction* of an arbour." But this "fantasy" is actually
reality. In the magic story, in fancy, what was "alive" has not petrified: the
arbor surrounding the dwelling place continued to grow, thus hiding/pro-
tecting the place and its occupant from the rest of the world. Nor has it
decayed: "the spell that used to set enchanted houses sleeping once upon a
time ... left their waking freshness unimpaired" (337). It is only in fancy
that the house is protected against both petrifaction and decay. Florence,
however, *is* immune against both. She is not petrified: "Florence lived alone
in the great dreary house, and day succeeded day, and still she lived alone;
and the blank walls looked down upon her with a vacant stare, as if they had
a Gorgon-like mind to stare her youth and beauty into stone" (337). Nor
does she decay: in an explicit contrast to a long description of the decay of
the house we read: "But Florence bloomed there, like the king's fair daughter
in the story" (339). If the reference to her "blooming" suggests her unimpaired physical beauty, her not turning into stone suggests that her feelings
remain alive (especially since the passage echoes Florence's meeting with

her father just before he left, during which "The glowing love within [her] breast" froze before his stare "and she stood and looked at him as if stricken into stone," [271]). The more Florence resembles the princess or the abode of the legend the less she resembles the house in its "grim reality."

A second difference between fancy and reality has to do with writing or engraving. In the "magic legend" there are "talismanic characters engraven on the portal"; here boys chalk the railings and pavement and draw ghosts on the stable door. The "talismanic characters" in the fairy tale prevent outsiders from invading the magic abode, thus protecting the house and its occupant; at the same time, they can be used by the hero in order to break the spell and bring the house and its occupant back to life. In the novel, on the other hand, the writings on the house represent its decay, its diminished status, and they foreshadow not the arrival of the hero but the invasion of the house by the world outside it. The boys' writings foreshadow the chalk writings—such as, " 'this room in panel. Green and gold' "—which will be scrawled on the walls by the various workers who will invade the house prior to Dombey's wedding; they also foreshadow the "men with pens and ink" who invade the house after Dombey's bankruptcy. In other words, these writings are another indication of the process of marking and wiping in preparation for further marking, of being in time. Once again, the house is *not* like the abode in the magic story, while Florence, who was supposed to be like it, becomes more and more like the princess in the fairy tales.

The decay of the house is presented as a consequence of Dombey's departure following the death of Paul. But Dombey's absence from the house with Major Bagstock, which ends with his return to the house in the company of Edith, soon to be his wife, could not have lasted more than a few months. During that short period, time seems to have unaccountably accelerated:

> Mildew and mould began to lurk in closets. Fungus trees grew in the corners of the cellars . . . . The grass began to grow upon the roof, and in the crevices of the basement paving. A scaly crumbling vegetation sprouted round the window-sills. Fragments of mortar lost their hold upon the insides of the unused chimneys, and came dropping down . . . . Through the whole building, white has turned yellow, yellow nearly black.   (338–39)

Thus, the decay of the house appears as a "monstrous fantasy," as if produced by fancy/magic rather than by a natural process. Only after two long pages describing the decay of the house, are we told that this decay has actually started a few years before, has been going on, in fact, "since the time when the poor lady died" (339). The decay of the house is not the consequence of Dombey's going away but of Fanny's death; it shows, as Paul's death did already, that Dombey's attempt at "preservation" has not been successful. Indeed, Dombey's attempt to arrest time could succeed only in legends, where the spell "that used to set enchanted houses sleeping . . . left their waking freshness unimpaired" (337). But in Dickens's reality this does not happen. The house—a real one—could not be protected against the effects of neglect that followed from Fanny's death. At the same time, though the house is inhabited by "a gentle figure moving through the solitude and gloom, that gave to every lifeless thing a touch of present human interest and wonder" (338) and who cannot be other than Florence, and although Dombey's rooms "were in every nook the better and the brighter for her care" (340), Dickens does not develop this possibility. Florence, who was told by her father before his departure, that "the whole house is yours above there . . . you are its mistress now" (272) did not turn into a little housekeeper jingling her keys but into a princess from a fairy tale.[9]

Besides mould and mildew and grass and fungus—growth that indicates neglect and decay—the house also undergoes more fanciful changes as when the "patterns of carpets" not only "faded" but also became "perplexed," the pictures "seemed to go in and secrete themselves," and the clocks, not only "never told the time" but also, "if wound up by any chance, told it wrong, and struck unearthly numbers, which are not upon the dial" (338). Patterns, pictures, and especially time, are here subject to uncanny processes. And, by its position in a paragraph that lists more and more uncanny phenomena, the most uncanny object of all is the staircase: "But, besides, there was the great staircase, where the lord of the place so rarely set his foot, and by which his little child had gone up to Heaven" (338). Within a long description that details all sorts of transformations, the staircase simply "was"—unchanged in the midst of natural and unnatural processes. And, by its simple "being," not subject to change, it ceases to be a "real" staircase and becomes associated with Heaven. Rather than linking the staircase, so avoided by Mr. Dombey, with Florence's care for her brother—she used to carry Paul up the staircase, singing—Dickens here strangely associates the ever-present staircase with the afterlife. There no care and no preservation are necessary, no decay occurs, time ceases to be. By exempting the material staircase, site of Florence's love and care for her brother, from change, the narrator already anticipates Dombey's view of Florence as the one whose love "never changed"; by linking this exemption from change to Heaven he shows that this, like Dombey's attempt to "preserve" the house, is possible only in the imaginary or imagined world of legends and religious belief.

In due time Dombey and Edith are engaged to be married and the house has a function once again. Dombey is sure that the beautiful and proud Edith will do the honors of his house even better than the meek Fanny. And there is every reason to believe that he hopes this second marriage will provide him with a son, which is why he feels that "his dead boy was now superseded by new ties" (532). And so the house must be made presentable so that it can once again conspicuously display Dombey's grandeur and be ready to receive a new son in due time. We are back at a point before the beginning of the novel, except that we now know that the renovation of the house, the creation of a new, fresh, and bright surface, is merely the wiping away of the marks of time in preparation for new marks. And we also know that the reproduction of the same, day in and day out, which creates the appearance of no change, of the abolition of time, requires constant labor and care which neither Dombey nor Edith seem to be able to undertake.

Upon Dombey's marriage to Edith the house is turned into "a perfect palace" (529) and it is now described as "bright" rather than as grim (525). On the eve of the "happy pair' ''s return from their honeymoon we are told that "Lights are sparkling in the windows this evening, and the ruddy glow of fires is warm and bright upon the hangings and soft carpets" (525) and when Edith passes through the suite of rooms we hear of "new and handsome garniture" (529). These short descriptions, suggesting brightness, warmth, softness, and beauty may make us think that the house is different and that, since the house's function is to represent Dombey (it is decorated for his "self glorification" [529]), Dombey has changed, maybe through his new love for Edith. But it soon becomes clear that this is not the case. In answer to Mrs. Skewton's compliments, Dombey replies: " 'I directed that no expense would be spared; and all that money could do, has been done, I believe" (529). Thus the beauty, brightness, warmth, and softness of the house are shown to be merely the effects of unlimited expense; the house now represents not so much Dombey's status as money's purchasing power.[10] Whereas in the first part of the novel Dombey's impersonality resulted from his view of himself as the temporary bearer of a name, in the part of the novel dealing with his relations with Edith—perhaps because in his association with an aristocratic lady his own name pales—the emphasis shifts from name to money. The relative personality of the name is replaced by the absolute impersonality of money.

The restoration of the house, like the new marriage, is therefore not a matter of care but of purchase. The agent in the process is neither Dombey nor Edith (who cannot bother to have an opinion on the matter except in the case of Florence's room) but rather money: "all that money could do, has been done." The formulation is reminiscent of Dombey's declaration that "the House . . . will be able to hold its own, and maintain its own, and hand down its own of itself" (50).

Since Florence does not see the house in terms of conspicuous display of either a name or the power of money but rather insists on seeing it as a home (even though it is so devoid of all the feelings and care normally associated with home) her view of the renovation of the house is quite different:

Florence passed [Towlinson] as if she were in a dream, and hurried up-stairs.
The garish light was in the long-darkened drawing-rooms, and there were steps
and platforms, and men in paper caps, in the high places. Her mother's picture
was gone with the rest of the moveables, and on the mark where it had been,
was scrawled in chalk, "this room in panel. Green and gold." The staircase
was a labyrinth of posts and planks like the outside of the house, and a whole
Olympus of plumbers and glaziers was reclining in various attitudes, on the
skylight. Her own room was not yet touched within, but there were beams and
boards raised against it without, baulking the daylight. She went up swiftly to
that other bedroom, where the little bed was; and a dark giant of a man with a
pipe in his mouth, and his head tied up in a pocket-handkerchief, was staring
in at the window.   (427)

From Florence's point of view the restoration of the house is an invasion and
a violation of its "sacred" parts—the staircase, Paul's room—and the removal of tokens of the past, such as Fanny's portrait, to be replaced by
new objects, symbolizing "new ties." To this the narrator opposes, at least
implicitly, Florence's state of mind. "Although the enchanted house was no
more," Florence has not changed:

In her thoughts of her new mother, and in the love and trust overflowing her
pure heart towards her, Florence loved her own dead mother more and more.
She had no fear of setting up a rival in her breast. The new flower sprang from
the deep-planted and long-cherished root, she knew. Every gentle word that
had fallen from the lips of the beautiful lady, sounded to Florence like an echo
of the voice long hushed and silent. How could she love that memory less for
living tenderness, when it was her memory of all parental tenderness and love!
       (446)

Florence's love for her mother is not subject to time, it is not wiped away to
make room for her new love for Edith, since her love "springs" naturally (it
is her nature to love) and because the love for her dead mother is subsumed
in a generalized, abstract concept of "parental tenderness and love." As
Florence continues to "bloom," like the princess in the fairy tale, the love
that is deep-rooted in her heart gives repeatedly and effortlessly new blos-
soms. Her love maintains and reproduces itself in a manner analogous to the
way Dombey hoped his name, his house, his money will—with little or
no labor.

The return to the new home, with all its "pomp and ornament" marks a
change in Dombey's feelings towards Florence which, though short-lived, is
important since it is the first glimpse of the final reversal: "The sight of her
in her beauty, almost changed into a woman without his knowledge" causes
him to see her as a "household spirit," "the spirit of his home," and makes
him think that he "had had a happy home within his reach" (532). From
"merely a piece of base coin that couldn't be invested—a bad Boy" (3),

Florence becomes an ornament—*the* ornament—a perfect wife: "a household spirit bending at his feet" (532). The narrator seems to endorse and approve of Dombey's feelings as finally doing justice to Florence; he only distances himself from Dombey in indicating that the motives for his feelings may not have been all pure. The narrator speculates that these may have come as response to "the sight of her in her beauty," or to "some simple eloquence distinctly heard, though only uttered in her eyes," or yet to "meaner and lower thoughts," concluding: "The mere association of her as an ornament, with all the ornament and pomp about him, may have been sufficient" (532). By multiplying the possible motives for the hypothetical thoughts and emotions that Florence unknowingly causes in her father, the narrator loosens the causal link between feelings and circumstances. Approving of the emotion while also linking it (at least hypothetically) to the commodified view of human beings (she is an ornament among others) that he previously satirized (as when Dombey thinks of Fanny as similar to "his plate and furniture") further helps diminish the importance of causes since now an attitude the narrator disapproves of can produce feelings he considers proper and an accurate response to Florence's real value.

The final collapse of Dombey and the house occurs in two steps: first the house as home and family is ruined and then the house as firm. Upon discovering Edith's flight, Dombey becomes momentarily blind to the difference between her and Florence, which he previously glimpsed, and thus sends Florence running out of the house. But "he does *not* think that he has lost her . . . He has lived too long shut up in his towering supremacy, seeing her, a patient gentle creature, in the path below it, to have any fear of that" (754; emphasis in the text). Thus Dombey's implicit belief in Florence's never changing love for him is here attributed to his blind pride and is presented as an error: she *is* lost to him, only he does not yet know it. It may be that the narrator takes this position in order to mislead the reader as to the outcome of the story and produce a little bit of suspense in a novel that has hardly any. But the result is a split in the narrator: whereas in this scene the narrator implicitly criticizes Dombey for his belief in Florence's unchanged nature, in the last scene of the novel the narrator will fully endorse this same view; indeed, the very closure of the novel depends on this view.

A year passes and its effects on the house of Dombey and Son are fully visible: "The ceaseless work of Time has been performed, in storm and sunshine. Through a whole year, the tides of human chance and change had set in their allotted courses. Through a whole year, the famous House of Dombey and Son had fought a fight for life . . . The year was out, and the great House was down" (856–57). From the description of the fall of the house of Dombey and Son the narrator moves to a description of the changes in the "great house in the long dull street": "Changes have come again upon the great house in the long dull street, once the scene of Florence's childhood and loneliness. It is a great house still, proof against wind and weather, without breaches in the roof, or shattered windows, or dilapidated walls; but it is a ruin none the less, and the rats fly from it'' (871). By saying that "changes have come again" and by referring to "Florence's childhood and loneliness" the narrator invites us to see these changes as similar to those brought upon the house after Paul's death and Dombey's departure. But, though the year that has passed was a year of neglect, (following the departure of Edith and Florence "Mr. Dombey's servants are becoming . . . quite dissipated, and unfit for . . . service" [763]), we don't find in this description any signs of the decay that marked the description of the deserted house in that previous instance. Here the house seems to be immune against the elements (it is "proof against wind and weather") and its "ruin" seems to be moral or affective rather than physical. It is as if the narrator, like Dombey before him, was confusing the "great house in the long dull street" with the House—and the name—of Dombey and Son since the latter can indeed be ruined without being dilapidated. The allusion to the rats flying away evokes the image of a sinking ship and thus again links the ruin of the house to the description of the demise of the firm, where the house of Dombey and Son was compared to a ship making battle against storms and tides. At the moment in which Dombey loses the firm after having lost his family, the two seem to be conflated. This conflation, however, cannot be attributed to Dombey's commodification of family relations; it is, rather, the result of the way the narrator, in his description of the changes brought about the house, dematerializes the house/home. This dematerialization is necessary for Dombey's subsequent discovery of "love."

Alone in the empty house after the bankruptcy, Dombey thinks about Florence and of "what might have been" had he not rejected her, just as Florence, solitary in the house after Paul's death and Dombey's departure, imagined what her life could have been had he loved her. Just like her he roams around the house unseen, in the dead of night. But whereas Florence's fancies vanished before the evidence of the real house, in Dombey's case it is the empty house that makes him aware of the opportunities he missed. With all the furniture gone, what is left is just an empty shell and this evacuation of the house of all material goods causes Dombey to see it as the site of affective bonds (which are thus dematerialized): "And now he felt that he had had two children born to him in that house, and that between him and the bare wide empty walls there was a tie, mournful, but hard to rend asunder, connected with a double childhood, and a double loss" (884). On the one hand, Dombey comes to realize that considering his house as but a conspicuous sign of his social status, commercial success or wealth prevented him from developing ties of affection to members of his family; on the other hand, linking the birth of this consciousness to the disappearance of material objects implies that they were the root of the problem. Discovering the power of family ties in the empty house, Dombey is led to dissociate them from all material reality and hence to see them as outside time and in no need of care.

This reasoning is implicit in Dombey's thoughts about the vanity of all worldly things: "His boy had faded into dust, his proud wife had sunk into a polluted creature, his flatterer and friend had been transformed into the worst of villains, his riches had melted away" (883). Dombey realizes then that matter is subject to decay and destruction; it is subject to change since it is subject to time. But rather than concluding that both people and possessions need to be cared for in order to protect them from such destruction, he concludes that he should have invested his attention in something which was not subject to time and change: his daughter Florence who "alone had never changed" (883), Florence as the incarnation of love—natural, overflowing, self-perpetuating love. Now she is not simply the "household spirit bending at his feet" (532), which he may have regretted as he saw the child growing into a woman, but a divine power comes to save him: as he (or more accurately "it" as Dombey is designated in this passage) "sat down, with its eyes upon the empty fireplace, and as it lost itself in thought there shone into the room a gleam of light; a ray of sun . . . at his knees, his daughter!" (886–89).[11]

In a final twist, as if in a reversed echo to Dombey's "she alone has never changed," one of Florence's first words to him are "I am changed" (889). Whereas he sees her as the never changing love he almost lost through his sins and may even refuse to the last through his pride ("So proud he was in his ruin . . . that if he could have heard her voice in an adjoining room, he would not have gone to her," 883), she presents herself as the prodigal daughter who came back penitent to ask the father's forgiveness. Whereas before she judged him by his behavior—"his cruelty, neglect and hatred" (704)—and concluded that she "had no father upon earth," now she repents of having left him, "knowing" what a sorrow to a parent's love a child's departure must be. In order to reach this "knowledge" Florence equates her own love for her child and her mother's love for her with Dombey's "love," declares parents' love to be above all others, and thus puts her father's love for her above her own love for him. By so doing she further separates love from behavior and specific acts. Not only is love indestructible, it is also generalized and abstracted and thus not related to acts. It is simply there, like a natural or divine force, and no particular "acts of affirmation and reinforcement"[12] are needed to create and recreate it, just as no acts of negation and destruction can undo it.

The effects of this affirmation are so strong that Dickens forgets what he has asserted at the very beginning of the novel. At the end of the novel we hear that though Dombey's face "bears heavy marks of care and suffering . . . they are traces of a storm that has passed on for ever, and left a clear evening in its track'' (920). The storm has passed, there will be no other storms, no more marks of care, no more care: ''Ambitious projects trouble him no more'' (920). Thus care is related to ambitious projects that may involve storms—they are part of the world of the House of Dombey and Son that Dombey gave up. In the family, surrounded by love, there are no cares. Time and his brother Care have ceased to be, vanquished by Love.

This love, as we have seen, transcends circumstances and particular acts. It is spontaneous and indestructible and therefore does not require any care—effort or labor—to reproduce. It thus uncannily resembles the view Dombey held of ''Dombey and Son'' at the beginning of the novel. The happy pronouncement that ''Dombey and Son should be/is indeed a daughter after all'' (241, 890) can now be seen as meaning something quite different from what it is usually taken to mean: that the love Florence represents is just a new version of the name which Paul was supposed to represent. But the house is another matter.

In debunking Dombey's view of the house and the objects within it as material signs of his name and firm, Dickens insisted on their being subject to time and care. In undermining Dombey's belief that time can be neutralized (arrested or accelerated), that objects can be artificially preserved, Dickens has shown that the house/home is subject to decay brought about by time and thereby negatively demonstrated the need for repeated acts of care to maintain it. The house as a physical space, in other words, cannot be subjected to the fantasy of indestructible love, independent of circumstance and acts, reproduced without labor. The materiality of the home is put at odds with the idealization of family feelings. Finally Dickens, like Dombey, has to empty the house of all its material objects, indeed deprive it of all materiality, transforming home from a physical space to an idealized affective state. Perhaps this is why the idyll of family love that marks the end of the novel cannot take place in a real house where time and care are always present.

NOTES

This essay was first presented as a lecture before the Dickens Universe at the University of California Santa Cruz. I would like to thank Bob Newsom and John Jordan for having invited me and the Universe participants for their questions and remarks, which were helpful to me in revising the lecture for publication.

1. *David Copperfield* (New York: Modern Library, 1950), 882, 884, 885; 540–41.
2. When acts of maintenance carried out by women *are* visible they are either portrayed as a child's play, ''self important busyness,'' as in the case of Bella in *Our Mutual Friend* (see Elizabeth Langland, *Nobody's Angels: Middle-Class*

Women and Domestic Ideology in Victorian Culture [Cornell UP, 1995], 109) or
judged to be detrimental to the happiness of the home, as in the case of Mrs.
Mac Stinger in *Dombey and Son*.

3. This is often expressed as Dombey's failure to abide by the separation of the
domestic and public spheres as dictated by domestic ideology. See, for example,
Catherine Waters's discussion of the novel in her *Dickens and the Politics of the
Family* (Cambridge UP, 1997), 38–57.

4. *Dombey and Son* (Oxford World's Classics, 2001), 892. All further references to
the novel will be to this edition and will be given parenthetically in the text.

5. Susan Nygaard has observed the lack of home at the end of the novel in her essay
"Redecorating Dombey: The Power of 'A Woman's Anger' versus Upholstery
in *Dombey and Son*," *Critical Matrix*, 8:1 (1994), 40–80. Her argument, however,
is different from mine and centers on the novel as a dramatization of "a sexual
struggle for control of domestic space" (56). Observing that "Dickens does not
rebuild Dombey's private house, nor does he replace it with Florence and Walter
Gay's house" and that the novel ends on the sea shore (68), she concludes:
"Erasing all the spatial boundaries and thresholds which provoked women's
anger, the novel's conclusion provides no point at which to anchor female resistance" (70).

6. Many critics discussed the novel's preoccupation with time, which most critics
understand as a preoccupation with change (rather than with repetition). Thus
Steven Marcus's chapter on *Dombey*, "The Changing World" (*Dickens: From
Pickwick to Dombey* [New York: Basic Books, 1965], 293–357) has been the
starting point for many subsequent studies of the novel's view of social transformation as symbolized by the introduction of the railroad. Whether Dombey himself represents this changing world or is its victim (or both) depends on the critics'
understanding of the kind of businessman Dombey is: as David W. Toise put it,
on whether he represents "nineteenth-century capitalism at its worse" or "an
increasingly archaic early modern ideology" associated with mercantilism (" 'As
Good as Nowhere': Dickens's *Dombey and Son*, the Contingency of Value, and
Theories of Domesticity," in *Criticism*, 41:3 [1999], 323–48, 326). On this question see also Jeremy Tambling, "Death and Modernity in *Dombey and Son*,"
Essays in Criticism 43:4 (1993), 308–29. On the representation of time in the
novel see, besides Marcus, John Lucas, *The Melancholy Man* (Totowa, NJ: Barnes
and Noble, 1980), 145–57; Michael Greenstein, "Measuring Time in *Dombey
and Son*," *Dickens Quarterly* 9:4 (1992), 151–57.

7. This is one of the reasons why, as Robert Newsom has observed, we have no
representation of any business transacted at the House. "Embodying *Dombey*:
Whole and in Part," *Dickens Studies Annual*, 18 (1989), 207.

8. For another kind of discussion of the presence of fairy tales in the novel see
Roger B. Henkle, "The Crisis of Representation in *Dombey and Son*," in *Critical
Reconstructions: The Relationship of Fiction and Life*, ed. Robert M. Polhemus
and Roger B. Henkle (Stanford UP, 1994), 92–95.

9. Florence's display of domestic skills when she runs away from home to the
Wooden Midshipman does not contradict this argument; rather it suggests that
her perfect wifely behavior is "natural" rather than learnt, spontaneous just like
her love.

10. On this distinction see Toise.
11. Gerhard Joseph has analyzed this scene as a "mirror scene" pointing out, rightly, that with Florence's reappearance, Dombey recovers his identity: he can see once more his image in the mirror, an image he has lost when he appeared to himself as other, an "it." This means, as Joseph puts it, that Florence "restore[s] him to himself," but, I will argue, not at all "as a radically altered being." "Change and the Changeling in *Dombey and Son*," *Dickens Studies Annual*, 18 (1989), 179–95.
12. Bourdieu, paraphrased by Jana Gohrisch, "Familiar Excess? Emotion and the Family in Victorian Literature," *Yearbook of Research in English and American Literature*, Giessen, Germany, 16 (2000), 163–83.

WORKS CITED

Dickens, Charles. *David Copperfield*. New York: Modern Library, 1950.

———. *Dombey and Son*. Oxford: Oxford World's Classics, 2001.

Gohrisch, Jana. "Familiar Excess? Emotion and the Family in Victorian Literature." *Yearbook of Research in English and American Literature* 16 (2000): 163–83.

Greenstein, Michael. "Measuring Time in *Dombey and Son*." *Dickens Quarterly* 9:4 (1992): 151–57.

Henkle, Roger B. "The Crisis of Representation in *Dombey and Son*." *Critical Reconstructions: The Relationship of Fiction and Life*. Ed. Robert M. Polhemus and Roger B. Henkle. Stanford: Stanford UP, 1994.

Joseph, Gerhard. "Change and the Changeling in *Dombey and Son*." *Dickens Studies Annual* 18 (1989): 179–95.

Langland, Elizabeth. *Nobody's Angels: Middle-Class Women and Domestic Ideology in Victorian Culture*. Ithaca: Cornell UP, 1995.

Lucas, John. *The Melancholy Man*. Totowa, NJ: Barnes and Noble, 1980.

Marcus, Steven. *Dickens: From Pickwick to Dombey*. New York: Basic Books, 1965.

Newsom, Robert. "Embodying *Dombey*: Whole and in Part." *Dickens Studies Annual* 18 (1989): 207.

Nygaard, Susan. "Redecorating Dombey: The Power of 'A Woman's Anger' versus Upholstery in *Dombey and Son*." *Critical Matrix* 8:1 (1994): 40–80.

Tambling, Jeremy. "Death and Modernity in *Dombey and Son*." *Essays in Criticism* 43:4 (1993): 308–29.

Toise, David W. " 'As Good as Nowhere': Dickens's *Dombey and Son*, the Contingency of Value, and Theories of Domesticity." *Criticism* 41:3 (1999): 323–48, 326.

Waters, Catherine. *Dickens and the Politics of the Family*. Cambridge: Cambridge UP, 1997.

The Illustrations in Dickens's *The Haunted Man and The Ghost's Bargain:* Public and Private Spheres and Spaces

Philip V. Allingham

Before Charles Dickens initiated his experiment in collaborative jour-nalism as the editor-in-chief of Household Words *(March, 1850–May, 1859), he engaged in a very different type of multipart collaboration with some of the leading illustrators of the 1840s to produce the four Christmas Books that followed* A Christmas Carol *(1843). His rôle as both writer and artistic advisor for these seasonal offerings is especially evident in the last of this series of novellas (and, in terms of the pictorial element, the most ambitious).* The Haunted Man *(1848) features seven-teen plates by four artists: John Leech and John Tenniel in the lead, with Clarkson Stanfield and Frank Stone supporting. Although Dickens's text explores the theme of the beneficial effect of memory on one's emotional existence, through the repeated references which culminate in the book's closing words, an abstract process (as opposed to scenes from memory, such as occur in* A Christmas Carol*) does not lend itself to illustration per se. Instead, the artists draw the reader's attention to the value of domestic and personal space in a society more and more obsessed with commercial, professional, and other specifically "mascu-line" pursuits outside the female-dominated sphere of home. In the life of an intellectual preoccupied with professional concerns and an unresolved past, the civilizing and harmonizing effects of memory are evident in his isolation, in contrast to the domestic felicity of the two family groups, the Swidgers and Tetterbys. Orchestrated by the novelist*

*himself, the plates become not mere visual translations of specific tex-
tual moments but interpolated elaborations of such interrelated social
issues as the necessity for a happy childhood in laying the basis for a
well-rounded, emotionally stable adult psyche, for giving free play to
the imaginative faculty that Dickens termed "Fancy," and for valoriz-
ing private and familial places and activities in our lives. The household
is not positioned in this text as a separate but equal sphere; rather,
Dickens and his illustrators imply that rest, refreshment, and solace
within the private sphere are necessary to the successful discharge of
responsibilities in the public.*

> Who that had seen him in his inner chamber,
> part library and part laboratory, . . . upon a win-
> ter night, alone, surrounded by his drugs and
> instruments and books; the shadow of his shaded
> lamp a monstrous beetle on the wall, motionless
> among a crowd of spectral shapes raised there by
> the flickering of the fire upon the quaint objects
> around him; . . . would not have said that the
> man seemed haunted and the chamber too?
> (Charles Dickens, "The Gift Bestowed," *The
> Haunted Man and The Ghost's Bargain*, 3–4)

Despite such evocative writing, prior to 1980 the prevailing critical view
of the last of Charles Dickens's Christmas Books was negative. Entirely
overlooking the story's implications about the "cash nexus," the Victorian
tendency to replace human relationships with possessions and business or
professional pursuits, contemporary critics seem to have resented the religious
tone and pious sentimentalizing in which Dickens indulges at the close of *The
Haunted Man*. For example, an anonymous reviewer in *Macphail's Edinburgh
Ecclesiastical Journal* for January 1849 pronounces Dickens unfit as a yuletide preacher: "He does not grace the chair of national instruction—he is both
too tiny and too playful" (Collins 180). The panning damns with faint praise:

> Had it not been for the very handsome exterior and the high price [5 shillings,
> the price of each of *The Haunted Man*'s progenitors] of this new Christmas
> book of Mr. Dickens, it was only worthy of appearing in the window of the
> small shop of *Tetterby & Co.*, the news-vendor, whom it celebrates. Let us now
> have a few more returns of Christmas, and Mr. Dickens will have destroyed
> his reputation as a tale-writer. We earnestly recommend him to quit the *twenty-
> fifth of December*, and take to the *first of April*.   (181)

Despite the book's initial sales of 17,775 copies, Robert Patten states that,
while *The Haunted Man* was "profitable" (by 31 December 1848 Dickens's

profits were £793.5.11), it was "not especially successful" (203), by which he presumably means that in the judgment of posterity the novella lacks enduring aesthetic interest.[1] In contrast, Dickens's monthly serialized novel of the late 1840s, *Dombey and Son*, had much larger sales, in the range of 32,000 to 35,000. However, Angus Wilson's pronouncing *The Haunted Man* "deservedly less successful in [its] own time" (181) must be put in the context of the sales of other well-known authors of the period: Thackeray's *Vanity Fair*, for example, "sold fewer than 5,000 copies per number" (Patten 189).Wilson's view is that *The Battle of Life* (1846) and *The Haunted Man* (1848) are the exhausted expressions of the highly original "domestic fairy-tale" that Dickens invented in "The Story of the Goblins Who Stole A Sexton" for the January 1837 number of *Pickwick* (issued just before Christmas 1836), and brought to perfection in December 1843, in *A Christmas Carol*.

None of the many Dickens biographers and only a handful of his modern critics have taken the trouble to analyze *The Haunted Man* as a deliberate, tightly-structured work of art that ingeniously synthesizes text and illustrations. This neglect is in sharp contrast to the ever-growing pile of essays, commentaries, and whole books (to say nothing of cinematic adaptations) on the prototype of the Christmas Books, *A Christmas Carol* (1843). Gradually, however, the later book has come to be regarded as more than a mere "quarry" for locating Dickens's "autobiographical obsessions" (Wilson 181). Sarah Solberg in 1980 drew attention to the fact that in its synthesis of text and illustration on the same page, *The Haunted Man* is not typical of nineteenth-century illustrated adult-oriented books: "Pictures and words [were] wedded in a manner which made them look as though they really belonged together" (110). In *The Haunted Man,* more than in any other of Dickens's Christmas Books, "As the text becomes part of the picture, so too does the picture become part of the text" (114). In contrast, consider the monthly instalments of *The Pickwick Papers* (or, for that matter, almost any other monthly serialized novel by Dickens), each containing 32 pages of text and two full-page illustrations. The plates for *Pickwick*, however, dominate our thoughts as we begin reading since they establish an anticipatory set, no matter what direction the text seems to be taking. The ratio of full-page plates to text is one to sixteen for *Pickwick*, and yet this ratio is belied by the power over the reader that the plates exert.[2]

On the other hand, in *The Haunted Man* the ratio of plates to text is seventeen to 188, which is to say approximately one uncaptioned illustration for every twelve pages of text. In Dickens's last little book for Christmas the reader is simultaneously reader and viewer of both text and illustration on the same page, experiencing one message in two media. The usual serial reading involves glancing back at the plate to compare both detail and narrative intention, as one might glance back at Allingham's second plate after reading chapter 6 and arriving at the bottom of page 136. But in reading the volume *The Haunted Man,* one is invited to go back and forth between two narratives on the same page, the viewing of the plate augmenting and enriching one's appreciation of the prose.[3]

As a result of a thorough analysis of the double-page plates of *The Chimes,* *The Battle of Life,* and *The Haunted Man,* the first such critical analysis conducted since the book's publication, Solberg concludes that, apart from their "special intimacy of tone" (Slater, *CB* I: vii) and seasonal setting, the Christmas Books—even those in which the note of social realism is muted and the supernatural nugatory (*The Cricket on the Hearth* and *The Battle of Life*)—are connected by the theme that "time affects Man" (104). That the plates treat the fanciful and the real aspects of *The Haunted Man* equally indicates that, as we read the text and simultaneously examine the artists' creative visualizations, "we [are] expected to accept the imaginative world of the text and its illustrations" (104). Dream time and dream space, as *A Christmas Carol* made clear five years earlier, are as influential in the lives of human beings as real time and real space, so that the "other-worldly" agents of *The Haunted Man and The Ghost's Bargain,* "A Fancy for Christmas-Time," like those of "A Ghost Story of Christmas" (*A Christmas Carol*) and *The Chimes: A Goblin Story of Some Bells That Rang an Old Year Out and A New Year In,* can and do have an impact on the protagonists' workaday selves and actions.

Further, as Solberg notes, these fairy-tales for the Industrial Age present in text and illustrations two types of reality: the everyday lives of ordinary, generally middle-class men and women and "the harsh world of miserable poverty" (108) that is the lot of the Victorian underclasses. Though apparently also set in the Hungry Forties, *The Cricket on the Hearth* (1845) possesses little of such social realism since the privations endured by blind Bertha and her poor but cheerful father hardly render them the realistic equivalents of the *Carol*'s allegorical figures of Ignorance and Want. Set in an eighteenth-century village, *The Battle of Life* (1846) offers a vision of the family that is even further removed from the institutional refuges, the "prisons and workhouses," upon which nineteenth-century businessmen such as Ebenezer Scrooge feel the stability of society depends. But in *The Haunted Man* Dickens returns to the dualistic vision of reality, and redefines the environments constructed by humanity as male- or female-dominated, domestic or private, recreational or public, professionally- and/or business-oriented, and performative. Although, as Wendy Carse has noted, Redlaw yearns for a home and a feminine, domesticated space whose "most explicit sign . . . [is] the hearth" (166), he has so intermingled his career and his private life that his laboratory, study, sleeping quarters, and lecture theater are contiguous and interconnected, as the illustrations make clear. His own solitary fireside, depicted in

Tenniel's frontispiece and Leech's "Redlaw and the Phantom," is hardly the source of comfort and companionship presented by its communal counterparts in Tenniel's "Illustrated Page to Chap.1" and Leech's "The Tetterbys."

Throughout the Christmas Books Dickens consistently adheres to the tight form of the novella, with a main and a subplot, a limited cast of characters, and a program of illustration which he both orchestrated and conducted, as his letters to the various artists reveal. The whole series involved 65 plates and seven artists in all:

–*A Christmas Carol* (1843) 8 plates: all by John Leech; *The Chimes* (1844) 13 plates: D. Maclise (2), R. Doyle (4), C. Stanfield (2), and J. Leech (5);
–*The Cricket on the Hearth* (1845) 14 plates: D. Maclise (2), R. Doyle (3), C. Stanfield (1), E. Landseer (1), and J. Leech (7);
–*The Battle of Life* (1846) 13 plates: D. Maclise (4), R. Doyle (3), Clarkson Stanfield (3), and J. Leech (3);
–*The Haunted Man* (1848) 17 plates: J. Tenniel (6), F. Stone (3), Clarkson Stanfield (3), and J. Leech (5).

Whereas *A Christmas Carol*, more modestly illustrated with eight plates by a single artist, did not even contain a list of illustrations, the later Christmas Books emphasized the pictorial element. In a sense, the second of these, *The Chimes: A Goblin Story of Some Bells that Rang an Old Year Out and a New Year In*, set the visual pattern for the series, having 13 plates by four accomplished artists. Ten illustrations are dropped into the text to synthesize the pictorial and textual narratives, the text guiding the reader into and out of the illustration which realizes the moment described in the accompanying prose. Dickens revived the "team" approach to illustration that he had first employed in *Master Humphrey's Clock* at the beginning of the 1840s, when H. K. Browne, George Cattermole, Samuel Williams, and Daniel Maclise collaborated on the untitled woodcuts dropped into the text at relevant points, as is the case with the Christmas Books. Dickens probably adopted this approach to illustration for the post-*Carol* seasonal offerings to ensure that all plates would be ready in time for the December publication date. His illustrators were busy in those days, contributing to *Punch* and other illustrated magazines, as well as working on other writers' books.

Thus, without realizing it, in creating the Christmas Books Dickens created what Marxist critic N. N. Feltes terms a "commodity-text," a union of prose text and illustrations that made each book a work of art still within the means of the upper range of the middle class. Despite the fact that the illustrations added considerably to the purchase price of Dickens's annual Christmas offering (especially if these were hand-colored) and would thereby decrease his profits (as was very much the case with the *Carol* five years earlier), Dickens did not merely maintain the number of illustrations that accompanied previous Christmas Books; he increased it.

For *The Haunted Man and The Ghost's Bargain*, Dickens devised an ample program of 17 plates, with John Tenniel and John Leech leading, and Frank Stone and Clarkson Stanfield supporting. Clearly Dickens placed great confidence in Leech throughout the Christmas Books, for he produced 43% of the total illustrations (28 out of 65 plates). In July 1836, through his illustrator for *Oliver Twist*, George Cruikshank, Dickens had met the self-taught illustrator and cartoonist John Leech, five years his junior, and subsequently recommended him to Chapman and Hall for their Library of Fiction. In fact, with the exception of Tenniel, the artists collaborating on the plates for *The Haunted Man* were all close friends of Dickens well before he commenced writing the novella in the summer of 1847. Dickens had first become acquainted with Stanfield in December 1837, and with Stone, secretary of the Shakespeare Society, in March 1838. Dickens's letter of 30 October 1848 to Leech indicates that the leading Christmas Book illustrator had yet to be introduced to Tenniel at that point, whom Dickens himself had just met: "Mr. Tenniel has been here today and will go to work on the frontispiece. We must arrange for a dinner here [Devonshire Terrace], very shortly, when you and he may meet. He seems to be a very agreeable fellow, and modest" (*Letters* 5: 431).[4] John Tenniel (1820–1914) was some three years younger than Leech (1817–64) and considerably younger than Clarkson Stanfield (1793–1867), but he had already exhibited at the Society of British Artists in 1836 and at the Royal Academy at various times from 1837 to 1842.

II: Production of and Commentary on the Plates

Ruth Glancy in "Dickens at Work on *The Haunted Man*" states that the Christmas Books offered Dickens as a novelist the rare opportunity "to correct an entire work before it went to press, a luxury not permitted by the serial publication of the novels" (83). In fact, in terms of instructing his artists regarding their illustrations, he had no such luxury at all. Working in conjunction with illustrator Hablot Knight Browne on the *Martin Chuzzlewit* plates from January 1843 through July 1844 must have been comparatively simple. In October 1843, while starting *A Christmas Carol*, Dickens was writing the November instalment, part eleven (chapters 27, 28, and 29):

> The routine during the composition and publication of *Chuzzlewit* in numbers was similar to that established for the previous monthly serials. The first half of each month was devoted to writing the new instalments, the second half to correcting proofs. Subjects for the plates were supplied [to Phiz] as early as possible, usually by the tenth . . . .   (Patten 132)

He would furnish Phiz with a clean set of proofs for a number of *Martin Chuzzlewit* and a list of suggestions for illustration. Phiz would produce sketches which Dickens could then critique; thus, month in and month out, Dickens controlled an orderly program of writing and illustration. Whatever subjects he and Phiz decided upon for the plates was immaterial, since the illustrations occupied whole pages and were included at the end of each part; the reader could locate their realized moments in the accompanying text and, if he or she so desired, have the plates bound in at those points once all nineteen numbers had been acquired.

In contrast to his usual leisurely pace at which he responded to illustrations for monthly serializations, in Dickens's letters we see how tight his creative timeline was for *The Haunted Man*. In under two months, Dickens completed the physical act of writing *The Haunted Man*, beginning on October 5, 1848, at Devonshire Terrace, London, and finishing on the night of November 30, at the Bedford Hotel, Brighton. By November 15, little more than a month before publication, he had received the proofs for the first part, including Tenniel's frontispiece and title-page, but not including Stone's "Milly and the Old Man," to which Dickens did not respond until November 23rd. The day before, Dickens wrote to his point man, John Leech, because he was still not in possession of Leech's illustration of the Tetterby family, which would have to be dropped into the text early in part 2. On November 27, writing Stone from Brighton, Dickens had no proofs for the artist, and had to describe what he had just written ("Sir, there is a subject I have written today for the third part, that I think and hope will just suit you."). By December 1, Leech was still not in possession of the corrected proofs for the third part, and Dickens, fearing Leech's other work was slowing him down, diplomatically asked him to pass the last illustration, the dinner in the great hall, over to Stanfield (who, though not much of a caricaturist, would handle well the architectural elements of the scene). And yet, by December 13, Dickens was able to send Mrs. Richard Watson an advance copy, even though Forster probably did not give him the corrected final proofs until about a week before. Having no rush proofs for part four, Dickens elected to go 29 pages without a single illustration. An added complication was that Dickens was supplying Mark Lemon with proofs to facilitate the staging of *The Haunted Man*; certainly this break-neck schedule was worse than the measured routine Dickens had followed in getting out each monthly serial instalment of *Dombey and Son* (October 1846, through April 1848).

In organizing the program of illustration, Dickens seems to have reserved certain scenes and themes for each artist: as befits his ornamental style, Tenniel's sequence (plates 1–3, 8a and 8b, and 13) is largely emblematic;[5] Stanfield's (plates 4, 11, and 16) architectural; Leech's (plates 6, 7, 8, 12, and 14) character studies; and Stone's (plates 5, 10, and 15) foreground the saintly Milly. Finally, in order to see that the plates were prepared on time, Dickens made use of four different engraving houses: Martin and Corbould produced seven of the Tenniel and Stone illustrations; T. Williams worked exclusively on the three Stanfield drawings; Smith and Cheltnam worked exclusively on Leech's five illustrations; and the much-occupied house of Dalziel was assigned only Stone's last picture.

In the illustrations as in the prose text, the professional and specifically male expertise of the protagonist is juxtaposed with the essentially feminine knowledge of domesticity and personal relationships. Redlaw, the professor of chemistry, like Scrooge the capitalist, is most comfortable in occupying a work-related space, an office full of the instruments and books associated with his professional pursuits. His knowledge, like Scrooge's, is essentially analytical and detached from personal considerations and relationships, breaking things down into their constituents, like the fluids in the glass vessels, vials, and beakers. As Scrooge is almost a fixture at the Exchange, Redlaw is present day and night at the old college. The domestic and personal knowledge of Milly Swidger, like that of the stroller's child, Sissy Jupe, in *Hard Times*, is almost an instinct; certainly, it is a knowledge that springs from the heart rather than (as is the case with Scrooge's accounting and Redlaw's chemistry) from the head. She exemplifies the theme that experiencing both joy and sorrow engenders empathy. While Redlaw's arcane science has the "power to uncombine" (3) the external, solid world of fact, Milly has innate ability to integrate and harmonize internal conflicts, discontent, bruised egos, and afflicted minds. Although hers is truly the domestic sphere, Dickens reveals that ultimately her power is greater than that of male science and striving in the greater world. These masculine and feminine elements and forces are contrasted throughout the pictorial program. Close examination of the plates seriatim will reveal the contribution each makes to the cumulative effect of the mixed-media presentation upon the reader.[6]

The process of illustration began in a leisurely enough way, with Dickens's interviewing John Tenniel about the initial plates on October 30, then reporting by letter to his lead artist. The frontispiece, a full-page illustration repeated and elaborated on later by Leech's "Redlaw and the Phantom," serves as an overture to the program, but is lacking a caption. Thus, without any mediating textual comment the reader is engaged in the psychomachia of a martial combat between angels and demons swarming around Redlaw and his double before the fire, the supernatural combatants forming a wreath. The frontispiece, then, prepares the reader-viewer for the closing words of the text, the overarching theme, delivered in the final plate on page 188, "Lord, keep my memory green." That the battle rages all around the vignette of an apprehensive man, seated before the fire, with a shrouded wraith whispering in his ear, suggests that he is the focal point of this opposition of

Figure 1. ''Frontispiece'' by John Tenniel. Original dimensions: 8.8 cm wide by 10 cm high, horizontally mounted.

LONDON:
BRADBURY & EVANS, 11, BOUVERIE STREET.
1848.

Figure 2. ''Title Page'' by John Tenniel (full-page illustration). Original dimensions: 8 cm wide by 9.5 cm high, horizontally mounted.

metaphysical forces. Ironically, caught up in his own thoughts, he is utterly oblivious to the battle going on around him. A horned demon, above, presides over the whole scene. To his left (stage right) angels rise, throwing spears and shooting arrows at demons to the right, as other demons drag human souls down. At the very bottom a soul struggles, enmeshed in latticework. The motif, as Stoker notes, seems to be modelled on those by Daniel Maclise for the title-page vignettes of *The Chimes* (1844) and *The Battle of Life* (1846); the human figures in the border are "beckoned to by angels and held back by devils" (Stoker, "Tenniel's Illustrations" 3). Although we do not encounter actual angels or demons in the printed text, the motif prepares us for a "fancy" with metaphysical and psychological overtones that involves the solitary professor (Dickens's only intellectual protagonist, although hardly matching the Victorian stereotype of the experimental scientist) and his ghostly double.

Tenniel's second plate, the title-page, again takes up a full page (9 cm wide by 17 cm high), but has text in a peculiar, sanserif ornamental font surrounding its circular vignette. The female angel with long hair who appears twice on the left-hand register of the wreath in the frontispiece points the way with her right hand as she takes the right hand of the child with her left. Continuing the right/left symbolism, Tenniel has the dark hooded figure (so reminiscent of the "Ghost of Christmas Yet To Come" in *A Christmas Carol*) hold the (apparently female) child's left hand. Again, the wreath motif is the unifying structural device, but occasionally these thorns bear a rose and leaves, unlike those in the frontispiece.

Thus, Tenniel's introductory plates make plain the nature of the allegory that the text will present: an acceptance of our lives, past and present, rose and thorn, painful and happy, is necessary for psychological integration and spiritual salvation.

> In his use of light and shadow as well as in the mix of angelic and sinister figures
> in the circular black-and-white border of the yellow-tinted frontispiece . . . and
> within the centered circle of the title page . . . , Tenniel implanted Dickens's
> theme that good is separate yet inextricable from evil. Throughout his illustra-
> tions for *The Haunted Man* he made light and shadow work symbolically as
> well as aesthetically.   (Cohen 155)

Dickens, perhaps initially unaware of Tenniel's artistic capabilities, confined him to ornamental subjects (the frontispiece, the title-page, and the fireside scene that opens the story proper), and later passed to him what Leech had insufficient time to execute, a managerial decision that resulted in the extremely wooden renditions of Mrs. Tetterby and her brood, and a muffled Redlaw.

For "Chapter I. The Gift Bestowed" on the very first page of text Tenniel has realized an early moment in the text, immediately after page 4. This is

Figure 3. "Illustrated Page to Chapter I" (page 1: full-page illustration) by John Tenniel. Area enclosed by border in original: 12.1 cm high by 6.9 cm wide.

the second of five plates that involve the emotional center of the Victorian home, the hearthside, and the second of nine plates depicting children. A mother and her five children, the youngest an infant with whom she is playing, are foregrounded by shadows as they sit by the fire. In darkness, the oldest child holds up a small book as he reads from it by the flickering light of the fire, which illuminates the other five figures, this performative reading reflecting Dickens's ideal of the family united in the appreciation of his art, the older sibling leading the others through the text. Emphasizing the pleasurable rather than terrifying aspects of creating images in the mind's eye from hearing the text, the plate captures the textual moment six pages later

> When little readers of story-books, by the firelight, tremble to think of Cassim Baba cut into quarters, hanging in the Robbers' Cave, or had some small misgivings that the fierce little old woman, with the crutch, who used to start out of the box in the merchant Abudah's bedroom, might, one of these nights, be found upon the stairs, in the long, cold, dusky journey up to bed.   (8)

Rising like smoke from the shadows are one-dimensional figures whose outlines fill the upper-left register of the page, benign creatures of the imagination and traditional fairy tales enclosing the text: an old woman (a witch?) with pointed hat and crutches; a turbaned Turk cut into five and thus transformed into a puppet; another Eastern warrior beside the first, a scimitar at his side (subtly implying that he is responsible for the dismemberment); four identical toy soldiers, all surmounted by mistletoe, a round fruit (a pumpkin, perhaps), and four mice running along a vine and seemingly pulling a pumpkin, at the front of which sits another mouse as the coachman, with a lady's shoe (Cinderella's slipper, one suspects) hung at the end of the vine. Tenniel has extended the fairy-tale allusions of the text to incorporate the Cinderella figures not merely to complement the oriental subjects, but also to suggest the world of Christmas pantomime. In short, in contrast to the gloomy metaphysical speculations of the philosopher in the frontispiece (which is also a hearthside scene), we have Tenniel's rendering of the real and imaginary worlds of childhood, male and female elements in balance, connected by the chime or rattle that is the original of the shadow that, transformed into an ornate shepherd's crook (suggestive of correction and guidance), dominates the left-hand side of the page. The controlling metaphor of the plate is the communal enjoyment of the performance of these weird and miraculous stories. The whole is contained in a border (7 cm by 12 cm) suggestive of rough-hewn poles lashed together, the bundle of memories that form the basis of a mature, well-balanced psyche.

Figure 3, we suddenly realize a few pages later, is actually an illustration of the passage after that realized by the fourth illustration; figure 3 complements the passage which describes children reading tales from the *Arabian*

Nights, specifically how Ali Baba's brother, Cassim, inadvertently trapped himself in the robbers' cave (as a result of his failing to remember the magic password), and was subsequently cut into quarters. They also read in James Ridley's *Tales of the Genii* and visualize how a diminutive old hag on crutches (Dickens mentions just one crutch on page 8) would nightly start out of the box belonging to the merchant Abudah, and exhort him to search for the talisman of Oromanes. While employing these allusions for their psychological implications, Dickens is also recalling his own childhood responses of terror and enchantment when reading these tales. The clause "When little readers of story-books trembled" (7–8) has been interpreted by Tenniel as involving one child reading to his or her younger siblings to reduce the ages and sizes of the other children, who become listeners *and* visualizers rather than "readers" whose rapt enjoyment of the hearthside ease, the quintessential domestic and shared space, is in complete contrast to Redlaw's ruminative depression is his anteroom adjacent to the lecture-theater.

Dickens may have chosen to allude to these tales in order to evoke the mystical atmosphere of the Eastern tale, which to him suggested the importance of retaining a childlike sense of wonder through memory, an aspect of Dickens's personal philosophy about the healing and transformative powers of the imagination found elsewhere in the Christmas Books. Dominated by the maternal figure (center), this family group need not be the Tetterbys, as Jane Cohen has suggested; however, the Tetterby children's enjoyment of each other and of their parents certainly may be threatened by "the monstrous shadows cast on the wall" (155) behind them. Stoker notes that the solid figure of the wondering child, back towards us, is pointing up at the shadow of what appears to be a nurse "about to eat the baby she is holding" (5), a distortion caused by the mother's outstretched hand (center) in juxtaposition to the shadow of the infant's head. Menacing the integrity of the family, these undefined, phantom shades (suggestive of future trials) "add an ominous prefatory note that is only partly relieved by the humorous Doyle-like figures in the upper portion of the scene" (Cohen 155). As in most of the other plates, the illustration here encloses printed text, thereby introducing both "stories" simultaneously.

Undoubtedly concerned that providing illustrations for *Punch* was occupying much of Leech's time as Christmas approached, Dickens sent the artist a letter via his publisher, William Bradbury, from the Bedford Hotel, Brighton, "explaining that not knowing how his time may serve, I have given the dinner subject to Stanfield" (*Letters* 5: 451). Slater observes,

> At a conference at the artist's [Stanfield's] house, Dickens gave the former seaman permission to execute "The Lighthouse" as one of his two subjects. Although it is not central to the narrative, the stormy seascape proved full of

AND THE GHOST'S BARGAIN.   7

against their
ponderous lanterns,
and fell dead.
When

Figure 4. ''The Lighthouse'' (page 7: three-quarter page illustration) by Clarkson Stanfield, R.A. Original dimensions: 7.6 cm wide by 12.5 cm high, dropped into text.

dramatic interest and motion—its curved sails, clouds, and waves contrasting
with diagonals of foam, rock, and birds (I, 386). Stanfield's versatility is evident
in his second subject, "The Exterior of the Old College," whose spare lines,
ordered white spaces, and stark atmosphere appropriately suggest the baleful
influence of the protagonist Redlaw.   (II, 441)

Moreover, when Leech found himself extremely pressed for time, Stanfield
willingly took over and executed the concluding dinner scene in which, as
the motto "Lord Keep My Memory Green" suggests, Redlaw finally accepts
the mixed blessings of memory (Cohen 181).

   Although both plates are essentially realistic in both style and subject, one
("The Old College") represents a dramatized setting in which we see characters from the story proper, while the other ("The Lighthouse") is drawn
strictly from three successive clauses in narrator's opening reverie:

   When mariners at sea, outlying upon icy yards, were tossed and swung above
   the howling ocean dreadfully. When lighthouses, on rocks and headlands,
   showed solitary and watchful; and benighted sea-birds breasted on against their
   ponderous lanterns and fell dead.
   (Text facing and for the last seven words incorporated into the plate, page 7)

Whereas the clauses may suggest discrete images, Stanfield has fused them
into a single illustration; although the yardarm is not icy, the four individual-
ized mariners are in a perilous circumstance. However, in the act of reefing
in the sail the youths are businesslike and unperturbed. Below them, three
gulls fly about the lighthouse, but none is dashed against the glass of the
lantern. Thus, Stanfield has not merely realized, but has subtly toned down
the accompanying text by muting the quality of menace, and by juxtaposing
the fellowship of the sailors against the fierceness of the storm. They perform
their duties as a group out-of-doors, in contrast to the solitary, in-door labors
of the university professor.
   Stanfield's first appearance in this text is admirably suited to his own
personal history (a sailor in the British merchant navy and then the Royal
Navy) and abilities as a painter of seascapes. In contrast to the domestic,
feminized interior of the previous plate, this illustration depicts four mer-
chant-sailors (two of them seemingly adolescents) struggling to reef in the
jib-sheet on the bowsprit of a sailing vessel. Beneath them, in the surf, is an
anchor. On a rock darkly rising from the breakers an owl-like lighthouse
stands, the small gulls indicating both its size and its distance from the ship
(which we must imagine, for only the bowsprit and its five supporting stays
are visible). The perilous scene is not allegorical but a visual realization
of a passage at the bottom of the (left) facing page: "When mariners at
sea . . . watchful" (6). The picture of a band of men braving the elements,

working as one, is bound up with the method of narration, which Dickens makes "wilder and stranger" by keeping Redlaw in the dark about how he communicates his "gift" of forgetfulness (21 November 1848, to Forster). Again, the illustration (7.5 cm wide by 12 cm high) encloses a few printed words, carrying the reader from the text preceding to the text after the plate.

This mention of a lighthouse on a rugged coastline, like the references in Stave 2 of *A Christmas Carol* to "A place where miners live" (100) and to "a solitary lighthouse" (101) beset by seabirds and breakers about a league from shore, is probably a reminiscence of the week-long excursion through Cornwall[7] taken by Dickens, Forster, and the artists Stanfield and Maclise late in October 1842 (exactly a year before he wrote the *Carol*). According to Peter Ackroyd, "Daniel Maclise was becoming much more difficult and reclusive" (386) about this time, perhaps furnishing Dickens with a model for Redlaw.

In Stanfield's plate we approach the unidentified lighthouse not as the landsman would—and not as Dickens and his companions regarded the Eddystone Light on the coast of Cornwall—from the shore. It is not a white speck in the distance surmounted by an oscillating beacon and surrounded by breakers, boulders, and clouds. Rather, Stanfield depicts it from the perspective of sailors making for home port. Thus, the lighthouse is at once an arbitrary symbol of danger, warning mariners of treacherous reefs, and a personal symbol of hope, a harbinger of homecoming and reunion with loved ones and family. The male science of navigation, implying a knowledge of charts and markers, is learned consciously, deliberately, as part of a masculine-oriented vocation, while the emotional associations are learned unconsciously, through direct experience: having made this passage before, the sailor recognizes the lighthouse not just as a menacing shaft suggestive of the powers of malignant nature, but a welcoming, white, feminine finger-post.

In a letter dated 21 November 1848 to Frank Stone, Dickens gives the artist a list of subjects from which to choose for chapter 2: the statement "you should keep Milly, as you have begun with her" (*Letters* 5: 444) suggests that the writer is concerned with pictorial-narrative continuity. Stone's sequence follows Milly Swidger: "Milly and the Old Man," "Milly and the Student," and "Milly and the Children," all executed with that firmness of line and Giotto-like solidity of figure for which his work was known. Milly is the central figure in each half-page illustration. On November 23, writing from Brighton, Dickens applauds Stone's first picture in the sequence: "The drawing of Milly on the chair [hanging holly with her father-in-law] is charming" (the last word twice underlined). However, Dickens, already formulating plans to use her presence as the counter-touchstone to Redlaw's contaminating touch that cancels out the ameliorating power of memory, insists that she be given a matronly cap to augment her age and dignity: "There is something

AND THE GHOST'S BARGAIN.   19

glistening burden in his arms, from which the quiet

Mrs. William took small
branches, which she
noiselessly trimmed
with her scissors, and
decorated the room
with, while her aged
father-in-law looked on
much interested in the
ceremony.

Figure 5. ''Milly and the Old Man'' (page 19) by Frank Stone. Original
dimensions: 6 cm wide by 11.5 cm high, dropped into text.

coming in the last part, about her having had a dead child, which makes it yet more desirable than the existing text does, that she should have that little matronly sign about her.—Unless the artist is obdurate indeed, and then he'll do as he likes'' (*Letters* 5: 446).

With what a subtle hand the writer directs the mixed-media project, always suggesting and pointing through praise, but never directly commanding his colleagues. The cheerful tact with which the writer addresses his illustrator demonstrates his conviction that the book is a collaborative artistic endeavor rather than a mere commercial, money-making venture. Dickens's initial response to this plate by Stone was delight, with the reservation that the artist give her a matronly cap because of the author's intending to introduce the subject of her dead child. In place of regulars Maclise and Doyle, Dickens enlisted Stone, a friend since their meeting at the Shakespeare Club in 1838, and Tenniel. The moment that Stone has realized is Milly's decorating the college with her father-in-law's assistance: "Mrs. William took small branches, which she noiselessly trimmed with her scissors, and decorated the room with, while her aged father-in-law looked on much interested in the ceremony" (19, accompanying the plate). In this scene, which Dickens had probably suggested to Stone in one of their face-to-face meetings in mid-October, we have moved from superstition, allegory, and psychomachia through reverie and tempestuous waves to a tranquil, domestic scene. The antique chair and small oil-painting admirably suggest the interior of the old college. We note that considerably more text shares the page with this plate (6 cm wide by 11.5 cm high), balancing textual and pictorial narratives. The review of *The Haunted Man* published in the *Athenaeum* praised Stone's realization of Milly as a positive counter-force to Dickens's failure to individualize his characters sufficiently (Cohen 187–88). The malignant spirit of Scrooge's anti-sentimentalism before his reformation is well demonstrated in *The Haunted Man* by old Philip's contrasting responses to the holly berries, which he initially enjoys as "seasonable" and values for the part they play in the ceremony of "greening" the home, but which he later regards as worthless because they serve no utilitarian function and are "not good to eat" (128).

John Leech's opening plate, his treatment of the *Doppelgänger* scene, compels the reader to return to Tenniel's earlier treatments of the same theme. This time, we have dialogue and explication on the previous page running over to the top of the illustration. How convenient that the sentence "This was the dread companion of the haunted man!" sits immediately above the figures. Leech's version of the dread spirit is more substantial than its counterpart in the frontispiece. Leech has made Redlaw's study lighter, permitting us to see far more detail in the bookcase at the back. We can see "his drugs and instruments and books" (3), but not "the shadow of his shaded lamp . . . ,

34   THE HAUNTED MAN

and gone already.   This was the dread companion
              the haunted man !

Figure 6. ''Redlaw and the Phantom'' (page 34) by John Leech. Original
dimensions: 7.6 cm wide by 12.1 cm high, dropped into text.

motionless among a crowd of spectral shapes'' (3). Both Tenniel's opening plates and a textual passage pages earlier have prepared us for this scene, the Ghost's second visitation. The moment captured is that immediately prior to Redlaw's noticing and addressing the Phantom. While the preoccupied Redlaw gazes into the fire (whose hearth does not echo to the laughter of children like that in the third plate), the sinister Phantom's thoughtful gaze is bent on the Chemist himself, and not on the flames: ''It took, for some moments, no more apparent heed of him, than he of it'' (35). Leech seems to have made this alteration in order to make his rendering of the two figures parallel Tenniel's rendering in the frontispiece. In both plates, Redlaw is literally surrounded by possessions and objects associated with his profession, intellectually insulated from external, emotional, and social realities by his learning, as exemplified by his books and various apparatuses, which constitute an alternative mode of existence to the domestic conviviality of the Tetterbys. Unlike the members of the story's family groupings, the Tetterbys and the Swidgers, Redlaw (despite his status as protagonist) is never designated by either a nickname or a Christian name, the outward and visible sign of membership in a community of the heart rather than one of the head.

Gone are the theological symbols of conscience and temptation, good angels and demons; in their place are commonplace objects, which nevertheless appear ominous in the half-light: is that a skull on the top shelf with a demon's mask above, or are these only ocular delusions? Redlaw's chair in Leech's plate is more prosaic: no carved gargoyle supports the arm of this chair, which lacks the elegantly twisting, serpentine back-support of Tenniel's. The specter does not whisper at Redlaw's ear like Satan at the ear of Eve in *Paradise Lost*; rather, Leech brings out the physical likeness in their features as Redlaw, seeing past wrongs re-enacted in the flames, is sardonically scrutinized by his double, whose body fades into the back of the chair and the curtain, right. Redlaw's hair is less full in Leech's version; his hairline recedes, giving him a more middle-aged and careworn aspect. His demeanor is not fearful, as in Tenniel, but bemused; although he sits with his legs crossed and his chin propped on his right hand in both plates, Leech's Redlaw sits further forward and his self-absorbed expression is fully visible. In addition to the small library, seen also in Tenniel's plate, the bookcase behind Leech's figures contains glass jars, indicative of Redlaw's scientific vocation. Thus, the plate underscores the fact that Redlaw's public life spills over into his private life, so that his workplace and his domestic space are one. Leech has captured the moment on the preceding page when ''As *he* leaned his arm upon the elbow of his chair, ruminating before the fire, it leaned upon the chair-back close above him'' (33). The curtain to the right appears again, but at the left, in the ninth illustration, thereby connecting the two in the pictorial narrative sequence.

There is little of Leech's usual sense of comedy and caricature here. However, he allows a strongly felt emotion to dominate, as in his "Scrooge and the Spirit of Christmas Yet To Come" in *A Christmas Carol*. Redlaw has entered, raising the lamp as the street urchin invited in by Milly cowers in the corner: "A bundle of tatters, held together by a hand, in size and form almost an infant's, but in its greedy, desperate little clutch, a bad old man" (47). The precise moment realized occurs as one turns the page: "Used, already, to be worried and hunted like a beast, the boy crouched down as he was looked at, and looked back again, and interposed his arm to ward off the expected blow" (47–48). The center of the printed page describes the child exactly as we see him at the right side of the plate. Is he, as John Butt suggests, a more "impressive" (136) or socially realistic treatment of the "*cartoon* figure" (136) Ignorance in the *Carol* plate? Leech's allegorical child in "The Second of the Three Spirits," a head shorter than his sister, Want, shivers in the cold, his clothing in tatters and his feet bare, despite the season. The savage street urchin or "slum child" (Butt 147) of *The Haunted Man* has more hair and his face is that of a fierce animal rather than an impassive façade. The street child cowers in anticipation of a blow from Redlaw rather than from the elements. The industrial smokestacks behind Ignorance and Want are symbols supplied by the radical *Punch* cartoonist to connect these social problems with the capitalistic factory system and Scrooge's Malthusian doctrine of "surplus population." Redlaw, too, is a theoretician who sees no necessary connection between his work and the human family. His work is "hermetic," insulated from contaminating emotion and a sense of social responsibility.

In "Redlaw and the Boy," Leech has placed a stack of folios on the chair that separates the characters, books that have no counterparts in the printed text. Once again, like the tomes in Redlaw's study on page 34, the books signify the sterility of mere data-gathering and book-learning when the springs of compassion—memory—have been allowed to dry up. Perhaps they mutely assert the upward climb that Redlaw has made from childhood through education—"I strove to climb!" (38), since, at a realistic level, the boy can hardly have placed them there in order to steal something from the bare wainscoting. The books, then, serve to connect the unloved slum child Redlaw once was with the deprived child he sees before him. They ironically suggest here as in *Hard Times* (1854) that the human heart cannot be schooled by mere facts alone, and that ideas, no matter how eloquently expressed, are no substitute for people. A society that is essentially pragmatic rather than sympathetic produces through ignorance and neglect thousands of children like the boy. The boy, if he is any sort of abstraction, is Hunger. However, the boy is described as being merely "*like* some small animal of prey" (emphasis added, 50). Dickens does not employ metaphor ("wolfish") or

48   THE HAUNTED MAN

back again, and interposed his arm to ward off the
expected blow.

Figure 7. "Redlaw and the Boy" (page 48) by John Leech. Original dimensions: 7.3 cm wide by 11.9 cm high, dropped into text.

allegorical terms ("Where angels might have sat enthroned, devils lurked"), and the artist has charged this boy with a feeling (well conveyed by the pose) quite absent from his *Christmas Carol* plate. Possessed of neither surname, Christian name, or nickname, the Boy has speech (unlike his mute counterpart in the *Carol* plate), but does not immediately recognize the meaning of "live" ("'Live! What's that?'" [50]). The street urchin and Professor Redlaw, despite their age and class differences, are connected by their social alienation: after he acquires his infectious gift and has lost both unhappy memories and the faculty of compassion, Redlaw becomes like the parentless waif, removed from human sympathy, imbuing others with a similar lack of concern for suffering. Both are outsiders, observers of rather than participants in social interactions, psychologically homeless, and emotionally alienated from the greater human family.

The closed curtain from the sixth figure becomes the just-opened curtain behind Redlaw (left), joining the two scenes. The printed text focuses on the "heavy curtain in the wall, by which he was accustomed to pass into and out of the theatre where he lectured,—which adjoined his room" (46). The curtain creates a sense of backstage or off-stage space, for Redlaw's study is the Green Room (so to speak) of a lecture theater[8], a juxtaposition which suggests that Redlaw is yet another of the novelist's self-projections. During the early stages of the composition of the book, Dickens confessed to Dr. James Kay-Shuttleworth (5 October 1848) that, in order to write *The Haunted Man* as a sustained narrative, "I . . . must hermetically seal myself up, in my own rooms here in the mornings" (*Letters* 5: 418), just as the chemist seals himself away from the rest of humanity to compose his lectures and conduct his experiments. Dickens was very much a writer who translated his intensely private visions, often created in the solitary hours of night or inspired by nocturnal walks, into textual and performative realties.

Coincidentally, much about *The Haunted Man* is "experimental." In our mind's eye we construct the "high amphitheatre of faces which his entrance charmed to interest in a moment" (46) after he would step through that curtain dividing public from private spaces and personas of the Chemistry professor. Both artist and novelist emphasize the palpable reality of the ghetto child as the product of societal and personal neglect: "A baby savage, a young monster, a child who had never been a child, a creature who might live to take the outward form of man, but who, within, would live and perish a mere beast" (47). Redlaw, with money, position, and education, has the ability, as Scrooge has, to alter the terrible course predicted.

"In the double illustrations introducing 'The Gift Diffused,' the children shrink from the dark figure of Redlaw, who himself is frighteningly dwarfed by his own shadow, a long symbol of the troubled past he wishes not to recall . . . '' (Cohen 155–157). Verbally and graphically, this is our first encounter with the domestic characters of the subplot, whom Dickens introduces

52   THE HAUNTED MAN

CHAPTER II.

THE GIFT DIFFUSED

———•———

A SMALL man sat in a small parlour, partitioned off
from a small shop by a small screen, pasted all over
with small scraps of newspapers. In company with

Figure 8A. ''Illustrated Double Page to Chapter Two'' (page 52) by John
Tenniel. Original dimensions: 7 cm wide by 5.9 cm high, dropped into text.

the small man,
was almost any amount
of small children you may
please to name—at least
it seemed so ; they made,
in that very limited sphere
of action, such an imposing
effect, in point of numbers.

Figure 8B. "Illustrated Double-Page to Chapter Two" (page 53) by John Tenniel. Original dimensions: 6.5 cm wide by 11.9 cm high, dropped into text.

simultaneously in the text, "Chapter II. The Gift Diffused." Here, Tenniel weakly anticipates the domestic theme struck by Leech in the eleventh illustration, depicting Mrs. Tetterby surrounded by five of her eight children and her husband (back turned to her, right). Redlaw, on the landing of the staircase, protects the flame of the candle he has just borrowed, his figure rendered more imposing by virtue of his tall hat and magnified double, his shadow a visual reminder of the nimbus weighing upon his spirit. Wrapped in his cloak, his face obscured, Redlaw is at once mysterious and self-contained. In Leech's conception, Mrs. Tetterby will be heavy and middle-aged; here, she is younger and thinner—indeed, one could confuse her with Milly. Dickens's distributing the responsibility for the plates in this manner has created a dissonance; furthermore, the text does not explicate the two-part scene until several pages later. The shadows in both plates are significant in that they suggest the doubt and despair connected to Redlaw's double. Redlaw's shadow, suggestive of his double, points us back, while Redlaw himself seems to point forward, towards the student's room and the textual counterpart of the plates.

Like all those that follow, except the concluding one, the ninth plate occupies somewhat less than a full page, and shares the page with the text. Leech had wanted a subject more congenial to his comedic tastes, and Dickens had proposed that he show this extended family of two adults, the infant Sally ("Moloch"), and the seven male children.[9] As we turn the page, we come upon the scene with Mrs. Tetterby setting the table and the children gathered about in anticipation. In this illustration, Leech conveys an impression of congested space and close living conditions with the small fireplace, insufficient table, inadequate floor space, and room full of small children. This is not the cheery yuletide repast of the Cratchits—the only food visible here is a small loaf. The plate's placement is masterful since it occurs at precisely the moment that one finds Mrs. Tetterby setting the table. Violating visual continuity, the small, square table behind Tenniel's youthful Mrs. Tetterby in the "Illustrated Double-page to Chapter Two" (page 52) has become a large oval in the foreground, increasing the sense of clutter, "while the screen pasted with news cuttings [upper left] . . . serves as a useful background device to make the room seem even more cramped" (Stoker, "Tenniel's Illustrations" 6). Whereas Tenniel's Tetterbys are essentially realistic, Leech's couple are caricatures. Despite the confined living conditions and constrained financial circumstances, the mantelpiece's ornaments have a humanizing influence on the domestic scene. An element that connects the newsvendor's family to earlier plates is Mr. Tetterby's reading (or, more properly, attempting to read) the newspaper; but his is a private rather than a performative reading which is abandoned, in contrast to the rapt attention of the listeners in Tenniel's "Illustrated Page to Chapter One," and the subject matter is

68   THE HAUNTED MAN

preparing the family supper; hitting it unnecessarily hard with the knives and forks, slapping it with the plates; dinting it with the salt-cellar, and coming heavily down upon it with the loaf.

Figure 9. ''The Tetterbys'' (page 68) by John Leech. Original dimensions: 7 cm wide by 10 cm high, dropped into text.

prosaic and ephemeral, rather than the enduring and imaginative text of a fairytale.

In his contributions to the visual program, Stone focuses on the figures, their states of mind, and the foreground, and avoids any suggestion as to background, creating an almost flat picture. The sacred atmosphere of "Milly and the Student" has affinities with the paintings of the German Nazarenes in that they share close attention to detail, a rejection of aerial perspective, a self-conscious religiosity in the unnatural stillness of the scene, and an avoidance of shadow in order to show everything clearly. Stone's first plate, depicting Mrs. Tetterby and her brood, lacks focus because it attempts to take in the whole scene. Stone's second production is more effective because it is a close-up that utilizes symbolic poses that convey both the characters' roles and feelings. Elegantly simple, the design (anticipating the manner of the Pre-Raphaelites[10]), is reminiscent of early Renaissance art, for Stone has foreshortened the daybed (as Giotto has done with the Virgin Mary's bed in his narrative-pictorial sequence of the life of Christ in the Arena Chapel, Padua) to frame the despondent student, Mr. "Denham," and emphasize his discomfort. The text and plate precisely coincide, since Milly is in the act of adjusting the student's pillow in both. We note that the student is grasping a locket which hangs on a chain about his neck, a detail not mentioned in the text but undoubtedly intended by the artist to suggest the source of the student's abstraction and melancholy. He does not look away towards the fire, as in the text. He does not seem to notice that his pillow is being adjusted, and appears neither uncivil nor ungrateful, would be suggested by the line at the top of the page. The young man's body language does, however, communicate Edmund's pensiveness: "you have often been thinking of late" (97).

Clarkson Stanfield's second plate is enclosed by textual description of the same scene, above and below. As in Tenniel's double-plate, the figure of Redlaw is distinguished by his large hat of seventeenth-century Puritan style. The mood of the scene is somber and tranquil, the white of the snow on the roof contrasting picturesquely with the shadowed portions of the courtyard. The scene depicted is actually several pages further on, for it involves both Redlaw and the boy. Seen as a series, Stanfield's plates are moving us from the limits of human habitation (the lighthouse) towards the center of urban civilization, not merely the metropolis or the university, but the extended family of his final offering, "The Christmas Party in the Great Dinner Hall" (p. 188). The skeletal trees (left), the shadows, and the night sky impart an appropriate gloominess as Redlaw's "gift" continues to be diffused. The Gothic architecture suggests the continuing presence of the past, and therefore reinforces the theme of the importance of memory in the forming of identity.

John Butt describes the boy as neither a type nor an abstraction like "Ignorance" in *A Christmas Carol*, but "a clearly recognizable slum child" (147).

" Tut ! " said the student, petulantly, " very little ails me."

A little more surprise, but no reproach, was expressed in her face, as she withdrew to the other side of the table, and took a small packet of needlework from her basket. But she laid it down again, on second thoughts, and going noiselessly about the room, set every thing exactly in its place,

Figure 10. ''Milly and the Student'' (page 96) by Frank Stone. Original dimensions: 7.3 cm wide by 8.2 cm high, dropped into text.

a little cloister outside, and from that sheltered place
he knew he could look in at the window of their
ordinary room, and see who was within.   The iron
gates were shut, but his hand was familiar with the
fastening, and drawing it back by thrusting in his
wrist between the bars, he passed through softly,
shut it again, and crept up to the window, crumbling
the thin crust of snow with his feet.

The fire, to which he had directed the boy last

Figure 11. "The Exterior of the Old College" (page 105) by Clarkson Stanfield, R.A. Original dimensions: 7.2 cm wide by 6.2 cm high, dropped into
text.

130   THE HAUNTED MAN

flung his body on it immediately, as if to hide it from him, lest the sight of it should tempt him to reclaim it ; and not until he saw him seated by his lamp, with his face hidden in his hands, began furtively to pick it up. When he had done so, he crept near the fire, and, sitting down in a great chair before it, took from his

Figure 12. "The Boy before the Fire" (page 130) by John Leech. Original dimensions: 5.6 cm wide by 8.4 cm high, dropped into text.

This child, for example, experiences various emotions: before, confronted by Redlaw, he was cringing in terror; here, he gives himself over to whole-hearted enjoyment of food, fire, and money. This is the sort of fire, a fire of blazing coals in a grate, that Scrooge initially forbids Bob Cratchit from building, but in conclusion exhorts him to construct with a newly-purchased coal-scuttle: in Stave 1, Bob cannot "replenish it, for Scrooge kept the coal-box in his own" (I: 47). Although coal is thus established in the *Carol*'s printed text as an expensive luxury, in *The Haunted Man* only the pictorial text makes coal a commodity.

Leech's boy, then, is no mere abstraction, but a child whose realism is conveyed through his various emotions and his size relative to the chair. The artist has given him tumbling mounds of hair, trousers far too short for his legs, and bare feet to emphasize his poverty. The passage illustrated is imme-diately above the plate, but the artist has positioned the boy sitting as near as possible to the fire, his feet approaching the fender. We have just read about an old man's being reduced to an egocentric sensualist by Redlaw's contagious gift, desiring to be waited on and fed, and seeing no merit in the holly-berries because they are inedible. He is more savage than the urchin because humanizing memory does not soften him as the physical warmth does the boy. Notes Cohen, "the way he positions the child before the fire-place (III . . .) not only recalls Redlaw's posture there in Tennicl's frontis-piece . . . as well as his own earlier portrayal (I . . .), but visually reinforces Dickens's linkage of the civilized, educated man and the wild, naturally tutored boy" (149).

In Tenniel's sixth and last plate, the feminine forces of light (the angels which have been identified with Milly in the printed text) sweep upward from the horizon, gathering in numbers and intensity as the vaguely apprehended forces of the night (identified by the stars and the hooded figure, upper right) retreat. Below, on a headland a lighthouse stands upon a rock (recalling Stanfield's "The Lighthouse," which Tenniel may have seen in the early proofs) above a small cove where the waves, such billowing breakers earlier, gently break. The plate promises an end to the storm, and implies that the Phantom's dubious "gift" (in fact, the modern fairytale's curse) will be reversed, just as Redlaw prays it will at the close of chapter 2. Stoker notes that, compositionally, this design is related to Stanfield's "The Lighthouse" (p. 7), although the moods and figures of the two plates are antithetical: storm versus tranquility, the human versus the metaphysical. The allegorical figures move upward to occupy the same space as the young sailors, but the later scene's only blackness is the figure of Night itself, clearly in retreat and being pushed out of the frame. "This figure is a pictorial echo, both of Redlaw in his cloak, and of the figure of Death in the title page design, while the female figures, symbolic both of the dawn and of a renewal of spiritual light in

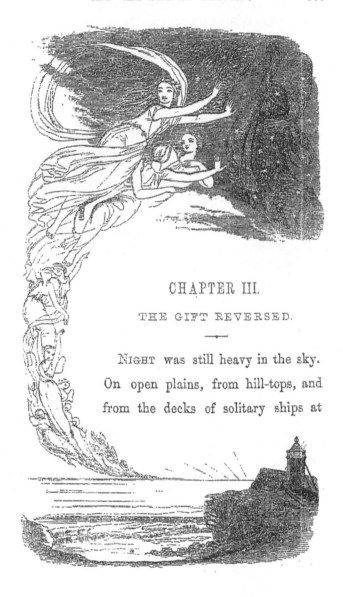

AND THE GHOST'S BARGAIN.   135

CHAPTER III.

THE GIFT REVERSED.

NIGHT was still heavy in the sky.
On open plains, from hill-tops, and
from the decks of solitary ships at

Figure 13. ''Illustrated Page to Chapter Three'' (page 135) by John Tenniel.
Original dimensions: 6.9 cm wide by 12.2 cm high, dropped into text.

Redlaw's life, are reminiscent of the angel" (Stoker, "Tenniel's Illustrations" 8).

While the figures suggestive of Day and Consciousness, the wingless young females in diaphanous, clinging dresses, rise from the distant horizon and a tranquil sea, apparently attempting to push the shaded figure of Night out of the frame, Night's dark wing is still outstretched to the left margin, its force blowing back the drapery of the leading figures of Day. Connecting Tenniel's angular Night to earlier figures are her dark drapery, reminiscent of Redlaw's obscuring cloak on page 53 and the Phantom's on page 34, and her rolled up curtain, recalling the drapery on page 48 which divides Redlaw's study from the lecturehall, the private from the public personae. In fact, Redlaw is never depicted in daylight, and his Phantom is consistently associated with the darker hours, and the realm of dream and nightmare. Rolling up her curtain to close the psychodrama of the subconscious, Tenniel's Night, hooded and androgynous, is vaguely reminiscent of Michelangelo's allegorical figure of Night from the Tomb of Guiliano de'Medici, built between 1526 and 1533 in Sagrestia Nuova, the Church of San Lorenzo, Florence.[11] Whereas, however, Tenniel's retreating, winged, half-awake figure is shrouded in drapery and is covered in symbolic stars, Michelangelo's is a sleeping nude, identified by a series of symbolic objects: the owl (suggestive of presiding over the dark hours), a gruesome mask (suggestive of both theatricality and nightmare), a bouquet of poppies (implying the medicinal benefits of slumber), and a diadem upon which the sculpture has superimposed stars and a crescent moon.

The enclosed text asserts that night is still in the ascendant, and that the result of the contest between light and darkness is still "remote and doubtful" (136). This moment signalling the triumph of the angelic and markedly feminine forces will not be realized in the printed text for a number of pages—"Soon, now, the distant line on the horizon brightened, the darkness faded" (144)—as we move in the text to the exterior of the Tetterbys' shop, with its leafless, potted plant suggestive of anything but the optimistic mood that figure 13 has established.

The spectre's discussion of the boy's emotional deprivation precedes Leech's humorous sketch of Johnny struggling to hold his infant-sister as his father removes the shutters from the shop's windows; as the text above proclaims, "The Tetterbys were up, and doing" (145). "The very looseness of Leech's lines in his pictures of Johnny coping with baby Moloch at home (II . . .) and abroad (III . . .) reinforces the good humor" (Cohen 149), but also underscores how such responsibility is devouring Johnny's childhood. Like the struggling Johnny in the subplot, the urchin of the street of the main plot is "the growth of man's indifference" (143). In the plate, Leech has conflated two different moments, for Mr. Tetterby has taken down the shutters

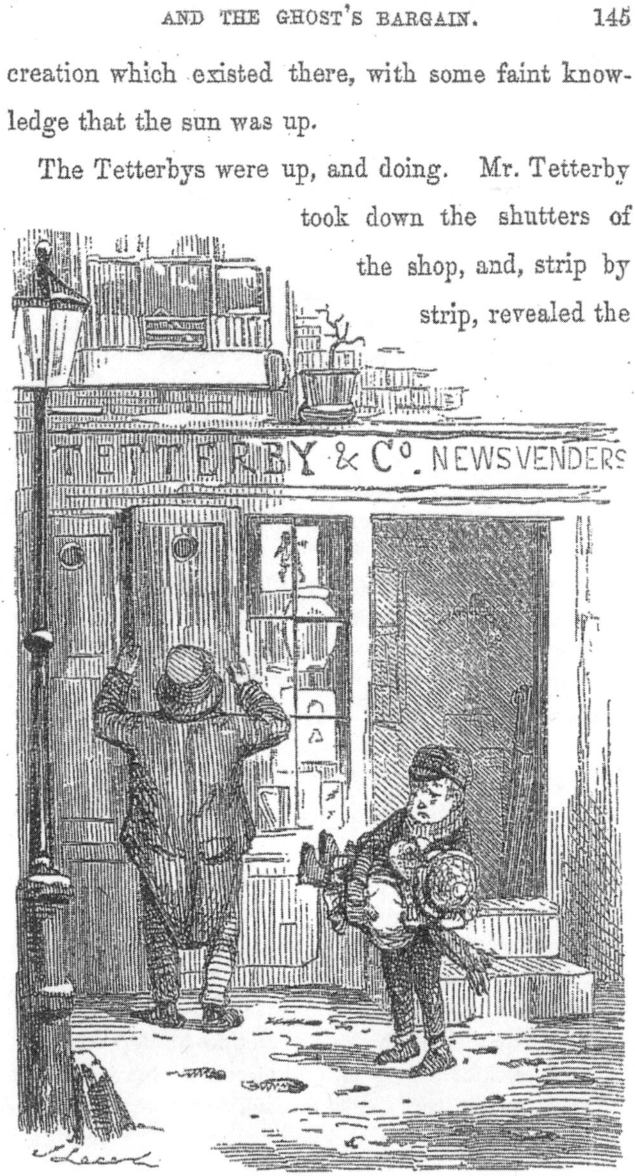

AND THE GHOST'S BARGAIN. 145

creation which existed there, with some faint knowledge that the sun was up.

The Tetterbys were up, and doing. Mr. Tetterby took down the shutters of the shop, and, strip by strip, revealed the

Figure 14. ''Johnny and Moloch'' (page 145) by John Leech. Original dimensions: 7.1 cm wide by 10.7 cm high, dropped into text.

of this "home business" before Johnny "stagger[s] up and down with his charge before the shop door" (146). Dickens here is perhaps critical of parents who exploit their older children by requiring them to mind their infant siblings, for the baby-minders are effectively robbed of their play time. Dickens renders this verdict on the otherwise caring Tetterbys through Johnny's nicknaming the infant in his charge "Moloch," the deity to whom the Canaanites sacrificed children to renew the strength of the sun's fires. To reinforce the novelist's criticism, the artist has juxtaposed Mr. Tetterby and Johnny to imply the elder's being absorbed in his business, and has given Johnny a doleful facial expression. To Victorian readers the very modern exterior of the shop and the gas lamp would have been reminders that this is a contemporary and middle-class fairytale.

Frank Stone in his third and final plate again depicts Milly with pictorial consistency (posture, form, costume, and scale) as Dickens had desired him to do, cap and all. This plate is considerably more realistic and less cartoonlike than Leech's final offering, but Stone's high seriousness is appropriate to his angelic, spiritually renewing subject. The moment captured textually appears right above the plate, synthesizing the two narratives. The tearful reconciliation between the Tetterbys which we have just read about is reinforced by the joy of the children here. Both text and plate proclaim that Redlaw's gift has been revoked. Stone's depiction of Milly recalls pictures of Christ with the children and Catholic Counter-Reformation artists' conceptions of Charity. Milly in the text is "like the spirit of all goodness, affection, gentle consideration, love, and domesticity" (160), those feminine qualities that the Christmas Books consistently celebrate. Owing to the time pressures involved in the artists' keeping pace with the production of the writer, the book now goes twenty-eight pages before the appearance of another illustration.

The essential tensions in the printed text are between the comic business of the Tetterbys and the melodrama surrounding Redlaw and the student; here, Milly clearly bridges the two plots and harmonizes these disparate elements in the same way that the country dance does at the close of *The Chimes*. A similar sort of tension exists in the pictorial narrative, between Leech's cartoon whimsy and Stone's quasireligious sobriety, reinforced by the natural forces depicted in Stanfield's marinescape and the architectural elements of his final plate. By confining the artists to those subjects which he perceived to be their forte, Dickens attempted to maintain pictorial-narrative continuity, although lapses do occasionally crop up, as in Leech's version of Johnny and the baby contrasted with Stone's in "Milly and the Children."

In the last plate of *The Haunted Man*, Stanfield has emphasized the architectural setting of "the Great Hall" at the expense of social reintegration of Redlaw implied in "The Christmas Party." The carefully delineated Gothic

AND THE GHOST'S BARGAIN. 159

So she was, and all the children with her; and as she came in, they kissed her, and kissed one another, and kissed the baby, and kissed their father and mother, and then ran back and flocked and danced about her, trooping on with her in triumph.

Figure 15. ''Milly and the Children'' (page 159) by Frank Stone. Original dimensions: 7 cm wide by 8.3 cm high, dropped into text.

188   THE HAUNTED MAN.

looked up at it ; and, clear and plain below, as if a
voice had uttered them, were the words,

Bradbury & Evans.]   [Printers, Whitefriars.

Figure 16. ''The Christmas Party in the Great Dinner Hall'' (page 188) by
Clarkson Stanfield, R.A. Original dimensions: 7 cm wide by 11.4 cm high,
dropped into text.

beams and elegant stained-glass window in the rear overwhelm the diners, a number of whom are obscured or have their backs to the viewer. Fred Guida's blowup of the final plate (Guida 150) corrects the dwarfing of the characters by the architectural setting, and permits the viewer to observe compositional details obscured in the much smaller original vignette, which occupies all but two lines of the last page. The largest child playing in the foreground is presumably Johnny Tetterby. The well-dressed diner facing away from us on the left (one is tempted to say "stage right," for the whole composition seems so much like one of Stanfield's theatrical sets) may be Professor Redlaw; Stanfield may have deliberately turned the figure so that we cannot see his face and thereby lose the visual continuity established by Leech and Tenniel.

Presumably the woman to the right is Milly, in which case the man seated in front of her is her husband, William, and the old man beside her is Philip Swidger, her father-in-law. The table's centerpiece appears to be a multilayered cake rather than the roast "beef" which Dickens specifically mentions. Appropriately, given the prominence of the pictorial element throughout the book, the final words of the text, "Lord, keep my memory green,"[12] are actually in the plate, thereby synthesizing visual and textual narratives at the final moment of the story. In "Dickens at Work on *The Haunted Man*," Ruth Glancy notes that Dickens deviated from the manuscript text to accommodate this effect: for the sake of illustration Dickens removed a statement that the scroll beneath the picture was in Latin, which, the manuscript said, translates as "Lord! keep my memory green!" As an illustration of the scroll appears on the final page of the book Dickens perhaps felt "old English letters" would be preferable to Latin.

The translation, of course, makes the motto more accessible to the common reader, albeit one who can afford the outlay of five shillings. Dickens's last little book induces the reader to respond to text and illustration simultaneously in twelve of the seventeen plates and in all illustrations after no. 7, "Redlaw and the Boy," which share space with printed text.

The warmth and geniality of the final scene inside the old college are a sharp contrast to the dark, icy, and forbidding exterior view of this mediaeval bastion of male learning in figure 11 (p. 105). "The Christmas Party in the Great Dinner Hall," the finale of the illustrated program, appropriately incorporates children (seen in no less than eight of the previous plates) and grownups into a harmonious, extended human family. In this final space, the past and present as well as the public and private converge. The Gothic beams support the roof and thereby emphasize the importance of the abiding presence of the past and of its contribution through memory to the individual's and the group's sense of identity. How can we know ourselves unless we retain awareness of our origins? The triple-paned stained-glass window complements the biblical language into which the reclaimed and resurrected Redlaw lapses under the influence of the Mary-like Milly, whose unconditional love is so well communicated in "Milly and the Children" (fig. 15, p. 159). Although she is "the embodiment of his better wisdom" (187), her presence in the great Dinner Hall is not immediately obvious. Like the protagonist himself, she has been absorbed into the figures so that the room with its occupants as depicted by Stanfield is an emblem of society as a whole.

Here in an ornate and beautiful space bequeathed by tradition and financed by a benevolent aristocracy (exemplified by the bearded Elizabethan gentleman in the portrait above the diners), the working-class Swidgers and lower-middle-class Tetterbys join with the upper-middle-class professional in communal celebration of Christmas. Here, too, the mundane—the teething infant, the rough-housing children, the great fire, and paneled walls—and the "marvellous" coincide: "shapes and faces on the walls, . . . gradually changing what was real and familiar there, to what was wild and magical" (187). In other words, the childlike faculty of imagination transforms the real into the wonderful. The public and ceremonial space is animated by the presence of young children, elders, the affianced couple, the mentor of young men who are metaphorically his children (Redlaw), and the epitome of domestic, feminine goodness who is a mother to the children of others (Milly).

Redlaw has removed himself from the isolation of his study, and abandoned his academic alienation for the common space of the great Dinner Hall, where people of all conditions and degrees and both genders meet to share a meal and after-dinner conversation. The "sedate" face from the past, staring benignly down upon the diners, has displaced the sardonic visage of Redlaw's doppelgänger, and a cheery communal fireplace of the "Illustrated Page to Chapter I" (p. 1) and of "The Christmas Party in the Great Dinner Hall" (p. 188) has replaced the barren, cheerless hearth of the chemist's study in the frontispiece and the sixth illustration (p. 34). Redlaw must return to his study as Scrooge to his countinghouse, but he will no longer bear into that confined space the burden of melancholy and the atmosphere of gloom that had hitherto invested it. A "bookend" effect occurs as the shadows enclosing the family gathering recall Tenniel's first plate:

> Stanfield's tailpiece design contains two reminders of Tenniel's Chapter I illustration: the same fireirons appear in the shadow at the lower border [and imply that the viewer's position is actually within the hearth], while four children, seated on the floor, have their shadows cast up behind them onto the white tablecloth of the Christmas feast.   (Stoker, "Tenniel's Illustrations," 8–9)

However, the final plate creates not only a synthesis but a serious divergence between text and illustration: the Swidgers present in Stanfield's plate are a mere handful compared to the text's legions of Swidgers, who are "so numerous that they might join hands and make a ring round England" (185), "by dozens and scores" (185), to say nothing of numerous Tetterbys. The jollity of Scrooge's prize-turkey, punch, and polkas has been boiled down to "beef," around which perhaps sixteen somber party-goers chat, rather than dance as at the close of *The Chimes* and *The Cricket on the Hearth.* The only spirits we are ever to credit fully in the Christmas Books in general and in particular are those of familial conviviality, charity, forgiveness, and compassion for our fellow man: in short, the Christmas Spirit. Sadly, in part owing to Stanfield's inability to convey the joyousness of the scene and in part to a growing want of something in Dickens's own life, the *bonhomie* that attends the close of each of the other Christmas Books seems lacking here. We have passed from the obvious allegory of *A Christmas Carol* and *The Chimes* to something more subtle. Dickens would construct collaborative framed-tales for *Household Words* and its successor *All the Year Round*, a Christmas blend he was certain suited the sentimental and popular if not the intellectual and critical tastes of the age.

   The overriding message of the plates in *The Haunted Man* is the hallowed nature of home and family, presided over by an "Angel in the House." In a manner consistent with Coventry Patmore's vision of cloistered femininity in that extended poem of 1854–56, Alfred, Lord Tennyson had already enunciated in 1847 the accepted societal rôles of the genders:

> Man for the field and woman for the hearth:
> Man for the sword and for the needle she:
> Man with the head and woman with the heart:
> Man to command and woman to obey:
> All else confusion.
>
> (*The Princess: A Medley,* Canto V: 437–40)

However, whereas contemporary, patriarchal views justified the repression and subjugation of the female to a patently inferior "domestic" sphere, Dickens asserts the emotional and personal superiority of that sphere in *The Haunted Man.* If one were to look for an analogue to Milly in Dickens's other fiction of the period, one would equate her with the benign Agnes Wickfield rather than the simple-minded Dora Spenlow of *David Copperfield*, since it is Agnes's and not Dora's healing influence on the novel's protagonist that becomes obvious as the novel draws to its conclusion. Although Michael Slater in *Dickens and Women* (1983) regards Milly as "simple" (308), he means "uneducated" rather than "stupid." Dickens extolled her virtue when writing to Frank Stone, who executed the illustrations of her, describing hers as "the very spirit of morning, gladness, innocence, hope, love, domesticity, &c" (*Letters* 5: 448). He and his artistic team, in the text and in the

illustrations, continually celebrate the ideal of the domestic, female-dominated space, for it was "in terms of personal relationships, especially within
a family grouping, that woman, for him as for most Victorians, realized her
full moral and spiritual potential" (Slater, *Dickens and Women*, 309). *The
Haunted Man,* in making Milly Swidger a modern-day fairy godmother, is not
a proto-feminist manifesto advocating the social, educational, and economic
emancipation of women, but it does question the validity of the generally
accepted assumption that the female sphere is necessarily inferior to the male.
The novelty of *The Haunted Man* is that it valorizes the redemptive, suc-
coring, and beneficent powers of the interior, domesticated space above the
worldly, commercial, and intellectual powers of the masculine arena.

NOTES

1. Steven Marcus concurs, describing Dickens's Christmas Books as "the minor
   fictional work" (272) of the 1840s. He feels that "The first of these, *A Christmas
   Carol,* is the only one of genuine literary interest" (272).
2. Robert Patten contends that Chapman and Hall's decision to reduce the ratio of
   illustrations to pages of prose text from 4:32 to 2:32 in the *Pickwick* instalments
   freed Dickens from his original role of commentator on Seymour's illustrations,
   reversing in fact the importance of writer and artist, and concomitantly the stipend
   paid to each: "At a single stroke something permanent and novel-like . . . was
   created out of something ephemeral and episodic: with sixteen pages between
   pictures, Dickens could expand his scenes and amplify his characterizations in
   ways he could not when he had to invent a new comic climax every six pages"
   (65).

   However, that there were seventeen separate illustrations in the 188 pages of
   The Haunted Man (a ratio of approximately 1:12) seems not to have restricted
   Dickens, possibly because he was (as his correspondence makes clear) in the
   position to control what appeared in the pictorial portion of the narrative. Another
   noteworthy difference between the full-page plate from *The Cornhill* and the
   illustrations for *The Haunted Man* is that the former is contained by a border
   which functions as a proscenium arch for this miniature drama some pages prior
   to its textual analogue, while the latter are integrated into the text so that text
   and visual complement coincide.
3. Although to modern readers the purchase price of five shillings seems small, it
   was not so modest in the 1840s, when a clerk such as Bob Cratchit earned
   only fifteen shillings per week. The first Christmas Book, with hand-colored
   frontispiece and elegant binding, was beyond the reach of those very lower-
   middle class readers to whom Dickens wished to be a seasonal benefactor. For
   the next in the series, *The Chimes,* Dickens decided to increase the number of
   illustrations from eight to twelve, and—to help Leech, add variety, and attract

more readers—''use four illustrators instead of one'' (Cohen 180). However, to keep production costs down, Dickens did not insist on hand-colouring of any of the illustrations. The same principle—increasing the scale of illustration, utilizing a team of artists, and yet curtailing production costs—Dickens applied to what proved to be the last of the series, *The Haunted Man*.

The Christmas Books were not the first popular, densely illustrated works of volume-length published in nineteenth-century Britain. Although written in the earlier eighteenth-century manner, in rhyming couplets, rather than the blank verse collection of his short tales *Italy* (1822–28), Samuel Rogers's two-part poem on the processes and benevolent powers of vivid recollection, *The Pleasures of Memory*, initially published in 1792, became one of the most successful late Romantic illustrated books when Moxon brought out a splendid new edition between 1830 and 1834, at a cost of £15,000, augmented by 114 steel-point illustrations produced by J. M. W. Turner and T. Stothard (the earliest editions had just the two plates by Stothard). Turner, in his program of illustration, suggests scenes set in memory rather than the present by throwing over such scenes a weird shimmering. Like Dickens's *The Haunted Man*, Rogers's poem demonstrates the power of memory to soften the harsher emotions of sorrow and despair into a gentle melancholy:

> When sleep has suspended the organs of sense from their office, she [Memory] not only supplies the mind with images, but assists in their combination. And even in madness itself, when the soul is resigned over to the tyranny of a distempered imagination, she revives past perceptions, awakens that train of thought which was formerly most familiar.
>
> (Rogers, 1793, ''Analysis of the Second Part,'' 39)

Like Dickens in the Christmas Books a full half-century later, Rogers describes the positive effects of memories both sad and pleasant through a process whereby objects and scenes serve as conduits to the images and associated feelings of bygone days. In both the Christmas Books and *The Pleasures of Memory*, the emphasis of the illustrations is on objective, external realities that are shaded and refined by the passage of time rather than on the process of association and remembrance itself. It is likely, given his relationship with the elder poet, that Dickens was familiar with the celebrated poem, and that the theme of memory's beneficent influence on the moral life of a desensitized individual such as Scrooge or Redlaw was suggested to the young novelist by Rogers's work.

4. Gill Stoker speculates that Dickens may have engaged Tenniel to assist in the illustrations of *The Haunted Man* because ''he may have been attracted by the illustrations to *Undine*, whose decorated page style reappears in Tenniel's frontispiece, title page and illustrations to Dickens's book'' (''Tenniel's Illustrations'' 1). There may even be, as Stoker notes, a prior connection since Dickens had met Tenniel's brother-in-law, the engraver Leopold Martin, in 1836; however, the surviving Dickens correspondence strongly suggests that Dickens and Tenniel had not been acquainted prior to the 1848 project. However, *Undine* is another

possible link, since Dickens's friend T. J. Thompson gave Christiana Weller a copy of Foque's book with Tenniel's illustrations in 1844 ("To T. J. Thompson," 11 March 1844, *Letters*, 4: 70); but nowhere in extant correspondence by Dickens is there proof that he had seen Tenniel's *Undine* illustrations. The letters we have that refer directly to Tenniel and his *HM* drawings show Dickens was well pleased with the frontispiece ("To L. C. Martin," 3 January 1849 [p. 468]) and that Dickens found the artist both "agreeable" and "modest" ("To John Leech," 30 October 1848 [*Letters* 5: 431]).

5. In terms of book illustration in the 1840s, ornamental work was *not* accorded lower status, as Gill Stoker has noted in an e-mail:

> Tenniel was good at intricate ornamental/symbolic work, and that's probably why Dickens allocated it to him. Similarly, when Tenniel joined *Punch* in the early 50s, he did mostly ornamental/decorative work at first (the kind of work that Doyle had done). Tenniel's representational, human-figure-type work was, I think, less strong in his early career.   (1 August 2004)

6. Solberg notes that the editors of the New Oxford Illustrated Edition "perverted' the original form of *The Haunted Man* with respect to the juxtaposition of illustration and text. Volume 2 of the Penguin edition (1971) shows the relationship more effectively, but is not faithful to the original. For example, although Penguin II, 245, corresponds to page 1 of the 1848 text of *The Haunted Man*, the Penguin edition has 50 words (exclusive of the chapter heading) on this page, whereas the original Bradbury and Evans page contains just 21 words, thereby according greater prominence to its illustration.

7. By virtue of its being located "a league" from shore and "Built upon a dismal reef of sunken rocks" (*A Christmas Carol*, Stave 3, page 101), Dickens's lighthouse would seem to be the famous Eddystone Light, the fourth tower (built between 1756–59) of which he, Forster, Maclise, and Stanfield must have seen eight miles off Start Point in the English Channel when they toured Cornwall (the locale suggested by "A place where Miners live" on the previous page of the *Carol*). In *The Haunted Man*, Dickens's reference to "lighthouses, on rocks and headlands" (6) again implies a coastline much like that of the Land's End area, which boasts "the greatest concentration of lighthouses anywhere in the world" ("Lighthouses of Cornwall"). Today, the area has thirteen lighthouses, but in October, 1842, the four friends would have seen only the following six: the Eddystone (re-built in 1759 to mark the dangerous reef called "The Hand Deep"), Wolf Rock (built in 1795 eight miles off Land's End), Lizard (1619), St. Agnes (1680), Longships (1795), and St. Anthony's Head (1835). Before Dickens published *The Haunted Man*, the new lighthouse at Trevose Head had just been completed 4.5 miles from Padstow on the shore. Ironically, despite the ominous description of the coastline, while travelling in Cornwall Dickens much enjoyed himself in the company of his three friends. Michael Hearn is probably incorrect in his assertion that the *Carol*'s "solitary lighthouse" in Stave 3 is "Likely the Longships" (131), since the lighthouse in Dickens's text is specifically "some league or so from shore" (p. 101), as the Longships light is "just

over a mile out to sea'' (''Penzance and West Cornwall Travel Guide—Land's End'').

8. The lecture theatre and the public stage connect Redlaw and his creator, who had already performed with other amateurs in the British regiment's theatricals in Montreal during his North American tour of 1842, and his own group in September 1845, and from May through July 1848 in London and the provinces.

9. With publication day drawing ever nearer and the bulk of the work depending upon the ever-busy Leech, Dickens had written him from Devonshire Terrace, urging haste (22 Nov. 1848). Although Dickens feels that ''speed is now of *transcendant importance*'' (the latter two words doubly underlined), he still manages his leading horse with a gentle hand: ''Your illustrations in the second part will be, I suppose, the Tetterby family and the boy at the fire. Unless anything else should strike you particularly, these would 'do', I think.'' In fact, to maintain visual continuity, Leech had to continue as he had begun, working on the character studies of Redlaw, the Phantom, the Boy, the Tetterbys in general, and Johnny with the gigantic baby (Sally), whom the narrator has whimsically dubbed ''Moloch'' (the Canaanite devourer of children). The writer correctly assessed Leech's strength as comedy from the first, and steered him towards the petit bourgeois family of newsvendors, who are *The Haunted Man*'s equivalents of the *Carol*'s Cratchits, reflecting in their bonhomie a social group (if not a class) so well known to the writer, his own family when he was a child.

10. Since the Pre-Raphaelite School was being founded by seven artists (led by Dante Gabriel Rosetti, John Everett Millais, and William Holman Hunt) at about the time that *The Haunted Man* was published, it would be a mistake to regard Stone's ''Milly'' illustrations as consciously ''Pre-Raphaelite'' in style. Stone, already forty-eight at the time, was a self-taught artist, while Pre-Raphaelites were younger and were associated with the Royal Academy schools, against the teachings of which they reacted.

11. Whether Tenniel was familiar with Michelangelo's neoclassical giantess from his few lessons at the Royal Academy is certainly disputable. The two allegorical figures reveal numerous differences. While Michelangelo's is obviously female in form, she is in a *contrapposto* repose (implying disturbed or uneasy slumber) to the left of the monumental tomb, balancing (and therefore equal to) the male figure of Day, right, Tenniel's figure on the illustrative page for the opening of chapter 3 (p. 135) is androgynous, and is crammed into the top-right of the page, a single figure straining against the multiple, obviously female figures rising from the bottom of the page. This figure raises its left hand ineffectually, closing its arm in upon its body. Michelangelo's well-muscled Day, a male giant, is awake but contorted, his face obscured, as if only coming to consciousness.

12. ''Keep my memory green,'' may, of course, be variously interpreted—Redlaw as a professor may well have conceived of it as a wish for a clear and retentive memory before his experiences with the Phantom, or perhaps even a wish that a man be remembered by succeeding generations on account of his achievements. That it may be a wish to remember both pleasant and unpleasant experiences in order to be able to experience sympathy for others is the meaning Redlaw apprehends as if he hears the words spoken by the figure in the portrait above them.

For this new understanding he thanks Milly, "who through the teaching of pure love, hast graciously restored me to the memory which was the memory of Christ upon the cross, and of all the good who perished in His cause" (184), rendering the tale a Christian allegory.

WORKS CITED

Altick, Richard D. *Victorian People and Ideas*. New York: Norton, 1973.

Bentley, Nicolas. "Dickens and his Illustrators." *Charles Dickens 1812–1870. A Centenary Volume*. Ed. E. W. F. Tomlin. London: Weidenfeld and Nicolson, 1969. 196–227.

Butt, John. "Dickens's Christmas Books" (1951). *Pope, Dickens and Others: Essays and Addresses*. Edinburgh: Edinburgh UP, 1969. 127–48.

Carse, Wendy. "Domestic Transformations in Dickens' 'The Haunted Man'." *Dickens Studies Annual* 23 (1994): 163–81.

Cohen, Jane R. *Charles Dickens and His Original Illustrators*. Columbus: Ohio State UP, 1980.

Collins, Philip, ed. *Dickens: The Critical Heritage*. London: Routledge and Kegan Paul, 1971.

———. "Dickens on Ghosts: An Uncollected Piece [from the *Examiner* for Feb. 26, 1848]." *Dickensian* 59 (Jan. 1963): 5–14.

———, and Edward Guiliano. *The Annotated Dickens*. 2 vols. New York: Clarkson N. Potter, 1986.

———. "Cornwall Calling." http://www.cornwall-calling.co.uk/lighthouses/Eddystone. htm

Davis, Paul. *Charles Dickens A to Z: The Essential Reference to His Life and Work*. New York: Facts On File, 1998.

Dickens, Charles. *The Christmas Books*. 2 vols. Ed. Michael Slater. Harmondsworth: Penguin, 1978. 2 vols.

———. *The Haunted Man, and The Ghost's Bargain*. London: Bradbury and Evans, 1848.

———. *The Letters of Charles Dickens*. Vol. 1: 1820–1839. The Pilgrim Edition, ed. Madeline House and Graham Storey. Oxford: Clarendon, 1965.

———. *The Letters of Charles Dickens*. Vol. 4: 1844–1846. The Pilgrim Edition, ed. Kathleen Tillotson. Oxford: Clarendon, 1977.

————. *The Letters of Charles Dickens*. Vol. 5: 1847–1849. The Pilgrim Edition, ed. Graham Storey and K. J. Fielding. Oxford: Clarendon, 1981.

Feltes, N. N. *Modes of Production of Victorian Novels*. Chicago: U of Chicago P, 1989. Forster, John. *The Life of Charles Dickens*. 2 vols. London: Chapman and Hall, 1874.

Glancy, Ruth. "Dickens and Christmas: His Framed-Tale Themes." *Nineteenth-Century Fiction* 35, 1 (June 1980): 53–72.

————. "Dickens at Work on *The Haunted Man*." *Dickens Studies Annual* 15 (1986): 65–85.

Guida, Fred. *A Christmas Carol and Its Adaptations*: *Dickens's Story on Screen and Television*. London and Jefferson, NC: McFarland, 2000.

Hearn, Michael Patrick, ed. *The Annotated* Christmas Carol. New York: Avenel: 1989.

Kaplan, Fred. *Dickens: A Biography*. New York: William Morrow, 1988.

"Lighthouses of Cornwall." http://www.nortonmede.com/lighthouses/page1.htm

Marcus, Steven. *Dickens: From Pickwick to Dombey*. New York: Basic Books, Clarion, Simon and Schuster: 1965.

Mitchell, Sally, ed. *Victorian Britain: An Encyclopedia*. New York: Garland, 1988.

"Moloch." *Encyclopedia Mythica*. http://www.pantheon.org/

Patten, Robert. *Charles Dickens and His Publishers*. Oxford: Clarendon, 1978.

"Penzance & West Cornwall Travel Guide—Land's End." http://www.chyor.co.uk/travel-tips/penzance/landsend.html

Rogers, Samuel. *"The Pleasures of Memory" with Some Other Poems*. Fifth edition. London: T. Cadell and C. Dilly, 1793. Pp. v-viii, 9–89.

————. *The Pleasures of Memory*. Il. J. M. W. Turner and T. Stothard. London: T. Cadell and E. Moxon, 1834.

Schlicke, Paul, ed. *The Oxford Reader's Companion to Dickens*. New York and Oxford: Oxford UP, 1999.

Slater, Michael. *Dickens and Women*. London: J. M. Dent, 1983.

Solberg, Sarah. " 'Text Dropped into the Woodcuts': Dickens' Christmas Books." *Dickens Studies Annual* 8 (1980): 103–18.

Stevens, Joan. " 'Woodcuts Dropped into Text': The Illustrations in *The Old Curiosity Shop* and *Barnaby Rudge*." *Studies in Bibliography: Papers of the Bibliographical Society of the University of Virginia* 20 (1967): 113–33.

Stoker, Gill. "A Prior Connection between Tenniel and Dickens?" 1 August 2004, 7:06 A. M. Personal correspondence.

———. "Tenniel's Illustrations to Dickens's 'The Haunted Man'." http://serendipity. p9.org.uk/dickens.htm

Stone, Harry. "*A Christmas Carol*: Giving Nursery Tales A Higher Form." *The Haunted Mind: The Supernatural in Victorian Literature*. Ed. Elton E. Smith and Robert Haas. Lanham, MD: Scarecrow, 1999. 11–18.

Tennyson, Alfred Lord. *The Princess: A Medley.* 1847. http://www.math.boisestate. edu/gas/other_gilbert/princess/tennv.htm

Tick, Stanley. "Dickens and *The Haunted Man*." Unpublished paper presented at the thirty-first annual meeting of the Dickens Society of America. De Paul University, Lincoln Park, IL, 15 October 2000.

Wilson, Angus. *The World of Charles Dickens*. London: Martin Secker & Warburg, 1970.

The Life of Our Lord Revisited

Gary L. Colledge

When Dickens composed The Life of Our Lord, *he did so as a novice theologian and Christian thinker intent on teaching his children "something about the history of Jesus Christ." This essay not only considers* The Life of Our Lord *a serious and deliberate attempt by Dickens to craft a harmony of the Gospels for his children, but also suggests that, as such, it plays a central role as a definitive source for our understanding of his basic religious orientation and worldview. Situating* The Life of Our Lord *in the context of the theological literature and biblical commentary of the day, the essay first examines Dickens's composition of* The Life of Our Lord *and its affinity with theological works of similar interests in the early to mid-nineteenth century. Attention turns in the second part of the essay to a discussion of selected theological themes that emerge from* The Life of Our Lord *and their significance for our understanding of Dickens's religious thought.*

For too long, *The Life of Our Lord* has been neglected as a source for a more complete and a more precise understanding of Dickens's religious thought. While there have been a handful of academic treatments of the book in the last two decades,[1] no sustained effort has yet been made by the scholarly community to incorporate it into the circle of serious discussion on Dickens's work. Under such circumstances, the value and necessity of *The Life of Our Lord* to the discussion not only of Dickens's religious beliefs, but also the larger Dickens corpus, has gone largely unrecognized or unacknowledged. Such circumstances, for the most part, seem to have arisen as the result of (1) failing to approach it in terms of its genre, a harmony of the Gospels,

Dickens Studies Annual, Volume 36, Copyright © 2005 by AMS Press, Inc. All rights reserved.

and (2) naively underestimating the value of its theological content. Both of these, in turn, have contributed to a lack of clarity concerning how this work should be read and understood.

A reassessment, then, of *The Life of Our Lord* along these lines is in order and will provide not only a better understanding of its importance and indispensability to Dickens studies but also will reveal its value as an index and definitive source for our understanding of Dickens's religious thought and his Christocentric worldview. To that end then, this article will consider, first, and of primary significance, *The Life of Our Lord* as Dickens's deliberate and serious effort toward composing a harmony of the Gospels. Understanding this work as a harmony can help us to begin to draw right conclusions about its content and Dickens's meaning in it. Then, having established an interpretive framework of sorts, we will be ready to examine selected portions of the work in order to reconsider the long underestimated value of its theological and biblical substance. Having accomplished this, a more productive basis for a conscientious analysis will have been established. Such a reassessment, it is hoped, will point to the book's considerable value as a source for a more precise understanding of Dickens and his religious thought.

The Life Of Our Lord as a Harmony of the Gospels

Central to Dickens's religious thought and worldview was the person and example of Jesus, particularly as set forth in the Gospels. Whether in his letters, his novels, or his essays, when the subject at hand was religion, Dickens ultimately defaulted to the teachings of the New Testament—which for him were the Gospels—and the life and lessons of Jesus.[2] He cared very little, if at all, for theological formulation and conjecture and, in fact, saw them as obstacles to the advance of what he called "real Christianity."[3] For Dickens, the whole of theology was essentially a practical or ethical Christology,[4] and it is this Christology that Dickens was so anxious for his children to understand. For this purpose, Dickens wrote his "History of Jesus Christ" (*TLOL* 11)[5] couched in the genre of a harmony of the Gospels to present to his children the person and example of Jesus unencumbered by what he saw as the trappings and distortions of an institutionalized Christianity.

The Life of Our Lord is an expressly private and personal composition from a father to his children to tell them what, from his perspective, was the most important thing they could know: the life and lessons of Jesus as found in the Gospels. In *The Life of Our Lord*, addressed to "My Dear Children," Dickens wrote from the very beginning, "I am very anxious that you should know something about the History of Jesus Christ. For everybody ought to know about Him'' (11). This, of course, is consistent with the central place that Jesus occupied in Dickens's religious orientation. Furthermore, Dickens's clear desire concerning the spiritual formation and moral development of his children was that they know about Jesus and imitate Him, and he was not reticent to encourage them in that endeavor. The familiar letter to his son, Edward (Plorn), upon his departure for Australia implored him to follow the teaching of Jesus. Dickens wrote, ''Try to do to others as you would have them do to you, and do not be discouraged if they fail sometimes. It is much better for you that they should fail in obeying the greatest rule laid down by Our Saviour than that you should.'' Dickens wrote further toward the end of the same letter, ''You will therefore understand . . . that I now most solemnly impress upon you the truth and beauty of the Christian Religion, as it came from Christ Himself, and the impossibility of your going far wrong if you humbly but heartily respect it'' (Forster 2: 379–80). A similar letter to his son Henry (Harry) included the timely advice, ''Deeply respecting it [the New Testament] and bowing down before the character of our Saviour, as separated from the vain constructions and inventions of men, you cannot go very wrong, and will always preserve at heart a true spirit of veneration and humility'' (Hogarth 2: 394). In each of these letters, he reminded both Edward and Henry that he had written to each of his sons, as they had gone away, quite similar words. Even in his will, Dickens's thoughts turned to the spiritual formation of his children. ''I exhort my dear children,'' he wrote, ''humbly to try to guide themselves by the teaching of the New Testament in its broad spirit, and to put no faith in any man's narrow construction of its letter here or there'' (Forster 2: 422). In each case, Dickens pointed to New Testament teaching as exemplified in Jesus as the unfailing rule for life and faith and encouraged his children to guide their lives and thinking by Jesus' example.

Dickens was quite fervent about this particular aspect of the spiritual formation of his children. For Dickens, the demonstration of ''real Christianity'' was not in subscribing to religious creeds or engaging in ecclesiastical exercises and pious behaviors. Rather, ''real Christianity'' was demonstrated in the effort toward following the example of Jesus as it is found in the Gospels. Accordingly, a document that deliberately and purposefully articulated Dickens's Christology to his children to the end that they understand and follow Jesus' example should surely be considered significant. Such genuine concern for the spiritual formation of his children, not to mention the fact that this was a document written exclusively for them and their own private religious instruction,[6] points to its value as an expression of Dickens's central spiritual concerns, an expression worthy of our careful consideration.

As has already been suggested, what most scholars and critics have failed to recognize is that *The Life of Our Lord* was intentionally and carefully crafted as a harmony of the Gospels.[7] It might best be described as a paraphrased selective juvenile harmony. By referring to *The Life of Our Lord* as a *paraphrased* harmony, I mean that Dickens preferred, for the most part, to paraphrase his basic narrative, although he typically used the King James Version verbatim in direct discourse. By calling it a *selective* harmony I mean that he did not include in his harmony all of the events and episodes recorded in the Gospels. Rather, he selected those representative portions that best served his purposes in telling his children "something about the History of Jesus Christ." By describing *The Life of Our Lord* as a *juvenile* harmony, I mean, of course, that it was written for a young audience—his children. It should be observed here that the *selective* process is of central significance in the study of *The Life of Our Lord*. As sole editor, Dickens's decision to include certain material can be as important as the content of the material itself.[8]

As a harmony, then, we should see in *The Life of Our Lord* the basic characteristics of a harmony and of harmonization. That is, it should exhibit an attempt throughout to combine—or harmonize—the New Testament Gospel accounts into a single and coherent running narrative of the life of Jesus. On the broadest level, a harmony should demonstrate an attempt to deal in some way with the chronology of the life of Christ as represented and informed by the four canonical Gospels.[9] At a second level, a harmony should reflect decisions made concerning harmonization of passages that seem to share certain affinities, yet possess their own discrete elements.[10] On a third level, a harmony should exhibit a sensible harmonization of parallel accounts that are shared by two or more of the Gospels.[11]

On the broadest level, Dickens shows little real concern for a detailed chronology in terms of the length of Jesus' public ministry or the number of Passovers he attended.[12] He does, however, demonstrate an awareness of this broader chronological concern. Obviously, Dickens has arranged his material in a chronological order. More importantly, it is clear that he has made decisions regarding the temporal arrangement of his material. In fact, Dickens's arrangement reflects, on the one hand, a knowledge of the basic chronology of the Gospel accounts and on the other hand, his own decisions about a chronological arrangement of events. This is one of the particular features of *The Life of Our Lord* that suggests Dickens gave some time and planning to this project.

On the second level, Dickens shows a remarkable sense of the issues involved in harmonization. One example in particular is noteworthy. While Dickens has been accused of carelessly and naively including two accounts of the Lord's Supper in *The Life of Our Lord* (Piret 182; Egan 265), he has, in fact, dealt knowledgeably and decisively with, what was in the nineteenth century, a difficult and debated issue. Even prior to the nineteenth century, the seeming dissonance between John and the Synoptic Evangelists regarding the celebration of the Passover just prior to Jesus' crucifixion was at issue.

The question was, were there two meals described in the Gospel accounts, the Passover meal in the Synoptics (Matt. 26.17–30; Mark 14.12–26; Luke 22.14–23) and another meal prior to the Passover described in John 13.1–30; or were these two one and the same? The 1807 edition of Daniel Whitby's *A Paraphrase and Commentary on the New Testament* supports the view that there were two separate meals described in the Gospels. Whitby included an extended discussion of the issues in an Appendix to Mark 14 (1: 284–6), but commented simply on John 13:1, "That this was not the paschal supper, but a supper they were at before the feast of the passover, [see] ver. 1" (1: 483). On the other side, Hermann Olshausen argued that the Passover observed in the Synoptic Gospels was one and the same with the meal described in John 13.1–30. In his *Biblical Commentary on the Gospels and On the Acts of the Apostles* (1850) Olshausen commented on John 13:1:

> The event to which John gives special prominence, in the period of this intimate fellowship, is the last meal of Jesus with his disciples. The identity of this δεῖπνον [*deipnon* = meal] with the last Supper is supported, *first*, by the parallel Luke xxii. 27, which evidently relates to the washing of the feet, and fixes it in the time of the Supper; *secondly*, John himself (xiii. 21, ff., 38, ff.) mentions the same conversations, as, according to the other Evangelists, took place at the Passover; and, *finally*, this interview, which is perfectly connected in itself, is immediately succeeded by the departure of Christ to Gethsemane (xvii. 26, xviii. 1.).   (4: 39)

These two examples from early-to mid-nineteenth-century commentaries, representative of the debate that continues even today in some circles, help to illustrate that Dickens was neither careless nor naïve in including accounts of two meals. Rather, he agreed with those like Whitby who saw two distinct meals described in the Gospels.

Dickens's own rendering of these Gospel accounts further indicates his deliberate inclusion of two meals. John's account of the meal at which the footwashing takes place begins with the rather imprecise, "Now before the feast of the passover" (John 13.1). Dickens's temporal designation to introduce the story of John 13.1–20 is simply, "One night" (*TLOL* 87).[13] Interestingly, he used a phrase similar to the Johannine account, "The Feast of the Passover being now almost come" (*TLOL* 90) to introduce his presentation of what is the Synoptic account of the preparation for the Passover meal and the meal itself. By eliminating the temporal designation used by John introducing the meal that followed the footwashing and by emphatically including a similar temporal designation to introduce the Synoptic account of the Passover, it seems that Dickens intentionally sought to keep the meal of John 13.1–20 distinct from the Synoptic account of the Passover meal.[14]

As to the third level of harmonization, one example in particular from *The Life of Our Lord* illustrates Dickens's more exacting work. In chapter 7,[15] a chapter that is developed almost exclusively from Luke's Gospel (Dickens's last two stories find their source in the Synoptics generally with some exclusive material from Mark), Dickens prefaced the Parable of the Good Samaritan (found only in Luke) with an introduction harmonized from the Synoptics:

> As Our Saviour sat teaching the people and answering their questions, a certain lawyer stood up and said, "Master, what shall I do, that I may live again in happiness after I am dead?" Jesus said unto him, "The first of all the commandments is, the Lord our God is one Lord: and thou shalt love the Lord thy God with all thy heart, and with all thy soul, and with all thy mind, and with all thy strength. And the second is like unto it. Thou shalt love thy neighbor as thyself. There is none other commandment greater than these." (65)

Even though Dickens interpolates his own setting in the clause, "As our Saviour sat teaching the people and answering their questions," it is obvious that he begins with Luke's account of the Good Samaritan but cleverly harmonizes it with the account of the controversy stories of Matt. 22.34–40 and Mark 12.28–34. While Matt. 22.35 mentions a "lawyer," only Luke refers to "a *certain* lawyer." In Matthew and Mark the issue at hand is Jesus' identifying "which is the first commandment of all" (Mark 12.28), whereas in Luke the issue is how one might obtain eternal life, or "live again in happiness" after death. After this initial sentence, however, Dickens departs from Luke and depends on Matthew and Mark. In the Lukan account, it is the lawyer who recites the greatest commandment in response to Jesus' question, "What is written in the law? how readest thou?" But Dickens, in a rather disjunctive way, has Jesus answering the lawyer's question immediately by stating the greatest commandment in a clearly Markan formulation: "The first of all the commandments is, the Lord our God is one Lord: and thou shalt love the Lord thy God . . . " (Mark 12.29). Only Mark includes the *Shema* (Deut. 6.4) in Jesus' initial words of response to his detractors, which Dickens transposes here. We also find only in Mark the order of "heart-soul-mind-strength" (Mark 12.30), the same order Dickens uses. Similarly, only Matthew uses the phrase, "And the second is like unto it" (Matt. 22.39), and only Mark reports Dickens's conclusion, "There is none other commandment greater than these" (Mark 12.31). Peculiarly, Dickens's manuscript shows that he began Jesus' words to the lawyer with "Thou shalt love the Lord they God with all" (25) from Matthew and Luke but then crossed it out and began instead with the Markan formulation.

It is a bit peculiar that Dickens saw the need to harmonize accounts here at all, but perhaps a clue to his decision lies in the fact that, in his manuscript, he has underlined these words of Jesus—six entire lines. It is rare to find such underlined passages in the manuscript (other than his chapter titles) and it seems that underlining, when it occurs, is always for emphasis. Considering, then, that this material is underlined, that it introduces the Parable of the Good Samaritan and that it includes the essence of The Golden Rule, it seems reasonable to conclude that Dickens has harmonized here to emphasize what he saw as a central aspect of the teaching of Jesus and a central lesson he would want his children to learn.

Examples like this may invite a number of fascinating observations about Dickens's harmony, but two in particular are immediately important for the present discussion. First, this example represents Dickens's careful and knowledgeable skill—and sometimes inventiveness—in harmonization. Obviously, a large number of such examples could be presented. A second observation, suggested by this example, and one that I will now consider more fully, is that the production of a harmony is no simple undertaking.

Although it might at first seem to be so, the genre of harmony is not static. While there are obvious parameters regarding subject, content, and even organization, nineteenth-century examples of harmonies indicate a rather wide variety in style and substance, and suggest that the genre was flexible and varied within its established boundaries. There were critical harmonies, academic harmonies, devotional harmonies and juvenile harmonies. Some harmonies were paraphrased, some were taken verbatim from the text of the King James Version, and some were the author's own translation from the Greek text. Some harmonies were comprehensive, some selective; most selective paraphrased harmonies possessed their own distinctive character.

In all of this, one thing remained common, however: a harmony, that was truly a harmony of the Gospels, was not simply an author's reflective thoughts on the life of Jesus or the New Testament Gospels, but rather a careful attempt to harmonize the Gospel accounts into a single and coherent running narrative. As such, the composition of a harmony was a more or less exacting and time-consuming task involving knowledge of the story of Jesus as a whole, some knowledge of the Gospels individually, and some knowledge of their affinities and their dissimilarities. In what has been considered above regarding harmonization in *The Life of Our Lord*, it seems reasonable to conclude that its design and composition were not the activities of just a few hours or even a few days.

Bolstered by comments Dickens made in a letter to Forster, 28 June 1846, it is often assumed that he wrote *The Life of Our Lord* in a very short time, perhaps in just a few days. In addition to other writing tasks and correspondence, Dickens wrote that he had, ''Half of the children's New Testament to write or pretty nearly,'' and adds, ''I set to work and did that'' (*Pilgrim Letters* 4: 573). This is typically understood to suggest that Dickens wrote almost half of *The Life of Our Lord* in perhaps a few hours. This seems unlikely, however, in view of the character of his harmony and the task of harmonization. As we have seen, *The Life of Our Lord* displays the characteristic signs that Dickens was, at least to some degree, aware of the fundamental aspects involved in the composition of a harmony and that he took care to be attentive to them. Even if Dickens were not formally acquainted with the fundamental aspects of harmony composition, he demonstrates in his work an intuitive knowledge of such composition. In this light, then, and in light of the nature and concerns of harmony composition, it would be careless to take the above comments to Forster indiscriminately to mean that he wrote "half of the children's New Testament" in a few hours one Sunday morning in June 1846. More likely, these comments referred to his drafting of previous work and research into manuscript form, or perhaps some other stage of the work.

That Dickens would give himself to such a task and such a discipline is significant. His doing so is consistent with the central role that Jesus played in his religious thought and worldview, and with the urgency that he felt to offer his children an account of the life and teaching of Jesus.

The Life Of Our Lord and Nineteenth-Century Harmonies

By the time Dickens attempted his hand at a harmony, the genre itself had enjoyed a long history extending as far back as the second century CE.[16] Harmonies, in a unique way, were early attempts to deal with the historical figure of Jesus. Prior to the Enlightenment, the harmonizing of the four canonical Gospels was the accepted method of constructing a biographical account of the life of Jesus. Such early attempts—and there were many—were, in fact, the predecessors of post-Enlightenment historical "Lives of Jesus" that in essence began to appear with the fragments "Concerning the Story of the Resurrection" and "The Aims of Jesus and His Disciples" by Hermann Reimarus published posthumously between 1774 and 1778 and which flourished in the nineteenth century behind the impetus of David Friedrich Strauss's *Das Leben Jesu, kritisch bearbeitet*, published in 1834 and translated by George Eliot in 1846 as *The Life of Jesus Critically Examined*. An important and significant difference between harmonies and "Lives," however, is that the harmonies, especially prior to the Enlightenment, were constructed upon the basic presupposition that the Gospels were reliable historical records revealing a true picture of Jesus. The real significance of this historical background is seen in the two-fold phenomenon that involved, on the one hand, Dickens's choice of method and genre, and on the other, the state of biblical studies in England in the first half of the nineteenth century.

While German theology was pioneering the historical-critical approach to the Gospels and thus turning the tide of Jesus studies toward "Lives" and determinedly away from harmonies, theological thought in England was essentially preoccupied with Anglican ecclesiastical issues. More significantly,

English theologians and churchmen were, for the most part, unreceptive to the new continental theology and methodology. This meant that this new approach had relatively little impact on British theology and that the new critical approach represented in "Lives of Jesus," even with the publication of Eliot's translation of Strauss, gained little scholarly or popular recognition prior to 1860.[17]

In this context, then, Dickens utilized a methodologically primitive, yet still very conventional and respected genre that in itself speaks emphatically to his basic theological orientation and his view of the Gospels, and especially to the fact that he saw in the Gospels a reliable, historical record of an authentic, historical Jesus. It is by no means clear to what degree Dickens knew or was even concerned about the scholarly subtleties of the interface between harmonies and Lives nor would that have been necessary in order for him to compose his own harmony. It appears, however, that he was aware of the harmony as a distinct genre and that he deliberately made use of it in an adept and familiar way.

A comparison between the two shows little influence of some of the important early to mid-nineteenth-century harmonies[18] upon *The Life of Our Lord* and no reliance by Dickens on either their chronologies or their arrangements. In fact, such a comparison suggests that Dickens, if he were at all familiar with any of the standard or popular harmonies, intentionally labored to keep his harmony distinct from them. If Dickens used any secondary sources, he did an outstanding job of disguising that fact. Accordingly, present investigation suggests that Dickens composed his own harmony according to his own chronological arrangement and his own thematic concerns.

This is not to suggest that Dickens's *The Life of Our Lord* is singularly unique as a harmony. After all, all harmonists are bound to work within the parameters established by the Gospels themselves as well as the harmony genre. Still, Dickens's structural arrangement and stylistic elements exhibit originality and independence, giving his harmony its own distinctive character. It remains possible, in theory at least, that he randomly selected the content and order of his harmony, or that he used an existing harmony as a template. However, the evidence strongly suggests that *The Life of Our Lord* was composed with at least a working knowledge of the fundamental principles of harmonization and a careful attention to them apart from any dependence on secondary sources. In other words, Dickens's harmony was his own creation.

Dickens's style as well as his treatment of the New Testament and his pedagogical method also indicates a distance between him and other early Victorian harmonists. Interestingly, Dickens did not engage in the type of extraneous commentary that some of his contemporaries did. Like other children's Gospel harmonies of his day, he freely added informative notes for his children, yet more economically than his peers. Likewise, Dickens refrained from the extraneous theological interpretation that was so characteristic of many of the early to mid-nineteenth-century juvenile harmonies, electing to work more often within the fixed parameters of the genre. Two examples will illustrate on a small scale the style and tone that distinguishes *The Life of Our Lord* from other juvenile harmonies.

In *Gospel Stories: An Attempt to Render the Chief Events of the Life of Our Saviour Intelligible and Profitable to Young Children*, a modified selective juvenile harmony that seems to have some linguistic affinities with *The Life of Our Lord*, the anonymous author included the following in recounting the story of John the Baptist:

> His father never forgot what the angel told him John was intended to do; so he took him, when he was a little boy, into a desert place, away from the rest of the people, and had him brought up to fear God in his youth; and John remained there till the time came when he was to preach to the people, and teach then to be good, and tell them that the SAVIOUR, God's own son, was soon to come and teach them himself; and he was, for a reason I will explain in another story, called John the BAPTIST.   (9–10)

Here, this author included as a part of the main narrative of the story the speculation that John was raised in the wilderness.[19] Dickens, on the other hand, stayed strictly within the boundaries of the Gospel accounts: "At that time there was a good man indeed, named John, who was the son of a woman named Elizabeth—the cousin of Mary. . . . He was poorly dressed in the skin of a camel and ate little but some insects called locusts, which he found as he traveled, and wild honey, which the bees left in the hollow of trees" (*TLOL* 20–3). While the writer of *Gospel Stories* felt free to report the beginning of John's ministry through a speculative lens, Dickens consistently avoided such liberties. On those few occasions when he wished to emphasize and teach a practical lesson or clarify words and ideas, even then he did not theologize or speculate, but only explained how the teaching might come to bear either on the lives of his children or on what the words and ideas meant.

In another place, the author of *Gospel Stories* related the story of Joseph and Mary taking their twelve-year-old son Jesus to Jerusalem for the Passover festival, going into detail to introduce the festival and explain its history. Dickens, much more economical and concise, and consistent with Luke's account, mentioned only a "religious feast" in Jerusalem and excluded any lengthy or nonessential explanations. Again, this is typical of Dickens's method and style. Contrary to what is understood about *The Life of Our Lord*, Dickens is especially accurate and conscientious in reporting the Biblical accounts that he includes in his harmony.[20]

Throughout *The Life of Our Lord*, it is clear that Dickens deliberately and purposefully employed the genre and methodology of a Gospel harmony. His work demonstrates both the skill and resourcefulness of the harmonist, the preparation and knowledge of the serious biblical thinker, and the affectionate care of a father. Had he simply wanted to pontificate or propagandize he certainly would not have chosen the harmony with its narrative and theological constraints nor would he have engaged in the rigors of analysis and harmonization that such a task demands. Dickens's decision to cast his Christian instruction to his children in the form of a harmony indicates his desire to compose a biblical portrait of Jesus that could stand on its own according to his own insistence that his children follow the teaching of Jesus in the Gospels apart from "the interpretations and the inventions of man." *The Life of Our Lord* is a serious attempt at a harmony of the Gospels in order to communicate to his own children the life and lessons of Jesus in an effective and formative manner. That Dickens was able to succeed in such an attempt and that he did so for his own children demands our attention and offers us, at the same time, a revealing display of his Christocentric worldview.

Christology in *The Life Of Our Lord*

In his 1989 article, "Dickens and Unitarianism," John Frazee wrote concerning *The Life of Our Lord*, "It must be considered theologically significant" (122). That Frazee did not go on to demonstrate effectively his assertion in the article should not reflect negatively on the importance of the assertion. Indeed, Frazee was right. Still, his statement flies in the face of conventional wisdom concerning the theological value of *The Life of Our Lord*. Noel Peyrouton wrote, in what is probably the seminal article on *The Life of Our Lord*, that it is easy to consider it as "a Gospel according to Dickens, an interpolation which, although written for his children, omits nothing essential of the author's own adult view. But this seems hardly reasonable; Dickens was much more sophisticated than this" (103). His article then goes on to point out what is missing in *The Life of Our Lord*, demonstrating that it is an inadequate and incomplete expression of Dickens's faith. Robert Newsom has remarked, "Given the intended audience [Dickens's children] it is hardly fair to infer the specifics of Dickens's faith from this slight work, which is in any case theologically rather inconsistent" (500).[21]

Such views fail to recognize *The Life of Our Lord* as a harmony of the Gospels and contribute to the consequent uncertainty concerning the means by which to approach it and study it effectively. Hence, many of the conclusions that are drawn concerning its theological significance and substance (or lack thereof) tend to be rather unsatisfying. Two interpretive observations, then, are pertinent. First, when *The Life of Our Lord* is understood as a harmony of the Gospels, it is understood properly as a biblical-theological document and is to be studied as such. Second, when it is recognized that Dickens is writing here not as a novelist or a journalist, but as an amateur theologian, a proper orientation is provided for a clearer understanding of its biblical-theological substance. *The Life of Our Lord* is intentionally a biblical-theological composition, not a literary one, and its literary value is quite beside the point. If *The Life of Our Lord* is viewed as a literary piece (however undistinguished we believe it to be) by Dickens the novelist and storyteller, it will not be fully appreciated or recognized for its value as theology. For that reason, it is imperative that *The Life of Our Lord* be studied and understood as an attempt at theology (however wanting we believe it to be) by Dickens as a Christian writer assuming the posture of theologian and biblical thinker.

A full consideration of the theology and theological thinking of *The Life of Our Lord* would, of course, be too lengthy to include in this article. However, a selective sampling of two of the more provocative themes will suffice to demonstrate the genuine theological substance that undergirds *The Life of Our Lord*. To that end, then, I will consider the Christological issue of the deity of Jesus and the soteriological issue of Jesus as Saviour-Redeemer. In both cases, *The Life of Our Lord* will be considered the touchstone while allowing other pertinent material from Dickens to corroborate observations.

For Dickens, as for the Gospel writers, Jesus was, of course, the central figure as well as the center of his harmony, and providing his children with a composite biblical portrait of Jesus was the expressed reason for his writing *The Life of Our Lord*. Dickens wanted to set before his children a portrait of the Jesus of the Gospels as the example and pattern for living their lives. But his portrait of Jesus is much more than that. It is, in fact, a rather orthodox portrait of Jesus. Two very important aspects of that portrait are Jesus as the Son of God and Jesus as Savior-Redeemer.

Janet Larson, in her *Dickens and the Broken Scriptures*, maintains that Dickens "articulates no clear doctrine of the incarnation" and as to the use of divine titles in reference to Jesus, such as the Son of God, "makes no such claims himself." Rather, she says, he is careful to put such ascriptions "in the mouths of characters who 'said' or 'believed' them" (11). This is surely to misread and misconstrue not only *The Life of Our Lord*, but also to ignore Dickens's use of harmonization. It is true that Dickens's account of the birth narrative includes no *clear* suggestion of incarnation,[22] but this is most likely a concession to his audience—his children—to avoid a theologically complex doctrine. Furthermore, that the title "Son of God" is found most often on the lips of observers is precisely what is found in the Gospels themselves.[23] That Dickens "makes no such claims himself" is not at all remarkable. What would be remarkable, not to mention suspect, is for Dickens to have forced his own assertions or claims that Jesus was the Son of God into his text when they were not in his Gospel sources.

The filial relationship between Jesus and God in *The Life of Our Lord* is consistent but subdued (e.g., 14, 34, 113). When Dickens used the term "Son of God," he used it economically and powerfully, and the more theologically nuanced Son of God terminology finds its significance not in the frequency of its occurrence but in the nature of its occurrence. Specifically, Dickens selected for inclusion in *The Life of Our Lord* the most Christologically charged "Son of God" passages in the Gospels. He reported God's declaration of Jesus as Son at both Jesus' Baptism and His Transfiguration, (24, 54) both recorded in the Synoptics, and absent in John; but he also included two other crucial Son of God passages. The Centurion's declaration at the Cross (113), reported in all three Synoptics, is found in Matthew and Mark as, "Truly, this was the Son of God." The confession of the disciples after Jesus had walked on water and calmed the sea (48–51), reported in Matthew, Mark, and John, is found in Matthew as, "Of a truth, thou art the Son of God." The significance of these passages in the Gospels is that they provide testimony of Jesus as the Son of God from the voice of God himself, from the Apostles, and from a representative from among the Gentiles. Dickens even included the important Gospel testimony of demons who also recognized Jesus as the Son of God (39).

Characteristically, this Son of God terminology, especially in these contexts, was understood by biblical scholars in Dickens's day to convey not only Jesus' messianic office but his deity as well. It is the deity of Christ that interests us here. That Dickens would include such terminology, and intentionally it seems, when he could have just as easily omitted it, is significant. In fact, Dickens's use of the designation "Son of God" throughout *The Life of Our Lord* seems simply to assume the deity of Jesus in some places and, in others, to assert it more directly. Such usage seems to qualify the claim by many that Dickens's Jesus is a thoroughly human one.[24]

While the "Son of God" passages cited above certainly are significant, there are other passages that provide further affirmation of the deity of Jesus. In an important episode toward the end of *The Life of Our Lord*, Dickens pointed out that the women who had gone to the sepulcher early on the day of the Resurrection actually *worship* Jesus. Dickens's narrative described Mary Magdalene finding the disciples and telling them that she had seen the risen Christ and that he had spoken to her. She found with the disciples the other women who had gone with her to the tomb, of whom Dickens wrote, "These women told her and the rest that they had seen at the tomb two men in shining garments, at sight of whom they had been afraid, . . . and also that as they came to tell this, they had seen Christ, on the way, and had held Him by the feet, and worshipped Him" (118). That Dickens included an explicit statement of Jesus being worshipped is remarkable in that it challenges the basic premise of those who hold that Dickens's Jesus is a thoroughly human

Jesus who is simply a good man, a good teacher, and a good example. Moreover, that "the women had held Him by the feet, and worshipped Him" is found in the Synoptics only at Matthew 28.9 and is absent from John. That such an almost incidental observation by Matthew could have been easily overlooked and easily omitted from *The Life of Our Lord*, coupled with its powerful statement, makes Dickens's inclusion of it especially conspicuous.

Perhaps even more significant is the inclusion of the account of Thomas' doubt in which he declared Jesus "my Lord and my God" (cf. *TLOL* 121 and John 20.28). This is important certainly in that Thomas confesses Jesus as his "God." Hermann Olshausen comments, "The words εἶπεν αὐτῷ [*eipen auto* = he said to him] demand that they should be referred to Christ personally. Hence, therefore, it only remains to say that Thomas styled Jesus 'God' "(4: 294). Yet, the inclusion of this episode is important for other reasons as well. First, structurally Dickens situated this episode in *The Life of Our Lord* at the climax certainly of his Resurrection story and perhaps his entire work. Following this climactic declaration is a very brief account (14 lines) in falling action, of other post-resurrection appearances and the ascension, which brings the narrative proper to a close. What follows is an epilogue of sorts in which Dickens rehearsed in two or three paragraphs the history of the early Church and the first Christians. So, as Dickens's climax of at least the Resurrection account, this story carries significant weight. If, indeed, it is the climax of his entire narrative, then Dickens has made the deity of Jesus central to his portrait of Jesus. Second, it was not uncommon in Dickens's day for Thomas' declaration to be seen not only as an affirmation of Christ's deity but also as a liturgical confession, an act of worship. Thomas Arnold remarked of this confession, "May we and all the whole Church join in the first fruits of Christian worship offered by the Apostle, now at last resigning himself to the fulness of his joy; may we from the bottom of our hearts say, as he did to our risen Saviour, "My Lord and my God!" (238–39).

Thus, Dickens developed a portrait of Jesus as the divine Son of God. He affirmed Jesus' deity by use of the formal designation (Son of God), by portraying Jesus as the object of worship, and by appealing to passages that declare Jesus' equality with God. The significance of such affirmation is that it does not emerge from any formal theological speculation about Jesus, but rather from Dickens's own concept of Jesus expressed in the use of his Gospel sources and his editorial selection of that material.

This same kind of affirmation is found in an intriguing passage of Dickens's *Dombey and Son*, the writing of which likely overlapped with the writing of *The Life of Our Lord*. When little Paul sees in his deathbed vision two figures standing on the shore apparently to greet him, we learn from Dickens's explanation and description that one of the figures is Paul's mother. The other figure, it becomes clear, is Jesus. "Mama is like you Floy. I know her by the face!'' Paul says to Florence of his mother. By the same sense of familiarity, Paul recognizes Jesus, and his impression of Jesus is one of divinity. He bids Florence, ''But tell them that the print upon the stairs at school is not Divine enough'' (241). This is quite a provocative statement by Dickens, especially as he seldom, if ever, engages in any sort of theological speculation in his novels. Having come face to face with Jesus in his vision, Paul recognizes something lacking in the earthly representations of Jesus. We are allowed such a ''revelation'' because little Paul is granted this deathbed vision. Dickens would have us understand that human representations of Jesus, while they may capture his humanity and his compassion and even his self-sacrificing love, cannot do justice to his deity (cf. Walder 133–34).

As deliberate as Dickens was, however, with his inclusion of Gospel passages in *The Life of Our Lord* that explicitly involve Jesus' deity, so was he also with passages that speak of Jesus as Saviour-Redeemer. While Dickens's favorite title for Jesus in *The Life of Our Lord* was either ''Jesus Christ'' or ''Jesus''—he refers to both titles well over fifty times each—he uses the term ''Saviour'' referring to Jesus no less than forty times. However, the question must be asked, what exactly did Dickens mean by Saviour? His very first use of ''Our Saviour'' occurs at the end of his third chapter, which itself has been an illustration of his description of the title. That description concludes the chapter, ''But he was always merciful and tender. And because he did such good, and taught people how to love God and how to hope to go to Heaven after death, he was called *Our Saviour*'' (*TLOL* 34). According to Dickens, Jesus is Saviour because he did three things: (1) he did good, (2) he taught people how to love God, and (3) he taught people how to hope to go to Heaven after death. At first glance, this seems to be a rather ambiguous and anemic understanding of Jesus as the Saviour, as it seems devoid of any overt suggestion of redemption and atonement. However, a more careful consideration of Dickens's portrayal of Jesus as Saviour produces a more substantial characterization.

Dickens's first use of the title ''Our Saviour'' (or Saviour) is bracketed by eight instances of the Saviour ''saving'': four preceding his introduction of the title and four following it. In the former case, there are three healings and the raising of Jairus' daughter; in the latter, there are a healing, the raising from the dead of the son of the widow of Nain, the calming of the sea and storm, and an exorcism. What is significant here is that Dickens illustrated in all of this the first characteristic in his description of ''Our Saviour,'' that is, that ''he did such good.'' But more than that, Dickens demonstrated in these miracles that Jesus had power over disease, over nature, over demons, and over death. In terms of New Testament theology, these are all illustrative of the in-breaking of the new age of Salvation inaugurated by Jesus (not to mention indicators of his deity). While Dickens may not have been fully aware of the theological subtleties at work here, he appears to have recognized, in this full catalogue of miracles, the saving activity of God in Jesus.

A further significance extends to the title of "Our Saviour" in Dickens's second characteristic, that Jesus taught people. When Dickens introduced and referred to the parables of Jesus, he called them "The Parables of Our Saviour" (*TLOL* 61). In fact, almost one-third of the occurrences of "Our Saviour" were used as the subject of teaching or were in some other way connected to teaching. Furthermore, the content of the teaching to which Dickens referred was "how to love God" and "how to hope to go to heaven after death." On the one hand, the phrase, "how to love God," for which Dickens provided no substantial explanation or illustration, seems to be used in an absolute sense. Certainly, Dickens included many of Jesus' parables that teach one's duty to God; and, of course, for Dickens, one's duty to God was most fully accomplished in one's fulfillment of his duty toward his fellow human beings. Still, Dickens included no explicit or sustained passage on simply loving God. On the other hand, Jesus' teaching on "how to hope to go to heaven after death" hints at a more fully developed thought and suggests that the title "Our Saviour" included for Dickens the idea of Redeemer and Mediator. In fact, under more careful scrutiny, what will be revealed is a broader soteriological theme for which the simplistic "works religion" that has usually been foisted upon *The Life of Our Lord* does not adequately account.

That Dickens's religion was a religion of works and good deeds only is commonly—and rather stubbornly—asserted.[25] It surely seems fair to say that Dickens connected good works in the Anglican sense, a technical term for Christian activity, with going to heaven after death. To suppose, however, that Dickens embraced a religion of good works with no concept of atonement or forgiveness of sin is refuted by *The Life of Our Lord*. In fact, it could be argued that Dickens embraced a popular Anglican view of salvation—a view that emphasized the importance of works along with justifying grace. In a letter to David Dickson (10 May 1843), apparently a response to Dickson's criticism of his discussion of the doctrine of the new birth in *The Pickwick Papers* (266–7), Dickens wrote, "That every man who seeks heaven must be born again, in good thoughts of his Maker, I sincerely believe. That it is expedient for every hound to say so in a certain snuffling form of words, to which he attaches no good meaning, I do not believe. I take it there is no difference between us" (*Pilgrim Letters* 3: 485). Dickens was not usually given to use the cant of the "snuffling" Evangelicals or Dissenters in a serious manner, yet here he was willing to affirm his belief in the necessity of being "born again" to make his point. Interestingly, however, he qualified his use of the term with the phrase, "in good thoughts of his Maker." But that does not dilute this affirmation or otherwise render his words hollow.

Rather, it seems to suggest subtly a more Anglican understanding of spiritual rebirth or conversion. What Dickens said straightforwardly, Edward Bouverie Pusey, an Oxford High Church Tractarian, seems to have said rather ornately: "In its widest sense 'conversion' is turning towards God . . . [it] is a course of being conformed to God, a learning to have Him more simply in our minds, to be turned wholly to Him, solely to Him, . . . opening our hearts to Him, to have their warmth, their health, their life, from Him" (3: 20). This, Dickens might say, is being "born again in good thoughts of his Maker." Clearly, Dickens would not use the term "born again" in the same sense as would an Evangelical. However, of crucial significance here is that Dickens affirmed, in a rather orthodox manner, the idea of conversion or regeneration. *The Life of Our Lord* illustrates more completely Dickens's understanding of conversion or regeneration by developing the fundamental themes of repentance and forgiveness.

The basic ideas of repentance and forgiveness are a dominant feature of *The Life of Our Lord*, and Dickens continued throughout to develop these themes, alternating freely between the concept of God's forgiveness of repentant sinners and human responsibility to forgive one another unconditionally. Yet, there is no lack of emphasis on God's forgiveness of repentant sinners. In a typical example of the manner in which he conveyed these themes, Dickens related the Parable of the Laborers in the Vineyard following it by his first of several interpretive asides in which he taught, "People who have been wicked . . . and who are truly sorry for it, however late in their lives, and pray God to forgive them, will be forgiven and will go to Heaven, too" (61). Here, Dickens presented simply the fundamental principles of sorrow for sin in repentance, seeking God's forgiveness, and the mercy of God extended in forgiveness. This is basic to the teaching of *The Life of Our Lord* and quite basic as well to the teaching of the Gospels.

The very first allusion to a Dickensian soteriology, however, occurred in the passage considered above in which Dickens identified Jesus as Our Saviour who taught people "how to hope to go to Heaven after death." This, of course, is far from any sort of a conclusive affirmation and yet, in its larger context, is notable. Shortly after that description, Dickens's first inclusion of Jesus forgiving sins was taken from the Lukan account of the woman who anointed Jesus' feet, washing them with her tears and drying them with her hair (Luke 7.36–50). She was, as Dickens described her, a woman "who had led a bad and sinful life and was ashamed that the Son of God should see her; and yet," he continued, "she trusted so much to His goodness and His compassion for all who, having done wrong were truly sorry for it in their hearts" (*TLOL* 43). To the utter dismay of his host, Jesus allowed such a woman as this sinner to touch him. Knowing the thoughts of his host, Jesus proceeded to relate a parable of forgiveness and then, to the amazement of the entire company present, declared to her, "God forgives you!" If some would argue here that Jesus is simply *announcing* God's forgiveness, it should be pointed out that Dickens immediately added to his narrative, "The company who were present wondered that Jesus Christ had power to forgive sins, but God had given it to Him" (44–45). Indeed, the entire account is couched in a salvific context of repentance and forgiveness in which Jesus is the chief protagonist, possessing the prerogative and the power to forgive sins.

Nevertheless, the question stands, did Dickens's Jesus possess the power in and of himself to forgive sins or was his power only derived? And what bearing might this have on his deity? In the passage that we have just considered, Jesus declared the sins of Mary Magdalene forgiven, the declaration of which caused an astonished reaction from those who heard it. Some might argue that Dickens's pronouncement on Jesus' power to forgive sins demonstrates rather conclusively that he understood that power as derivative not inherent, thereby implying that Jesus was somehow less than God. On the contrary, Dickens's statement is thoroughly consistent with Jesus' deity and with the biblical data concerning Jesus and his power and authority to forgive sins.

This is seen most clearly in a similar passage, at least in terms of Dickens's intent, involving the legitimacy of Jesus' power and authority to forgive sins, reported by the Synoptic Evangelists. All three (Mark 2.3–12, Matthew 9.2–8, and Luke 5.18–26) report the miracle story of the paralytic lowered through the roof of a house in order to get him close to Jesus for healing. Not only did Jesus heal him, but, to the consternation and the outrage of many of those present, also pronounced the man's sins forgiven. It is Matthew who adds, "But when the multitude saw it, they marveled, and glorified God, which had given such power unto men" (Matt. 9.8). Most likely, this is where Dickens borrowed the notion of God giving Jesus the power to forgive sins. It is a basic Scriptural affirmation. The Matthean account, harmonized with the two other Synoptic Evangelists, would affirm for Dickens that God had given Jesus the power and authority to forgive sins while at the same time it would allow him to hold in tension next to it the expressed deity of Jesus consistent with the principles of biblical interpretation in his day.[26]

In his novels, we see Dickens's emphasis on patient forgiveness in personal relationships and encounters, and yet, it is clear that he saw such behavior and attitudes as predicated upon Jesus' example. In a letter to David Macrae, Dickens emphasized that Jesus was the model and pattern for his "good people." "One of my most constant and most earnest endeavors," Dickens wrote, "has been to exhibit in all my good people some faint reflections of the teachings of our great Master . . . . All my good people are humble, charitable, faithful, and forgiving. Over and over again, I claim them in express words as disciples of the Founder of our religion" (127).

That Dickens's "good people" are "disciples" who are themselves very much an expression of the forgiving and merciful "Founder" of Christianity is exemplified throughout *David Copperfield*, but rather poignantly in one particular episode. In chapter 51 of *David Copperfield*, Dickens included what could easily be taken as a scene of repentance, confession, and forgiveness as Em'ly knelt before the feet of Mr. Peggotty "humbled, as it might be in the dust our Saviour wrote in with his blessed hand" (690). The allusion to the adulterous woman brought before Jesus in John 8.1–11 is too clear and places the scene of Em'ly before her uncle, at least in Dickens's mind, in the context of sin and forgiveness in the Gospels. Clearly, Em'ly understood herself as having sinned and was humbled in repentance; and clearly Mr. Peggotty was the one who would offer grace, mercy, and forgiveness. This is precisely the same pattern we saw in Dickens's teaching concerning the Parable of the Laborers in the Vineyard in *The Life of Our Lord*, a pattern found repeatedly there.

Yet, beyond this emphasis on forgiveness and repentance, stands Dickens's gesture toward Jesus as the Saviour-Redeemer, even the one who made atonement for sin. In addition to the clear soteriological implications there, it is in his account of the raising of Lazarus that Dickens remarked, "At this sight, so awful and affecting, many of the people there believed that Christ was indeed the Son of God, come to instruct and save mankind" (*TLOL* 81–82). Larson would want to attribute this to an intentional dodge by Dickens by only reporting what "many of the people there believed," rather than what he himself thought (11). In that case, it would be strange that Dickens added his own interpolation of what the "many" believed, "that Christ was indeed the Son of God, come to instruct and save mankind." John has simply, "Many . . . believed on him" (John 11.45). "That Christ was indeed the Son of God, come to instruct and save mankind," is Dickens's own construction, one that represents central and significant themes in *The Life of Our Lord*. In the larger Johannine context, that Jesus was the Son of God and that He had come to teach and affect salvation would clearly be understood as the content of what the many believed here in the Lazarus story. Dickens's inclusion of this interpolation here speaks not only to his understanding of the Johannine formulation but also to his own perception of the life and ministry of Jesus.

Similarly worth noting is the passage in the account of the crucifixion in which Dickens curiously had the crowd taunting Jesus saying, "He came to save sinners. Let Him save Himself" (*TLOL* 109). Again, the taunt, "He came to save sinners," is an interpolation by Dickens of the Synoptic Evangelists', "He saved others; himself he cannot save" (Matt. 27.42; Mark 15.31; cf. Luke 23.35, "He saved others; let him save himself."). The occurrence is conspicuous not only as to its presence here but also as to its content—Jesus, at least in Dickens's mind, had given people the impression that he had come to "save sinners." As above, it represents Dickens's filling out the meaning of the "save" or "saved" of the Evangelists with his own understanding of what that "saving" entails.

That Jesus is given a redemptive role by Dickens in *The Life of Our Lord* seems clear, and that he is the Redeemer in some real sense is a reasonable conclusion. The title "Redeemer," a designation with clear New Testament associations and clear soteriological connotations, was one of Dickens's favorites. While it is not found in *The Life of Our Lord*, there are significant examples of it exterior to *The Life of Our Lord*. In "In Memoriam to W.M. Thackeray," originally published in *Cornhill Magazine*, February 1864, Dickens appealed to it: "God grant that on that Christmas Eve when he laid his head back on his pillow and threw up his arms as he had been wont to do when very weary, some consciousness of duty done and Christian hope throughout life humbly cherished, may have caused his own heart so to throb, when he passed away to his Redeemer's rest!" (*Selected Journalism*, 593). At the death of Stephen Blackpool in *Hard Times*, Dickens observed, "The Star had shown him where to find the God of the poor; and through humility, and sorrow, and forgiveness, he had gone to his Redeemer's rest" (292). He made use of it, too, in the article "Pet Prisoners" from *Household Words*, 27 April 1850: "Now God forbid that we, unworthily believing in the Redeemer, should shut out hope, or even humble trustfulness, from any criminal at the dread pass; but it is not in us to call this state of mind repentance" (Philip and Neuburg 78).

Obviously, Dickens found the term "Redeemer" a fitting designation for Jesus.[27] Furthermore, the portrait that Dickens paints of Jesus in *The Life of Our Lord* is one that not only allows for, but also encourages our understanding Him as a Saviour-Redeemer. On the one hand, there is no explicit statement that the most significant thing Jesus did was to die on the Cross as the atonement for the sins of humanity, which, of course, would be consistent with Dickens's broader purpose of writing moral instruction to his children. There is, on the other hand, much to suggest in the Christological titles and in his soteriological themes that Dickens held to some sort of pattern of atonement wherein Jesus was the Saviour-Redeemer. This is not to say that Dickens embraced an Evangelical view of vicarious atonement. Still, Jesus, in Dickens's evaluation, was more than just one who announced God's forgiveness; more than a Messenger or Mediator of God's good news. For Dickens, Jesus was "indeed the Son of God, come to instruct and save mankind."

A citation that seems to have broad significance in this regard lies outside of *The Life of Our Lord*, in a letter to Angela Burdett-Coutts dated 28 October 1847.[28] Dickens enclosed in that letter "An Appeal to Fallen Women," which he had written and which had been read to the women of Urania House to encourage them and to impress upon them a sense of accountability and discipline. Exhorting them to their responsibility toward others, he wrote:

But you must solemnly remember that if you enter this Home without such constant resolutions, you occupy, unworthily and uselessly, the place of some other unhappy girl, now wandering and lost; and that her ruin, no less than your own, will be upon your head, before Almighty God, who knows the secrets of our breasts; and Christ, who died upon the Cross to save us.

(Letters Coutts 100)

Certainly, Dickens was not attempting to teach soteriology here, which perhaps gives this assertion even more force, but such a statement, taken with what we have seen above, underlines the fact that he understood Jesus as Saviour-Redeemer as well as Son of God in quite an orthodox way.

Conclusion

To continue to insist, then, that *The Life of Our Lord* is not to be taken seriously or that it lacks theological substance can no longer be sustained in light of a proper and conscientious study brought to bear upon it. When it is examined according to its genre and within a biblical-theological approach, we find in *The Life of Our Lord* a theology, or Christology, from Dickens himself that provides a more profound understanding of Jesus, the central element not only of his perception of Christianity but of his broader worldview, than has sometimes been recognized. With such a resource and a more finely textured view of his Christian thought, we can begin to move beyond the stale and questionable reaffirmations of Dickens's "broad Christian views" toward a more informed understanding of, in Tolstoy's words, "that great Christian writer" and toward a more informed knowledge of the role of Dickens's Christianity in his life and work.

NOTES

1. Most notably see, Madonna Egan; Michael Piret; Robert Hanna, "Charles Dickens' 'Life of Our Lord' " and *The Dickens Family Gospel.*
2. See, for example, Dickens's *Little Dorrit* 756; *Bleak House* 322–23; "Two Views of a Cheap Theatre" and "A Fly-Leaf in Life" in *The Uncommercial Traveller* 35–39, 353–57. See also letters to R.H. Davies in Forster 2: 469; to David Macrae in Macrae 127; to J.M. Makeham in Forster 2: 469; to Mrs. Charles Smithson in *Pilgrim Letters* 4: 108.
3. Dickens uses this phrase in the oft-quoted letter to Rev. R. H. Davies. See Forster 2: 469.
4. When I use the term Christology here, I am using it in a broader, more popular sense to refer to basic and familiar Gospel notions of Jesus rather than the more

specialized sense in which theologians use it to refer to the discussion of the intricacies and details of the ontological and theological concepts of Jesus in the New Testament. Qualifying "Christology" with the designation "practical" or "ethical" is to suggest that Dickens looked at Jesus primarily, although not exclusively, in terms of how his life and example came to bear on daily living, thinking and behaving.

5. In citations, where necessary, *The Life of Our Lord* will be abbreviated *TLOL*.

6. Robert Hanna has presented a compelling argument for understanding *TLOL* as a pedagogical tool read by Dickens to his children. Compare Egan on this as well.

7. A harmony is an attempt to combine the accounts of the four New Testament Gospels into one continuous narrative (one of the best examples of a contemporary harmony of the sort Dickens wrote, though a bit wooden and even awkward at times, is Cheney's *The Life of Christ in Stereo*). In the nineteenth century, a harmony might also be referred to as a "diatessaron" (composed of four) or a "monotessaron" (four in one). As early as the sixteenth century, what is referred to today as the "synopsis" appeared (although some hold that it was Johann Griesbach who pioneered the synopsis with his *Synopsis Evangeliorum Matthaei Marci et Lucae cum Ioannis Pericopis Parallelis* in 1776). A synopsis arranges the Gospels in four parallel columns rather than a running narrative (the standard synopsis today is Aland's, *Synopsis*).

8. Obviously, what is omitted invites our attention as well. However, it would be counterproductive here to speculate about excluded material at the expense of an examination of the material that Dickens provided. This article, then, will focus on what is present in the document.

9. This, of course, is no easy task. Nevertheless, the harmonizer is faced with the necessity of at least establishing some sort of relative chronology. The watershed for this task is typically understood to involve establishing the length of Jesus' public ministry by determining the number of Passover celebrations that he attended as reported in the Gospels. This endeavor is in turn plagued by the apparent discrepancies between the Gospel of John and the Synoptic Gospels relative to the number of Passover feasts. For most nineteenth-century harmonists, John's directly mentioned Passovers were understood to give a basic framework, and Synoptic events were arranged within that framework.

10. E.g., Matthew's Sermon on the Mount and Luke's Sermon on the Plain; the two Gergesene demoniacs of Matthew and the one Gadarene demoniac of Mark and Luke; the Feeding of the 5,000 and the Feeding of the 4,000; the discussions of the Greatest Commandment in Matt. 22.34–40, Mark 12.28–34, and Luke 10.25–37. This last example will be considered further on in the article and can be seen to illustrate at once both the second level and the third level of harmonization. It should be noted that at this second level, very often other textual and historical elements will come to bear on decision-making.

11. These passages would differ from those of the second level in that they are clearly the same story, or a parallel account, but they may differ in minor linguistic or minor narrative elements, or both.

12. Although there are a few intimations that Dickens may have been alert to this concern, they are rather vague. See for instance the multiple references to the

Passover in chapter 8 of *TLOL*. Dickens informs us of only this one Passover. While taken alone, this would suggest a short public ministry that included only one Passover. However, Dickens would have to give us much more than this if we are to draw any persuasive conclusions.

13. Dickens's use of the phrase, "The Feast of the Passover now drawing very near" (*TLOL* 86) to introduce the Triumphal Entry (following John's account) seems to be related exclusively to that event and only incidentally to what follows.

14. Other examples of Dickens's harmonization at this second level, which are too extensive to deal with here, would include his account of the Crucifixion and Resurrection, and his harmonization in his Epilogue of Jesus' post-Resurrection appearances and Ascension (with the allusion to I Cor. 15.6), and the Acts material.

15. This passage could also be taken as an example of harmonization at the second level in that Dickens has decided to combine the accounts of the controversy stories of Matt. 22.34–40 and Mark 12.28–34 with the account of the conversation that lead to the telling of the Parable of the Good Samaritan. My use of it here calls attention to both the second and third levels of harmonization. While I emphasize the third level, it is clear that Dickens has made decisions about harmonization at the second level as well.

16. Tatian's *Diatessaron*, the first known harmony, was composed ca. 150 CE.

17. Not until the publication of Darwin's *Origin of the Species* (1859) and more significantly, the publication of *Essays and Reviews* (1860) did British theology begin to utilize and grapple with, on a broader scale, the methodological advances in theological and biblical studies.

18. The more important harmonies in Dickens's day were Edward Greswell's Greek *Harmonia Evangelica* (1830) and Johann Griesbach's Greek *Synopsis Evangeliorum Matthaei Marci et Lucae cum Ioannis Pericopis Parallelis* (1776). Other significant popular and scholarly harmonies of the early nineteenth century include: Dr. Lant Carpenter's *Apostolical Harmony* (1838); Rev. Edward Bickersteth's *Harmony of the Four Gospels* (1832); Rev. John Fleetwood's, *The Life of Our Lord And Saviour Jesus Christ* (1832). Some notable juvenile harmonies were Lucy Barton's *The History of Our Lord and Saviour Jesus Christ* (1837); Henry Ware's *The Life of the Saviour* (1833); Robert Kinniburgh's *The Life of Jesus Christ* (1814).

19. Although much speculation about John's origin has ensued since the discovery of the Qumran scrolls in 1947, this author's observations likely are derived from inferences from the Gospel accounts of John's asceticism and his arrival on the scene from the wilderness. Perhaps this author was also familiar with the speculations based on inferences from Josephus and Philo concerning John's association with the Essenes.

20. There are certainly examples to be pointed out in which Dickens takes some liberties or even makes mistakes (apparently), but these tend to be the exception rather than the rule.

21. To one degree or another these two statements tend to represent more recent scholarly opinion on *TLOL* as to its being a serious expression of Dickens's theology. See also Zemka 117–47 and Collins 53–60 for similar evaluations.

22. It should not be assumed that his language here categorically disallows for incarnation. The language is sufficiently ambiguous to support incarnation, for "God will love Him as His own Son." In light of how Dickens uses the title Son of God, even more credence could be given to the suggestion that his lack of a "clear doctrine of incarnation" is, in fact, a concession to his children rather than a categorical denial of Incarnation. See *TLOL* 18. Furthermore, the work as a whole seems to imply the deity of Jesus.

23. Of the 28 times the ascription "Son of God" is found in the Gospels (18 occurrences in the Synoptics and 10 in John), it is found only four times on Jesus' lips, all four of which occur only in John; and three of those occurrences are spoken in the third person.

24. Most often this is cast in terms of the alleged Unitarian emphasis in *TLOL*. See Frazee, Piret, Larson 10–14, and Johnson 2: Notes, 50. The discussion of Dickens's connection to Unitarianism and its bearing on *TLOL* is beyond the scope of this article. It should be pointed out here, however, that I do not believe that a compelling argument for an alleged Unitarian emphasis in *TLOL* can be sustained in light of a proper study of it. Some of the reasons for that position emerge from my discussion here of the deity of Jesus as it is understood by Dickens. Frazee's discussion is excellent and informative, but his argument for Dickens's Unitarianism turns on dubious claims concerning Forster's motives and R.V. Holt's questionable observations.

25. See for instance, House 111–13, 131–32; Newsom 499–502; Brown 178–79; Orwell 55–60; Larson 10–12.

26. Nineteenth-century commentaries acknowledge the tension without seeking to resolve it. See, for instance, Whitby's comments on Matt. 9.6, "Moreover, that Christ here speaks of a power inherent in him, and not only of the power of God assisting him, as it did the apostles, when they healed diseases, is evident; because if Christ had only pronounced, that the sins of this paralytic were remitted by God, and the cure performed by his power, the Pharisees could have had no cause to be offended with him, and much less to have accused him of blasphemy" (Whitby 1: 81); note also D'Oyly and Mant on the same passage: "The principle on which this accusation went, our Lord plainly allows; but then He clears Himself of it by this consequence, that, as no power but God's could forgive sins, so none but God's could work this miracle of healing, If therefore He could give them a sensible proof of His divinity in one of the instances, they ought to be satisfied that He had done no more than became Him in the other" (see D'Oyly and Mant II, 11K4–5).

27. That Dickens used this term to describe Jesus (not God the Father) is suggested not only by the normal Christological use of the term but also by his uses of it in, for instance, *Pictures from Italy* (see Dickens, *American Notes* 276) and "Mugbie Junction" (see Dickens, *Christmas Stories* 494).

28. It should be noted incidentally that this is a letter written during the time in which Dickens could well have been still working on *TLOL*.

WORKS CITED

Aland, Kurt, ed. *Synopsis of the Four Gospels. Greek-English Edition of the Synopsis Quattor Evangeliorum.* 9th ed. Stuttgart: German Bible Society, 1989.

Arnold, Thomas. *Sermons Chiefly on the Interpretation of Scripture.* London: B. Fellowes, 1845.

Brown, Ivor. *Dickens in His Time.* London: Thomas Nelson, 1963.

Cheney, Johnston. *The Life of Christ in Stereo.* Ed. Stanley Ellisen. Portland: Western Conservative Baptist Seminary, 1979.

Collins, Philip. *Dickens and Education.* London: Macmillan, 1964.

Dickens, Charles. *American Notes and Pictures from Italy.* London: OUP, 1966.

———. *Bleak House.* New York: Norton, 1977.

———. *Christmas Stories.* London: OUP, 1968.

———. *David Copperfield.* London: J.M. Dent & Sons Ltd., 1965.

———. *A December Vision and Other Thoughtful Writings.* Eds. Neil Philip and Victor Neuburg. New York: Continuum, 1987.

———. *Dombey and Son.* Oxford: OUP, 1999.

———. *Hard Times.* London: Penguin Books, 1985.

———. *The Letters of Charles Dickens.* Ed. Georgina Hogarth and Mamie Dickens. Vol. 2. London: Chapman and Hall, 1880.

———. *The Letters of Charles Dickens.* Ed. Madeline House, Graham Storey, Kathleen Tillotson, et al. Pilgrim Edition. 12 vols. Oxford: Clarendon, 1965–2004.

———. *Letters From Charles Dickens to Angela Burdett-Coutts, 1841–1865.* Ed. Edgar Johnson. London: Jonathan Cape, 1953.

———. *The Life of Our Lord.* The Dickens Collection. The Free Library of Philadelphia.

———. *The Life Of Our Lord.* London: Associated Newspapers, 1934.

———. *Little Dorrit.* London: Penguin, 1998.

———. *The Pickwick Papers.* Oxford: OUP, 1986.

———. *Selected Journalism 1850–1870.* Ed. David Pascoe. London: Penguin, 1997.

———. *The Uncommercial Traveller and Reprinted Pieces.* London: OUP, 1968.

D'Oyly, George and Richard Mant. *The Holy Bible, According to the Authorized Version; with Notes, Explanatory and Practical; Taken Principally from the Most Eminent Writers of the United Church of England and Ireland. For the Use of Families.* 4 vols. Oxford: Clarendon Press, 1817.

Egan, Madonna. "Telling 'The Blessed History': Charles Dickens's The Life of Our Lord." 2 vols. Diss. University of Minnesota, 1983. Ann Arbor: UMI, 1983. 8318061.

Forster, John. *The Life of Charles Dickens.* 2 vols. London: Dent, 1950.

Frazee, John P. "Dickens and Unitarianism." *Dickens Studies Annual.* 18 (1989).

Gospel Stories: An Attempt to Render The Chief Events of The Life of Our Saviour Intelligible and Profitable to Young Children. 2d ed. London: John Murray, 1833.

Greswell, Edward. *Dissertations upon the Principles and Arrangement of a Harmony of the Gospels.* 3 vols. Oxford: OUP, 1830.

Hanna, Robert. "Charles Dickens' 'The Life of Our Lord' as a Primer for Christian Education." Diss. U. of North Carolina at Greensboro, 1995. Ann Arbor: UMI, 1995. 9531839.

———. *The Dickens Family Gospel: A Family Devotional Guide.* San Diego: Legacy, 2000.

House, Humphry. *The Dickens World.* London: OUP, 1941.

Johnson, Edgar. *Charles Dickens: His Tragedy and Triumph.* 2 vols. New York: Simon, 1952.

Larson, Janet. *Dickens and the Broken Scripture.* Athens: U. of Georgia P., 1985.

Newsom, Robert. "Religion." *The Oxford Readers Companion to Dickens.* Ed. Paul Schlicke. Oxford: OUP, 1999.

Macrae, David Rev. *Amongst the Darkies and Other Papers.* Glasgow: John S. Marr, 1880.

Olshausen, Hermann. *Biblical Commentary on the Gospels and on the Acts of the Apostles.* Trans. Rev. John Gill and Rev. William Lindsay. Vol. 4. Edinburgh: T& T Clark, 1850.

Orwell, George. *Critical Essays.* London: Secker and Warburg, 1960.

Peyrouton, Noel C. "*The Life of Our Lord*: Some Notes of Explication." *Dickensian* 59 (1963): 102–12.

Piret, Michael. "Charles Dickens's 'Children's New Testament': An introduction, annotated edition, and critical discussion." Diss. U. of Michigan, 1991. Ann Arbor: UMI, 1991. 9208623.

Pusey, E.B. *Parochial Sermons*. Rev. ed. Vol. 3. London: Rivingtons, 1873.

Walder, Dennis. *Dickens and Religion*. London: George Allen and Unwin, 1981.

Whitby, Daniel. *A Paraphrase and Commentary on the New Testament*. 2 vols. 10th ed. Edinburgh: Ogle & Aikman, 1807–08.

Zemka, Sue. *Victorian Testaments: The Bible, Christology, and Literary Authority in Early-Nineteenth-Century British Culture*. Stanford: Stanford UP, 1997.

"This Most Protean Sitter": The Factory Worker and Triangular Desire in *Hard Times*

David M. Wilkes

René Girard's model for triangular desire provides the framework for understanding the "muddle" that plagues Hard Times. *To date, the critical tendency towards reductionism has distorted Stephen Blackpool's relationship with both Rachael and the Coketown union. Girard's relational geometry diagrams the complexities and ambivalences of working-class life by examining the interplay among the subject, the mediator, and the object. What is more, Dickens anticipates this psychosocial indexing when he casts Rachael as the mediating* angel *in the factory,* Stephen *as the* discipulus *(subject),* Mrs. Blackpool *as the* drunkard *(object, in the first triangulation), and* Slackbridge *as the* rebel *(object, in the second triangulation)—all stylized depictions of the factory worker that later appear in John Tenniel's* Punch *illustration titled* The Working-Man from the Westminster Exhibition.

"Our thoughts . . . were fast becoming cloddish. Our labor symbolized nothing, and left us mentally sluggish in the dark of the evening. Intellectual activity is incompatible with any large amount of bodily exercise" (85).
Nathaniel Hawthorne, *The Blithedale Romance*

"People who are immersed in sensual appetites and desires are not very well prepared to handle abstract ideas" (114).
Thomas Merton, *The Seven Storey Mountain*

In a comic review of the Royal Westminster Exhibition of 1865, a staff writer for *Punch*—that "bastion of upper-middle-class ideology" (Kunzle 40)—confidently announced that "THE WORKING-MAN seems to be quite *the* fashionable subject within a group of Westminster painters"[1] ("Pictures" 205). On a subsequent page (see fig. 1 and Appendix), the "mysterious" workingman is then sketched according to the "fine imagination" of Sir John Tenniel (205), *Punch*'s "chief pictorial satirist and commentator on great affairs" known for "the purity of his line, the loftiness of his conception, the boldness and fidelity of his treatment, the wonderful strength of it all" (Hancher 139). In fact, Tenniel provides his viewers with four telling specimens: the first worker is a refined (and somewhat effeminate) *angel*; the second is an after-hours *discipulus*, a self-help philosopher of sorts; the third Hand is a faceless rebel who blatantly attacks authority; while the fourth is a despondent drunkard—a "most extraordinary variety" that leaves *Punch*'s readers unsure as to the real nature of the "puzzling original" ("Pictures" 205). Of course, when the names of the parliamentarian painters are added to their respective portraits, thus establishing the piece as political satire, the figures themselves readily fall into two categories regarding one very seminal Victorian issue, namely, the enfranchisement of the working class as first seen by pro-universal suffrage advocates John Bright and William Forster, and their staunch opponents, Robert Lowe and Edward Horsman. Indeed, Quakers square off with Adullamites in *Punch*'s comic arena as part of the ongoing national debate that eventually leads to the passage of the Second Reform Bill.[2] What is more, the year 1865 also produces the People's Edition of Charles Dickens's *Hard Times* (reissued ten years after its weekly serialization in *Household Words*), an industrial novel that clearly anticipates the social indexing of Tenniel's four working-class illustrations.[3] To be more specific: if Rachael is labeled the *angel* and Stephen Blackpool deemed the novel's *discipulus* (despite Dickens's off-handed disclaimer in Book the First, chapter 10, that "Old Stephen might have passed for a particularly intelligent man in his condition. Yet he was not" [68]); and if Slackbridge is given the role of *rebel* while the *drunkard* is embodied in the incorrigible Mrs. Blackpool, then Dickens has managed, once again, to fictionalize a key mid-nineteenth-century issue—here it is "The Working-Man Question"—with many of its relational and psychological permutations. Siding with Bright and Forster, Dickens extols working-class virtues such as loyalty and long-suffering by allowing the angel to care for the drunkard, yet the novelist also aligns himself with Lowe and Horsman when he marginalizes both the discipulus

Figure 1. John Tenniel's "Working-Man" Illustration

and the rebel. But where Tenniel separates his factory workers into non-relational cubicles, Dickens puts his Hands into the same narrative in order to demonstrate the complexities of working-class relationships—a far messier and more organic composition. In fact, both the novelist and the illustrator resist the urge to oversimplify the worker as a whole. Tenniel depicts both the Hand's ethereal industry and his temporal dissipation just as Dickens gives his readers both a working-class hero and a societal "monster" (Carlyle 203), a martyr and an idle man—the last of which even Karl Marx placed in the "dangerous class" and labeled as "social scum, that passively rotting mass thrown off by the lowest layers of old society" (qtd. in Ruis 116).[4]

In his book *Engels, Manchester, and the Working Class*, Steven Marcus provides yet another set of working-man portraits, sketched by German socialist Fredrich Engels, a decade prior to the novel's publication:

> First, there are those that are beaten down and either perish, or drop out of the proletariat into the urban underclasses and their subgroupings, or who rub along in demoralized misery without hope yet without active despair. . . . Then there are those who acquiesce in the openly declared values of society at large and try to live according to them; sometimes they are rewarded for this allegiance, sometimes—in Engels' view more often than not—they get no reward at all. In addition to these there are a further series of responses that sociologists like to class as deviant . . . [i.e., beggars, criminals, trade unionists]. (220–21, 227)

The three sketches here line up with Tenniel's drunkard, angel, and rebel, respectively, with the discipulus conspicuously absent, a fact that Marcus inadvertently accounts for when he describes the worker's "tendency to be impulse-ridden" (209). According to Engels, workers in the "industrial proletariat" evince "impulsive and promiscuous sexuality, general improvidence, lack of foresight, inability to plan for the future, insufficient internalization of disciplines, regularities and normative controls, and adaptive inflexibilities" (210)—all of which are counterproductive to serious study and self-improvement.[5] There is, to a large extent, a disproportionate sense of the working-man's debilities (a type of class-profiling that omits any virtues and contributions) which, despite Marcus's footnote about Engels's mythologizing "the preindustrial past, largely but not entirely out of ignorance. His mythologization of the future . . . [being] an extremely complex matter" as well (232), sounds like a reductive dismissal.[6] Simon Trezise notes that Dickens must be "squeezed" to reveal his affinity with the *Communist Manifesto* (127), while Patrick Brantlinger has observed that "whenever Dickens scores the ugliness and monotony of Coketown, there is a hint of the 'esthetic socialism' of Ruskin and Morris, but there is no suggestion of a return to handicrafts or any other preindustrial condition, no outline of a future utopia, and only equivocal sympathy for working-class brands of radicalism" (281).

Much has also been said about mythmaking of a different sort wherein fairy-tale, moral fable, and classical allusion codify the condition of the working class, with varying degrees of success.[7] One critic has suggested that *Hard Times*, in particular, can be reduced to "one major idea . . . . a very important idea, but it is also a protean one taking different names" (Samuels 13–14). Proteus, in fact, displays himself in a series of familiar binaries ranging from Fact/Fancy to Coketown/Circus to Bitzer/Sissy, to which "sociological imagination"/ "literary" imagination is added (14). Yet the fullest and most illustrative range of critical identities is found, it seems, in the *Hard Times* factory portraits whose conflicting variety argues against reducing the working-man to a single demographic equation—a cold statistic or abstract generated by an odious "ology." And rather than being ignorant with regard to *real* workers, Dickens simply records a plurality that, like life itself, defies easy categorization and often produces paradox.[8]

The assumption that most mid-nineteenth-century workers were the "unwitting victims of 'false consciousness'," mindless dupes who are "unable to perceive their own 'indigenous' values" and thus "all too easily persuaded to accept the values of their oppressors, to be 'moralized' and 'socialized' against their own best interests," has recently been challenged (qtd. in Himmelfarb, *Demoralization* 30). The counter-assertion argues that Victorian values— which "included not only the familiar ones of work, thrift, cleanliness, temperance, honesty, self-help, but also less obvious ones that were crucial to the 'work ethic': promptness, regularity, conformity, rationality" (29)—were shared by working and middle classes alike (30), even if they were, at times, honored more in the breach. "They affirmed, in effect, the principles of morality even if they could not always act in accordance with those principles" (26). Moreover, these commonly held virtues "were summed up in the idea of 'respectability' " (31), which "was a function of character" (32): "Working-class memoirs and the evidence of oral history testify poignantly to the efforts to remain respectable, to have a good character . . . in spite of all the difficulties and temptations to the contrary" (32). Factory workers like Rachael and Stephen would have struggled to avoid drunkenness, murder, adultery, and social rebellion because they, like their culture, valued respectability and sought to do what was morally expected of them. Yet even so, there is a complication in their seemingly innocent friendship since the married man and the single woman develop an emotional intimacy that vacillates between *philia* and *eros* so as to produce a relational portrait that remains ambivalent to the very end of the novel.

That Dickens initially intended for his readers to see Rachael as an angel is quite clear yet more often than not, her critics have reduced her to a simple moral influence exerted over her struggling friend (not her unattainable lover).[9] "Stephen's impeccable virtue," we are told, "is not simply another instance of the difficulty of presenting a 'good' character; he must be completely without offense if Dickens is to persuade his more conservative readers to sympathize with Stephen, and wish for his release'' (Baird 407). He is "the good, victimized working-man, whose perfect patience under infliction we are expected to find supremely edifying and irresistibly touching as the agonies are piled on for his martyrdom" (Leavis 259).[10] Yet such reductionism only partially accounts for the constant "muddle" of their personal lives; nor does it, in Stephen's case, account for the "inconsistency in Blackpool's character" (Pittock 179). More recently, the entire Coketown labor force has been placed within the intriguing (and Foucauldian) "framework of the 'factory-monastery' in order to contrast Stephen and Rachael's "idealized form of religious acceptance" (Stiltner 205)—a sign of "their resignation to the social inequities that their class endures" (205)—with the non-engaged resistance of the other "Hands against norming procedures" (204). But here again, the workers (now religious) are reduced to a predictable signifier while the complexity of moving from ideology to practical living is obfuscated by the rhetoric of class and gender. To further understand Rachael's role as *angel* and Stephen's role as *discipulus*, and their relationship as "star-crossed lovers" in an industrial age, we must turn to the relational geometry of René Girard's model for triangular desire.[11]

I

As a "systematic metaphor" for the "transparent yet opaque [mystery] of human relations" (2), Girard's triangle is anchored at the corners by *a mediator* (as model/obstacle), *a subject* (as disciple/rival), and *an object* (as "means of reaching the mediator") (53). The subject "pursues objects which are determined for him" (2) by the mediator and, in the process, the mediator is revered—and, to some degree, resented or hated—(13) while the object itself is transfigured or even obliterated (17, 47). According to Girard, there are three essential "triangular emotions"—"envy, jealousy, and impotent hatred"—which make up the "universal vanity" that lies behind all desire (14). Furthermore, desire is never spontaneous but rather the product of imitation (16) played out according to the "spiritual" distance between the mediator and the subject (9): "external mediation" indicates that the distance between the two agents is great, thus "eliminat[ing] any contact between the two spheres of *possibilities*," while "internal mediation" indicates that "this same distance is sufficiently reduced to allow these two spheres to penetrate each other more or less profoundly" (9). In the end, healthy metaphysical desire can displace its physical counterpart (85) so as to produce transcendency in the mediator and "polymorphosis" (i.e., "atomization of the personality") in the enlightened subject (92).

Applying Girard's theory to Dickens's novel produces two sets of triangulation involving Stephen-as-subject and Rachael-as-mediator. The first internal mediation involves the husband, the female friend,[12] and the debauched wife:

Rachael (Angel as mediator)

Stephen (Discipulus as subject)   *Mrs. Blackpool* (Drunkard as object)

Stephen-as-subject is trapped in a bad marriage with a woman who has been reified by her alcoholism and "moral infamy" (Dickens 72; bk.1, ch.10).[13] Rachael functions as the scenario's mediator who is inscribed with the supernatural attributes of the angel.[14] The subject's desire to possess the mediator and to transfigure the object is clearly seen in Book the First, chapter 10 where all three figures are initially triangulated. While waiting for Rachael to appear after work, Stephen anxiously scrutinizes each of "the shawled figures" only to find his model of encouragement in the "brightness of a lamp" at the very last, epiphanic minute (69; bk.1, ch.10). The ethereal signification continues as Rachael is described "with a quiet oval face, dark and rather delicate, irradiated by a pair of very gentle eyes, and further set off by the perfect order of her shining black hair." A seemingly innocent question then follows:

> "I thought thou wast ahind me, Rachael?"
> "No." (70; bk.1, ch.10)

The answer, of course, implies that she is in front of him, leading him in the right direction. The mediator-as-model is predetermining the type of desire that Stephen-as-subject will pursue, namely, to maintain the constancy of their friendship. Yet from the beginning, due to the intimate nature of internal mediation, Rachael also functions as *an obstacle* that blocks Stephen's desire to possess her romantically, as the next section of dialogue demonstrates:

> "Early t'night, lass?"
> "Times I'm a little early, Stephen; 'times a little late. I'm never to be counted on, going home."
> "Nor going t'other way, neither, 'tseems to me, Rachael?"
> "No, Stephen."

Stephen's attempt to circumvent Rachael-as-obstacle is countermanded by her strategic unpredictability, which the mediator uses to create instability and to re-direct the subject's desire. "Going t'other way" reveals the rival's willingness to buck conventional morality either as an adulterer or perhaps as a polygamist, [15] especially since "a woman who committed adultery lost her position in society, but a man did not" (Baird 403). With Rachael's emphatic "No, Stephen," the rival is led back into his role as compliant *disciple*: "He looked at her with some disappointment in his face, *but with a respectful and patient conviction that she must be right in whatever she did.* The expression was not lost upon her; she laid her hand lightly on his arm a moment, as if to thank him for it" (italics added, Dickens 70; bk.1, ch. 10). The light touch here both quells and inflames his desire to possess her in a further instance of the mediator's "double role" as "model and obstacle" (Girard 42) for Stephen is both discouraged from potential adultery and encouraged to maintain their intimate relationship, the source of his ongoing temptation. When Rachael next says that "We are such true friends, lad, and such old friends, and getting to be such old folk, now," the mediator-as-model attempts to re-emphasize the non-erotic quality of their interaction, a cue that Stephen ignores as he shifts the conversation onto to the topic of her age: "No, Rachael, thou'rt as young as ever thou wast" (Dickens 70; bk.1, ch.10). Her later admonition "to not walk too much together" again calls forth the disciple's reverence: "But thou'rt right; 'tmight mak fok talk, even of thee. Thou hast been that to me, Rachael, through so many year: thou hast done me so much good, and heartened of me in that cheering way, that thy word is a law to me. Ah lass, and a bright good law! Better than some real ones" (70; bk. 1, ch. 10). The model's spoken word is the disciple's established rule, a benevolent guideline that attempts to steer Stephen away from "envy, jealousy, and impotent hatred" caused by prejudicial divorce laws. His submission translates into dejection, however, as the subject de-clares that all "'tis a muddle," a conclusion that marks Stephen's paradoxical "lucidity and blindness" due to the increased presence of the mediator whose double role as model and obstacle has produced emotional ambivalence (Gi-rard 74).[16] In her attempt to relieve him of his pain, Rachael again gently touches Stephen on the arm with an "instantaneous effect" that both calms and re-stimulates his forbidden desire (Dickens 71; bk.1, ch.10). Later still, Rachael put "her hand in his" before slipping into the darkness in yet another "muddling" act. In a passage deleted from the original manuscript, Dickens apparently intended to wrap up the scene with a comment on the power of individual "affections and passions"—two indicators of internal mediation (qtd. in Flint, notes 307).

Triangulation continues as the subject enters his own home and "stumbles against" his drunken wife (as-object) who is "barely able to preserve her sitting posture by steadying herself with one begrimed hand on the floor" (72; bk.1, ch.10). Stephen's earlier description as *discipulus*, "a rather stooping man, with a knitted brow, a pondering expression of face, and a hard-looking head sufficiently capacious, on which his iron-grey hair lay long and thin" (68; bk.1, ch.10),[17] is dramatically contrasted with his wife's inhuman portrait as "a disabled, drunken creature . . . . so foul to look at, in her tatters, stains, and splashes, but so much fouler than that in her moral infamy" (72; bk.1, ch.10). Having internalized both sets of Rachael's desires, Stephen imitates her benevolence and her obstructionism, as reflected in his initial (and only) comment in the scene: "Heaven's mercy, woman! . . . Hast thou come back again!" Predictably, the attempt to transfigure the object gives way to the desire to obliterate it when, at the end of the scene, Stephen "throw[s] a covering over" his unconscious wife, "as if his hands [which covered his own face] were not enough to hide her, even in the darkness" (73; bk.1, ch.10). The disciple becomes the rival who now challenges the model's mediation in a figurative attempt to remove the object. As Girard states, the subject's "impassioned admiration and desire to emulate stumble over the unfair obstacle with which the model seems to block the way of his disciple, and then these passions recoil on the disciple in the form of impotent hatred, thus causing [a] sort of psychological self-poisoning . . . " (11). "Poisoning the self" triangulates into "poisoning the other," especially after Stephen's futile visit with Bounderby in chapter 11. Later, while walking to his home, Stephen reflects on "being placed in some new and diseased relation towards the objects among which he passed" (Dickens 85; bk.1, ch.12)—a telling symptom of his conflicted role. The source of this "diseased relation" is inferred at the beginning of the next chapter, during an exchange with Rachael in which he tells her that "he had had a fright" while coming home:

"A fright?"
"Ay, ay! coming in. When I were walking. When I were thinking. When I—"
It seized him again.   (88; bk.1, ch.13)

The rival terrorizes the disciple in a diseased *intra-personal* conflict that is mirrored in the external relationship between husband and wife. In short, self-disgust *and* triangular desire are at the heart of Stephen's fear.

Prior to this conversation, Rachael's double role is readily apparent in the tableaux drawn at the opening of chapter 13 wherein Stephen is holding his breath at the door, Rachael is sitting quietly by the bed, and the wife is sleeping behind a curtain. The subject's trepidation in approaching the object is mediated by the model's stabilizing influence. Rachael functions initially as *a guardian angel* who attends to the physical needs of her debauched friend ("she worked with me when we were girls both, and for that you courted her and married her when I was her friend") and to the metaphysical needs of her male co-worker (87; bk.1, ch.13). The model, however, is displaced by the obstacle when we learn that Rachael has "put a curtain up" (86; bk.1, ch.13) to block Stephen's view of his wife in yet another "muddling" attempt to obliterate the object. Reverence appears to dominate the scene, however, as subject and mediator draw closer together thus intensifying their desires while emptying the object "of its concrete value" (Girard 85). Like an angel's aura, Rachael's mediation envelops everything around it until "it appeared to [Stephen] that he saw all this in Rachael's face, and looked at nothing besides" (86; bk.1, ch.13). Her shaping influence asserts itself in a series of directives wherein the mediator-as-model "tells" the subject-as-disciple what to feel and how to act: "And next, for that I know your heart, and am right sure and certain that 'tis far too merciful to let her die, or even so much as suffer, for want of aid . . . . Thou art not the man to cast the last stone, Stephen, when she is brought so low" (87; bk.1, ch.13). But Stephen *is* tempted to be that man, and when he inadvertently reads "what was printed on [the medicine bottle] in large letters, . . . a sudden horror seemed to fall upon him" (87–88; bk.1, ch.13). The subject-as-rival is prompted to defy the mediator in order to fulfill his desire for the object's destruction, that is, until Rachael temporarily "cast[s the desire] out; she would keep it out; he trusted to her to defend him from himself" (88; bk.1, ch.13). The vacillation continues as "his eyes again fell on the bottle, and a tremble passed over him, causing him to shiver in every limb." That Stephen understands the conflict between model and obstacle is implied in his subsequent refusal to have any physical contact with Rachael: "She was coming to him, but he stretched out his arm to stop her." Already tempted to become the rival, Stephen cannot endure the mediator's "muddling" touch: "No! Don't please; don't! . . . . Let me see thee, a' so good, and so forgiving. Let me see thee as I see thee when I coom in. I can never see thee better than so. Never, never, never!" (88; bk.1, ch. 13). Girard notes that "the closer the mediator comes, the more feverish the action becomes" (85). The "violent fit of trembling" that seizes Stephen before he slumps lifelessly into a nearby chair marks the compressed distance between mediator and subject (88; bk.1, ch.13). Yielding to the model's imitative desire, Stephen then sees Rachael in supernatural terms, "as if she had a glory shining round her head. He could have believed she had. He did believe it . . . " (89; bk.1, ch.13). At this point, physical desire diminishes as its metaphysical counterpart grows since the two desires "always fluctuate at the expense of each other" (Girard 87). Yet the subject's struggle is by no means over.

In "a long, troubled dream" that circumvents his defense mechanisms, Stephen again revisits the forbidden desire to obliterate the object thus defying the mediator (89; bk.1, ch.13). The dream sequence opens with his marriage to "one on whom his heart had long been set—but she was not Rachael" in the subject's first and only *positive desire for* the object. Debauchery then follows in the form of symbolic "darkness" that is overcome by "a tremendous light . . . from one line in the table of commandments at the altar," presumably the sixth commandment to "not murder." Instantly, Stephen stands as a convicted felon before a crowd that "abhorred him"—the tragic act, as Horace requires in the *Ars Poetica*, having occurred offstage. Stephen is executed only to be mysteriously brought back to life in order to wander alone, never "to look on Rachael's face or hear her voice" (90; bk.1, ch.13), a reference perhaps to his metaphysical hell where demons like himself are separated from angels like Rachael, a place where *rivals* have no contact with *models*. Moreover, Stephen is tormented by the recurring shape of the bottle (as murder weapon) in what amounts to a metonymic reference to the subject's plight as a receptacle for the mediator's desires; he has become a repository for both poisonous and medicinal longings. The final image in this bizarre dream sequence is the unarticulated word (i.e., "poison") printed on the label—a reminder that for the subject, poisoning the other ultimately becomes poisoning of the self.[18]

In a hypnagogic state, Stephen then sees the actual bottle sitting on a three-legged table next to the bedside. Just as Oliver had watched Fagin "finger his loot" in the twilight of that novel, so Stephen turns voyeur in the firelight as he peers at his wife's "debauched features" (91; bk.1, ch.13). Illicit desire prompts Stephen to remain silent, "as if a spell were on him," so as to become a passive but willing participant in his wife's attempt to destroy herself. Yet at that very moment, "Rachael started up with a suppressed cry" and wrestled the cup from the wife's hand in an ironic twist of events wherein "the mediator's 'virtue' acts on the [voyeur's] senses *like a poison* which constantly spreads and slowly paralyzes" the subject-as-rival (Italics added; Girard 87); the model now blocks the very desire created by its dual role as obstacle.[19] In fact, the mediator's metaphysical coup d'état strongly encourages Stephen to remain a devoted disciple for the rest of the novel—a shift immediately seen in his genuflection: "As she looked at him, saying 'Stephen?' he went down on his knee before her, on the poor mean stairs, and put an end of her shawl to his lips" (92; bk.1, ch.13). Stephen's posture here signifies that "the positive mediation of the saint [or angel]" has replaced "the negative mediation of anguish and hate" generated by the obstacle/ rival relationship (Girard 60). The religious devotee, the fiancée, and the chivalric knight collapse into one expression of adoration that marks Stephen's deep devotion and Rachael's temporary transcendency: "Thou art an Angel. Bless thee, bless thee! . . . Thou changest me from bad to good. Thou mak'st me humbly wishfo' t be more like thee, and fearfo' to lose thee when this life is ower, an a' the muddle cleared awa'. Thou'rt an Angel; it may be, thou hast saved my soul alive!'' (92; bk.1, ch.13). The subject's desire to imitate the model (and not the obstacle) intensifies Stephen's longing to clear away "the muddle" caused by the mediator's double role. When Stephen next confesses the premeditated intent of his rivalry and his own temptation to "poison the self," he not only acknowledges his "ontological sickness" whose "fatal outcome . . . is, directly or indirectly, a form of suicide" (Girard 280) but he hints at the second working-class triangulation, namely, the relationship between Rachael, Stephen, and Slackbridge (the collective representative of "onreasonable" Hands):

> I coom home desp'rate. I coom home wi'out a hope, and mad wi' thinking that when I said a word o' complaint, I was reckoned a onreasonable Hand. I told thee I had had a fright. It were the Poison-bottle on table. I never hurt a livin' creetur; but happenin' so suddenly upon't, I thowt, "How can *I* say what I might ha' done to myseln, or her, or both!'' (92–2; bk. 1, ch.13)

Rachael reacts by putting "her two hands on his mouth" in a physical gesture that threatens to subvert the model's positive influence. But like "electric current in a battery" running from subject to mediator and back again (Girard 99)—a circuit that Girard defines as "double mediation" (100)—Stephen's strong desire to emulate Rachael-as-angel begins the process of transforming him into a "subject-mediator." Removing her hands, he then accelerates his choice to be an impassioned disciple by repeating his triangular vows:

> But I see thee, Rachael, setten by the bed. I ha' seen thee, aw this night. In my troublous sleep I ha' known thee still to be there. Evermore I will see thee there. I nevermore will see her or think o' her, but thou shalt be beside her. I nevermore will see or think o' anything that angers me, but thou, so much better than me, shalt be by th' side on't. And so I will try t' look t' th' time, and so I will try t' trust t' th' time, when thou and me at last shall walk together far awa', beyond the deep gulf, in th' country where thy little sister is.
> (93; bk.1, ch. 13)

Stephen's vows mark the end of the first triangulation in addition to establishing the possessive relationship between the mediator and the object. In fact, *Hard Times* will close with the image of "a woman of a pensive beauty, always dressed in black" having "compassion on a degraded, drunken wretch of her own sex, who was sometimes seen in the town secretly begging of her, and crying to her" (297; bk. 3, ch. 9). Grief becomes the nexus connecting Stephen to both female characters who, in mourning the loss of the same subject, preserve the first set of triangulated desires. As for Stephen, he undergoes "polymorphosis" in the last two books of the novel wherein the "atomization of [his] personality" circumscribes his developing role as mediator (Girard 92). In what amounts to a "chain of triangles" (73), Stephen goes from subject to mediator-as-model/obstacle despite Rachael's opposition to his joining the union and Slackbridge's vilification of that same resistance.

II

In the second major triangulation, Stephen assumes the more complex role of subject-mediator while Slackbridge becomes the new object (reified by his strident "all-or-nothing" advocacy) and Rachael functions as the mediator—both the *angel in the factory* (i.e., the model worker) who maintains her "sweet-tempered and serene, and even cheerful" disposition while "working, every working, but content to do it, and preferring to do it as her natural lot," and the *obstacle* who blocks the developmental progress of her dedicated subject (Dickens 297; bk. 3, ch. 9).

Rachael (Mediator)

Stephen (Subject-mediator)   *Slackbridge* (Object)

That Rachael belongs to the very union she implicitly asks Stephen not to join—although her membership is unofficial and the "prohibition" placed on Stephen "did not yet formally extend to the women working in the factories" (148; bk. 2, ch. 4)—is indeed strange. Why would she not want her clandestine lover to be a part of that same warp and woof? Would it not be a comfort to have him nearby, to know that such proximity would allow their relationship to continue through a series of familiar, after-hour rendezvous? Yet in Book the Third, chapter 6, Dickens implies that Stephen's decision to remain outside of the union has its genesis in Rachael's prayer: "I didn't seek it of him, poor lad. *I prayed him to avoid trouble for his own good*, little thinking he'd come to it through me" (italics added; 162; bk. 2, ch. 6). The off-screen exchange (i.e., shared prayer?) between the star-crossed lovers draws attention to Rachael's double role as model and obstacle wherein her love for Stephen is set against the triangulated emotions of envy and jealousy, both of which are produced by the increasing intimacy of internal mediation (Girard 14). Perhaps having Stephen in secretive fits and snatches is no longer enough. Or perhaps the monogamous commitment demanded by marriage and organized labor (for each type of "union" abhors the deviant other, the mistress and the scab) has created a quiet desperation that exacerbates Rachael's role as obstacle. For when Stephen responds to her implanted desire "to avoid trouble" and remain safe, thus reaffirming Rachael's role as benevolent mediator, "No one, excepting myseln, can ever know what honour, an what love, an respect, I bear to Rachael, or wi' what cause. When I passed that promess, I towd her true, she were th' Angel o' my life. 'Twere a solemn promess. 'Tis gone fro me, for ever" (162; bk. 2, ch. 6), he not only drops his inclination to join the union—"I'd coom in wi' th' rest," he has said, though "I doubt their doin' yo onny good" (145; bk. 2, ch. 4)—but willingly places himself outside of his own working-class community. In being fired from his job and stripped of his livelihood, Stephen is also denied access to the very model that inspires his devotion as *discipulus*: "Not only did he see no Rachael all the time, but he avoided every chance of seeing her . . . . [because he] dreaded that Rachael might be even singled out from the rest if she were seen in his company" (148; bk. 2, ch. 4). The implications here are that Rachael's ongoing affiliation with the Coketown union must be protected and that Stephen's "promess" has indeed become a "positive muddle" producing nothing but isolation and ignominy. Once again, the mediator has blocked the subject's growth by manipulating his devotion. In the final analysis, Rachael *does not want* to share Stephen with his wife or his co-workers, due to the possessive nature of her role as obstacle.

The psychology of such a desire is certainly understandable, for Rachael's life is filled with little more than deprivation and dull physical labor. Her relationships are confined to the short intervals between her shifts and to the people she has immediate contact with. Although she would never bind herself to an unworthy husband in the name of Utilitarianism, as Louisa does; or play the sycophant to gain temporary security, as Mrs. Sparsit does; or adopt Sissy's optimistic view of the industrialized world (Rachael is too experienced to do that), or fall hopelessly into alcoholism and slatternliness, as her girlhood friend, Mrs. Blackpool, has done; still, Rachael distorts the one significant relationship she does have in pursuit of personal happiness and conjugal respectability. She cannot legally partner with Stephen and she knows it, and perhaps the pain of such an understanding compels her to do the very thing she despises when she supplants Stephen's wife and work in the name of friendship, the results of which are destabilization and the constant temptation of illicit desire. Dickens, of course, has purposely shifted our sympathies to the star-crossed lovers in order to emphasize the futility of their plight. Yet the fact remains that Rachael has added significantly to the "muddle" of Stephen's marriage and livelihood.

On the opposite slope of the same triangle, the mediator has created an insurmountable distance between herself and the object. That Rachael has no direct contact with Slackbridge at any point in the novel is telling, as is

Stephen's choice to internalize Rachael's prohibition and subsequently challenge Slackbridge's legitimacy during a public meeting. Here the subject demonstrates that he too is distanced from the object. Standing with "propriety" and "dignity" before a crowd of his peers (Dickens 145; bk. 2, ch. 4), Stephen begins by rejecting the kinship claims of union solidarity: "My brothers . . . and my fellow-workmen—for that yo are to me, *though not*, as I knows on, *to this delegate heer*—" (Italics added). Just prior to this passage, Dickens sketches Slackbridge as a disagreeable caricature and then sets him against the rough sincerity of the Coketown operatives:

> He was not so honest, he was not so manly, he was not so good-humoured; he substituted cunning for their simplicity, and passion for their safe solid sense. An ill-made high-shouldered man, with lowering brows, and his features crushed into an habitually sour expression contrasted most unfavourably, even in his mongrel dress, with the great body of his hearers in their plain working clothes.   (142; bk. 2, ch. 4)

The Delegate's disparaging laughter, his folded arms, his sarcastic frown (Dickens 145; bk. 2, ch. 4), and his "bombastic rhetoric" (Fowler 393) all point to the sardonic reification of the object.

By contrast, Stephen speaks in plain but measured terms, with a full understanding that he will be despised and rejected for doing so. His speech, in fact, marks his transposition from compliant subject (in Rachael's mediated triangle) to mediator-as-role model in a contiguous triangle that keeps labor as the object but posits the factory worker as the new subject:[20]

> my fellow-workmen . . . I ha but a word to sen, and I could sen nommore if I was to speak till Strike o' day. I know weel, aw what's afore me. I know weel that yo are aw resolved to ha nommore a do wi' a man who is not wi' yo in this matther. I know weel that if I was a lyin' parisht i' th' road, yo'd feel it right to pass me by, as a forrenner and stranger. What I ha getn, I mun mak th' best on.   (145–6; bk. 2, ch. 4)

Stephen's rhetoric certainly resonates with "the regional, uneducated and oral properties of the language of the Hands" (Fowler 396). Yet it also contains a profundity based on shared experience that deeply humanizes Stephen at the very moment he sacrifices himself. When he gestures toward Slackbridge—whose surname ironically connotes both a *stoppage* and a *pathway*—Stephen creates his own definition of solidarity that hinges on commiseration, and not on class-consciousness, and, in the process, reduces the trade unionist to a parenthetical interjection. The pun on "Strike o' day" (i.e., closing of day = closing of factories) contains Dickens's own distrust of those who foment working-class agitation: "His essential complaint was that the organisers of the strike ' . . . are, sometimes, not workmen at all, but designing persons who have, for their own base purposes, immeshed the workmen in a system of tyranny and oppression' '' (qtd. in Ackroyd 690).[21] Stephen's reference to his impending isolation is then followed by the analogue of the Good Samaritan wherein Stephen becomes the abused (and robbed) traveler, emotionally bloodied and abandoned, while his fellow-workers are cast as the priest and the Levite condemned for their unwillingness to get involved. The Good Samaritan, who ignores class and ethnic distinctions and acts out of compassion, is nowhere to be found. As an emerging mediator, Stephen parlays his public "trial" into a parabolic teaching on individual integrity that directly challenges the "One united power" of trade unionism (141; bk. 2, ch. 4). When Stephen asks for the universal right to work, Slackbridge employs his own brand of "violent, biblical rhetoric" (Fowler 393) to assert that "private feelings must yield to the common cause" (147; bk. 2, ch. 4). He then atomizes Stephen's personality: Blackpool becomes "a traitor and a craven and a recreant" (143; bk. 2, ch. 4), an Esau "who sold his birthright for a mess of pottage . . . [a] Judas Iscariot . . . and [a Lord] Castlereagh" (144; bk. 2, ch. 4).[22] Before long, Bounderby adds "waspish, raspish, ill-conditioned [and unemployed] chap" to the denigrating list (155; bk. 2, ch. 5). Later still, Slackbridge completes the atomization by proclaiming that Stephen is "A thief! A plunderer! A proscribed fugitive, with a price upon his head; a fester and a wound upon the noble character of the Coketown operative!" (249; bk. 3, ch. 4). Blackpool, he concludes, has shamed his "class" family by first going his own way and then by committing an egregious crime (which, of course, he has not committed).[23]

Yet the name-calling, the false accusations, and the ostracism, all mark the subject's transposition to public mediator: "Thus easily did Stephen Blackpool fall into the loneliest of lives, the life of solitude among a familiar crowd" (147; bk. 2, ch. 4). According to Girard, the emerging hero (i.e., subject) who is plagued by disappointment and deprivation is also "in danger of falling into the abyss of the present like a well-digger whose rope breaks" (Girard 89). In fact, Stephen's downward movement is required as part of the novel's forward progress: "There is always the same meaning behind the adventure of the hero of a novel; it takes us from the upper to the lower regions of a particular novelistic domain. The career of the hero is a descent into hell which almost always ends in a return to the light, by means of a metaphysical, nontemporal conversion" (253). This "descent into hell" is symbolically rendered in *Hard Times* when Stephen falls down the Old Hell Shaft after wandering over "dangerous country at such a dangerous time" (271; bk. 3, ch. 6). Grotesquely contorted and "buried alive" in a Dantesque pit (268; bk. 3, ch. 6), Stephen nevertheless fixes his attention on a single star overhead which he thought to be the very one that "guided [the shepherds] to Our Saviour's home" (274; bk. 3, ch. 6). The "imagery of vertical transcendency" (Girard 285) now guides the rescuers to Stephen's broken body. But the biblical typology cannot sustain the weight of both the mediator-as-model and the subject-as-conflicted rival—the salvific figure and the fallen sinner—and so it collapses into what becomes Stephen's own problematic double role. In a sense, there is a clash between his public and private triangles that produces more indeterminacy. When he is finally lifted (i.e., resurrected) out of the mineshaft, a familiar pattern follows: Stephen sees Rachael's face; *she grabs* his hand; *he tells her* that all is "a muddle! Fro' first to last, a muddle!" (Dickens 272; bk. 3, ch. 6). In triangulated terms, Rachael's physical contact (as obstacle) stimulates Stephen's inordinate devotion (as subject) which, in turn, blocks his intentions (as mediator). Throughout the novel, Stephen reiterates and rejects Rachael's implanted desire to "avoid trouble" but as a result of this vacillation, he is unable (or unwilling) to "repudiate [ ] his mediator" (294) or to "contradict his former ideas" (292). "Genuine conversion," Girard implies, is marked by reversal wherein "deception gives way to truth, anguish to remembrance, agitation to repose, hatred to love, humiliation to humility, mediated desire to autonomy, deviated transcendency to vertical transcendency" (294). Yet such a clear and dramatic reversal eludes each of the star-crossed lovers. Hand-in-damaged-hand under the cover of darkness, Rachael and Stephen maintain their forbidden relationship up to the very end, until mortality, and not English law, ultimately blocks their consummation.

Stephen's "promess" and his subsequent death have certainly produced a wide range of critical responses. While some "do their best to ignore this part of the novel" (Fielding and Smith 22), others see Stephen's "sacrifice" as "one of the mysterious aspects of *Hard Times*" in which "the reader is never quite sure why Stephen refuses to join the union and assure his outcast status" (Stiltner 210); it is simply "incomprehensible" (Malone 84). Others have assigned values based on Christian, Marxist, and humanist paradigms, although the propitiatory mechanisms are never fully explained.[24] Yet the emotional logic of triangulated desire seems to account for Stephen's impractical albeit devoted "decision" to remain outside the union and inside his personal relationship with Rachael, despite the destructive consequences. If Stephen were truly a religious martyr or a heroic victim of capitalism, his death would profoundly affect the commercial, religious, and educational structures of the novel but none of these are radically altered by his "sacrifice." Bounderby (the middle-class manufacturer) does not change at all; Thomas Gradgrind (the middle-class educator) changes *before* Stephen's death, as does Louisa; James Harthouse (the drifting gentry) is affected by a different mediator, Sissy Jupe; Tom Jr. sheds tears of sorrow at not seeing his beloved sister instead of tears of remorse for framing Stephen ("died in penance" is vague at best [Dickens 297; bk. 3, ch. 9]); Slackbridge drops out of the picture, and even Rachael returns to the factory, "always dressed in black,'' as if she were Stephen's true widow—a gesture that is tender but presumptuous, one which implies that love and manipulation are strangely mixed into Rachael's desire for respectability. In short, "muddled Saint Stephen" is filled with unresolved conflict: the disciple wars with the rival, the husband fights with the lover, the weaver squares off with the union outcast, the honest man is set against the accused thief, the private subject clashes with the public mediator. Although his struggle with temptation in the first triangulation is laudable, as is his indictment of industrial malfeasance in the second, they are personal victories at best, not social triumphs. Stephen's greatest worth is found in the strength of his convictions, despite his failures, and in the battle he wages to maintain both his love and his respectability.

Yet time and time again, triangulated desire produces a muddling effect that not even money, divorce, power, or class can eradicate, as is suggested by Louisa's ill-fated entanglement with James Harthouse. Even when Dickens removes the mediator (Harthouse is the desirable model, the passionate lover who becomes an obstacle in Louisa's marriage) and dismisses the object (Bounderby is reified by his self-fictionalizing egoism), he is still unable to repair the damage done to Louisa as a divided subject. Perhaps her inability to remarry—her assumed "from bed and board only" form of divorce does not change the fact that Louisa is still "legally married to Bounderby" (Baird 402, 411)—finds its working-class counterpart in Rachael's choice to remain single since both scenarios suggest a surviving attachment to a previously mediated desire. And perhaps Dickens is rehearsing the implications of his own triangulated (albeit incipient) relationship with Ellen Ternan, born out of his own "family troubles," and Catherine (Gallagher 289, fn.6). Some three years later, this triangulation is destined to make Dickens feel that "his married life was unbearable, yet there seemed nothing he could do except bear it"—a frustration that is very much in line with Stephen Blackpool's (Johnson 448). Whatever the source, the muddled ending of Stephen's life rings true with the complexities of human desire.

Returning once more to Stephen's last meeting with Rachael in book 3, we find a final image of the divided subject. Walking beside his stretcher, Rachael holds Stephen's "broken right hand lying bare on the outside of the covering garments, as if wanting to be taken by another hand" (272; bk. 3, ch. 6) while the rest of the man lies paralyzed. Stephen is once again reduced to a synecdoche, but this time the "hand" signifies his role as broken discipulus—a failing devotee who is losing his grip on the mediator-as-model. His voice, however, resonates with the rival's intention to pursue forbidden desire: "Rachael, beloved lass! Don't let go my hand. We may walk together t'night, my dear!" (274; bk. 3, ch. 6). Under the guise of friendship, the two lovers express their feelings through physical touch in what amounts to an ambiguous conflation of *philia* and *eros*. In the face of death, Stephen yields to his greater desire as a rival and, in the process, the object (Mrs. Blackpool) is temporarily erased thus flattening the relational geometry into a single, albeit illicit, line that Stephen seeks to preserve by calling for his death shroud prior to his own physical demise: "Will soombody be pleased to coover my face!" Predictably, the covering reifies Stephen as the rescue attempt turns into "a funeral procession" (275; bk. 3, ch. 6) and the once conflicted subject becomes an inert (and possessed) object in the hand of the surviving mediator.

Dickens keenly understood the pathos generated by Stephen's death and Rachael's longing, despite the vagueness of the novel's social programming. Slackbridge's absence and Mrs. Blackpool's disappearance are hardly noticeable when set against another triangulated relationship, that of a broken-hearted father who makes the irrational choice to rescue his errant son from the pursuant authorities in the closing chapters.[25] On the whole, the ending of *Hard Times* does seem to be "more pessimistic than promising" (Thomas 132) as borne out by Louisa, Thomas Gradgrind, Tom Jr., Bounderby, Mrs. Sparsit, James Harthouse, Rachael, Stephen, and Mrs. Blackpool—all of whom have been deeply affected by triangulated relationships. Only Sissy Jupe is projected into a happy futurity, "she holding this course as part of no fantastic vow, or bond, or brotherhood, or sisterhood, or pledge, or covenant, or fancy dress, or fancy fair; but simply as a duty to be done" (298; bk. 3, ch. 9). In fact, her ability to facilitate healthy mediation marks her as one of the book's "two good angels" (Friedman 257), and as the only mediator capable of implanting transformational desire at several social levels. What is more, in the final paragraph of the novel, Dickens himself mediates between the reader-as-subject and the working-man-as-object: "Dear reader! It rests with you and me, whether, in our two fields of action, similar things shall be or not. Let them be!" (298; bk. 3, ch. 9). The author-as-mediator first underscores our need to choose and then follows it up with the imperative to "Let them be!"—an injunction loaded with the dualism of internal mediation: "Let them [i.e., good things] be" a part of working-class life is an implanted desire generated by the mediator-as-model while "Let them [i.e., the workers] be" (i.e., leave them alone) signifies the presence of the mediator-as-obstacle. The closing combination of "Lighter bosoms" and "ashes of our fires turn[ed] grey and cold" contains the same bifurcation, one that can be extended profitably to the "Working-Man Question" as a whole: To what extent is Victorian society *modeling* or *obstructing* working class growth? And is the factory hand to be seen as a casualty to be resurrected or an object to be obliterated? In the last lines of the novel, Dickens seeks to implant his own desire for working-class transcendency so as to convert his dear readers on the very "hearth" of their private lives. He enjoins them to imitate Sissy rather than Bitzer, to pursue respectability instead of deviation, to value individuals before institutions, to model benevolence rather than obstructionism—despite the muddling threat of triangulated desire—and to do so whether the times are extremely easy or deplorably hard.

APPENDIX

In its original context, John Tenniel's slender and fastidious *angel*, with finishing hammer in hand, satirizes the personality and politics of John Bright, a Liberal parliamentarian and "a sincere Quaker [with] . . . a genuine spiritual humility" (Briggs 199). In fact, Bright's pacifism so worked against him during the Crimean War that his constituency in Manchester finally burned his effigy in protest (216). In response, Bright delivered his eloquent "angel of death" speech to a spellbound House in 1854, as the war with Russia dragged on: "The angel of death," he declared, "has been abroad throughout the land; you may almost hear the beating of *his* wings" (italics added; qtd. in Briggs 217). Tenniel cleverly combines Bright's famous trope with the latter's strong belief in the political rectitude of the working class in order to create his heavenly factotum. Add Bright's teetotal advocacy to the mix (the figure is drinking water from a public fountain) and the satire is complete.

Patrick Brantlinger has noted that "Dickens seems to have found it easier to support the Anti-Corn Law League than to support the Ten Hours Movement" (277), two positions that Bright himself agreed with: as a leader among Corn Law reformers *and* a free-trader, Bright saw "all legislative interference with labour market, all attempts of Government to fix the wages of industry, all interference of a third party between employers and employed . . . [as] unjustifiable in principle and mischievous in their results" (qtd. in Briggs 210). By contrast, Peter Ackroyd points out that "in a later letter [Dickens] attacked what was generally known as the 'Manchester School' of political economics for what he called ' . . . its reduction to the grossest absurdity of the supply-and-demand dogmatism' and its belief that self-interest was the major factor in human decisions" (qtd. in Ackroyd 697). When it came to the Temperance Issue, Dickens was a staunch moderationist, as his running argument with teetotaler George Cruikshank demonstrated.

In the illustration attributed to William Forster, the *discipulus* (or afterhours philosopher) is plagued by a hidden inconsistency that is described in the article accompanying the visual text: despite his "noble, benevolent, and intellectual" demeanor, he keeps "a pewter pot and a pipe . . . under the table" and has "an emblematical design . . . for the seven deadly sins" beneath his feet ("Pictures" 205). The real thirst, *Punch* suggests, is not for knowledge; and what little information is acquired will converted to gluttony and greed, not enlightenment. This "Galileo in his cell" is nothing more than a social heretic who wants to change the nature of the English political universe by calling for working-class enfranchisement. Five years later, Forster will oversee the passage of the "Elementary Education Act (1870) which provided aid for existing schools, established supplementary nondenominational 'board schools,' and was the foundation for the English system of national compulsory education" ("Forster")—a Galilean vindication for Forster and a black-eye for Punch.

In the *rebel* illustration assigned to Edward Horsman, the factory worker is fervently "sawing down the beam which supports the Crown, regardless of the fact that he himself will certainly come down with it" ("Pictures" 205). The source of such violence is found in his "habitual defiance of rule," as if it were a genetic predisposition. According to Horsman, the uninformed masses were a threat to orderly governance, a faceless rebel whose notions of reform constituted a "militant radicalism" that had to be rejected for the good of the country (Briggs 231). Interestingly enough, Dickens does connect Bounderby (the capitalist) to such hegemonic symbolism when he writes that strangers in the novel "made [Bounderby] out to be the Royal arms, the Union-Jack, Magna Charta [sic], John Bull, Habeas Corpus, the Bill of Rights, An Englishman's house is his castle, Church and State, and God save the Queen, all put together" (49; bk. 1, ch. 7). To attack the industrialist is to attack the Crown.

Tenniel's portrait of the *drunkard* is assigned to Robert Lowe, and it shows the working-man slouched "over his pipe and pewter while BRITANNIA [not shown] holds before his eyes a balance containing the franchise in one scale, and 240 pots of beer in the other" ("Pictures" 205). The worker, of course, stares at the beer and ignores his own social progress. Such perceived ignorance was at the heart of Lowe's resistance to working-class enfranchisement since he, like his followers, believed that "it would transfer political power to the ignorant, . . . destroy real leadership . . . . [and] undermine national unity and prosperity" (Briggs 242). In other words, Lowe "attacked reform not as a Whig apologist defending an order but as an intellectual pleading for government by the educated against government by the [unenlightened] masses" (Briggs 232). *Punch* apparently agreed since the portrait reinforces the working-class stereotype that laborers are "naturally" bent toward dissipation.

NOTES

1. David Kunzle notes that the working-class magazine *Fun*, launched in 1861, had already run a comic series by James Sullivan titled "The British Working Man" (40).

2. Asa Briggs discusses John Bright's Quakerism (pp. 202–05) and Robert Lowe's leadership role with the "Adullamites" (p. 229), a term used by Bright in a speech referencing I Samuel 22:1–2 wherein a younger David, after feigning madness before King Achish, "left Gath and escaped to the cave of Adullam . . . . All those who were in distress or in debt or discontented gathered around him, and he became their leader." Briggs writes, "Lowe soon gathered around him a small group of members of the Liberal party who were opposed, like himself, to any lowering of the franchise. They included Lord Elcho, Lord Grosvenor, and Mr. Horsman; 'unattached' men or unrepentant Palmerstonians who felt no special loyalty to Russell or Gladstone; and some of the members for small boroughs who feared changes in the distribution of seats. In all, they numbered more than forty, and they were not without influential supporters outside, like Delane, who believed that they were capable of becoming 'a third party' " (237). Gladstone's 1866 Reform Bill was defeated, despite "mass demonstrations in Manchester, Birmingham, Edinburgh, Leeds, Liverpool and Rochdale [Bright's birthplace]."

   William Forster was the son of a Society of Friends minister, had a Quaker education, but "left the Society of Friends" when he married the daughter of Dr. Thomas Arnold, "Jane Martha Arnold (a non-Friend) in 1850" ("Dressed in Simplicity").

3. P.J. Keating identifies "six kinds of working class character[s]" that loosely correspond to Tenniel's index: (1) Respectable, (2) Intellectual, (3) Poor, (4) Debased, (5) Eccentric, and (6) Criminal (pp. 26–27). David Lodge divides all of the characters in *Hard Times* into four class-inscribed groups: (1) the Gradgrind family, (2) the Bounderby ménage, (3) the workers, and (4) the circus folk ("How Successful" 384). Hilary Schor has noted that "*Hard Times* works less by argument than by such metaphorical or analogical groupings" (69).

4. John Bright placed idle individuals in what he called the "residuum," those who should not be enfranchised "because they have no independence whatever" (qtd. in Briggs 247). Despite this shared assessment, with regard to the Second Reform Bill, Marx referred to Bright as " 'Father Bright' and held him largely responsible for 'the period of corruption' in the middle years of the century during which the workingmen became 'henchmen of the capitalists' " (qtd. in Briggs 200).

5. Like Nathaniel Hawthorne (see epigraph), Henry David Thoreau understood (in *Walden*) that "incessant labor with my hands . . . made more study impossible" (69).

6. Phyllis Deane states that Engels's book "is one of the most vivid and angry denunciations of the factory system" in which he "makes no bones about his political motives" (238–39). Engels goes on to "charge the English middle classes with mass murder, wholesale robbery, and all the other crimes in the calendar" (qtd. in Deane 239) in yet another reductive portrait.

7. See F.R. Leavis's *The Great Tradition* (chapter 5), David Lodge's *Language of Fiction* (chapter 3) and "How Successful is *Hard Times*?" from *Working With Structuralism*. Kate Flint in her introduction to *Hard Times* remarks that "mythmaking . . . can be turned to falsifying, destructive ends as well as good ones"

(xvii). See also Robert Barnard's "Imagery and Theme in *Hard Times*," pp. 368, 376, and Rodney Stenning Edgecombe's "*Hard Times* and the Moral Fable."

8. Gertrude Himmelfarb cites George Gissing, George Bernard Shaw, and George Orwell as critics who see Stephen Blackpool as "unrepresentative of his class," and Dickens as being "ignorant of the plight of the industrial worker" (*The Idea of Poverty* 485). In his introduction to *Hard Times*, Terry Eagleton states that "Dickens's presentation of the trade unions is seriously one-sided, reflecting middle-class prejudice and panic more than precise observation" (336, fn 43).

9. David L. Cowles remarks that Rachael "exhibits standard Victorian feminine virtues: extraordinary devotion (especially to a needy male), remarkable love-based powers of intuition, firm but modest assertion of heart-felt values, great spiritual strength and endurance" (80). Stanley Friedman identifies Rachael's angelic demeanor (256). See Katherine Retan's recap of "feminist critics" who explore "the domestic angel and her 'demonic' other" (184–85). Even Rachael's deceased little sister, whose arm was to be "torn off by a factory-machine," is described as "angelic," as if the symbolism runs in the family (Ford and Monod 278).

10. Leavis does note, later on, that Stephen "is too good and qualifies too consistently for the martyr's halo," only then to make a pejorative comparison to Harriet Beecher Stowe's "Uncle Tom" (270).

11. Mary Poovey has recently written about "the triangular structure of anxiety" in *Hard Times*, a Freudian derivative comprised of an "Endangered Subject," a "Source of Danger," and the "Protector Ego" (163, 155). This fascinating "anti-metaphyical model" (153) brings together political economy and nineteenth-century novel writing, and focuses primarily on the middle-class. John Baird, without referring to it as such, has triangulated "suffering virtue (Stephen), active virtue (Rachael), and loathsome vice (Stephen's wife)" in his oft-quoted article on Victorian divorce (408).

12. Although "Stephen's resemblance to his Biblical namesake has often been noticed" (Lampard 113), little has been said about Rachael's connection to Genesis 29 (see Philip Allingham pp. 29–30). In fact, Laban's younger daughter who "was lovely in form and beautiful" functions as a symbol of deferred happiness in a triangulation involving Laban (mediator), Jacob (subject), her older sister, Leah (undesired wife-as-object) and Rachel (desirable wife-as-object).

13. Himmelfarb observes that "the common problem, even among the 'roughs,' was not the absence of a father but the presence of one who was irregularly employed and regularly drunk and abusive, or, somewhat less commonly, a mother who was drunk and slatternly" (*Demoralization* 42).

14. There are many examples of triangulation involving the angel-as-mediator in both the Old and New Testaments: Hagar (S)/Angel (M)/Sarai's legitimacy (O) in Genesis 16:7–16; Lot (S)/Angel (M)/Sodom's judgment (O) in Genesis 19:15–26; Abraham (S)/Angel (M)/Isaac's sacrifice (O) in Genesis 22: 9–18; Israelites (S)/Angel (M)/Pharaoh's threat (O) in Exodus 14:19; Moses (S)/Angel in burning bush (M)/God's calling (O) in Exodus 3:1–22; Balaam (S)/Angel (M)/Donkey as mouthpiece (O) in Numbers 22:21–35; Gideon (S)/Angel (M)/God's calling (O) in Judges 6:11–24; Manoah (S)/Angel (M)/ Samson's birth (O) in Judges

13:1–25; Zechariah (S)/Gabriel (M)/John's birth (O) in Luke 1:11–22; Mary (S)/ Gabriel (M)/God's anointing (O) in Luke 1:26; Joseph (S)/Angel in a dream (M)/Mary's virginity (O) in Matthew 1:20–25; Cornelius (S)/Angel in a vision (M)/Peter's message (O) in Acts 10:1–48; Philip (S)/Angel (M)/Ethiopian eunuch's understanding (O) in Acts 8:26–40; Peter (S)/Angel (M)/Herod's judgment (O) in Acts 12:1–19; the various churches (S)/Angel (M)/God's judgment (O) throughout the Book of Revelation.

15. Girard argues that "the subject is torn between two opposite feelings toward his model—the most submissive reverence and the most intense malice. This is the passion we call hatred. Only someone who prevents us from satisfying a desire which he himself has inspired in us is truly an object of hatred" (10). To make Rachael his mistress would be to ruin the woman he loves but cannot legally marry, yet he is tempted nonetheless.

16. Critical readings of "muddle" range from historically based observations about the Crimean War, the failed Reform Bill, and daughter Mary's cholera (see Edgar Johnson p. 411) to poor labor relations (see Brantlinger p. 280) to "instances of neglected responsibility" (see Sanders 324) to "an eschatologically deferred explanation" that accomplishes nothing (see Edgecombe 198).

17. Throughout the novel, Stephen is described in contemplative terms: he lives a "life of solitude among a familiar crowd" (147; bk. 2, ch. 4), and is "a quiet silent man . . . used to companionship with his own thoughts" (148; bk. 2, ch. 4); he evinces "the quiet confidence of absolute certainty" while talking with Bounderby (153; bk. 2, ch. 5) and during the scene with Louisa, Stephen "remained quietly attentive, in his usual thoughtful attitude, with his hand at his chin" (162; bk. 2, ch. 6). His "appearance and manner" are always "very honest" (255; bk. 3, ch. 4).

18. John Baird speculates that the poison might literally be "perchloride of mercury, otherwise known as corrosive sublimate, a widely used medicine for syphilis" (408), hence explaining why it appears on the nightstand in the first place: Stephen's wife is infected.

19. Valerie L. Wainwright has written about "Dickens' picture of the psychological make-up of moral excellence" in the novel, stating, in particular, that "in developing his dramatic interpretation of the powers of the will in the scene where Rachel saves both Stephen and his wife, Dickens' account becomes at once more complex and enigmatic, and undoubtedly for some readers more problematic" (171, 181). Awakened by her "clairvoyance," Rachel stops the suicide attempt (181). Her moral (and angelic) nature never waivers while Stephen remains debilitated throughout by his "moral helplessness"—two reductive consistencies that can be disputed using Girard's model.

20. The chain of triangles would appear as follows, with Stephen's role as *subject* marking his private triangulation with Rachael while his role as *mediator* identifies his public triangulation involving his brother workers. In the latter, Stephen becomes the working-man's model of self-respect and honesty while his refusal to join the union marks him as an obstacle. The Coketown operatives, however, are eventually persuaded to reject Stephen. See his "their work be murder to 'em" speech for the reference to "public muddle" (272–3; bk. 3, ch. 6).

Rachael (*M*)

△

(*M*) Stephen (*S*)   Slackbridge (*O*)

△

(*S*) Workers   (*O*) Slackbridge

21. R. D. Butterworth says that Dickens's "description of the [Preston] leaders reflects his view that they are suspicious characters leading the gullible workers astray" (132). Edgar Johnson writes that "*Hard Times* made clear [that Dickens] believed labour leaders were often corrupt demagogues" (413). Alexander Welsh states that "*Hard Times* makes it clear that its author was opposed to collective action: it is not merely the Slackbridges who are the problem, but the danger of many men moving as one and what they will do" (165).

22. According to Kate Flint, "Lord Castlereagh (1769–1822) [was] a politician considered oppressive by the working classes and by radicals, especially because of his role in suppressing the open-air meeting held on 16 August 1819 on Peterloo Fields, Manchester, in favour of Parliamentary reform. As a result of the charge on the meeting by cavalry and yeomanry, about eleven people were killed and some six hundred injured" (notes 312, fn 1).

23. If the union functions as one of the novel's "family-society metaphor[s]," then it, like the other socio-familial tropes, must succumb to the same faltering "metaphoricality" that plagues *Hard Times* as a whole, namely, that "metaphors often break down or reveal themselves to be pure illusions, mere shows that conceal (and often ill-conceal) seamy actualities" (Gallagher 149, 166, 160). Slackbridge's diatribe contains an intolerance that actually threatens working-class solidarity since fear, and not loyalty, becomes the driving force behind membership. See Wainwright's comment that "Stephen's experiences highlight the costs of solidarity when unity is obtained through conformist bigotry" (173).

24. For example, Stephen represents "emotional transcendence in self-sacrifice" based on "his loyalty to Rachael" and "his religious sentiments" (Gallagher 152); he is a "saint and martyr, dialect spokesman for religious morality" (Gardner 143); he is "in keeping with their religious beliefs" when he "vow[s] not to join the union" (Hill 120); he is true to "his principles" and "has promised not to [join the union]: nothing else" (Pittock 179); he "maintains a higher [nondescript] loyalty to Rachael" (Cowles 83); he is "a scapegoat" that "the novelist will raise up in order to shame all those who have scorned him—and the readers of the novel as well—into reconcilement of their differences" (Welsh 163); he illustrates that "working-class suffering is an essential and permanent feature of the social order" (Sanders 324); he underscores "the need to close the rift between classes in mid-Victorian England" (Friedman 260); he symbolizes the "repudiation of *laissez-faire*" practices (Shaw 339); he marks Dickens's opposition "to any change in the political and economic structure of society" (Lodge, *Language* 156); he "refuse[s] to join the union because of a mysterious and

apparently meaningless promise'' (Lodge, *Language* 310, fn 13); he ''represents nothing at all; he is a mere model of meekness'' (Gissing 333); he is associated with ''wanton and sadistic sentimentality'' in ''a wholly inadequate—indeed a thoroughly false—moral'' (Barnard 376); he constitutes ''one of the flaws in the novel'' because he fails ''to explain his reason for not joining the union, except for a passing reference to a mysterious 'promise' '' (Himmelfarb, *The Idea of Poverty* 479).

25. The triangulation would appear as follows, with Sissy Jupe functioning as a mediating agency on Gradgrind's behalf. Tom's reification is registered in his outrageous ''comic livery'' (283; bk. 3, ch. 7) while Bitzer's devotion as a student of Utilitarianism has subsequently turned him into Gradgrind's rival. Tom Sr. models the ''wisdom of the Heart'' (226; bk. 3, ch.1) but also serves as an obstacle to the execution of justice.

Thomas Gradgrind (*M*)

△

Bitzer (*S*)   Tom Jr. (*O*)

WORKS CITED

Ackroyd, Peter. *Dickens.* New York: HarperCollins, 1990.

Allingham, Philip V. ''Theme, Form, and the Naming of Names in *Hard Times For These Times.*'' *The Dickensian* 87.1 (Spring 1991): 17–31.

Baird, John. ''Divorce and Matrimonal Causes: An Aspect of *Hard Times.*'' *Victorian Studies* 20 (1977): 401–12.

Barnard, Robert. ''Imagery and Theme in Hard Times.'' *The Norton Critical Edition of Hard Times.* Ed. George Ford and Sylvère Monod. 2nd ed. New York: Norton, 1990. 367–79.

Brantlinger, Patrick. ''Dickens and the Factories.'' *Nineteenth-Century Fiction* 21 (1971): 270–85.

Briggs, Asa. *Victorian People: A Reassessment of Persons and Themes 1851–1867.* Chicago: U of Chicago, 1955.

Butterworth, R. D. ''Dickens the Journalist: The Preston Strike and 'On Strike.' '' *The Dickensian* 89.2 (Summer 1993): 129–38.

Carlyle, Thomas. *Past and Present.* Ed. Richard D. Altick. 1843. Boston: Houghton Mifflin, 1965.

Cowles, David L. "Having It Both Ways: Gender and Paradox in *Hard Times.*" *Dickens Quarterly* 8.2 (June 1991): 79–84.

Deane, Phyllis. *The First Industrial Revolution.* Cambridge: Cambridge UP, 1965.

Dickens, Charles. *Hard Times: For These Times.* 1854. New York: Penguin, 1995.

"Dressed in Simplicity." Tottenham Quaker Meeting (Religious Society of Friends). Google. June 10, 2003. <http://www.nanning.nildram.co.uk/quakers/history/Forsters007>

Edgecombe, Rodney Stenning. "*Hard Times* and the Moral Fable." *Dickens Quarterly* 18.4 (Dec. 2001): 186–201.

Fielding, K.J. and Anne Smith. "*Hard Times* and the Factory Controversy." *Dickens Centennial Essays.* Ed. Ada Nisbet and Blake Nevius. Berkeley: U of California P, 1971. 22–45.

Flint, Kate. Introduction. *Hard Times.* By Charles Dickens. New York: Penguin, 1995. xi-xxxiii.

———. Notes. *Hard Times.* By Charles Dickens. New York: Penguin, 1995. 299–319.

Ford, George, and Sylvère Monod, ed.s. *The Norton Critical Edition of Hard Times.* 2nd ed., New York: Norton, 1990.

"Forster, William Edward." *Columbia Encyclopedia.* Academic Search Premier. October 10, 2003. <http://web18.epnet.com/citation>

Fowler, Roger. "Modes of Speech in *Hard Times.*" *The Norton Critical Edition of Hard Times.* Ed. George Ford and Sylvère Monod. 2nd ed. New York: Norton, 1990. 392–401.

Friedman, Stanley. "Sad Stephen and Troubled Louisa: Paired Protagonists in *Hard Times.*" *Dickens Quarterly* 7.2 (June 1990): 254–62.

Gallagher, Catherine. *The Industrial Reformation of English Fiction: Social Discourse and Narrative Form, 1832–1867.* Chicago: U of Chicago P, 1985.

Gardner, Joseph H. "Dickens's Dystopian Metacomedy: *Hard Times*, Morals, and Religion." *The Victorian Comic Spirit: New Perspectives.* Ed. Jennifer A. Wagner-Lawler. Brookfield: Ashgate, 2000. 141–52.

Girard, René. *Deceit, Desire, and the Novel: Self and Other in Literary Structure.* Trans. Yvonne Freccero. Baltimore: Johns Hopkins UP, 1965.

Hancher, Michael. "Tenniel's Allegorical Cartoons." *The Telling Image: Explorations in the Emblem.* Ed. Ayers L. Bagley, Edward M. Griffin, and Austin J. McLean. New York: AMS Press, 1996. 139–70.

Hill, Nancy K. *A Reformer's Art: Dickens' Picturesque and Grotesque Imagery*. Athens: Ohio UP, 1981.

Himmelfarb, Gertrude. *The De-Moralization of Society: From Victorian Virtues to Modern Values*. New York: Knopf, 1995.

———. *The Idea of Poverty: England in the Early Industrial Age*. New York: Random House, 1983.

Johnson, Edgar. *Charles Dickens: His Tragedy and Triumph*. 1952. New York: Penguin, rev. and abridged 1986.

Keating, P. J. *The Working Classes in Victorian Fiction*. London: Routledge & Kegan Paul, 1971.

Kunzle, David. "The First Ally Sloper: The Earliest Popular Cartoon Character as a Satire on the Victorian Work Ethic." *Oxford Art Journal*. 8.1 (1985): 40–48.

Lampard, Ron. "The New Church in *Hard Times*." *The Dickensian* 93.2 (Summer 1997): 109–15.

Leavis, F. R. *The Great Tradition: George Eliot, Henry James, Joseph Conrad*. 1948. Harmondsworth: Penguin, 1962.

Lodge, David. "How Successful is *Hard Times*?" *The Norton Critical Edition of Hard Times*. Ed. George Ford and Sylvère Monod. 2nd ed. New York: Norton, 1990. 381–89.

———. *The Language of Fiction: Essays in Criticism and Verbal Analysis of the English Novel*. London: Routledge, 2002.

Malone, Cynthia Northcutt. "Surveillance and Discipline in *Hard Times*." *Readings on Hard Times*. Ed. Jill Karson. San Diego: Greenhaven Press, 2002. 77–87.

Marcus, Steven. *Engels, Manchester, and the Working Class*. 1974. New York: Norton, 1985.

"Pictures of the Working-Man at the Royal Westminster Exhibition." *Punch*. 20 May 1865: 202, 205.

Pittock, Malcolm. "*Hard Times* Once More." *Readings on Hard Times*. Ed. Jill Karson. San Diego: Greenhaven Press, 2002. 175–94.

Poovey, Mary. "The Structure of Anxiety in Political Economy and *Hard Times*." *Knowing the Past: Victorian Literature and Culture*. Ed. Suzy Anger. London: Cornell UP, 2001. 151–71.

Retan, Katherine. "Lower-Class Angels in the Middle-Class House: The Domestic Woman's 'Progress' in *Hard Times* and *Ruth*." *Dickens Studies Annual*. 23 (1994): 183–204.

Ruis. *Marx for Beginners*. Trans. Richard Appignanesi. New York: Pantheon, 1976.

Sanders, Mike. "Manufacturing Accident: Industrialism and the Worker's Body in Early Victorian Fiction." *Victorian Literature and Culture* (2000): 313–29.

Schor, Hilary. "Novels of the 1850s: *Hard Times, Little Dorrit*, and *A Tale of Two Cities*." *The Cambridge Companion to Charles Dickens*. Ed. John O. Jordan. Cambridge: Cambridge UP. 2001. 64–77.

Shaw, Bernard. "*Hard Times*." *The Norton Critical Edition of Hard Times*. Ed. George Ford and Sylvère Monod. 2nd ed. New York: Norton, 1990. 333–40.

Stiltner, Barry. "*Hard Times*: The Disciplinary City." *Dickens Studies Annual*. 30 (2001): 193–213.

Tenniel, John. Cartoon. "The Working-Man, From the Royal Westminster Exhibition." *Punch*. 20 May 1865: 203.

Thomas, Deborah. *Hard Times: A Reader's Companion*. New York: Twayne, 1997.

Thoreau, Henry David. *Walden and Civil Disobedience*. Ed. Sherman Paul. Boston: Houghton Mifflin, 1960.

Trezise, Simon David. "The Making of Dickens: The Evolution of Marxist Criticism." *Dickens Quarterly* 11.3 (Sept. 1994): 127–37.

Welsh, Alexander. *Dickens Redressed: The Art of Bleak House and Hard Times*. New Haven: Yale UP, 2000.

Wainwright, Valerie L. "On Goods, Virtues, and *Hard Times*." *Dickens Studies Annual* 26 (1998): 169–86.

Dickens and Naming

John R. Reed

Charles Dickens was perfectly aware of the power of names and nam-
ing. Within his fiction, some characters have the power of naming oth-
ers, something that Dickens calls attention to as potentially dangerous.
Characteristic of Dickens's narratives is his alluding to this power and
to the act of naming itself. Through this artistic pointing to one of his
most distinctive traits, Dickens also reveals the ultimate power he re-
tains over his text and indicates his distance from the realist approach
to storytelling.

Names are important in literature. Although in serious literature names tend
to be non-directive until characters's natures are manifested through actions,
in many cases a name itself defines a character's nature or hints at it. Especially in comic literature, we willingly accept names that typify. We accept
them as a writer's shorthand, a way of conveying quickly and without complication the basic "humor" of his character. But we tend also to accept this
shorthand passively, without considering the immense power that such naming confers upon the writer. In this essay, I wish to explore the ways in which
Dickens exploits a wide range of possibilities in the naming of characters as
a means of sequestering the force of his narratives to his own authority, a
gesture at odds with the conventions of realism which seek to create the
illusion of transparent or "natural" narrative. Moreover, it is my contention
that he purposely uses names to call attention to his own performance as the
force behind naming both within and beyond the diegesis, the fictional world
created by the narrative.[1]

Dickens Studies Annual, Volume 36, Copyright © 2005 by AMS Press, Inc. All
rights reserved.

This power shows itself in many types of fiction, sometimes in quite subtle ways. At one point in Proust's *Remembrance of Things Past*, for example, Marcel refers to Rachel as "Rachel when from the Lord," a puzzling denomination for the general reader. J. Hillis Miller remarks that this is "a striking example within the novel itself of naming as a sovereign speech act making or remaking the one who is named" (*Speech Acts* 207). Miller emphasizes that, while Marcel's act of naming is part of the diegesis, it is actually Proust, not his character, who wishes to *convey* the multiple significances of the allusive name. If it were his character who wished to transmit this information, Proust would presumably have confirmed or explained Marcel's reason for employing this name. Instead, it remains a mystery to all but the initiate, though it is possible that Proust felt the allusion to Jacques Halévy's opera *La juive* (*The Jewess* [1835]) would be evident to his contemporaries.[2] Whatever the case, it is possible to make a distinction between the author's power to name and the significance of the act of naming within the diegesis, which, as Miller brilliantly demonstrates, requires an energetic intertextual exercise on the part of the reader.

Miller calls naming a "sovereign speech act," thereby himself indirectly alluding to the sovereignty granted to Adam and Eve over Eden, when God assigned them the privilege of naming the beings and objects of their world. Naming is widely understood to embody power in language. Few speech acts have more sustained effect, with the exception of such dramatic utterances as "Off with his head!" and the like. Some women influenced by feminist activism from the middle of the twentieth century acknowledged the power of naming by refusing to yield the surname they were born with to take that of a husband, despite the fact that both names usually came to them from men. Stage names, pseudonyms, and aliases also indicate a strong human impulse to appropriate the power of naming to oneself. What concerns me in this essay, beyond a general interest in Charles Dickens's practice of naming in his fiction, is the distinction hinted at, but not explored in depth in Miller's comments on Proust, between the author's and the narrator's or character's acts of naming.

Charles Dickens was acutely aware of the power of naming both within his narratives, as exercised by his characters or his narrators, and on his own part as author. From the beginning of his career, Dickens was deeply involved with and interested in the act of naming.[3] He began his writing career, as we all know, under a false name as Boz and relished such self-naming as The Inimitable and the Sparkler of Albion. But from the *Sketches* onward, he was conscious of the resonances of names, most often in the early works for their comic qualities, a feature he shared with and borrowed from the numerous comic writers of his own and earlier times. Jingle aptly suggests the garrulousness of that character, as Winkle, Tupman, and less effectively, Snodgrass suggest the respective characters of these humorous sidekicks. Pickwick itself is a comical name. Similarly, names that carry an allegorical quality were familiar in literary tradition and often used by some of Dickens's favorite writers. Henry Fielding's Squire Allworthy is a good example. Dickens's contemporary and friend Captain Frederick Marryat was in the habit of naming his protagonists according to their supposed or actual attributes, such as Peter Simple, Jacob Faithful, Masterman Ready, and Jack Easy.

Often the names Dickens selects have connotative value only, as with Quilp, a name that sounds both foolish and nasty. Other names suggest a character trait as with Miss Nipper and Mrs. MacStinger in *Dombey and Son*. Still others have associational power, as with Solomon Gills and Captain Cuttle, both connected to maritime activities. But some names also carry denotative power, as with Bradley Headstone, whose name was first tried in Dickens's notes as Amos Headstone or Deadstone, before becoming Bradley Deadstone and finally Headstone.[4] To thrust home his point, Dickens has Rogue Riderhood remark on the churchyard associations of the name. Michael Cotsell observes the resemblance of Fascination Fledgeby's name to "fledgling" (150). And, of course, there are the transparent Veneerings. There are even those well-known instances where Dickens directly borrowed or alluded satirically to real names, as he did with Fagin in *Oliver Twist*. All of these acts of naming by Dickens as author are significant. However, I am particularly interested in those instances where characters call attention to the act of naming and, in doing so, signal Dickens's own ultimate authority as the source of all such naming.

Garrett Stewart offers a good example of Dickens's complicated naming activity as early as *The Old Curiosity Shop*. Dick Swiveller achieves a kind of poetic apotheosis when he names the Brasses's anonymous servant girl the Marchioness. As Stewart puts it, he effectively brings the girl into being, a beingness that will be crucial to his recovery from illness and to his achieving a degree of success in life. But, Stewart continues, if Dick is something of a wordmaster and takes to himself the privilege of naming, he is himself, through Dickens's authority to name him, an example of the complex force that names can suggest:

> Many have noted the importance of the name "Dick," one syllable of his author's last name, as a clue to the inherence in this comic character of at least a part of the author's own personality, one phase of his artistic temperament. Further, the family pronunciation of Sam's last name, "Veller," is also contained in Dick's own surname. And there is surely something in "Swiveller" that catches his directionless vitality, that willingness to take the prevailing wind which often makes him seem as though he is merely going in circles. But Dick not only swivels, he seeks; he himself wonders about his first name in connection with that prototypical Richard who became Lord Mayor of London.

"Perhaps the bells might strike up 'Turn again, Swiveller, Lord Mayor of London.' Whittington's name was Dick." (105–06)

Stewart demonstrates the possible connections between Dickens and his character, the possible echoes between characters from different books, and the use of traditional lore to give weight to characters. The most significant attribute of this instance is its dual function: while it characterizes Dick, it also highlights the function of his name as a turner or swiveller. So, while Dick is focusing on his first name, Dickens is showing us the substance of his last name and hinting proleptically at Dick's ultimate turning from his trivial existence to a purposeful life.[5]

Stewart also points to some functions of naming in *Our Mutual Friend*. Again, it is characteristic for characters to manifest their own sense of superiority by naming others. So Eugene feels free to refer to Riah as "Mr. Aaron" and "Patriarch," claiming that he does so in a complimentary fashion, although, for the reader, his taking liberties with the Jew's name can be seen as a form of appropriation (Stewart 212). More telling is Stewart's example of self-naming in Jenny Wren. "Fanny Cleaver," he writes, "has bestowed upon herself a liberating pseudonym, a *nom de plumage* whose assonant lift is meant to carry her fancy above the sordidness of her cares and labors" (205). Jenny sometimes smells flowers and hears songbirds that recall her dream of angelic visitors, and Stewart notes that "Jenny Wren has named herself a songbird—developing an eye as 'bright and watchful as the bird's whose name she had taken (2:11)—and has grown herself a bower" (209). Jenny has consciously renamed herself with a view to redemption, or at least removal from her sordid reality. Stewart shrewdly remarks that, "Like Dickens himself, Jenny Wren is also a tireless coiner of names ironic and otherwise" for others (204). However, Stewart does not directly note that it is Dickens who named this character Fanny Cleaver, whose ironic tongue is so sharp and cutting. Much as Jenny tries to wrest command of her character from her creator, he remains in control of her sardonic nature. His name for her—Cleaver—still fits. Moreover, it is also Dickens who has permitted Fanny to choose the name Jenny Wren, which has its ironies for her, but perhaps others for Dickens himself.[6]

David Copperfield offers a clear and simple example of the power of naming in atmosphere of coercion within its diegesis.[7] When Mr. Murdstone wants to warn his associates to be prudent in their speech around the young David, he says someone is very sharp, identifying this someone as "Brooks of Sheffield," an allusion to the city of Sheffield's reputation for good cutlery.[8] Murdstone's humor here bears a surprising resemblance to some of Dickens's own metaphorical and metonymic naming techniques. Steerforth names David "Daisy," to indicate his innocence as well as his subjugation to Steerforth himself. In neither instance does David realize that the act of denomination is belittling and manipulative. Aunt Betsey renames David with her own name Trotwood as a mark of her command over him, just as Dora's nickname for him, Doady, signifies possession. Harry Stone observes that the new name Trotwood also signals a new phase in David's life ("Names" 193). The same could be said of Dora's nickname for David. David says that Doady is Dora's "corruption of David," an ambiguous statement. Dora is not a wise choice as a partner for a young man like David, and hence she does represent a "corruption" of his true course in life.[9] Within the narrative, therefore, it is clear that the act of naming involves an assumption of power over the person named (Penguin 667). Oddly enough, David, who begins his career as a story-teller early, seldom names other people in this way.

Personal names are intriguing in *David Copperfield* in various ways, one of which is the way they intimate rather than declare authorial intention. It is interesting how some of the important names in the novel suggest a natural setting—Copper*field*, Trot*wood*, Wick*field*, Murd*stone*. Arguably, these names suggest a pastoral quality in *Copperfield* that is more persistent than in most of Dickens's novels. In other novels, names of this sort also indicate characters who ultimately figure positively in their stories, such as *Woodcourt* and Light*wood*, whereas characters with names like Murd*stone* and Small*weed* suggest the unappealing aspects of the natural world. Even David's birthplace, Blunderstone, suggests the same outdoor atmosphere, though the "blunder" in the word implies error and misfortune and is therefore not pleasantly combined with the hard suggestions of "stone." The name is also a forecast of Clara Copperfield's second husband, the cruel Mr. Murdstone, whose name Betsey Trotwood confuses when she complains that David's mother "goes and marries a Murderer—or a man with a name like it" (Penguin 253). In passages such as this, Dickens calls attention to his own authority in the act of naming. Harry Stone indicates that Dickens's selection of the name Murdstone combines ideas of murder and hardness with equal emphasis and openness, but also shows how the name connects him with David's real father by way of its allusion to the father's gravestone ("Names" 194–95). Names including w's often but not always (Sam Weller is a prominent exception, though he would have pronounced his name "Veller") suggest behavioral handicaps and include most notably Mr. Wilkins Micawber, but also Mr. Wickfield, and both Dora Spenlow and her father. Dickens also tries out a pattern he later uses effectively in *Great Expectations* by contrasting names with the same number of letters, though with different connotative sounds. Thus, the steady and alert Mr. Peggotty, is set against the glum and morose Mrs. Gummidge. More significant, perhaps, are the names of David's friendly companion and Steerforth's evil servant. Though Micawber's name may suggest weakness, its open vowels and soft consonants also imply a kindly, accommodating nature, whereas Littimer's pinched vowels and pointy consonants hint at a prickly, unappealing character.[10] Several characters' names are ambiguous. Hence, Steerforth itself calls up heroic possibilities, but these possibilities are, as we discover by the end of the novel, misapplied. Tommy Traddles's name is both comic and balanced, and it is the combination of a humorous and an industrious character that brings him success in life.

What interests me in *Copperfield* is that it is Dickens, not his first-person narrator, who is in charge of this naming. The water imagery of this novel supports a complex pattern of danger, salvation, and death. Steerforth's name evokes the image of a sea captain, but this "hero" corrupts Little Em'ly and carries her off in his sailing vessel, a reversal of the ideal of the rescue at sea. And Steerforth dies retributively in both literal and metaphorical shipwreck. Dickens reinforces the moral design of his novel by showing the morally compassless Steerforth coming to misfortune through the abuse of his considerable powers.[11] By contrast, Peggotty keeps an ark that has come to rest not on Ararat, but the Yarmouth sands, where he shelters his extended family, including the appropriately named Ham, named after a son of the original ark owner, Noah. Ultimately, it is a ship that will carry the Micawbers, Em'ly, and Martha to a new world of opportunity in Australia. Dickens, not his characters, links appropriate names to a water-related theme by way of obliging his readers to interpret his narrative in the manner he directs, not in some capricious reading of their own. This aim on his part might be misguided, given the researches of modern critics, especially those employing what is known as reader-response criticism, but there is little doubt in my mind that this was his purpose.[12]

Dickens himself took delight in naming his characters, from the simplest and most theatrical to more subtle and complicated instances, but it is also interesting to observe the ways in which he delegates the authority for naming to his third-person and first-person narrators. Esther Summerson and David Copperfield tend not to be big namers, whereas third-person narrators name as freely as Dickens himself, if any distinction is to be made between author and narrator. The ironic voice of the narrator of *Our Mutual Friend* even dispenses with proper names, to call a few of the stylized characters Boots and Brewer, and, in a much slyer manner, to refer to the Veneerings' servant as the Analytical Chemist.

Dickens was fully aware of what one might call the sins of naming. Michael Ragussis has shown the discordance between a person's or place's name and actual nature. In fact, he indicates that this discordance is part of a larger problem with language itself in *Bleak House*, arguing that "language is London's communicative/communicable disease" (263). Even Esther Summerson's apparently positive name is misleading; unlike other characters who are robbed of histories by their names, "it is not the name itself that robs her: it is the absence of a name" (257). But if Dickens offered numerous indications about the perils involved with naming, he also offered as many indications of his own authority and control where naming was concerned, and Ragussis, without making this case, gives an appropriate instance. Hawdon, Esther's unknown father, is referred to in several ways: the Captain, Nemo (his own alias), Our Dear Brother (the narrator's ironic term), and Nimrod, Mrs. Snagsby's misunderstanding of Nemo. But, as Ragussis demonstrates, this incorrect name referring to the mighty hunter of the Old Testament nonetheless connects Hawdon to the theme of confused language indicated by references to the tower of Babel and carried out in the thematic network of language as confusion in "Dickens's brilliant use of 'the great wilderness of London' (xlviii, 583), that 'immense desert of law-hand' (xlvii, 567), as the Old Testament desert, but with this difference: the Law of God, the divine Word, has itself degenerated into babel, and the Father has become the tyrannous, and dead, Pharaoh" (262). Thus, while confusion might reign within the diegesis, and names not connect signified and signifier, Dickens makes certain that his story retains its tightly-woven meaning and even opens up occasional windows for readers alert enough to draw the threads together.

Sometimes it might appear that Dickens or his narrator has slipped up. Why, for example, would an author name his titular character Chuzzlewit? Such a name suggests an inferior, comic character—much more so than Pickwick, which is simply playful. Dickens did not come to the name easily, but considered several others, including Sweezlewag, Sweezlebach, Sweezleden, Chuzzletoe, and the favored Chuzzlewig. Only at the last stage did it become Chuzzlewit, certainly far the best of these names. But why such a pejorative name for the book's hero? The full early versions of the book's title provide the clue to an answer, for they indicate that this is not merely the story of young Martin, but forms "a complete key to The House of Chuzzlewig" (Stone, Notes 33). A glance at the novel's opening paragraph reveals that the so-called House of Chuzzlewit is the human race, that traces its heritage back to Adam and Eve. Hence, the Chuzzlewit family is all of us; we are all confused and selfish. And lest anyone think that this is a late interpretation, it is necessary only to observe that from Dickens's earliest notes for the novel, he wrote his intention that for the readers of this novel "Your homes the scene. Yourselves the actors here" (Stone, Notes 31).

The power to name is enormously significant, though it also permits an illusion of command.[13] A notable example of this is Pip in *Great Expectations*, who names himself by a slip of the tongue. This novel is also an interesting exception to the division between the non-naming first-person and the naming third-person narrators of Dickens's novels. Pip is a notable example of the importance of naming, if for no other reason than because Dickens calls such attention to this speech act at the very outset of his novel, when his protagonist first becomes conscious of his own being. This sovereign speech act, however, is reported to us in the midst of much confusion on Pip's part, which includes his misunderstanding of what is written about his dead parents and siblings on their cemetery markers, and then the perturbation prompted by Magwitch's account of his bloodthirsty partner. It could be said that Pip has *misnamed* himself, since he has shrunk himself from the complete Philip Pirrip to the diminutive Pip. From this point of view, one might conclude that Pip lives out his early career under a false name. As is frequently the case in Dickens's later fiction, he offers a redundancy of clues for the reader to grasp his full intentions, if not while reading, then when the reading is complete and all information is in. One such clue about Pip and names is in the brief episode when the young and still largely illiterate Pip writes a letter for Joe in which he shortens Joe's name to JO, an act of abbreviation resembling the shortening of his own name and hinting at his misvaluing of the man Joe as well, though interestingly, Joe can recognize his name when he sees Pip's written JO, though he is otherwise no reader (75).

Appropriately, Pip's false name mirrors the falseness of his situation. His great expectations are to become a wealthy gentleman and Estella's husband, though in reality he will become an overseas merchant who is single when the narrative ends. Pip's misnaming of himself is thus consistent with the illusory life he leads through most of the narrative. By mistakenly assuming control of his own name, he loses command of his actual nature, accepting a form of secular destiny instead of forging his own fate. The verb "to forge" stems from the Old French *forgier*, derived from the Latin *fabricare*, to make or fashion. There are many modes of making, some true and some false, though *forge* suggests arduous creation. But to forge money is to be so false as to constitute criminality. Whereas Joe is true to the right purpose of forging, Pip forges an identity which he passes off as real in the world around him, despite the fact that several characters see through this specious form of specie, from Biddy to Trabb's boy to Dolge Orlick. The latter names Pip "wolf," a displacement of Pip's identity, but not inexplicable from Orlick's point of view, to whom Pip has not been kind. There are many reasons for Pip's pervading sense of guilt and association with criminality, not the least of which is that he is living an alias. I am myself here playing with words to a specific end. The Forge is one of the most important place names in *Great Expectations,* and it carries the weight of many kinds of making because it is here that the core mystery of the plot is worked into shape, a fact that Dickens signals throughout the narrative by the recurring allusions to equipment associated with the Forge—a file, manacles, and chains.

Herbert Pocket changes Pip's name, preferring to call him Handel because of that musician's well-known composition "The Harmonious Blacksmith." A blacksmith is a man of physical power who can shape what is otherwise resistant to change through his mastery of the forge. Joe is true to the simple identity he did not make, but over which he takes control. Ceding domestic power to his wife is a sign of his real authority. Only those who hold power can lease it to others. No one offers to call Joe by anything but his given names. But by renaming Pip Handel, Herbert displaces Pip from his false identity without providing him with a true one, unlike the renamings of David Copperfield. Not he, but Dickens is calling attention to the parallel between Handel's translation of the rough work of the blacksmith into art and Pip's transformation from a blacksmith in fact into a role-playing gentleman. It is, after all, Herbert's father who has the task of coining this new gentleman. So Dickens's allusiveness, put in the mouth of Herbert as a thing of little significance, is actually a clue to the correct understanding of the entire novel. This name game comes full circle when, near the close of the novel, we learn that Joe and Biddy's child has been named Pip. This will be his proper name and his proper identity to fulfill. The original Pip has presumably by this time achieved his true identity, which permits him to become the narrator of his own history; presumably he is now Philip Pirrip again and not that false construction known as Pip. Although in Dickens's original ending of the novel Estella calls Pip by that name, in the published ending she does not.

Naming plays an important part throughout *Great Expectations*. Some names are neutral, as is Joe Gargery's. Others intend a comic sound, as with the guests gathered at the Gargery home—Wopsle, Hubble, and especially Pumblechook. Other names bear varying degrees of more intense meaning. Abel Magwitch links an edenic name with suggestions of sorcery and wicked power.[14] Dolge Orlick, with its rolling vowels, possibly echoes the moroseness of its owner. Other names similarly play with sounds that are compatible with the characters they name, such as Drummle and Startop. A minor character, the Pockets' neighbor is clearly skewered by being named Mrs. Coiler. But important characters are similarly well defined. Estella suggests a stellar inaccessibility, an apt name considering Dickens's initial ending of the novel, in which Pip does not attain his female prize. More evident is the meaning of Miss Havisham's name, for her entire life is a sham. These are necessary, but unoriginal observations. What is interesting to me is that Dickens in this novel gives Pip, a first-person narrator, a tendency to naming that resembles that of his third-person narrators. Pip the narrator has not named the characters mentioned above, but Pip the subject of the narration does rename Pepper, his unnecessary servant, as the Avenger. And something fairly complex is going on with the narrative when this happens. Pip the narrator has used many images of entanglement, such as golden chains and the reappearing file, to indicate a pattern of entrapment in Pip's career, but that is because he is narrating the account after the important events have occurred and have become a story that can be woven together with a clear teleological purpose.

But Pip the subject of narration creates the minatory name for his servant while he is in the midst of that story, before it even is a story. Yet he fulfills Dickens's need to retain control of his narrative by putting in place the allusive and connotative blocks that constitute the edifice of his narrative. It is Dickens, too, who gives the narrating Pip his powers of metaphor.

Dickens exploits his naming game best in this novel with Jaggers and his clerk, Wemmick. While at first the two seem aptly paired—both secretive and solitary and devoted to the business of the law—in fact, they are eventually distinguished from one another. Their names make this distinction precisely evident. Jaggers is as jagged and rough a name as one might wish for with its harsh vowels and consonants. Wemmick, by contrast, is almost a mellifluous name with its softened consonants, though the hard consonant at the end of the name might signal a connection to Jaggers. More intriguing is that the two names align perfectly, each consisting of seven letters with contrasting consonants and vowels matching exactly, a precise development of examples I gave earlier from *David Copperfield*. There is no accident in this kind of naming. Moreover, the place names associated with both men have a similar effect. Little Britain, though a real place, nonetheless has a spikey quality that makes it sound unattractive, whereas Walworth has a gentle, inviting tonality. These contrasting names, both of persons and of place, show what power Dickens could convey through his naming, for entire personalities and contexts are evoked in these names before any actions flesh them out. In some ways, they are Dickens's clues to his readers about how to receive each of his fictional personalities. We know before the secret is out that Wemmick is a better man than he seems. Walworth and Walworth sentiments are already implied in his name.

In her study of realism, *All is True*, Lilian R. Furst identifies the eighteenth century as the period when location and actual place became important to fiction. Previously places bore symbolic and allegorical significance. "Only in the late eighteenth and early nineteenth centuries does fiction begin to develop environment as a matrix in which character is formed, and with this, the close articulation of places and people" (98). At the end of the eighteenth century, the romantic enthusiasm for landscape combines with curiosity about practical industrial matters and details of social organization. "The stark symbolism of allegory combines with the digressive prolixity of travel writing to produce the technique of detailed and cumulative notation of place normally associated with realism" (98). Furst notes that since Ian Watt's *The Rise of the Novel*, particularity of place has been considered a hallmark of realism. Because place names in fiction can and often do refer to real sites, they "can act as a bridge of continuity, along which readers may move from one sphere to the other without becoming conscious of the transition" (102). This easy flow between fiction and reality enhances the illusion of transparency to which realism aspires.

Here again, Dickens, though a master at particularity, does not employ his details for the same strategic ends as realism. Even with place names he often tries to evoke an emotional response, whether positive in a place like Dingley Dell, or negative, with the allegorically named Dotheboys Hall or Pocket Breaches, the town for which Veneering becomes a Member of Parliament. The first is comprehensible even by a twenty-first-century American student; the second requires some historical information. The name suggests a pocket borough—one controlled by a single individual or family, and hence a certainty for a favored parliamentary candidate. That such favor often involved cash payment is suggested by the name Dickens chose for the town, but even more by the names he listed in his mems, but then discarded—Ticklepocket and Twitchpocket.[15] If his characters exert or try to exert control over their environment and other characters through assuming the power to rename, Dickens himself overtly claims a similar authority through the reverberating significance of the names he gives to persons and things.[16] But Dickens also extends his own yen for naming places to his characters. Not many seriously realistic novelists would have their characters offer place names such as Bleak House, Satis House, or the Golden Bower. But Dickens does not want to be a realist in the accepted sense of that term. Richard Lettis puts the matter well.

> Above all, he thought that writing should enable the reader to see the essential affirmative "truth" of life—this was for him the best that writing could achieve. He disliked the obvious, and approved always of subtlety, but knew that judicious use of the commonplace, of carefully-selected detail, could bring reality to a story—but it must always be the kind of reality he found in drama: "wonderful reality"—the world as we know it, but "polished by art" until it assumed values not felt in the dull settled world itself. For him reality was not what it was to the realists; it was neither commonplace as in Howells nor sordid as in so many others. (*Dickens* 60–61)

I would add that Dickens wanted a wonderful reality not only polished by art, but specifically by the art of Charles Dickens.

When Dickens names a voting town Eatanswill, he is thumbing his nose at what was to become the realist convention because he wants his audience to be conscious of the author as a performer, as master of the sovereign act of naming.[17] When he confers that power upon his narrators and characters, he means to show his audience how important that power of naming is and how it remains ultimately the province of the author who is permitting his characters to name others and even themselves. But he also calls attention to the *sins* of naming in characters like Steerforth or Murdstone, and the *mistake* of naming in Pip. By telling the stories of those who do not understand how sovereign the act of naming is, Dickens reinforces his own power by using that act correctly and to its proper end.

NOTES

1. S. D. Powell calls attention to the well-established tradition of interest in Dickens's naming of characters in a long footnote, listing Elizabeth Hope Gordon as among the first to attempt to categorize those names (63).
2. Miller observes that this allusion to Halevy's aria compounds a pattern of other references to Jewishness and antisemitism pervasive in Proust's narrative.
3. Harry Stone examines the intricacies of Dickens's practicing of naming and calls it a "carefully calculated and artfully articulated system that gives up its secrets only to the initiate" ("Name" 193). It is possible that naming had greater resonance in the nineteenth century than it does today, since naming was recognized as part of formal church practice. Michael Cotsell remarks in reference to a passage in *Our Mutual Friend* that the second question in the Catechism of the Church of England is Who gave you this Name, for which the answer is: "My Godfathers and Godmothers in my Baptism; wherein I was made a member of Christ, the child of God, and an inheritor of the kingdom of heaven" (173). The narrator makes direct reference to this situation in chapter 40 of *Bleak House*, when he notes that on the occasion of Woolwich's last birthday, "Mr. Bagnet certainly did, after observing on his growth and general advancement, proceed, in a moment of profound reflection on the changes wrought by time, to examine him in the catechism; accomplishing with extreme accuracy the questions number one and two, What is your name? And Who gave you that name? But there failing in the exact precision of his memory, and substituting for number three, the question And how do you like that name?" (Oxford 666).
4. Harry Stone examines the significance of Headstone's name in some detail ("Name" 198ff). Joel J. Brattin offers a detailed look at Headstone's name and more by way of a reading of Dickens's manuscript (147ff).
5. Viewing naming as an assertion of power is my suggestion, not Stewart's.
6. Michael Cotsell reminds us that Jenny Wren is a character out of nursery lore, notably as the partner of Robin Redbreast or Cock Robin. He reproduces a poem in which Jenny Wren falls sick and gets well, but is hostile to Robin Redbreast (140).
7. *David Copperfield* has attracted the most attention about naming among Dickens's novels. I refer here to two recent articles, one by S. D. Powell and one by Richard Lettis.
8. Richard Lettis says that Brooks is a conventional British alias ("Names" 75).
9. S. D. Powell has this to say about Dora's nickname for David:

> His willing acceptance of this name, however, and the narrator's refusal to criticize himself for it, should be an immediate tip-off that his attraction to Dora is wrongheaded, that the narrator recognizes, as we do that "Doady" represents a step back from the mature freedom of "Trotwood" and the family that bestowed that name.   (56–57)

10. Richard Lettis comments that nobody knows Littimer's Christian name ("Names" 71).

11. Harry Stone shows how Dickens fits Murdstone into a similar larger pattern.

> "The notes, therefore, not only show Dickens carefully fashioning the name 'Murdstone,' but shaping the name and controlling the attendant imagery (and the motifs that the name and the imagery embody) so that each enriches and illuminates the other"
>
> ("Name" 196).

12. I find J. Hillis Miller's reading of *Bleak House* compatible with my argument about Dickens's mode of incorporating his names into a larger network of imagery:

> *Bleak House* is properly allegorical, according to a definition of allegory as a temporal system of cross references among signs rather than as a spatial pattern of correspondence between signs and referents. Most people in the novel live without understanding their plight. The novel, on the other hand, gives the reader the information necessary to understand why the characters suffer, and at the same time the power to understand that the novel is fiction rather than mimesis. The novel calls attention to its own procedures and confesses to its own rhetoric, not only, for example, in the onomastic system of metaphorical names already discussed, but also in the insistent metaphors of the style throughout.
>
> (Introduction, 29)

13. Juliet McMaster observes an interesting pattern of naming in *The Old Curiosity Shop*. Whereas there is detailed naming in Quilp's side of the narrative, the naming is intentionally vague and general in Nell's, in keeping, she suggests, with the interests of a generalized allegorical fable (114). She also comments on Quilp's fascination with naming as an "almost fiendish device" (115).

14. Tom Lloyd examines some of the consequences of names in regard to Pip and Magwitch (104ff.).

15. Cotsell notes that Dickens was given to this kind of naming, especially for voting constituencies—the most memorable, perhaps, being the town of Eatanswill in *Pickwick Papers* (144). Judith Flynn offers an interesting examination of place-naming with the name of Cloisterham (passim).

16. McMaster, again, notes that place names are particular where associated with Quilp, but unspecific when associated with Nell (116). Dickens uses a far different approach in *Hard Times*, beginning with the appropriate Coketown for the name of its chief city.

17. Harry Stone does not highlight the difference between Dickens's aims in writing and those of the realists, but his description of those aims is highly compatible with my own:

> What then can we conclude from the process I have just been tracing? Simply this: that Dickens' names are quintessential embodiments of what one sees everywhere in his art, a fusion of the

wild, the portentous, and the fantastic with the rational and the everyday. His names, like his whispering houses, terrifying streets, primordial storms, and spell-casting witches are at once wildly expressionistic and improbable and profoundly real and ordinary. Dickens conveys with the same stroke the surface of things and the hidden springs of meaning. His world is discrete, tangible, and familiar, but also interconnected, fantastic, and mysterious.

("Name" 203)

WORKS CITED

Brattin, Joel J. "Dickens' Creation of Bradley Headstone," *Dickens Studies Annual* 14 (1985): 147–65.

Cotsell, Michael. *The Companion to* Our Mutual Friend. London: Allen & Unwin, 1986.

Dickens, Charles. *Bleak House*. London: Oxford UP, 1967.

———. *David Copperfield*. Harmondsworth: Penguin, 1983.

———. *Great Expectations*. London: Oxford UP, 1953.

———. The Old Curiosity Shop. London: Oxford UP, 1951.

———. *Our Mutual Friend*. London: Oxford UP, 1966.

Flynn, Judith. " 'Fugitive and Cloistered Virtue': Innocence and Evil in *Edwin Drood.*" *English Studies in Canada* 9:3 (Sept. 1983): 312–25.

Furst, Lilian R. *All is True: The Claims and Strategies of Realist Fiction*. Durham NC: Duke UP, 1995.

Lettis, Richard. *Dickens on Literature: A Continuing Study of His Aesthetic*. New York: AMS, 1990.

———. "The Names of David Copperfield." *Dickens Studies Annual* 31 (2002): 67–86.

Lloyd, Tom. *Crises of Realism: Representing Experience in the British Novel, 1816–1910*. Lewisburg, PA: Bucknell UP, 1997.

McMaster, Juliet. *Dickens the Designer*. Houndsmill, Basingstoke: Macmillan, 1987.

Miller, J. Hillis. "Introduction." *Bleak House*. Ed. Norman Page. Harmondsworth, Middlesex: Penguin, 1972. 11–34.

———. *Speech Acts in Literature*. Stanford: Stanford UP, 2001.

Powell, S. D. "The Subject of David Copperfield's Renaming and the Limits of Fiction," *Dickens Studies Annual* 31(2002): 47–66.

Ragussis, Michael. "The Ghostly Signs of Bleak House," *Nineteenth-Century Fiction* 34:3 (December 1979): 253–80.

Stewart, Garrett, *Dickens and the Trials of Imagination.* Cambridge: Harvard UP, 1974.

Stone, Harry, "What's in a Name: Fantasy and Calculation in Dickens." *Dickens Studies Annual* 14 (1985): 191–204.

———, ed. *Dickens's Working Notes for His Novels.* Chicago: U of Chicago P, 1987.

Novels by Literary Snobs: The Contentious Class-coding of Thackerayan Parody

Michael J. Flynn

In 1847 Thackeray and Dickens had the first of the quarrels which would periodically punctuate their relationship. John Forster had taken offense at Thackeray's series of parodies Novels by Eminent Hands; *Dickens acted as his second, and performed his part so zealously that he was still lecturing Thackeray about the series seven months after the quarrel had formally ended. What makes the episode puzzling is that neither Forster nor Dickens was among the authors Thackeray parodied. Why, then, their reaction? Joss Marsh's work on blasphemy has illustrated the fact that certain literary forms carried class connotations for Victorian readers. A look at "George de Barnwell," Thackeray's parody of* Eugene Aram, *will show that the quarrel arose because in 1847 parody carried two conflicting sets of such connotations. Thackeray was writing in a genteel tradition, in which parody was the pastime of university men; Dickens was reading in a very different tradition, in which it was the province of Grub Street hacks. It was a setback to Dickens's cherished hopes for the professionalization of literature to see the author of* Vanity Fair *behaving like such a hack, so he came down hard on Thackeray—and in so doing, cast a long shadow over their future relationship.*

In January 1847, William Makepeace Thackeray wrote to Albany Fonblanque about a new series he was starting for *Punch*. "The Snobs of England" had just about run its course, and Thackeray had decided to follow its general satires with more specific ones—parodies of the most popular novelists of the day. The new series commenced in April and ran throughout the year under the title "Punch's Prize Novelists"; it is now more commonly known as *Novels by Eminent Hands*, the title Thackeray gave it when it was republished in 1856 as part of his *Miscellanies*.[1] January 1847 had also seen the publication of the first installment of *Vanity Fair*, so the parodies were not the work uppermost on Thackeray's mind. But the *Fair* was his first full-length novel, the first work published under his own name, and it was hardly ensured of success; the *Novels by Eminent Hands* were an insurance policy, something that would keep the money coming in and allow him to support an insane wife and two young daughters. Thackeray's letter to Fonblanque reflects this: "I cant afford to give up my plan. It is my bread indeed for next year" (*Letters* 2: 270).

In the end, of course, *Vanity Fair* succeeded beyond the expectations of everyone involved, and as a result, the series of parodies tailed out, the last extended magazine fiction of Thackeray's long apprenticeship. The year 1847 saw Thackeray wildly popular with the public, "all but at the top of the tree . . . and having a great fight up there with Dickens" (*Letters* 2: 333). But 1847 also saw Thackeray wildly *un*popular with some of his fellow novelists, and having another fight of a more personal kind with Dickens, among others. Thackeray ascribed this second fight to the same cause as he did the first: the success of *Vanity Fair*, he felt, had made his brother authors jealous. But in this he miscalculated. "Jerrold hates me, Ainsworth hates me, Dickens mistrusts me, Forster says I am false as hell, and Bulwer curses me," Thackeray wrote to his mother in July, then added that "he [Bulwer-Lytton] is the only one who has any reason" (*Letters* 2: 308). That reason was the first of the *Novels by Eminent Hands*, "George de Barnwell," a vicious parody of Bulwer-Lytton's *Eugene Aram*. What Thackeray seems not to have understood is that Dickens, Forster, Bulwer-Lytton, and the party of professional writers that was coalescing around them in 1847 saw parody as an attack on all of them, whether they were specific targets of his series or not. The *Novels by Eminent Hands* posed a far greater professional challenge to them than did the surprising success of *Vanity Fair*—a challenge arising from their very status as parodies.

Thackeray isn't the only one that this fact escaped. It is rare that the *Novels by Eminent Hands* are treated by modern criticism at all (the parodies were so effective at destroying the taste for their originals that they've ceased to be topical, and are now largely unread), and the limited terms in which they have been examined have never adequately explained Dickens's and Forster's hostile response to them. Thackeray's original introduction to "George de Barnwell," for instance, certainly indicates that some of Bulwer-Lytton's stylistic traits—"the splendid length of the words, the frequent employment of the Beautiful and the Ideal, the brilliant display of capitals, the profuse and profound classical learning" (12: 136)—are about to come under fire. But while such satire might well have given Bulwer-Lytton a reason to curse Thackeray, it would hardly have made Dickens and Forster mistrust him. Again, "George de Barnwell" certainly takes issue with *Eugene Aram*'s lack of realism—Thackeray's protagonist loftily proclaims that "The Ideal . . . is the true Real, and the Actual but a visionary hallucination" (12: 137)—in the same way that, say, *Northanger Abbey* takes issue with the Gothic novel. Still, it is hard to imagine that Thackeray's questioning of Bulwer-Lytton's realism would have had Dickens and Forster up in arms against him.

We need another, extra-literary context in which to read the *Novels by Eminent Hands* if we are to make sense of Dickens and company's resentment of them. Just such a context is provided by Joss Marsh—though what she gives with one hand, she takes away with the other. Marsh's book *Word Crimes* is primarily concerned with highlighting the class-coded nature of blasphemy in nineteenth-century England. It argues that the ideas and sentiments which Huxley could set out with impunity in his essays on agnosticism, which Arnold could publish with prestige in *Literature and Dogma*, were not only scandalous but legally indictable if published in cheap formats affordable by the lower class or in coarse or vulgar language understood by the lower class. Such class-coding was Victorian England's way of protecting itself from its own religious doubt.

Where Marsh's work intersects with parody is in her discussion of the three trials of William Hone, London publisher and bookseller, in December 1817. Hone had written and published, earlier that year, three cheap pamphlets satirizing the leading Tory ministers of the day and their repressive social policies—satires which took the form of the catechism, the creed, and the Litany. Thus, *John Wilkes's Catechism* reads in part: "OUR Lord who art in the Treasury, whatsoever be thy name, thy power be prolonged, thy will be done throughout the empire, as it is in each session. Give us our usual sops" (qtd. in Marsh 26). Because the three satires parodied religious texts, Hone was brought up on charges of blasphemy; but the intent of the government was, of course, to silence these politically seditious texts. Standing trial for the three charges of blasphemy on three consecutive days, in what became a full-blown public spectacle with more than twenty thousand onlookers, Hone defended himself on the grounds that the pamphlets he had written followed a long line of parodies of sacred texts, parodies written by such luminous figures as Martin Luther, Bishop Latimer, and even George Canning—then a member of the very ministry that had initiated Hone's prosecution (Marsh 33). What Hone made clear was that he was being prosecuted not

for writing and selling parody, but for writing and selling lower-class, politically radical parody: what was literature when written by and for the upper
classes was sedition when written by and for the lower classes.

Hone was acquitted on all three counts of blasphemy. But, Marsh argues,
his trials showed that the government could, and in the right circumstances
would, prosecute parody as a legal offense; and the specter of such prosecution
quickly led to the depolemicizing of parody in England. Thus the 1847 quarrel
between Thackeray and the Dickens party over the *Novels by Eminent Hands*
cannot be explained by reference to the class polemics or class-coding of
parody, because by 1847 such polemics and coding had evaporated:

> Within two decades of Hone's trials, ridicule could be found criminal, and
> parody was subject to careful limitations. The *Essays of Elia* by Hone's friend
> Charles Lamb were blackballed for "levity" by Woodbridge Quakers in 1823;
> "levity" helped his reputation dwindle quickly after his death in 1847. Victo-
> rian literature disengaged from overt relationship with "personalities" and
> public affairs; parody became "general" and private, self-consciously middle-
> class. It also became strenuously "purely literary": only when the parodist was
> "legitimate" could parody achieve legitimacy in the later nineteenth centu-
> ry . . . . Hone came to epitomize the Victorian conception of "the objectionable
> form of parody." Not one of the works collected in Walter Jerrold and R.M.
> Leonard's 1913 Oxford volume *A Century of Parody and Imitation* had any
> political bearing.   (Marsh 37)

When Marsh claims that "strenuously 'purely literary' " parody was the only
variety one could write after 1837, she's bringing us right back to where
we started.

There's no doubt that her argument about the depolemicizing of parody is
accurate in the long run. Late-Victorian and Edwardian volumes such as C.
S. Calverley's delightful *Fly Leaves* (1872) contain parodies so unpolemical
that they might often be better termed imitations or pastiches. Still, it's a
long span of years between Hone's trial in 1817 and Jerrold and Leonard's
collection of parodies in 1913, and the process of "purification" could easily
have been more gradual than Marsh feels it was. There is, in fact, a good
deal of evidence to suggest this. H. M. Paull's book on *Literary Ethics*,
published in 1929, is one of the key sources for Marsh's contention that
parody became less acceptable as the nineteenth century went on and the
Victorian age gave way to the Edwardian. It's organized from the most hei-
nous literary crimes to the least culpable, and places parody early, following
only theft, forgery, piracy, and plagiarism. Yet Paull's brief comment on
political parody ("indecent," "malicious," "obscene," "objectionable,"
"in bad taste" [134–36]) is absolutely vitriolic—so much so that it suggests
he is reacting not to a long-defunct historical mode, but to a form that had
managed to survive to his own day, despised and discredited or not. George

Kitchin, reviewing the history of parody two years after Paull, gives more positive proof. Kitchin believes that the Victorian age's great contribution to parody was turning it away from religious and political targets and towards purely literary ones, but he admits that *Punch* was still happily wallowing in the old, polemicized parodic forms as late as 1872 (202–03). Moreover, he codes such remnants socially low, while describing purely literary parody as "a polite art," a "gentle art," an art which is primarily the province of university-educated men (143). Parody continues to have class implications for him even in 1931.

Marsh, it seems, is actually doing herself a disservice by making the depolemicizing of parody such an abrupt process. The class-coding of the form which she's uncovered might in fact be used to shed light on literary problems of a much later date than Hone's trials in 1817. If we examine the 1847 quarrel between Dickens and Thackeray, we'll see that it suggests Hone's defense did not so much depolemicize parody as *confuse* its polemics: the quarrel—and, in fact, a significant portion of the disagreements between the two novelists over the next decade—can be seen to arise from a confusion about what class of author writes parody, over whether parody is a strictly polite art or a form naturally suited to the uses of a radical pamphleteer like Hone. Focusing on the first and most apparently objectionable of the *Novels by Eminent Hands*, "George de Barnwell, by Sir E.L.B.L.BB.LL.BBB.LLL., Bart.," we'll want to examine the ways in which even a parody of a literary genre can contain explicit positions on questions of class politics; next, we'll look at Thackeray's use of the parodic voice, and see in it highly polemical implications about the relative class status of a parodist and his target; and finally, we'll consider Dickens's "distrust" of Thackeray and the parodic mode, and see that a completely different class-coding of the form is at work in his mind, and at the root of the 1847 quarrel.

I

Eugene Aram, published in 1832, was Edward Bulwer-Lytton's second Newgate novel; like all the novels of that subgenre, it takes a real-life criminal from the pages of the *Newgate Calendar*—in this case, the notorious mid-eighteenth-century scholar-murderer Aram—and heavily romanticizes his history. Bulwer-Lytton's tale starts in a rural English village, where the middle-aged Aram has staked out a reclusive existence; his keen intellect, gentle manners, and impeccable morals have contributed to his being held in high esteem by the surrounding villagers, and to his being loved passionately by Madeline Lester, the daughter of the local squire. Madeline's cousin Walter, who has long pined after her, despairs when he sees her affections directed elsewhere, and goes on a grand tour to drown his sorrow; during his travels he stumbles upon a series of clues and discovers the fate of his father, a dissipated rascal who'd vanished under mysterious circumstances years before. It turns out that his father had been murdered by Aram. The scholar had been at the ragged edge of poverty at the time, and was convinced by a ne'er-do-well kinsman to kill Walter's father for his money—which he, Aram, had intended to use for the betterment of mankind, instead of frittering it away on gambling and drink as its owner had been doing. Walter returns home and has Aram arrested, to the dismay of the admiring county; Aram is found guilty and is sentenced to death; Madeline dies in horror; and the scholar takes his own life on the eve of his execution, leaving only a half-remorseful, half-defiant confession behind him.

From the first, *Eugene Aram* was tainted by the stigma of radicalism because of its status as a Newgate novel. The genre, though largely a combination of the picaresque and the Gothic, also owed a good deal to the Godwinian novel of purpose, in its portrayal of the criminal as a hero free from the oppressive constraints of conventional society; Bulwer-Lytton (who'd had Godwin's support when he'd first run for parliament in 1830) actually parades that debt, proudly relating in his 1840 preface how the political philosopher had once told him that Aram's history would make a great subject for a story (11).[2] And the novel's very first episode hits a Godwinian note that will develop into a major theme. An ill-favored man walks into the village and sits down outside the local inn; the innkeeper, suspicious of his looks, warns him off, and threatens to have him arrested for vagrancy. The stranger asks what a vagrant is, and is told that "a vagrant is a man what wanders, and what has no money"; he pulls a handful of silver coins from his pocket, and the innkeeper's distrust immediately disappears (15). From the beginning of *Eugene Aram*, then, crime is defined less by action than by wealth and class.

This inequity is addressed by Aram himself at various points in the novel. For instance, he and Madeline's father cross paths with two rural clowns while they are strolling through the countryside; the men are not tenants of Lester's, and the squire wonders whether they might not belong to a gang of housebreakers who've been terrorizing the neighborhood. Aram, chiding him, complains that society automatically despises the simple, natural appearance of the poor, and just as automatically respects the artificial trappings of the rich. He mourns the way the rich pass legislation against the poor, "how we scowl upon his scanty holydays, how we hedge in his mirth with laws, and turn his hilarity into crime." And he laments that society punishes mercilessly the crimes it drives the poor into—crimes it has invented for the sole purpose of entrapping them (198). All of this is, of course, just preparing the reader for Aram's climactic justification of his own crime, set out in his written confession. Aram says there that he had committed the murder in order to gain the financial means to do good: "I was shut out from all uses by the wall of my own poverty" (399). And that poverty he blames on conventional society, which respects family rather than talent: "Society is my foe.—Laws order me to starve . . . . I might wrest from society, to which I owed nothing, the means to be wise and great" (400–01). Aram's robbery of Walter Lester's father is no mere crime, but a heroic blow for the poor and the lower-class against the rich and the upper-class. The victim is portrayed not merely as a dissipated man, but as a dissipated *gentle*man, whose behavior shows just enough signs of breeding to make it clear that he'd had, and had thrown away, a good education and upbringing which should have made him a better man (403). The murder is a redistribution of wealth, taking money from a corrupt and undeserving upper class and giving it to a morally sound but underprivileged lower class.

It might be objected that these sentiments are dramatized—that Bulwer-Lytton has put them into the mouth of a murderer in order to discredit them, to make them seem mere rationalization. But Aram's reasoning is actually echoed by the narrator, and thus given formal authority. In a note appended to Aram's self-justifying confession, the narrator says that "The chain of reasonings . . . , which [Aram] wrought around his act, it was, in justice to him, necessary to give at length, in order to throw a clearer light on his character—and lighten, perhaps, in some measure the heinousness of his crime" (409). The "perhaps, in some measure" is augmented by further hemming and hawing for the remainder of the long note, but the general thrust is clear. While the narrator might not be willing to espouse or even acquit lower-class murder, he is certainly asking us to admit social provocations to it and ethical justifications for it. The note serves no other purpose.

The radicalism at the core of *Eugene Aram* contributed heavily to the critical backlash against it in the 1830s; it is worth remembering that the book was first published during the agitation for the Reform Bill. Early responses to the novel, including parodies like Thackeray's own *Catherine* (1839–40), jumped on this radicalism, and were carried largely by conservative periodicals (*Catherine*, for instance, appeared in William Maginn's vehemently Tory *Fraser's Magazine*). More important for our investigation is the fact that the stigma of radicalism was still there when Thackeray read Bentley's reprinted edition of the novel in 1847, a year when Chartist agitation was swelling for the final time and democratic movements across Europe were building toward the conflagrations of the following year. "George de Barnwell," which is, after all, a relatively late response to Bulwer-Lytton's novel, still makes the radical implications of its target the center of its satire.

The plot of "George de Barnwell" mirrors *Eugene Aram*'s fairly closely. Barnwell is a poor scholar whose intellect has fitted him for better things; his uncle is a wealthy man, but, in his nephew's opinion, unworthy of that wealth;

Barnwell kills him so that he can put the money to use in a way he feels will better serve mankind. He's convicted of the deed and sentenced to death, and gives a ringing speech of self-vindication, surrounded by weeping admirers, before he goes to his doom. The major change that Thackeray makes, the shift that pushes "George de Barnwell" into parody, isn't a change to the plot at all, but a downward shift in the principal characters' class: "George de Barnwell" is, essentially, a piece of mock-heroic. The primary effect of this downward shift is to emphasize and thereby make ridiculous *Eugene Aram*'s justification of lower-class crime.

Let's step back a moment. Bulwer-Lytton's novel has a radical premise, the notion that Aram's crime is legitimized by society's unjust relegation of him to a life of poverty. But it manages to avoid outright revolutionary sentiment by adding a second justification that obscures and softens the first. Aram may be poor, but he has an intellect that ensures the noblest and most impeccable morality; his victim may be genteel, but he's a man who's thrown aside his education and become a cheat, a thief, and a rapist. Aram's crime is justified, in other words, not simply because he is poor and needs money, but because he is poor and learned, and both needs money and knows how to use it better than his social superiors do. Thackeray's downshifting of the protagonist's class in "George de Barnwell" is intended to make Bulwer-Lytton's second, more complex justification of Aram's crime—his intellectual superiority—look ludicrous; the result is that we are forced to look at the first justification—Aram's lower-class stature—in its starkest form, and asked to see it as mere mercenary rationalization.

The following passage introduces us to our protagonist—not the noble recluse Aram, but Barnwell, a grocer's boy working behind a counter in Cheapside:

> Among the many brilliant shops whose casements shone upon Chepe, there stood one a century back (about which period our tale opens) devoted to the sale of Colonial produce. A rudely carved image of a negro with a fantastic plume and apron of variegated feathers, decorated the lintel. The East and the West had sent their contributions to replenish the window.
> The poor slave had toiled, died perhaps, to produce yon pyramid of swarthy sugar marked "ONLY 6$^1/2d$."—That catty box, on which was the epigraph STRONG FAMILY CONGO ONLY 3s. 9d., was from the country of Confutzee—That heap of dark produce bore the legend "TRY OUR REAL NUT"—'Twas Cocoa—and that nut the Cocoa-nut, whose milk has refreshed the traveller and perplexed the natural philosopher. The shop in question was, in a word, a Grocer's.
> In the midst of the shop and its gorgeous contents sate one who, to judge from his appearance (though 'twas a difficult task, as, in sooth, his back was turned), had just reached that happy period of life when the Boy is expanding into the Man .... Immersed in thought or study, and indifferent to the din around him, sate the Boy. A careless guardian was he of the treasures confided

to him. The crowd passed in Chepe; he never marked it. The sun shone on Chepe; he only asked that it should illumine the page he read. The knave might filch his treasures, he was heedless of the knave. The customer might enter; but his book was all in all to him.

And indeed a customer *was* there.

The customer, a pretty young woman who drops her "h"s, tries and fails to get Barnwell's attention:

> "*Ton d'apameibomenos prosephe*," read on the Student, his voice choked with emotion. "What language!" he said; "How rich, how noble, how sonorous! *Prosephe podas—*"
>
> The customer burst out into a fit of laughter so shrill and cheery, that the young Student could not but turn round, and, blushing, for the first time remarked her. "A pretty Grocer's boy you are," she cried, "with your applepiebomenos and your French and lingo. Am I to be kep waiting for hever?"
>
> "Pardon, fair Maiden," said he, with high-bred courtesy; " 'Twas not French I read, 'twas the Godlike language of the blind old bard. In what can I be serviceable to ye, lady?" . . .
>
> "I might have prigged this box of figs," the damsel said, good-naturedly, "and you'd never have turned round."
>
> "They came from the country of HECTOR," the boy said. "Would you have currants, lady? These once bloomed in the island gardens of the blue Ægean. They are uncommon fine ones, and the figure is low; they're fourpence-halfpenny a pound." (12: 136–37)

The humor here is aptly summed up by the young woman's comment: "A pretty Grocer's boy you are, with your applepiebomenos and your French and lingo." Thackeray clearly thinks it ridiculous to describe sixpence-halfpenny sugar as if it were something out of an epic poem; a grocer's is nothing more than a grocer's, and to pretend otherwise is absurd. The idea of Barnwell making an allusion to Homer is designed to appear equally ridiculous; grocer's boys are nothing more than grocer's boys, and pretending that such lower-class figures and learning go together, as Bulwer-Lytton did in *Eugene Aram*, is equally absurd.

Taking this satiric angle was a conscious choice on Thackeray's part, and a choice with some significant implications. A modern-day parody of *Eugene Aram*, for instance, would be far more likely to satirize an entirely different angle: Bulwer-Lytton's assumptions that, because Aram is blessed with a brilliant intellect, he must consequently have impeccable morals. "George de Barnwell" doesn't show the slightest skepticism of those assumptions; rather than questioning the association of education with moral authority, Thackeray laughs at the absurd idea that the lower class could *have* a good education—and thereby at the idea that it could have moral authority. That's not a politically neutral joke, and was certainly not a politically neutral joke in

1847, a time when other, more liberal novelists were earnestly portraying lower-class scholars in fiction (Gaskell would do so with *Mary Barton*'s Job Legh just a year later, and in 1850 Kingsley would make such a figure the central character of *Alton Locke*). Thackeray's satire is coming from a distinctly conservative position, and is intended for a distinctly conservative audience—one which would assume that education and the moral authority that goes with it are the province of the upper and middle classes.

The first of "George de Barnwell" 's three installments thus laughs at Bulwer-Lytton's secondary justification of Aram's crime. Barnwell is not, like Aram, a lower-class figure whose education has fitted him for spending and distributing money; the idea that he could have an education is shown to be absurd, and so he's just a lower-class figure with his eye eagerly on the till. The third installment of "George de Barnwell" continues this satire: if the first number strips away Barnwell's intellectual credibility and leaves him starkly lower-class, the third strips away his victim's moral debasement and leaves him starkly middle-class. Remember that Aram's victim had thrown away a gentleman's education and become a dissipated cheat and a thief, a man who might possibly be said to have deserved his fate. Barnwell's victim is nothing of the kind; he's simply a lower-middle-class grocer, reputedly philistine, whose vast crime is that he has "very little taste for the True and the Beautiful" that so consumes his nephew (12: 146). Barnwell relates his murder of this man to the prison chaplain shortly before his execution, in a passage which Thackeray (as *Punch*'s editor of this prize novel) identifies as a "gross plagiarism" by E.L.B.L.BB.LL.BBB.LLL. of "the ingenious romance of *Eugene Aram*":

> "And wherefore, Sir, should I have sorrow," the Boy resumed, "for ridding the world of a sordid worm; of a man whose very soul was dross, and who never had a feeling for the Truthful and the Beautiful? When I stood before my uncle in the moonlight, in the gardens of the ancestral halls of the DE BARNWELLS, I felt that I was the NEMESIS come to overthrow him. 'Dog,' I said to the trembling slave, 'tell me where thy Gold is. *Thou* hast no use for it. I can spend it in relieving the Poverty on which thou tramplest [i.e., Barnwell's own—his uncle has "trampled" on him by giving him a job in his grocery]; in aiding Science, which thou knowest not; in uplifting Art, to which thou art blind. Give Gold, and thou art free!' But he spake not, and I slew him."
>
> (12: 155)

Barnwell's justification for killing his uncle—that he is more cultured than his victim, and can spend his money better—is the same as Aram's for killing Walter Lester's father. But Thackeray has already asked us to be suspicious of this justification, by insinuating in the first installment that Barnwell couldn't possibly be cultured; now, he casts further doubt on it, by intimating that Barnwell's uncle couldn't possibly be as philistine as his nephew makes him out to be. Barnwell's uncle, the "sordid worm . . . whose very soul was dross, and who never had a feeling for the Truthful and the Beautiful," is actually shown in the third installment's illustration to be reading a book when Barnwell assaults him (see figure 1). The murder, Thackeray is saying, is not about the just redistribution of wealth, but about the simple redistribution of wealth from the victim to the culprit. Thackeray detested Bulwer-Lytton's overuse of capitalized words, and parodied it mercilessly throughout his career, but in the passage quoted above, the capitalization of "gold"—twice—is more than a stylistic satire: it's used to elevate money to the status of the Truthful and the Beautiful, to show Gold as being on a par with Barnwell's other ideal virtues. The whole murder is premised on money, is mere robbery; it's Barnwell's very soul, not his uncle's, that is dross.

The chaplain's response to Barnwell's vindicatory speech concludes Thackeray's highlighting of the class implications of *Eugene Aram*:

> "I would not have this doctrine vulgarly promulgated," said the admirable chaplain, "for its general practice might chance to do harm . . . . Think what would be the world's condition, were men without any Yearning after the Ideal to attempt to reorganize Society, to redistribute Property, to avenge Wrong."
>
> (12: 155)

The word "vulgarly" is crucial here, carrying the dual meanings of "commonly," i.e., without Barnwell's would-be genius, and "among the vulgar," i.e., among the lower class. Thackeray's point is, of course, that since there are no hero-scholars in the lower class, the promulgation of the defense of lower-class crime is *always* dangerous—and in its "attempt to reorganize Society," always revolutionary. *Eugene Aram* is covertly but firmly radical; "George de Barnwell" is less covertly and just as firmly conservative.

Thus, the first of the *Novels by Eminent Hands* shows that even as late as 1847, parody did not have to be strictly stylistic or purely literary. "George de Barnwell" identifies a radical position on class politics in the genre it satirizes, and takes up an opposing position. But Thackeray's parody of Bulwer-Lytton's novel also demonstrates something even more interesting: not simply that parody *could* be polemical, but that it was constitutionally, *inherently* concerned with some highly contentious questions of class. To establish this, we must return briefly to *Eugene Aram*.

II

Jacob Bunting is a resident of the village in which Eugene Aram lives, a retired corporal who prides himself on having become a "man of the world" during his years of military service. Bunting is a minor character, used mostly

Fig. 1. Barnwell and his uncle, by Thackeray.

to provide local color and comic relief, but in his endless pontificating about London life, he occasionally serves as a mouthpiece for Bulwer-Lytton. At one point in the novel, he describes his experience of London's literary circles to Walter Lester:

> [Authors] be so damned quarrelsome . . . wringle, wrangle, wrongle, snap, growl, scratch . . . . then, too, these creturs always fancy you forgets that their father was a clargyman; they always thinks more of their family, like, than their writings; and if they does not get money when they wants it, they bristles up and cries, "not treated like a gentleman, by God!" (170)

Literary quarrels, according to Bunting, are less about literary matters than about class. London authors "thinks more of their family, like, than their writings," and when they snap, growl, and scratch, it's because their class status has been called into question, not because their work has been attacked.

Now, it might be argued that Bunting is speaking in a novel set in the mid-eighteenth century, and that his comments need to be read in that context. That's probably giving Bulwer-Lytton's historical technique more credit than it deserves (the middle installment of "George de Barnwell" has a field day parodying the anachronisms in his fiction); besides, the dedication of the novel strongly suggests that Bulwer-Lytton was thinking of his own time when he composed Bunting's critical observation. The original 1832 dedication, to "SIR WALTER SCOTT, BART. &c. &c.," briefly applauds the quality of the Waverley novels, but then turns its attention to Scott himself. Bulwer-Lytton most admires Scott not for his literary technique, but for his ability to rise above literary quarrels: "It is a great lesson to all cultivators of letters, to behold one who, in winning renown, has at last conquered envy, and who is at once without an equal and without a detractor" (vi). Clearly Bulwer-Lytton envies Scott's freedom from critical pursuit, which is understandable, since his own career had begun to be dogged by it at every step. His first Newgate novel, *Paul Clifford*, had been published two years earlier, and had immediately come under fire—partly, as we've said, because of the radicalism inherent in the genre. The hostile response to *Eugene Aram* made the criticism of *Paul Clifford* look mild by comparison.

But that response varied in kind as well as in degree. The campaign against *Paul Clifford* was carried on mostly by reviewers; the campaign against *Eugene Aram* began increasingly to be waged by parodists. *Elizabeth Brownrigge*, a parody that used to be ascribed to Thackeray, appeared in *Fraser's* in 1832, scant months after the publication of *Eugene Aram*; it was followed over the next decade by Thackeray's own *Catherine* and several other parodies. The unrelenting pressure of this parodic campaign led Bulwer-Lytton to revise the dedication to *Eugene Aram*. He rewrote the passage about Scott's freedom from critical opposition, now giving a reason for that freedom rather than simply applauding it: "That nature must indeed be gentle which has conciliated the envy that pursues intellectual greatness, and left without an enemy a man who has no living equal in renown" (5). The crucial word in this revision is "gentle," which has the usual slippage with "genteel"; Scott is above literary quarrels—above parody—not because his work is better than anyone else's, but because he is a member of the gentility. Presumably, Bulwer-Lytton felt that the criticism directed against him was a result of his *not* being a member of that gentility—that it had less to do with *Eugene Aram*'s literary merits than with the class of its author.

Here we are near the end of Joss Marsh's twenty-year window for the depolemicizing of parody, and Bulwer-Lytton is intimating that parody is both polemical and personal, that it has little to do with imitating the style of an author and everything to do with scorning his class. Led by his suspicions, we might look again at "George de Barnwell," where we'll find that even in 1847—ten years after the end of Marsh's twenty-year window—Thackeray's parody of Bulwer-Lytton is indeed as much about his class as about his novel's style or politics. And in this discovery, we'll find what we need to understand Dickens's objection to the *Novels by Eminent Hands*, and indeed much of Thackeray's relationship with Dickens over the next decade.

"George de Barnwell" 's assault on Bulwer-Lytton's class starts early—even before the text itself, in fact. One of the parody's primary jokes, we've seen, is that its protagonist is extremely lower-class, a grocer's boy. Thackeray is simply following his source here, George Lillo's play *The London Merchant, or the History of George Barnwell* (1731). But he makes a significant change to Barnwell's name, adding an aristocratic "de" that Lillo's protagonist does not possess. This small addition is a very pointed joke, aimed at the boy's absurd fantasies about coming from an aristocratic family; in essence, it is a radically simpler version of the joke contained in the title of *Tess of the d'Urbervilles*. But the real payoff for Thackeray is in the ascription of authorship, "by SIR E.L.B.L.BB.LL.BBB.LLL., BART.," because here, he can ridicule Bulwer-Lytton for precisely the same sin which Barnwell has committed: just as the grocer's boy has spiced his name up to the aristocratic "de Barnwell," plain old Edward Bulwer had, upon inheriting Knebworth from his mother in 1843, expanded his name to Sir Edward George Earle Lytton Bulwer-Lytton, Bart. That step had galled Thackeray, who now saw in it an opportunity to compare Bulwer-Lytton with the protagonist of his parody—to accuse Bulwer-Lytton, just as he'd accused Barnwell, of pretending to a higher class status than he really possessed.

The clear implication is that Bulwer-Lytton is lower-class, just as Barnwell is. Such an implication is patently false, of course; Bulwer-Lytton may not have become a landed gentleman and a baronet until 1843, but he came from two families that had been entitled since the Conquest, and he'd always moved in the fashionable circles of London. Still, the Bulwer of the 1830s had always had a taint of the shabby-genteel about him—his mother having cut off his generous allowance after his marriage to Rosina Wheeler, a blow that had steered him towards writing novels in the first place—and his expansion of his name to Bulwer-Lytton seemed pretentious to many in London's literary circles. What Thackeray resented in fact was a middle-class colleague's assumption of upper-class airs; what he mocks in the parody is a lower-class writer's assumption of upper-class airs.[3]

This exaggeration is a long-standing facet of Thackeray's non-parodic satire of Bulwer-Lytton; two of the final *Yellowplush Papers*, for instance, imply that he is primarily appreciated by and best suited for the company of subliterate Cockney footmen. And Thackeray seized an opportunity to push the point home when he designed the illustrations to "George de Barnwell." In all three he gives the protagonist of his prize novel an absurdly prominent nose, almost certainly in an effort to caricature Bulwer-Lytton himself (see figure 2).[4] The baronet is thus quickly made into a grocer's boy, and one who would be well advised to spend less time reading Plato—or writing Newgate novels—and more preventing customers from prigging boxes of figs.

The portrayal of Bulwer-Lytton as lower-class, however inaccurate, allows Thackeray to introduce yet another class comment. For "George de Barnwell" does not simply represent its target as lower-class and leave it at that; it also implies that the parodist is of a higher class. Let's look, for example, at a passage from the beginning of the parody's second installment, where E.L.B.L.BB.LL.BBB.LLL. addresses *Punch*'s readers:

> Those who frequent the dismal and enormous Mansions of Silence which society has raised to Ennui in that Omphalos of town, Pall Mall, and which, because they knock you down with their dullness, are called Clubs, no doubt; those who yawn from a bay-window in St. James's Street, at a half-score of other dandies gaping from another bay-window over the way; those who consult a dreary evening paper for news, or satisfy themselves with the jokes of the miserable *Punch*, by way of wit; the men about town of the present day, in a word, can have but little idea of London some six or eight score years back. [Thou dandiacal genteel readers of *Punch*,] in fancy, in taste, in opinion, in philosophy, the newspaper legislates for you; it is there you get your jokes, and your thoughts, and your facts and your wisdom—poor Pall Mall dullards.   (12: 146)

The passage seems to insult *Punch*'s readers because they are members of a brass generation instead of an earlier, golden one. But in actuality, those readers are abused as much for their class as for their place in history: E.L.B.L.BB.LL.BBB.LLL. is attacking newspaper-reading gentlemen, club gentlemen, St.-James's-Street and Pall-Mall gentlemen—and from what sounds like a lower-class position. The claim the passage makes is to educational superiority over such men. They think they know their history, having

Fig. 2. Left: From Thackeray's "George de Barnwell." Right: Edward Bulwer-Lytton.

learned it at university, but E.L.B.L.BB.LL.BBB.LLL. contends that they don't, and that he, by contrast, does.

In the rest of the installment Thackeray systematically refutes this claim, showing that the sneering prize author does *not* know better, and assuming that *Punch*'s readers do—that they will be able to get the joke. The installment satirizes the anachronisms that Thackeray saw everywhere in Bulwer-Lytton's fiction: muffins are served to customers decades before they're invented, and someone uses the word "springald" in a conversation with Samuel Johnson, even though Johnson listed the word as obsolete in his dictionary.[5] But the jokes aren't just designed to show E.L.B.L.BB.LL.BBB.LLL.'s educational inferiority; some of them have class implications. The scene is confidently set, for example, at "BUTTON'S IN PALL MALL"—but Button's wasn't in Pall Mall; it was in Russell Street, in Covent Garden. After abusing all the fashionable wits of the "Omphalos of town," the prize author of "George de Barnwell" has pretended to knowledge of it—only to reveal his ignorance, and to show that his own experience of the city comes from rather lower quarters. Truly fashionable readers would know this, and laugh at the pretensions of an outsider.

Thackeray's parody in "George de Barnwell" is not simply stylistic, then; it's highly polemical. Nor does it limit itself to satirizing the radical politics of its target text; Thackeray implies that the author of that text is pretending to a class status not properly his, and that he himself is of a higher class than his victim. Nor is "George de Barnwell" a peculiar example, a singular result of Thackeray's inordinate dislike of Bulwer-Lytton; the rest of the *Novels by Eminent Hands* follow its lead. The second, "Codlingsby," may in fact be an even better example of the way Thackeray's parody satirizes authors as well as texts. It could be argued, after all, that the satire in "George de Barnwell" is primarily focused on the radical politics in *Eugene Aram*, and that the personal slight on Bulwer-Lytton is just a supplementary comment on the type of person who would promote such views. In "Codlingsby," however, Thackeray completely ignores the political content of his overtly political target, Disraeli's *Coningsby*, while still making fun of the class pretensions of its author—a choice which suggests that the class-coding of his parody is its primary feature, not one dependent on a prior polemical stance in the work being parodied.

Thackeray reduces Sidonia, *Coningsby*'s aristocratic power broker, to Rafael Mendoza, an old-clothes merchant with a shop in Holywell Street, just as he'd reduced the gentlemanly Aram to Barnwell, Cheapside grocer's boy. He laughs at the absurdity of Mendoza's hobnobbing with Louis Philippe, just as he'd laughed at Barnwell's reading Greek. And in his illustrations, he makes Mendoza look like Disraeli, just as he'd drawn Barnwell as Bulwer-Lytton, so that all of his jokes about the class of the character apply with equal force to the writer.[6] Thackeray also pokes fun at Disraeli as the supposed author of the story, in the same way he'd laughed at Bulwer-Lytton through E.L.B.L.BB.LL.BBB.LLL. "Codlingsby" is by "B. de Shrewsbury, Esq.," a man whose name contains the same aristocratic "de" that George Barnwell so groundlessly assumes, and who's labeled himself an esquire—that vaguest sign of respectability—to boot. And when de Shrewsbury flashes back to his protagonist's Cambridge career in the second installment of "Codlingsby," he exposes himself by mixing that school's customs up with Oxford's, and delivering "a series of clangers that a university man would never be guilty of" (McMaster 321). Similar jokes recur throughout the other *Novels by Eminent Hands*; the only parodied author whose class is not visibly questioned is the last, James Fenimore Cooper.

Very likely, it is Cooper's nationality that exempts him from such satire; after all, when Thackeray had anatomized the subject of class pretensions in his previous series for *Punch*, he had called that series "The Snobs of England."[7] Two installments in that series support the contention that class was on Thackeray's mind when he was writing the *Novels by Eminent Hands*. Having described military snobs, clerical snobs, university snobs, and others, Thackeray turned in the sixteenth and seventeenth chapters to his own profession; he assured the readers of *Punch* that he had no qualms about satirizing his fellow authors, but that it had proved impossible to do so because "the fact is, that in the literary profession THERE ARE NO SNOBS." No English man of letters had any need to assume the airs of a class he didn't belong to, because he was already "the great lion of society":

> He takes the *pas* of Dukes and Earls; all the nobility crowd to see him: I forget how many Baronesses and Duchesses fall in love with him. But on this subject let us hold our tongues. Modesty forbids that we should reveal the names of the heart-broken Countesses and dear Marchionesses who are pining for every one of the contributors of this periodical.
>
> If anybody wants to know how intimately authors are connected with the fashionable world, they have but to read the genteel novels. What refinement and delicacy pervades the works of MRS. BARNABY! What delightful good company do you meet with in MRS. ARMYTAGE! She seldom introduces you to anybody under a Marquis! I don't know anything more delicious than the pictures of genteel life in *Ten Thousand a Year*, except perhaps the *Young Duke*, and *Coningsby*. There's a modest grace about *them*, and an air of easy high fashion, which only belongs to blood, my dear Sir—to true blood.
>
> (10: 271)

This passage shows Thackeray making several of the same accusations he makes in the *Novels by Eminent Hands*, and of many of the same authors. Disraeli's novels of aristocratic life are designed to make readers think he has "true blood"; Catherine Gore's fiction is designed to make readers think she's writing about her own life in fashionable society (''Mrs. Armytage'' is one of her silver-fork novels, but Thackeray's syntax makes it sound like her pen name). They couldn't possibly be shamming, Thackeray opines, because authors only write about what they know: ''For what do we admire SHAKS-PEARE so much as for his wondrous versatility? He must have *been* everything he describes: *Falstaff, Miranda, Caliban, Marc Antony, Ophelia, Justice Shallow''* (10: 281).

Other previews of the *Novels* follow. The use of French in fiction, which Thackeray ridicules in ''Lords and Liveries,'' isn't a stylistic tic; it's a way for Bulwer-Lytton and Gore to show off their knowledge of fashionable lingo. G. P. R. James's prolixity, satirized in ''Barbazure,'' isn't a stylistic flaw; Thackeray attributes it to literary snobbery (10: 271). Five of the seven authors parodied in the *Novels by Eminent Hands* are called out by name in the first chapter on literary snobs, the result being that reading the *Novels* without thinking of their authors as snobs is as great an oversight as coming across Dobbin in *The Newcomes* without realizing that he's one of the central characters in *Vanity Fair*. The two *Punch* series are extensions of one another, the way most of Thackeray's novels are.

And when Thackeray revised the series of parodies for publication in volume form in 1856, he turned it into an extension of still another of his attacks on literary snobbery. The series could no longer be called ''Punch's Prize Novelists,'' since it was being reprinted outside the framework of that magazine; Thackeray needed a new title, and chose one which invoked what was by then a decade-old joke. In June 1845, Harrison Ainsworth had bought *The New Monthly Magazine* from Henry Colburn and taken out an advertisement boasting about the ''eminent'' contributors that the periodical would henceforth feature. Thackeray's reaction in *Punch* had been scathing:

MR. AINSWORTH, ''on whom the Editorship of the *New Monthly Magazine* has devolved,'' parades a list of contributors to that brilliant periodical, and says he has secured the aid of several writers *''eminent not only for talent,* BUT FOR HIGH RANK.''

Are they of high rank as authors, or in the Red Book? MR. AINSWORTH can't mean that the readers of his Magazine care for an author because he happens to be a lord—a flunky might—but not a gentleman who has any more brains than a fool. A literary gentleman who respects his calling, doesn't surely mean to propitiate the public by saying, ''I am going to write for you, and—and Lord Fitzdiddle is going to write too.''

Hang it man, *let* him write—write and be—successful, or write and be—unsuccessful, according to his merits. But don't let us talk about high rank in the republic of letters—let us keep *that* place clear. Publishers have sought for lordlings, we know, and got them to put their unlucky names to works which they never wrote; but don't let men of letters demean themselves in this way.

(''Immense Opportunity'' 14)

Thackeray was so irritated by what he perceived to be Ainsworth's snobbery that he intermittently revived the "eminent authors" issue in *The Book of Snobs* and elsewhere over the following two years, long after the advertisement itself would have faded from most readers' memories. By retitling his series of parodies *Novels by Eminent Hands*, he was making a final indication that the authors being parodied had made themselves targets not because of their literary flaws, but because of their class—or, more to the point, because of the class to which they had snobbishly pretended.

Gordon N. Ray has argued that *The Book of Snobs* was a turning point for *Punch*, the point at which it left behind its early radicalism and assumed a more genteel position, one which it would hold for the rest of the century (373). The *Novels by Eminent Hands* are written in just this vein; they're parodies written by a socially respectable author against socially marginal ones. This genteel parody is hardly an invention of Thackeray's: we've seen that William Hone based his whole defense on the contention that parody had been allowed to upper-class authors from time out of mind, and that George Kitchin sees parody primarily as a pastime of university men who used the form to satirize those with less literary breadth than they had themselves. Thackeray is participating in this tradition—consciously participating, too, because most of the jokes in the *Novels* (E.L.B.L.BB.LL.BBB.LLL.'s mistakes in describing fashionable London, for instance) demand that his audience also be aware of that tradition. Class-coding is part of the basic makeup of parody as practiced by Thackeray; full understanding of the *Novels by Eminent Hands* requires a sensitivity to it.

In fact, the quarrel we've set out to explain arose precisely because Thackeray was so confident that his parody would be read in this tradition—that it was the only tradition it could be read in. And, of course, it wasn't. What Marsh's work does brilliantly is to show that Hone's trials inaugurated a *new* tradition, one in which parody figured as the work not of upper-class writers, but of lower-class writers satirizing their social betters. For Marsh, this second tradition quickly stigmatized parody and eradicated the first tradition; more likely, the two traditions coexisted for a long period of time—possibly without anyone consciously realizing that there *were* two traditions. Thackeray, for instance, writes a parody saturated with class implications, but there is nothing in the *Novels by Eminent Hands* which suggests that he realizes parody could be understood as properly the work of a Grub Street hack. If we turn to Dickens's reaction to the series, we will see that he, too, sees parody as inherently tied up with issues of class—but also that he shows not the slightest awareness that parody could be penned by anyone *other* than a Grub Street hack. The two are working under fundamentally opposed conceptions of what parody is, and each is utterly oblivious of the existence of the other's conception. Hence the disagreement.

III

The quarrel which caused Thackeray to lament that "Dickens mistrusts me" started in mid-1847, with John Forster reading the *Novels by Eminent Hands* as they appeared in *Punch*. Forster was apparently reminded by them of a caricature or caricatures of himself that Thackeray had once drawn,[8] and in a fit of spleen he remarked to Tom Taylor that Thackeray was "false as hell." Taylor, a regular contributor to *Punch* himself, indiscreetly passed the comment on; and when Thackeray next met Forster, at Bryan Waller Procter's on 8 June, he cut him, refusing to shake his hand. Forster indignantly inquired as to the reason for this in a letter written the next day, and was duly answered by a note written by Thackeray in high dudgeon; a small avalanche of correspondence followed, with Dickens becoming involved when he took it upon himself to act as Forster's second. The squabble took about a week to settle, and was nominally put to rest by Thackeray's opinion that "Forster ought not to have used the words: Taylor ought not to have told them: and I ought not to have taken them up" (*Letters* 2: 300). But apparently there were lingering hard feelings: it was almost three weeks later that Thackeray wrote to his mother saying, "Jerrold hates me, Ainsworth hates me, Dickens mistrusts me, Forster says I am false as hell, and Bulwer curses me."

Thackeray clearly attributed this hate and mistrust to the success of *Vanity Fair*; the same letter continues, "I was the most popular man in the craft until within ab^t 12 months—and behold I've begun to succeed. It makes me very sad at heart, though, this envy and meanness" (*Letters* 2: 308). But such reasoning says more about Thackeray's preoccupations at the time (the letter goes on to elaborate the themes he was trying to work into *Vanity Fair*) than the real causes of the quarrel. Forster was angered by the *Novels by Eminent Hands*, not *Vanity Fair*, even though he was not parodied in that series; Dickens, too, objected to the series of prize novels, though he was neither parodied in it nor reminded of caricatures of himself by the same hand, as Forster was.

Dickens's objection to the *Novels*, in other words, was not personal but professional, but if anything, this made his objection stronger, not weaker; the author least involved in the parodies themselves—not Bulwer-Lytton, not Forster—was the one longest bothered by them. This is shown by the postscript to the quarrel, which had been more or less settled by 12 June 1847 and formally closed with a reconciliation dinner on 21 June. The issue never arose again between Thackeray and Forster, but it did between Thackeray and Dickens—*seven months later*; it had been sitting between them all that time, even though Dickens had only been involved as a go-between. The burst of friendly sentiment with which Dickens begins a letter to Thackeray on 9 January 1848 (in reply to a letter from him which has been lost) has the feel of a sudden thaw, suggesting that the two men had been giving one another the cold shoulder for more than half a year:

> My dear Thackeray,
> I need not tell you that I have been delighted—and cut tender, as it were to the very heart—by your generous letter. You would never have written it if you had not known how truly and heartily I should feel it. I will only say the spirit in which I read it, was worthy of the spirit in which you wrote it, and that I think there is nothing in the world or out of it to which I am so sensitive as the least mark of such a manly and gallant regard.
> I *do* sometimes please myself with thinking that my success has opened the way for good writers. And of this, I am quite sure now, and hope I shall be when I die—that in all my social doings I am mindful of this honour and dignity and always try to do something towards the quiet assertion of their right place. I am always possessed with the hope of leaving the position of literary men in England, something better and more independent than I found it.
> There's a wild and egotistical fancy for you! See what it is to get into my confidence so thoroughly!
> It is curious, about Punch, that I was so strongly impressed by the absurdity and injustice of my being left out of those imitations, that I several times said at home here I would write to you and urge the merits of the case. But I never made up my mind to do so, for I feared you might misunderstand me.
> I will tell you now, candidly, that I did not admire the design—but I think it is a great pity to take advantage of the means our calling gives us with such accursed readiness, of at all depreciating or vulgarizing each other—but this seems to me to be one of the main reasons why we are generally more divided among ourselves than artists who have not those means at their command—and that I thought your power thrown away on that series, however happily executed. So now I have made a clean breast too, and have nothing more to confess but that I am saving up the perusal of Vanity Fair until I shall have done Dombey.   (*Letters* 5: 227–28)

This letter becomes involved in the issues we've been examining when it conjoins two apparently very different things: Dickens's criticism of the basic premise or "design" of the *Novels by Eminent Hands*, and the preceding effusion about the stature of authors in England—a section so high-flown and idealistic that Dickens himself seems to have been momentarily embarrassed by it, as the letter's third paragraph shows. But the conjunction is far from coincidental. The first section, which is overwhelmingly about class, provides the context for Dickens's sentiments in the second, and shows how vastly different his conception of parody is from Thackeray's. It is hard not to be reminded of Bulwer-Lytton's remark in *Eugene Aram* that authors care more about their families than their writings; Dickens's rhapsodizing about the "assertion of [authors'] right place" echoes Bulwer-Lytton's "not treated like a gentleman, by God!" The paragraph reminds us that the elevation of writing into a profession—with all the class implications which that word carried in Victorian England—had been one of Dickens's concerns since at least 1843, when he tried and failed to establish a Society of Authors, and also that it would continue to occupy his mind, so that in 1851 he would succeed in getting incorporated the Guild of Literature and Art (helped in the cause by, not coincidentally, Bulwer-Lytton).

That first section casts a long shadow, and forces us to recognize those same class concerns as they suffuse the section more particularly about Thackeray's parodies. None of Dickens's criticism of the series is at all literary in nature; indeed, he implies that Thackeray's execution was quite good. Instead, it is treated as a social indiscretion: if Dickens claims to have minded the honor and dignity of his profession "in all my social doings," the implication is that in the *Novels by Eminent Hands* Thackeray had committed a social faux pas, one that disgraced not only him but all his fellow authors. And when Dickens describes parody as "depreciating" or "vulgarizing" the position of the author, it becomes clear that he sees this social indiscretion as indelibly lower-class. He elaborates on this association in a letter written to Forster during the quarrel itself, grousing that the *Novels by Eminent Hands* "did no honor to literature or to literary men, and should be left to very inferior and miserable hands" (*Letters* 5: 82). The comment is a little cryptic if "inferior and miserable" is read as relating to literary quality; it's not at all clear why parody by an untalented writer would be more acceptable than parody written by a talented one. But it makes perfect sense if "inferior" means "socially inferior" and "miserable" means "poor"—a connotation it almost always does have in Dickens's fiction: now parody should be left to such hands because, in Dickens's mind, that's who it's always been written by. Thackeray's error was being a successful, prosperous, respectable author writing parody; in this, his notion that *Vanity Fair*'s success had something to do with his quarrel with Dickens and Forster was correct.

But note how different Dickens's ideas about parody are from Thackeray's. Dickens shows not the slightest comprehension that parody could be thought of as a gentlemanly pursuit, that it might, as George Kitchin argues, be the province of university men. For him, parody is profoundly ungentlemanly, a form used only by lower-class hacks—such as William Hone. Certainly this makes sense. Dickens never attended university as Thackeray did, and would not there have been exposed to the earlier parodic tradition; his experience with parody was with borderline forgeries such as *The Posthumous Notes of the Pickwickian Club*, *Oliver Twiss*, and *Nichelas Nickleberry*, which truly were trash written by Grub Street hacks to make a quick hit at the expense of a respectable novelist. There's clearly a grain of respect contained in all such parodies, since it doesn't make any sense for a hack to parody anyone but a well-known, popular, and prosperous author; this may be why Dickens admitted to Thackeray that he'd talked to his family about "the absurdity and injustice of my being left out of those imitations." For a series of parodies of popular authors of the day not to contain a takeoff of the inimitable Boz is, in this sense, no mean slight. But this is clearly outweighed in Dickens's mind by the idea that anyone writing such parodies is vulgar, disreputable, and not to be admitted into polite society; the fact that the man who was joining him "at the top of the tree" was just such a parodist was a serious threat to his hopes that he could make their profession socially respectable. Apparently Dickens had not the slightest awareness of the parodic tradition in which Thackeray was writing; his own conception of parody was part of the new tradition which William Hone's trials had introduced into English literary history. The quarrel over the *Novels by Eminent Hands* shows that both traditions were alive and kicking in 1847—and that they were entirely ignorant of one another's existence.

IV

Joss Marsh's history of the depolemicizing of parody thus needs some revision: Thackeray was saturating his parody with pointed comments about class a decade after Marsh says the literary climate should have made it impossible for him to do so. William Hone's three trials for blasphemy seem not to have ended the polemicizing of parody, but to have confused it, to have created a situation where parody was still read polemically, but could be read in different ways by different people. Thackeray is apparently reading parody as an upper-class, gentlemanly form; Dickens is clearly reading it as lower-class and not at all respectable. But it can hardly be supposed that these two authors are the only such confused readers; Hone's trials were such a landmark event, such a public spectacle, that they must have caught up all of literary London in this dilemma of how to read parody. Such a theory might help explain some of the odd quirks of the history of Victorian parody. Thackeray, for instance, wrote *Catherine*, a parody of Bulwer-Lytton's Newgate and historical novels, early in his career, and had it published in William Maginn's fiercely Tory *Fraser's Magazine*. When he wrote "George de Barnwell" eight years later, he reused many of his earlier jokes (the second installment of the prize novel is in places almost a quotation from *Catherine*), yet published the parody in *Punch*, which, though mellowing, still had a decidedly radical reputation. This somewhat odd fact might be partially explained if we see that both liberal and conservative editors might look at a piece of parody and see it as being a form inherently suited to them. The early years of *Punch*'s history also make for odd reading; at a time when literary magazines were still fiercely partisan (if not so baldly as they had been twenty years before), *Punch* survived, even thrived, with a staff pretty evenly split between thundering radicals like Douglas Jerrold and relatively conservative gentlemen like Thackeray. But *Punch* was a magazine composed almost entirely of parody, and if the form itself had two traditions of class coding, it may have helped members of a socially and politically diverse staff to coexist.

Our investigations suggest another revision to Marsh's history. The forces pressing for the depolemicizing of parody need to be reconsidered, at least as much as does the time span over which that depolemicizing occurred. For Marsh, the pressure comes from outside the literary community: Hone's trials showed that the government could, and would, prosecute parody, and even if Hone was acquitted on all counts, the risk of conviction was enough to steer any but purely stylistic satirists away from the form. The history of the quarrel over the *Novels by Eminent Hands* suggests something different. "George de Barnwell" does concern itself with larger political matters, but its most inflammatory facets deal with the pecking order in the literary world. The parody in the *Novels by Eminent Hands*, in other words, was subjected to censorship not by the government, but by the heavyweights of literary London, who were apparently much more sensitive to its implications than the average man in the street. This suggests that the depolemicizing of parody over the course of the nineteenth century might in fact be an afterthought, a side effect of another change—the gradual shift of parody from a respectable literary form to a subliterary one. In 1847, when the gentlemanly tradition of parody was still competing with the tradition initiated by Hone, it was possible for an author such as Thackeray to write the *Novels by Eminent Hands* with one hand and *Vanity Fair* with the other (and, in fact, to include passages of outright parody in the sixth chapter of *Vanity Fair* itself). His work might cause problems with his peers, as it did with Dickens, but it was still possible to do that work. By the end of the century, this was no longer the case. Instead, authors like C. S. Calverley could enjoy great popularity as parodists, but no reputation as serious artists; Calverley did classical translations as well as parody, but such translations were the exercises of a university man, not real literature. This change (which persisted until well into the twentieth century, when Pound and Eliot and continental writers like Proust forced a revaluation) could hardly have come about because of legal pressure; but if the Dickensian view of parody had gradually supplanted the Thackerayan, then parodists would have found themselves increasingly stigmatized. The price of entrance into literary London would have been to renounce the form—not for literary reasons, but for social ones.

It is, in any case, the response of authors, not audiences, to his parody which made life difficult for Thackeray in 1847, and which would continue to undermine his relationships with his professional brethren. For Thackeray and Dickens were only briefly reconciled in January 1848; two years later they found themselves on opposite sides in the "dignity of literature" debate, and by the end of the 1850s they were almost at legal odds, and were openly feuding. A difference of opinion about the class status of authors is central to this feud, a fact which Mark Cronin stresses in a series of recent articles, but so is the class-coding of parody, a fact which hasn't generally been appreciated. Thackeray ended the *Novels by Eminent Hands* in late 1847, and with it his career as a magazine journalist; and he ended it without the parody of Dickens that he had projected in his initial prospectus of the series for Albany Fonblanque. But that series had professionally challenged the Inimitable Boz, as surely as if it had parodied his work directly, and it indelibly affected the relationship of the two novelists now fighting "at the top of the tree."

NOTES

1. The series originally consisted of parodies of Bulwer-Lytton, Disraeli, Catherine Gore, G. P. R. James, Charles Lever, Thackeray himself, and James Fenimore Cooper. Most of the parodies consist of three installments (the better to mimic the format of the three-volume novel); each installment ran a full page, more or less, in *Punch*, and included an illustration or two by Thackeray. Only the first five parodies were collected in 1856; later editions of the series normally print all seven, and often add "A Plan for a Prize Novel," a short piece that Thackeray contributed to *Punch* in 1851.

   The 1856 edition makes several significant revisions to the serial text. The short introduction to the series which Thackeray wrote for *Punch* is omitted, since it doesn't make much sense outside of its original context. That framing piece had introduced the first parody as "GEORGE DE BARNWELL, by SIR E.L.B.L.BB.LL.BBB.LLL., BART.," and once it was omitted, Thackeray had to provide an independent title for his prize novel; in 1856 this is "GEORGE DE BARNWELL, by SIR E.L.B.L., BART." The name of the reputed author of "Codlingsby" undergoes a similar change, from "B. de Shrewsbury, Esq." to the less pretentious "D. Shrewsbury, Esq." The significance of such revisions will soon become apparent. I've therefore chosen to quote from the original magazine version of the *Novels* rather than from one of the three collected editions usually used by Thackeray scholars; since the series spans more than one volume of the bound edition of *Punch*, citations are to volume and page.

2. Bulwer-Lytton would revise *Eugene Aram* in 1849, in response to Thackeray's criticism of it in "George de Barnwell." The revisions were designed to eliminate the radical sentiments which had by then become an embarrassment to their author: in the years since the original publication of *Eugene Aram*, Bulwer-Lytton had become a landed gentleman and a conservative; when he was elected to parliament in 1852, it was with the support of Disraeli, not Godwin. Because the

1849 revisions so significantly change the political valence of the text, I have found it essential to quote from a pre-1849 version of *Eugene Aram*. An 1832 first edition has proved hard to acquire, so Bentley's 1846 reprint seemed the next best choice, it being the edition Thackeray read just before writing his parody (Ray 391). All citations from the body of the novel are from this edition.

However, the 1846 *Eugene Aram* appears to be a simple reprint of Bentley's earlier 1836 edition, meaning it contains only an early version of the dedication, and lacks the prefaces which Bulwer-Lytton later wrote for the novel. Citations from this prefatory material have thus had to be taken from a later edition; here, I've used the New Knebworth edition of the novel, the one usually cited by modern critics.

3. It is interesting to note that as time passed and literary London got used to Bulwer-Lytton as a baronet, Thackeray resented him less. When the *Novels by Eminent Hands* were republished in 1856, "George de Barnwell" was ascribed to "SIR E.L.B.L., BART."; Thackeray now identifies the author being parodied without sneering at his class pretensions. There is, of course, no one simple explanation for Thackeray's softening towards his erstwhile target; still, one starts to think that Bulwer-Lytton may not have been far off the mark when he suggested in the revised dedication to *Eugene Aram* that Scott was immune to literary criticism because of his class.

4. Admittedly, the caricature is a poor one; Bulwer-Lytton had a hatchet nose rather than the bulbous one sported by Barnwell. But this is probably more a result of Thackeray's artistic talent—or lack thereof—than anything else. It's also possible that Thackeray had only the vaguest familiarity with his victim's nose: in 1848 he told Lady Blessington that he'd only met Bulwer-Lytton once (*Letters* 2: 485).

Whatever the explanation for the quality of the caricature, I'm confident about its intent. I've been delighted to find that Juliet McMaster seconds my guess. Her work in annotating the *Novels by Eminent Hands* has led her to believe that the illustrations to all seven prize novels caricature the authors being parodied—including those to "Crinoline," in which Thackeray parodies himself (see figure 3, which compares the famous self-portrait in the third number of *Vanity Fair* with an illustration of Jools de Chacabac, the protagonist of "Crinoline." When Thackeray is caricaturing a face he's familiar with, his intent becomes readily apparent). McMaster does admit that she can't prove her conjecture about the illustrations to the *Novels by Eminent Hands*; it's hard to find portraits of people like Catherine Gore and G.P.R. James that would confirm it. But she's confident about Thackeray's caricature of Bulwer-Lytton in "George de Barnwell" (315–16).

5. I'm indebted to McMaster, again, for elucidating the jokes discussed in this paragraph (312).

6. Claire Nicolay, in an article on anti-Semitism in *Punch*, agrees that Thackeray expected his readers to take Mendoza as Disraeli himself, and that his primary intent in "Codlingsby" is to deflate Disraeli's threatening class pretensions (135). But her focus is on Disraeli as a Jew, not as an author, and so she does not see that such deflation goes on in several of the other *Novels by Eminent Hands*.

Fig. 3. Left: Thackeray's *Vanity Fair* self portrait. Right: Thackeray's Jools de Chacabac from "Crinoline."

7. When Thackeray collected this series and republished it as *The Book of Snobs* in 1848, he decided to omit several of the original chapters, including one of the two "On Literary Snobs" which are my primary focus here. This means that, as was the case with *Novels by Eminent Hands*, I've had to quote from the original magazine version rather than from a collected edition of Thackeray's works.

8. The correspondence regarding the quarrel does not identify the offending sketches, nor does it specify the angle they took in satirizing Forster. But Thackeray's surviving letters and private papers contain several caricatures of Forster, almost all of which poke fun at his girth. It's worth noting the conjunction in Forster's mind between literary parody and drawn caricature, since the same connection appears between the text and the illustrations of the *Novels by Eminent Hands*: Forster instinctively associated literary parody, which Marsh says should have "disengaged from overt relationship with 'personalities' " by 1847, with the openly personal satire of drawn caricature. It is entirely possible, in fact, that Forster's irritation arose from the illustrations rather than the text of the *Novels*. Dickens's letters, however, make it clear that he was responding to the text, and that his irritation was with Thackeray as an author, not as an illustrator.

WORKS CITED

[Bulwer-Lytton, Edward.] *Eugene Aram: A Tale.* 1832. London: Bentley, 1846.

[————.] *Eugene Aram: A Tale [The New Knebworth Edition].* 1832. London: Routledge, [1900].

Cronin, Mark. "Henry Gowan, William Makepeace Thackeray, and 'The Dignity of Literature' Controversy." *Dickens Quarterly* 16 (1999): 104–15.

————. "The Rake, the Writer, and *The Stranger*: Textual Relations between *Pendennis* and *David Copperfield*." *Dickens Studies Annual* 24 (1996): 215–40.

Dickens, Charles. *The Letters of Charles Dickens [The Pilgrim Edition].* Ed. Madeline House, Graham Storey, and Kathleen Tillotson. 12 vols. Oxford: Clarendon, 1965–2002.

Kitchin, George. *A Survey of Burlesque and Parody in English.* Edinburgh: Oliver, 1931.

Marsh, Joss. *Word Crimes: Blasphemy, Culture, and Literature in Nineteenth-Century England.* Chicago: U of Chicago P, 1998.

McMaster, Juliet. "*Novels by Eminent Hands*: Sincerest Flattery from the Author of *Vanity Fair*." *Dickens Studies Annual* 18 (1989): 309–36.

Nicolay, Claire. "The Anxiety of 'Mosaic' Influence: Thackeray, Disraeli, and Anglo-Jewish Assimilation in the 1840s." *Nineteenth-Century Contexts* 25 (2003): 119–45.

Paull, H. M. *Literary Ethics: A Study in the Growth of the Literary Conscience.* New York: Dutton, 1929.

Ray, Gordon N. *Thackeray: The Uses of Adversity, 1811–1846.* New York: McGraw, 1955.

[Thackeray, William Makepeace.] "Immense Opportunity." *Punch* 5 July 1845: 14.

———. *The Letters and Private Papers of William Makepeace Thackeray.* Ed. Gordon N. Ray. 4 vols. Cambridge: Harvard UP, 1945–46.

[———.] "Punch's Prize Novelists." *Punch* 3 Apr. 1847: 136–37; 10 Apr. 1847: 146–47; 17 Apr. 1847: 155; ff.

[———.] "The Snobs of England, by One of Themselves." *Punch* 28 Feb. 1846: 101; 7 Mar. 1846: 111–12; 14 Mar. 1846: 115; ff.

Wilkie Collins, Narrativity, and Epitaph

Jolene Zigarovich

This essay closely examines the complicity between writing and mortality, especially the epitaphic function of writing, in Collins's fiction. These novels constantly warn us that texts, including epitaphs, may be subjectively interpreted, have multiple interpretations and referents, and in addition, are often susceptible to rhetorical slippage. False and premature pronouncements of death—as well as the writing and rewriting of death—are rhetorical situations in which Collins exposes his own participation in the expansion of narrative boundaries and the exploration of the subversive nature of language. Collins's attention to typographical detail furthers the argument that the gravesite is a locus for the workings of language and truth in his fiction. The insistence that epitaphs be graphically reproduced in his work reminds us visually of the paradox and ensuing problem of writing the dead.

Every great writer senses the presence of death in the act of creation he performs through written language. During the act of writing, every artist becomes, momentarily, a carver of gravestones.[1]

Taking the epitaph as a paradigm for writing is one of the great power plays in humanism's history.[2]

In ''Essay Upon Epitaphs—I'' (1810) William Wordsworth defines the epitaph as a form of writing ''intended to be permanent and for universal perusal.'' Yet the tombstone, like any other text, can be miswritten or lie. The inscriptions of tombstones, as Peter Brooks recognizes, are "authoritative texts that nonetheless require decipherment" (297). Tombstones appear often in the nineteenth-century novel, for instance in Charles Dickens's *A Christmas Carol* (1843) where Scrooge uncannily reads "upon the stone of the neglected grave his own name, EBENEZER SCROOGE" and, most memorably, in *Great Expectations* (1860–61), which overlapped publication with *The Woman in White* in *All the Year Round*.[3] As Brooks has notably interpreted, the opening scene of the novel dramatizes quite remarkably the role of the epitaph, not only as narrative, but as a visual marker. Here young Pip confronts his parents' graves:

> As I never saw my father or my mother, and never saw any likeness of either of them (for their days were long before the days of photographs), my first fancies regarding what they were like, were unreasonably derived from their tombstones. The shape of the letters on my father's, gave me an odd idea that he was a square, stout, dark man, with curly black hair. From the character and turn of the inscription, "Also Georgiana Wife of the Above," I drew a childish conclusion that my mother was freckled and sickly.   (3)

This alignment of the body and corpse with narrative and visual representation demonstrates in an interesting manner one of the more creative functions of epitaph. In this scene Dickens has the orphaned Pip face the tombstone (the meeting place of corpse and text) in order to develop some sort of image of how the dead appeared when alive. It is as if the graphic symbols—the manner in which the engraved letters are painted and shaped—have become directly mimetic. Though Pip does not tell us the full content of the inscription, we do know that simply "the shape of the letters" made an impression on him—they inspired him to conjure an imaginative mental picture of his absent parents. The epitaph has thereby become a decipherable and interpretive narrative; the visual and textual switch places or are somehow conjoined.

As in *Great Expectations*, Collins's novels constantly warn us that texts, including epitaphs, may be subjectively interpreted, have multiple interpretations and referents, and in addition, are often susceptible to rhetorical slippage. For this discussion, we will investigate not only the rhetorical significance of the language of death, but the possible reasons behind Collins's own fascination with buried texts. From the tomb-tending in *Antonina* (1850) and *Hide and Seek* (1854), to the themes of forgery and the erasure of identity and writing in *Basil* (1852), to the ghost-like figures and cemetery scenes in *The Dead Secret* (1857), Collins's early fiction demonstrates his preoccupation with the susceptibility of identity and writing to misreading. Buried texts and unmarked graves are favorite images and plot elements, evident in later novels such as *The Moonstone* (1868). While others have remarked on the deconstructive implications of blank and white spaces or of the Gothic and feminist symbols in *The Woman in White*,[4] this study will demonstrate how in Collins's fiction, writing (and righting) the dead proves epitaphic: it is problematic, uncanny, and, at intervals, vacant. If we interpret the tombstone as a visual metaphor for dichotomy (life-death, presence-absence, engraved-blank, speaking-silent, and so on) then we can more closely look at Collins's dramatization of epitaphs, absent forms of writing ("vacancies"), and the act of authoring to reveal and demonstrate Collins's intuitive understanding of the various manipulations of writing and representation. Unearthing the meanings behind the tombstone—Collins's touchstone for narrative and death—casts new light on the implications of *logos* and *thanatos*.

I

Critics and biographers of Collins have repeatedly pointed to the sources of the "sensation" plots employed throughout his fiction, yet none have looked at the way in which the provocative "presumed dead—returned to life" plot works on a narrative level. His labyrinthine plots, emphasis on body doubling, and narrative duplicity all contribute to not only his "modern" sensibility (what Walter M. Kendrick terms "a tentative breach of the mid-Victorian realist contract"), but create an unstable environment in which writing cannot be trusted. And as we shall discover, we must focus our attention on the places where writing, death, and absence merge. What narrative complications are created when a supposed posthumous character is pronounced dead? In what way is Collins figuratively demonstrating through the "epitaph" that in the fictional world, death is not always final and writing is not always truthful? For Collins, the tombstone and its inscription are integral places in his fiction where paradox is found at its apex: body and corpse, writing and erasing, truth and fraudulency, and exhumation and burial merge at the gravesite.

The theme of the presumed dead returning to life can be seen in Collins's early works such as *Sister Rose* (1855) and "The Dead Hand" (1857), the play *The Red Vial* (1858) where a supposed corpse awakens in the Frankfurt morgue, most notably in *The Woman in White* (1860), and then later in *Armadale* (1866), *John Jago's Ghost* (1873–4), *The New Magdalen* (1873), and *Jezebel's Daughter* (1880). The dramatic device of digging a false grave and erecting a tombstone while the person supposedly dead is still alive becomes Collins's sensation marker, to be adopted by Mary Elizabeth Braddon for *Lady Audley's Secret* (1862). Due to the popularity of Collins's and Braddon's novels, readers learned to expect a supposed dead character to return. Kathleen Tillotson aptly remarks, "Eventually readers must have learnt never to believe anyone dead unless they had a complete corpse (not charred bones), certified as of the right identity and safely buried" (xxv).[5] In fact, "dead, yet not dead" became one of the most adopted stereotypes of the sensation novel. What these types of plots create is posthumous narrative. False and premature pronouncements of death—as well as the writing and rewriting of death—are rhetorical situations in which Collins exposes his own participation in the expansion of narrative boundaries and the exploration of the subversive nature of language.

In order to recognize Collins's insistence that the gravesite—especially the epitaph—should be the center of narrative plot, we must look at his intentions. John Sutherland has noted that Collins was meticulous about the typography of his work. In his note on the manuscript of *Armadale*, Sutherland remarks that "throughout his manuscript, Collins paid minute attention to details of interruptive typography: the italics, white and black lines . . . and dynamic typography which break up the narrative flow" (vii–viii). Collins is particular in instructions to the compositor regarding such things as small caps, new paragraphs, "white lines," dashes, and spacing. This attention to typographical detail is evident in most of his manuscripts, but blatantly so for the graphic replication of epitaphs.

Though not a sensation novel, *Antonina; or, The Fall of Rome* (1850) represents the commencement of Collins's interest in epitaph, grave-tending, and the paradox of writing death. Antonina, wooed by the chieftain Hermanric, later devotes herself to tend his grave out of respect for the warrior who had "died in her defense and for her love." In fact, the novel ends at the graveyard (a place of "righting" the dead for Collins) where Antonina and her father pay their respects.

> The trees, the flower-beds, and the patches of grass, all remained in their former positions; nothing had been added or taken away since the melancholy days that were past but a change was visible in Hermanric's grave. The turf above it had been renewed, and a border of evergreen shrubs was planted over the track which Goisvintha's footsteps had traced. A white marble cross was raised at the end of the mound; the short, Latin inscription on it signified, "PRAY FOR THE DEAD."   (436)

As a crossroads, the grave is also the setting where the repentant Vetranio bids goodbye to Antonina before he retires to the country. Indeed, Vetranio is no stranger to the epitaph. Earlier in the novel, when the invasion of Rome by the Goths is imminent, he addresses the Romans. At "The Banquet of Famine," Vetranio accepts defeat and uncannily speaks "a funeral oration over his friends and himself" as he unveils his own epitaph "scratched on the marble in faint, irregular characters" (see fig. 1). It is a pagan symbol to others in the suicide pact of his resoluteness to honorably accept death. Yet Vetranio escapes death, leaving the self-authored epitaph as a marker for

𝕾𝕿𝕺𝕻, 𝕾𝕡𝕖𝕔𝕥𝕒𝕥𝕠𝕣!

If thou hast reverently cultivated the pleasures of the taste,
pause amidst these illustrious ruins of what was once
a palace;
and peruse with respect, on this stone,
the epitaph of
VETRANIO, a senator.
He was the first man who invented a successful
Nightingale Sauce;
his bold and creative genius added much, and would have
added more, to
THE ART OF COOKERY;
but, alas for the interests of science!
he lived in the days when the Gothic barbarians besieged
THE IMPERIAL CITY;
famine left him no matter for gustatory experiment;
and pestilence deprived him of cooks to enlighten!
Opposed at all points by the force of adverse circumstances,
finding his life of no further use to the culinary
interests of Rome,
he called his chosen friends together to assist him,
conscientiously drank up every drop of wine remaining
· in his cellars,
lit the funeral pile of himself and his guests
in the banqueting-hall of his own palace,
and died, as he had lived,
the patriotic CATO
of his country's gastronomy!

Figure 1. Graphic of Vetranio's epitaph. *Antonina*. Harper and Brothers illustrated edition, 1873. Courtesy of Honnold/Mudd Library for The Claremont Colleges, Claremont, California.

one who still lives. This "burial plot"—the fact that death is announced prematurely—is a strangely ironic, reoccurring theme in Collins's fiction (and also foreshadows his own epitaphic self-authoring).

The Dead Secret (1857) anticipates *The Woman in White* in its theme of buried secrets and ghosts, as well as its insistence on the gravesite as a locus for plot, character, and paradox. Early in the novel Sarah Leeson visits the grave of her former love, Hugh Polwheal, before she leaves her position as maid following the death of her mistress. She then picks a few leaves of grass from the grave and embalms them in a little book of *Wesley's Hymns*, a gift from the deceased. She is next seen much later in the novel, following a sixteen-year absence. Again, she visits "the grave which had stood apart in the bygone days" and now had "companion-graves on the right hand and on the left."

> She could not have singled it out but from the weather-stains on the head-stone, which told of storm and rain passing over it, that had not passed over

the rest. The mound was still kept in shape ; but the grass grew long, and waved
a dreary welcome to her, as the wind swept through it. She knelt down by the
stone, and tried to read the inscription. The black paint which had once made
the carved words distinct was all flayed off from them now. To any other eyes
but hers, the very name of the dead man would have been hard to trace. She
sighed heavily as she followed the letters of the inscription mechanically, one
by one, with her finger:

SACRED TO THE MEMORY

OF

HUGH POLWHEAL,

AGED 26 YEARS.

HE MET WITH HIS DEATH

THROUGH THE FALL OF A ROCK

IN

PORTHGENNA MINE,

DECEMBER 17TH, 1823.

Her hand lingered over the letters after it had followed them to the last line ;
and she bent forward and pressed her lips on the stone.
  'Better so!' she said to herself, as she rose from her knees, and looked down
at the inscription for the last time, 'Better it should fade out so! Fewer strangers'
eyes will see it; fewer strangers' feet will follow where mine have been—he
will lie all the quieter in the place of his rest!'[6]   (34)

This scene foreshadows the textual drama that ensues at Mrs. Fairlie's
gravesite in *The Woman in White*. Here the epitaph has virtually lost its power
of inscription; it now stands in as a tabula rasa for any or every dead person.
Though buried and stained, what remains of the inscription is simply a
"trace" of the anonymous body it stands for. This early scene exemplifies
that, for Collins, the act of writing can be seen as epitaphic. Here, Sarah
Leeson emotionally and physically bonds with the site of the corpse (the
grave), the pronouncement of death (the engraved tombstone), and the slow
erosion of signification (the fading epitaph). It is a cryptic scene where con-
traries mingle and complicate interpretation.
  The importance of the graphic becomes more apparent when its reproduction history is illuminated. The serial publication of the novel twice includes
the graphic of Hugh Polwheal's tombstone. In fact, it is the only significant
graphic in the issue. We can only assume that Collins's manuscript depicted
these typographical instructions for the manuscript of the novel has not been
located. (This is a mysterious example of Collins's own "buried writing" or
"dead secret").[7] The serial publication of the novel in *Household Words* must
then be used as the earliest evidence of Collins's typographical directions for
the epitaph in the novel. Despite the space and font limitations of a serial
publication, Hugh Polwheal's tombstone is reproduced twice. It is distinctive
from the rest of the publication due to spacing and capitalization and is a

powerful visual marker (fig. 2). Without the graphic of the tombstone, the significance of the scene and the symbol of death would be diminished.

In the Bradbury & Evans two-volume first edition (1857) and the Harper and Brothers illustrated edition (1873), Hugh Polwheal's epitaph is again reproduced. Details such as spacing, small caps, and more ornate fonts such as Gothic script are designated for a more realistic effect (fig. 3). It is here that Collins demonstrates the literal problem of "writing" the dead. The typographical significance is more powerful than in *Household Words*; it is a realistic depiction of a tombstone as well as a visual reminder of epitaphic paradox.

The Woman in White's blending of sensation and detective genres aptly suits Collins's further exploration of metaphors that reflect the symptoms (and difficulties) of writing death. While the novel compiles multiple narratives and enlists the experiences of multiple narrators, its mysteries are hinged upon both the absence and presence of various forms of writing. Yet at the same time the text repeatedly works to expose the forgeries, duplicities, and inherent arbitrariness of narrative. In order for buried truths to be uncovered, textual gaps, blanks, and lies must be exposed and then written (or erased and rewritten) with truth. Bodies are in essence "blanks" waiting to be inscribed, literal epitaphs are incapable of sustaining meaning, and writing speaks for yet defies the body. Here Collins has clearly developed the use of the epitaphic function to include not only the literal but the figural; the living are confused with the dead. In the novel's opening, we find a figure who represents the paradox of "the dead alive:"

> There, in the middle of the broad, bright high-road—there, as if it had that moment sprung out of the earth or dropped from the heaven—stood the figure of a solitary Woman, dressed from head to foot in white garments; her face bent in grave inquiry on mine, her hand pointing to the dark cloud over London, as I faced her. I was far too seriously startled by the suddenness with which this extraordinary apparition stood before me, in the dead of night and in that lonely place to ask what she wanted.[8]   (15)

This passage, noted by Charles Dickens to be one of the two most dramatic descriptions in all of literature and directly inspiring his re-narrating of it in the figure of Miss Havisham in *Great Expectations* (1860–61),[9] is the first of the novel's two most climactic, "sensational" scenes. Here the figure is described as an "extraordinary apparition" that appears alone in the "dead of night," is garbed in white, and seems transfixed in her pointing stance. Though writing from retrospect, Walter chooses to suspend belief and allow his readers to imagine that the figure he has encountered is truly a ghost. Most disturbing is that Walter describes the figure as a recently exhumed object: "As if it had that moment sprung out of the earth." The apparition she had restrained since leaving her room, began to flow again. Urgent as her reasons now were for effecting her departure without a moment's loss of time, she advanced, with the strangest inconsistency, a few steps towards the nursery-door. Before she had gone far, a slight noise in the lower part of the house caught her ear, and instantly checked her further progress. While she stood doubtful, the grief at her heart—a greater grief than any she had yet betrayed —rose irresistibly to her lips, and burst from them in one deep gasping sob. The sound of it seemed to terrify her into a sense of the danger of her position, if she delayed a moment longer. She ran out again to the stairs, reached the kitchen-floor in safety, and made her escape by the garden-door which the servant had opened for her at the dawn of the morning.

On getting clear of the premises at Porthgenna Tower, instead of taking the nearest path over the moor that led to the high road, she diverged to the church; but stopped before she came to it, at the public well of the neighbourhood, which had been sunk near the cottages of the Porthgenna fishermen. Cautiously looking round her, she dropped into the well the little rusty key which she had brought out of the Myrtle Room; then hurried on, and entered the churchyard. She directed her course straight to one of the graves, situated a little apart from the rest. On the headstone were inscribed these words:—

SACRED TO THE MEMORY OF
HUGH POLWHEAL,
AGED 26 YEARS.
HE MET WITH HIS DEATH
THROUGH THE FALL OF A ROCK
IN
PORTHGENNA MINE,
DECEMBER 17TH, 1823.

Gathering a few leaves of grass from the grave, Sarah opened the little book of Wesley's Hymns which she had brought with her from the bed-room at Porthgenna Tower, and placed the leaves delicately and carefully between the pages. As she did this, the wind blew open the title-page of the Hymns, and displayed this inscription on it, written in large clumsy characters:—"Sarah Leeson, her book. The gift of Hugh Pol-

followed the moorland path on her way to the high road.

Four hours afterwards, Captain Treverton desired one of the servants at Porthgenna Tower to inform Sarah Leeson that he wished to hear all she had to tell him of the dying moments of her mistress. The messenger returned with looks and words of amazement, and with the letter that Sarah had addressed to her master in his hand.

The moment Captain Treverton had read the letter, he ordered an immediate search to be made after the missing woman. She was so easy to describe and to recognise by the premature greyness of her hair, by the odd, scared look in her eyes, and by her habit of constantly talking to herself, that she was traced with certainty as far as Truro. In that large town, the track of her was lost, and never recovered again. Rewards were offered; the magistrates of the district were interested in the case; all that wealth and power could do to discover her, was done— and done in vain. No clue was found to suggest a suspicion of her whereabouts, or to help in the slightest degree towards explaining the nature of the secret at which she had hinted in her letter. She was not seen again, not heard of again, at Porthgenna Tower, after the morning of the Twenty-Third of August, eighteen hundred and twenty-nine.

THE GIFT OF TONGUES.

An interesting feature in the late war was the multiplicity of languages with which it brought the western armies into contact. They occupied the soil of a people whose half barbarous speech was made up of contributions from Greek, Roman, Scythian, Median, Celt, Gothic Venetian, and Mongol Tartar. They heard the tongues of Wallachian, Bulgarian, Slovak, and Circassian. There was spoken among them English, French, Italian, German, Berber, Turkish, Egyptian, Modern Greek, besides some little Abasian, Persian, Croatian, and so forth. They were opposed to Russian, Polish, Usbec Nogars, and all Cossack forms of speech. In the midst of such a Babel who was so much at a loss for the gift of tongues

Figure 2. Graphic of epitaph. *The Dead Secret* serialized in *Household Words*, January–June, 1857. Special Collections, Honnold/Mudd Library for The Claremont Colleges, Claremont, California.

SACRED TO THE MEMORY

OF

𝕳𝖚𝖌𝖍 𝕻𝖔𝖑𝖜𝖍𝖊𝖆𝖑,

AGED 26 YEARS.

HE MET WITH HIS DEATH

THROUGH THE FALL OF A ROCK

IN

PORTHGENNA MINE,

DECEMBER 17TH, 1823.

Figure 3. *The Dead Secret.* Harper and Brothers illustrated edition, 1873. Courtesy of Honnold/Mudd Library for The Claremont Colleges, Claremont, California.

wears shroud-like garments and, with no subtle pun, has "grave" eyes and is bent in "grave enquiry."

This scene is later repeated by another astonishing entrance of a woman in white:

> There stood Miss Fairlie, a white figure, alone in the moonlight; in her attitude, in the turn of her head, in her complexion, in the shape of her face, the living image, at that distance and under those circumstances, of the woman in white! The doubt which had troubled my mind for hours and hours past, flashed into conviction in an instant. That 'something wanting' was my own recognition of the ominous likeness between the fugitive from the asylum and my pupil at Limmeridge House. (51)

Laura Fairlie, as "living image," is the complement to Anne Catherick ("T'ghaist of Mistress Fairlie") who is associated with "fatality." Though quite alive, Anne is figured as an apparition that haunts the likeness of Laura and the mind of Walter. The "something wanting" that both women embody emerges as the symbol of a blank space awaiting inscription, of the ghostly attributes that haunt the workings of language and meaning.

While Anne writes anonymously and Laura refuses to "mark" her identity, Mrs. Fairlie's absence-presence is encrypted on the white surface of her tombstone. Carolyn Dever remarks that Mrs. Fairlie's gravesite "is the locus of difference," the center of the dead mother plot (115). Tamar Heller observes, "The novel's most central symbolic site is the grave of Laura and Marian's mother, which functions as an image for women's lack of identity"[10] (114). I would agree that the site is the symbol of female lack and difference (or "otherness"), and would further argue that it is the symbol of the dichotomous workings of representation. Loss of origin, misreading, and the problematic of identity are bound up here, specifically in relation to the mingling of engraved and buried lies. In the novel, not only the gravesite but also the gravestone's inscription itself is overtly fetishized: the epitaph is repeatedly visited and gazed at, kissed, cleaned, traced, erased, amended and re-engraved. Walter describes it as such:

> The natural whiteness of the cross was a little clouded, here and there, by weather-stains; and rather more than one half of the square block beneath it, on the side which bore the inscription, was in the same condition. The other half, however, attracted my attention at once by its singular freedom from stain or impurity of any kind. I looked closer, and saw that it had been cleaned and the part that had not, was traceable wherever the inscription left a blank space of marble—sharply traceable as a line that had been produced by artificial means. Who had begun the cleansing of the marble, and who had left it unfinished? (78)

This "blank space" and the cleaning of the marble, of course, foreshadow Walter's later removal of Laura's name from the tombstone in the same churchyard at the end of the novel, but the scene also has a more symbolic significance. Reminiscent of the tombstone in *The Dead Secret*, Mrs. Fairlie's tombstone embodies a trace—here between legible and non-legible. The "traceable line" visually cuts the tombstone in half—it leaves "a blank space of marble." The line divides the readable and unreadable, life and death, body and text, presence and absence. Anticipating that the person who cleaned half of the stone will return to complete the cleaning, Walter decides to hide in the cemetery in order to survey the gravesite. He soon describes the appearance of a woman: "I saw the woman in a cloak approach close to the grave, and stand looking at it for a little while" (82). The woman proceeds to dip a white cotton cloth into the brook, kiss the tombstone, and then clean the inscription.[11] Walter learns that the grave tender is indeed the woman in white, Anne Catherick: "There, speaking affrightedly for itself—there was the same face confronting me over Mrs. Fairlie's grave, which had first looked into mine on the high-road by night" (83). Evidently Anne's power as the tomb-cleaner is not only in erasure but in revelation.[12] While the identity of Mrs. Fairlie is once again clearly legible (and legitimate), her epitaph stands in contrast to Anne, the embodiment of anonymity and illegitimacy.

If the epitaph is the uncanny voice of both life and death, it isn't surprising to find Anne drawn to the object that so exemplifies her existence. As she cleans the gravestone, Anne's near-necrophilic exclamations are overheard by Walter, " 'Oh, if I could die, and be hidden and at rest with *you*!' Her lips murmured the words close on the grave-stone; murmured them in tones of passionate endearment, to the dead remains beneath" (90). And similar to Sarah from *The Dead Secret*, she merges her body with the stone: "I heard her lips kissing the stone: I saw her hands beating on it passionately." And in an ironic foreshadowing, she states: "*I* shall not rest under the marble cross that I washed with my own hands, and made so white and pure for her sake" (255). (Indeed, she will be anonymously buried under the cross). Once again Anne enacts the merging of her dead body with the tombstone: "She crouched down over the flat stone of the grave, till her face was hidden on it," and she "never moved her face from the stone" (90). She tells Walter of Mrs. Fairlie: "Ah! she was fond of white in her lifetime; and here is white stone about her grave—and I am making it whiter for her sake" (89). Unlike Sarah Leeson who chooses to leave Hugh Polwheal's epitaph unreadable, by "making it whiter" Anne erases in order to reveal its decipherability as she creates a textual space for her own pronouncement of death.

The connection between Anne, Laura, and Mrs. Fairlie's grave is subsequently intensified (and perverted) by Sir Percival and Count Fosco's sensational death-plot, during which Anne subsequently dies, and most importantly, before the true Lady Glyde was to arrive in London. Count Fosco writes in his narrative: "When I got back, Anne Catherick was dead. Dead on the 25th; and Lady Glyde was not to arrive in London till the 26th!" (567).[13] The body-swapping plot, described by John Sutherland as "bizarre" and "cumbersome"[14] ("Wilkie Collins" 255), is further complicated by the fact that Laura's body must stand in for Anne at the asylum. The novel indeed forces the issue of metaphoric replacement. Laura later admits to Marian and Walter that she herself was unsure of her own identity after seeing the written "proof" of her existence as "Anne." Walter writes:

> This was the Asylum. Here she first heard herself called by Anne Catherick's name; and here, as a last remarkable circumstance in the story of the conspiracy, her own eyes informed her that she had Anne Catherick's clothes on. The nurse, on the first night in the Asylum, had shown her the marks on each article of underclothing as it was taken off, and had said, not at all irritably or unkindly, "Look at your own name on your own clothes, and don't worry us all any more about being Lady Glyde. She's dead and buried and you're alive and hearty. Do look at your clothes now! There it is, in good marking-ink; and there you will find it on all your old things, which we have kept in the house—Anne Catherick, as plain as print!" (393–94)

Again, body and text merge. The label, as metaphoric epitaph, embodies the identity of the dead. Laura has now become the walking epitaph for Anne Catherick, the textual voice for the presence-of-absence. It is only when Marian visits "Anne" at the asylum that the true identity of Laura is confirmed.

> Miss Halcombe advanced on her side, and the women advanced on theirs. When they were within a dozen paces of each other, one of the women stopped for an instant, looked eagerly at the strange lady, shook off the nurse's grasp

on her, and, the next moment, rushed into Miss Halcombe's arms. In that
moment Miss Halcombe recognized her sister—recognized the dead-alive.
(387)

It is a troubling scene: Marian (along with the reader) must instantly and
simultaneously bury Anne and raise Laura from the dead. Once again the
novel's burial-exhumation theme resurfaces; the cathartic sensation of recognizing "the dead-alive" is replayed.

In *Hide and Seek* (1854) Collins sets the revelation of buried identity in a
graveyard. Searching for his sister, Matthew Grice is told that a girl named
Mary was buried behind the church where "the poor were buried."

A few of the mounds had stained moldering tombstones at their heads. He
looked at these first; and finding only strange names on them, turned next to
the mounds marked out by cross-boards of wood. At one of the graves the
cross-board had been torn, or had rotted away, from its upright supports, and
lay on the ground weather-stained and soiled, but still faintly showing that it
had once had a few letters cut in it. He examined this board to begin with, and
was trying to make out what the letters were, when the sound of some one
approaching disturbed him. He looked up, and saw a woman walking slowly
toward the place where he was standing.   (349)

Here Mary Grice's identity is unknown; she is buried in a pauper's grave,
the initials "M.G." marked on a rotten wooden board at the foot of an
unkempt grave "in a dark corner among the trees." As with Collins's previous graveyard scenes, the visitor struggles with deciphering the epitaph; it is
a sign of the corpse's anonymity and the slippery workings of writing death.
Mary is virtually nameless; her identity is erased as the epitaph "M.G."
literally decomposes. It is mere coincidence that Mrs. Peckover, the sole
mourner of Mary, approaches the grave where Matthew is standing, his sister's braided hair bracelet in hand (fig. 4). It is a powerful scene, in which
Mary's identity and family are soon after revealed, and the grave in Bangbury
churchyard is later properly and "rightly" marked.

If for Collins the gravesite is the morbid apex of drama and narrativity, as
found in *Hide and Seek*, this is where *The Woman in White*'s most sensational
moment must occur. First, a visitor must enact the uncanny element of epitaph: he must attempt to read the slippery inscription. Upon his return to
England, Walter hears of Laura's death and proceeds to visit her grave to
mourn. "There was the marble cross, fair and white, at the head of the
tomb—the tomb that now rose over mother and daughter alike" (376).
Though fully aware of her death, Walter is incapable of reading Laura's name
on the headstone.

I stopped before the pedestal from which the cross rose. On one side of it, on
the side nearest to me, the newly-cut inscription met my eyes—the hard, clear

"LORD SAVE US!" SHE EXCLAIMED, RECOGNIZING IT.

Figure 4. *Hide and Seek*. Harper and Brothers illustrated edition, 1873. Courtesy of Honnold/Mudd Library for The Claremont Colleges, Claremont, California.

cruel black letters which told the story of her life and death. I tried to read
them. I did read, as far as the name. 'Sacred to the Memory of Laura——...'
    A second time I tried to read the inscription. I saw, at the end, the date of
her death; and above it——
    Above it, there were lines on the marble, there was a name among them,
which disturbed my thoughts of her. I went round to the other side of the grave,
where there was nothing to read—.   (376)

Eerily reminiscent of Matthew Grice in *Hide and Seek* and then later Sarah
Leeson in Collins's *The Dead Secret* who visits the grave of her lost love
and attempts to read the inscription, Walter finds the epitaph difficult, if not
incapable, to read. As the name "Glyde" slides off the stone, it is as if
Walter somehow realizes the inscription is a lie—that his faltering reflects
the hesitation to believe in Laura's death, reflects the indecipherability of
death itself. The blank side of the tombstone provides relief, for literally,
instead of figuratively, he cannot read it.
    Next, for the sensational element of narrative to be enacted, the symbol of
destabilization must be the site for figural exhumation.

The veiled woman with her cried out faintly. I stopped. The springs of my life
fell low; and the shuddering of an unutterable dread crept over me from head
to foot . . . the veiled woman had possession of me, body and soul. She stopped
on one side of the grave. We stood face to face, with the tombstone between
us. She was close to the inscription on the side of the pedestal. Her gown
touched the black letters.
    The voice came nearer, and rose and rose more passionately still. 'Hide your
face! don't look at her! Oh, for God's sake, spare him!——'
    The woman lifted her veil.

> ### *Sacred*
> TO THE MEMORY OF
> **LAURA,**
> LADY GLYDE,——

Laura, Lady Glyde, was standing by the inscription, and was looking at me
over the grave.[15]   (378)

Despite the appearance of her name on the gravestone (written testament of
her death), Laura, recently "escaped" from the asylum, is very much alive.[16]
Later to be used by Dickens in *Great Expectations*, where the haunting figure
of Magwitch (a surrogate parent of sorts) appears near the tombstone of Pip's
parents for shocking and symbolic effect (fig. 5), the scene is uncanny for
at once Laura appears to be both Anne Catherick and her own ghost; she
simultaneously appears and disappears, unveils and veils. This marks the
height of sensation for the novel and is illustrated in the 1873 edition (fig.
6). As in Pailthorpe's illustration "The Terrible Stranger in the Churchyard,"

The Terrible Stranger in the Churchyard

Figure 5. F. W. Pailthorpe. ''The Terrible Stranger in the Churchyard.'' 1885. *Great Expectations. The New Oxford Illustrated Editions.*

LAURA, LADY GLYDE, WAS STANDING BY THE INSCRIPTION, AND WAS
LOOKING AT ME OVER THE GRAVE.

Figure 6. Harper and Brothers illustrated edition. 1873. *The Woman in White*.
Courtesy of Honnold/Mudd Library for The Claremont Colleges, Claremont, California.

the body and epitaph appear to merge; the dichotomies of alive-dead and voice-silence are conflated. Here Walter is re-living the experience of young Jacob Postlethwaite in reverse: he sees the ghost of Laura who must in reality be Anne, the true corpse that the tombstone fails to mark. The appearance of Laura's own body denies the text; she is the haunting presence of the physically impossible. As ''the dead-alive,'' Laura is in fact the living embodiment of the unreadable epitaph—she has inherited Anne's previous role as her own walking tombstone.

For added drama and realism, Collins graphically reproduces the epitaph in part, and visually marks with a drawn line Walters inability to read her death in its entirety: Lady Glyde,—. The line drawn after Glyde, not drawn in the manuscript, also represents the blankness of death and is not reproduced

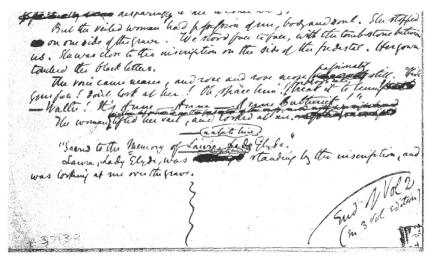

Figure 7. Manuscript. *The Woman in White*. Courtesy of The Pierpont Morgan Library (MA79).

in the second half of the novel (fig. 7). The manuscript shows that Collins did instruct that white lines be placed above and below the partial epitaph, which are reproduced, but he also included a line extracted from subsequent publications:—Walter! Its Anne—Anne—Anne Catherick! (also fig. 7). Clearly Collins wanted Laura to announce that it is Anne who is dead and buried in her wrongly marked grave. This line most likely was deleted by Collins from the serial publication so that the morbidly ironic position of Laura at her own gravesite would be sensationalized, but it also contributes to Collins's perpetuation of the shifting nature of signification and inscription where names, identities, and mortalities are interchangeable.

III

In Wilkie Collins's early novel *Basil* (1852), the attempt to destroy identity is violently dramatized. Here Basil, the narrator, is textually illegitimized for dishonoring his father's wishes. Taking out the family Bible, Basil's father opens it to the page displaying the family tree. "At the top, a miniature portrait of me, when a child, was let into the leaf. Under it, was the record of my birth and names . . . below, a large blank space was left for the entry of future particulars" Basil relates (201–2). His father then proceeds to destroy the page:

> "In this record your place is destroyed—and destroyed for ever. Would to God I could tear the past from my memory, as I tear the leaf from this book!" . . . My father rent out from the book before him the whole of the leaf which contained my name; tore it into fragments, and cast them on the floor.   (203)

Being forced to abandon his father's name, Basil describes that this act of destruction incurred a blank "wherever my father's name should appear." This scene of ripping out the proof of identity and leaving a blank space where the record of legitimacy previously was located is mirrored in *The Woman in White*. Peter Brooks designates the parish register as "the most important text of all" (170), and Collins was so pleased with the register plot that he later recycles it for *Armadale*. Ironically "copies" of writing determine the illegitimacy of Sir Percival. In fact, it is a blank space that signifies his origins. Walter relates this discovery as such:

> I turned to the month of September, eighteen hundred and three. I found the marriage of the man whose Christian name was the same as my own. I found the double register of the marriages of the two brothers. And between these entries at the bottom of the page? Nothing! Not a vestige of the entry which recorded the marriage of Sir Felix Glyde and Cecilia Jane Elster, in the register of the church!   (470)

The absence of Sir Felix Glyde's marriage—the blank—signifies.[17] In a metaphoric doubling of the troublesome link between Philip Fairlie's legitimate and illegitimate daughters, Laura and Anne, Glyde forges himself into legitimacy. The name "Glyde"—literally denoting that words (whether true or false) are slippery and intangible—is important. Sir Percival's attempt to fictionally legitimize himself (in opposition to Anne's power to erase and reveal) has been exposed—his aristocracy "glides" off of him. The forged, textual evidence of a marriage ceremony, squeezed into the blank space of the register, is a textual rape, much like Fosco's forced entry into Marian's diary.[18] Ultimately, Sir Percival, just as Walter and even Collins himself, can be seen as a type of fictional author, filling up gaps with writing. Here the scene in *Basil* is reversed: Sir Percival fills the blank space with legitimacy while Basil's father creates a blank space by attempting to render his son "illegitimate," figuratively "dead" to the family. Walter further describes this textual gap:

> The marriage was not there. The entries on the copy occupied exactly the same places on the page as the entries in the original. The last entry on one page recorded the marriage of the man with my Christian name. Below it, there was a blank space—a space evidently left because it was too narrow to contain the entry of the marriages of the two brothers, which in the copy, as in the original, occupied the top of the next page.   (470–71)

The multiple narration of the novel is reflected not only by Mrs. Fairlie's tombstone, but in the marriage register itself, for its three versions lead Walter to unveil Sir Percival's secret. With this blank space, Collins demonstrates the power of absence to signify.

> That space told the whole story! There it must have remained, in the church register, from eighteen hundred and three (when the marriages had been solemnized and the copy had been made) to eighteen hundred and twenty-seven, when Sir Percival appeared at Old Welmingham. Here, at Knowlesbury, was the chance of committing the forgery, shown to me in the copy—and there, at Old Welmingham, was the forgery committed, in the register of the church!
>   (471)

The buried secret is paradoxically exposed by a "space that told the whole story," an exposed grave symbolizing the demise of his forged identity.

Engraved and buried signs are crucial to the identification of Sir Percival in death (his engraved watch in this case) as well as the accomplice in Laura's legal death, Count Fosco. Unlike Laura and Anne, Count Fosco is more than pleased to apply his signature to the blank page. He signs his narrative which admits his crimes and duplicities, and upon his forced entry into Marian's diary, he signs it with aplomb: "FOSCO." Important for this discussion are the ways in which Collins conflates notions of the body and text. With Professor Pesca's assistance, Walter discovers that Count Fosco is an exiled member of an Italian Brotherhood that marks all its members with a distinct tattoo. Pesca informs Walter: "We are identified with the Brotherhood by a secret mark, which we all bear, which lasts while our lives last" (536). It is a mark directly linked to mortality—somehow the sign changes at death. He then shows Walter the identification mark:

> He raised his bare arm, and showed me, high on the upper part of it and on the inner side, a brand deeply burnt in the flesh and stained of a bright blood-red color. I abstain from describing the device which the brand represented. It

will be sufficient to say that it was circular in form, and so small that it would
have been completely covered by a shilling coin.   (537)

Reminiscent of Anne, who carried on her body the symbol of living death,
the presence of absence, Fosco also harbors a brand that is the marker of his
mortality: the emblem of epitaphic gesture.

Fished out of the Seine and then exhibited (as anonymous) at the infamous
Paris dead-house, the Morgue (notably visited by Collins and Dickens on
several occasions),[19] Fosco's dead body contains the sign of his assassination.
Walter describes the particular markings of death:

> The wound that had killed him had been struck with a knife or dagger exactly
> over his heart. No other traces of violence appeared about the body, except on
> the left arm; and there, exactly in the place where I had seen the brand on
> Pesca's arm, were two deep cuts in the shape of the letter T, which entirely
> obliterated the mark of the Brotherhood.   (581)

Assassinated, Fosco's identity and mortality are usurped by the Brotherhood,
just as he usurped Anne and Laura's. Walter describes further: "The two
cuts, in the form of a T, on the left arm of the dead man, signified the Italian
word, 'Traditore,' and showed that justice had been done by the Brotherhood
on a Traitor" (581). Philip O'Neill remarks, "By erasing the scar, the society
put things to right. All signs now reflect reality" (124). But Fosco's body,
just as Marian's diary, is textually raped. The spectacle of his corpse demonstrates that even in death the body is able to signify. This reinscription foreshadows the reinscription of Laura's tombstone (and is an odd reversal of
Pip's personification of his parents' tombstone). We learn that he is a double
agent; his duplicitous identity becomes symbolized by double writing. It is
also appropriate that the man whom has discovered a "means of petrifying
the body after death, so as to preserve it, as hard as marble, to the end of
time" (199) is not preserved; his corpse is defiled, designated traitor, and
"performs" in death. Resembling Sir Percival's corpse that was suspended
in anonymity, Fosco's corpse is displayed, naked and nameless, to the Pari-
sian public. Incidentally, Walter writes, "The body was identified, the day
after I had seen it, by means of an anonymous letter addressed to his wife"
(582). Similar to Anne's earlier letters of warning, the anonymous body,
signed by the mark of the Brotherhood and then re-signed, is ironically identified by the absence of a signature.

IV

Through an accumulation of evidence and speculation, Walter discovers that
the "fatal resemblance" between Anne and Laura is genuine: they both share

the same father.[20] This complicates Anne's burial even further, for as the illegitimate daughter of Philip Fairlie, she is indeed buried in the proper grave, next to her father's wife, marked "Daughter of the late Philip Fairlie Esq." The epitaph, in part, thus "writes" Anne correctly. Yet Anne still "claims the name, place, and the living personality of dead Lady Glyde," her half-sister, complicating a unique reversal of mortalities (380). Laura as well is a phantom-figure, alive in the eyes of Marian and Walter, but dead to everyone else: "In the eye of reason and of law, in the estimation of relatives and friends, according to every received formality of civilized society, 'Laura, Lady Glyde,' lay buried with her mother in the Limmeridge churchyard" (380). While Anne underwent a loss of identity as an inmate of the asylum, Laura too undergoes a similar obliteration. The novel must now rewrite itself and give a credible explanation for Laura as "living" so that Anne can be properly interred (and referred).

For Collins, the tombstone repeatedly lies, for it embodies the voice of the impossible. It is as if the novel itself—through the metaphor of the tomb-stone—desires to expose the problems of narrating death. Walter explains his desire to re-engrave the tombstone with truth: "Lady Glyde . . . has been cast out as a stranger from the house in which she was born   a Lie which records her death has been written on her mother's tomb." Inevitably, the stone must be cleansed. "That house shall open again to receive her," he continues, "in the presence of every soul who followed the false funeral to the grave; that lie shall be publicly erased from the tombstone" (410). Walter desires to "right" the dead by re-performing the funeral rites (a textual exorcism of sorts), and by correctly "writing" the dead.[21] And that is in fact Walter's task: as textual excavator, he must legally resurrect Laura from the grave of Sir Percival and Count Fosco's inheritance plot. This task involves him in countering physical objects that have been turned into forged "narratives" such as "The Narrative of the Doctor" and "The Narrative of the Tomb-stone," "the most evil false text in the novel" (Kendrick 29). The documents are a doubling of the epitaph's lie; they embody the triumph of false narrative. For realistic effect, Collins chooses to graphically reproduce these documents, as illustrated in subsequent volume editions.

THE NARRATIVE OF THE DOCTOR

To The Registrar of the Sub-District in which the under-mentioned Death took place.——I hereby certify that I attended *Lady Glyde*, aged *Twenty-one* last Birthday ; that I last saw her, on *the 25th July*, 1850 ; that she died *on the same day at No. 5, Forest-road, St. John's Wood* ; and that the cause of her death was

CAUSE OF	DURATION OF
DEATH	DISEASE
Aneurism	Not known

Signed,
Alfred Goodricke

Prof. Title. *M.R.C.S. Eng. L.S.A.*
Address. 12, *Croydon Gardens, St. John's Wood.*

Collins's reproduction of "The Narrative of the Tombstone" is striking:

Sacred
TO THE MEMORY OF
LAURA
LADY GLYDE,
WIFE OF SIR PERCIVAL GLYDE, BART.,
OF BLACKWATER PARK, HAMPSHIRE;
AND
DAUGHTER OF THE LATE PHILIP FAIRLIE ESQ.,
OF LIMMERIDGE HOUSE, IN THIS PARISH.
BORN, MARCH 27TH, 1829.
MARRIED, DECEMBER 22ND, 1849
DIED, JULY 25TH, 1850.

Collins's attention to detail is again evident in the manuscript and serial publication. The manuscript emphatically demonstrates the desire for veracity. For "The Narrative of the Doctor" Collins draws the small box representing the certificate and designates which words are to be italicized and capitalized (fig. 8).

Considering the narrow columns and limited space, it is quite amazing that these directions were approved for *All the Year Round* as well (fig. 9). "The Narrative of the Tomb Stone" also incurs some typographical changes from the manuscript, but the power of the tombstone is apparent. In the manuscript, Collins designates that "a black line" be drawn above and below the epitaph and that capitals be used for the first letter of certain words (fig. 10). "Sacred" and "Laura" are to be all capitals. In *All the Year Round* a box is drawn around the epitaph, an addition that helps the narrative resemble a true marker (fig. 11). "Sacred" is in script and only the "S" is capitalized, while "Laura" is printed largest and in all capitals. The remainder of the narrative is in small yet all capital letters, a change from the manuscript instructions.

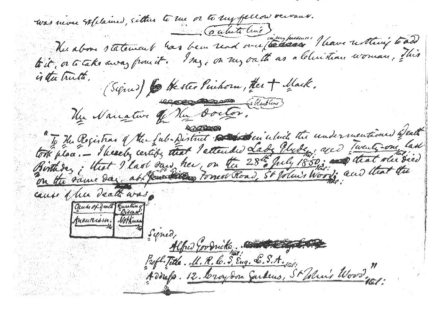

Figure 8. "The Narrative of the Doctor." Manuscript. *The Woman in White*. Courtesy of The Pierpont Morgan Library (MA79).

While attention to type and spacing is emphasized, Collins mistakenly writes the incorrect marriage date as "December 23rd" and it is printed thus in *All the Year Round*.[22] Interestingly, H. P. Sucksmith chose to use the serialized version of the novel in *All the Year Round* as the basis for his Oxford edition, which thereby reproduces the death certificate and tombstone as shown in Collins's manuscript. Subsequent scholarly editions of the novel have unfairly ignored Collins's intentions, diminishing the emotional and visual impact of the narratives.

In the end, the novel must return to Mrs. Fairlie and Laura's gravesite, the textual locus of the novel that embodies shifting and erroneous narratives. This will be the last lesson in epitaphic function. After gathering the proof of Anne's death and illegitimacy, and of Laura's survival and true identity, Walter is equipped with enough textual evidence to erase the false tombstone. For evidence, Walter takes a copy, a tracing, of the epitaph: "My last labor, as the evening approached, was to obtain 'The Narrative of the Tombstone,' by taking a copy of the false inscription on the grave, before it was erased" (575). In a way, this "tracing" of the false narrative perpetuates a false-hood—it leaves a trace of the lying text. The next day the redramatization of the funeral occurs. It is a pseudo-legal reenactment that "rights" Anne's burial rites. Walter explains: "I invited all the persons present . . . to follow over the sick lady. He looked very serious, all on a sudden, at the sight of her; and put his hand on her heart.

My mistress stared hard in Mr. Goodricke's face. "Not dead!" says she, whispering, and turning all of a tremble from head to foot.

"Yes," says the doctor, very quiet and grave. "Dead. I was afraid it would happen suddenly, when I examined her heart yesterday." My mistress stepped back from the bedside, while he was speaking, and trembled and trembled again. "Dead!" she whispers to herself; "dead so suddenly! dead so soon! What will the Count say?" Mr. Goodricke advised her to go down stairs, and quiet herself a little. "You have been sitting up all night," says he; "and your nerves are shaken. This person," says he, meaning me, "this person will stay in the room, till I can send for the necessary assistance." My mistress did as he told her. "I must prepare the Count," she says. "I must carefully prepare the Count." And so she left us, shaking from head to foot, and went out.

"Your master is a foreigner," says Mr. Goodricke, when my mistress had left us. "Does he understand about registering the death?" "I can't rightly tell, sir," says I; "but I should think not." The doctor considered a minute; and then, says he, "I don't usually do such things," says he, "but it may save the family trouble in this case, if I register the death myself. I shall pass the district office in half an hour's time; and I can easily look in. Mention, if you please, that I will do so." "Yes, sir," says I, "with thanks, I'm sure, for your kindness in thinking of it." "You don't mind staying here, till I can send you the proper person?" says he. "No, sir," says I; "I'll stay with the poor lady, till then. I suppose nothing more could be done, sir, than was done?" says I. "No," says he; "nothing; she must have suffered sadly before ever I saw her: the case was hopeless when I was called in." "Ah, dear me! we all come to it, sooner or later, don't we, sir?" says I. He gave no answer to that; he didn't seem to care about talking. He said, "Good day," and went out.

I stopped by the bedside from that time, till the time when Mr. Goodricke sent the person in, as he had promised. She was, by name, Jane Gould. I considered her to be a respectable-looking woman. She made no remark, except to say that she understood what was wanted of her, and that she had winded a many of them in her time.

How master bore the news, when he first heard it, is more than I can tell; not having been present. When I did see him, he looked being most beautiful. The dead lady's husband was away, as we heard, in foreign parts. But my mistress (being her aunt) settled it with her friends in the country (Cumberland, I think) that she should be buried there, in the same grave along with her mother. Everything was done handsomely, in respect of the funeral, I say again; and master went down to attend the burying in the country himself. He looked grand in his deep mourning, with his big solemn face, and his slow walk, and his broad hatband—that he did!

In conclusion, I have to say, in answer to questions put to me,

(1) That neither I nor my fellow-servant ever saw my master give Lady Glyde any medicine himself.

(2) That he was never, to my knowledge and belief, left alone in the room with Lady Glyde.

(3) That I am not able to say what caused the sudden fright, which my mistress informed me had seized the lady on her first coming into the house. The cause was never explained, either to me or to my fellow-servant.

The above statement has been read over in my presence. I have nothing to add to it, or to take away from it. I say, on my oath as a Christian woman, This is the truth.

(Signed)   Hester Pinhorn, Her + Mark.

THE NARRATIVE OF THE DOCTOR.

"To The Registrar of the Sub-District in which the under-mentioned Death took place.— I hereby certify that I attended *Lady Glyde*, aged *Twenty-one* last Birthday; that I last saw her, on *the 28th July*, 1850; that she died on *the same day at No. 5, Forest-road, St. John's Wood;* and that the cause of her death was

CAUSE OF DEATH.	DURATION OF DISEASE.
Aneurism.	*Not known.*

Signed,
        Alfred Goodricke.
Prof'. Title. *M.R.C.S. Eng. L.S.A.*
Address. 12, *Croydon Gardens, St. John's Wood.*

THE NARRATIVE OF JANE GOULD.

I WAS the person sent in by Mr. Goodricke, to do what was right and needful by the remains of a lady, who had died at the house named in the certificate which precedes this. I found the body

Figure 9. "The Narrative of the Doctor." *The Woman in White* serialized in *All the Year Round*, May 1860. Special Collections, Honnold/Mudd Library for The Claremont Colleges, Claremont, California.

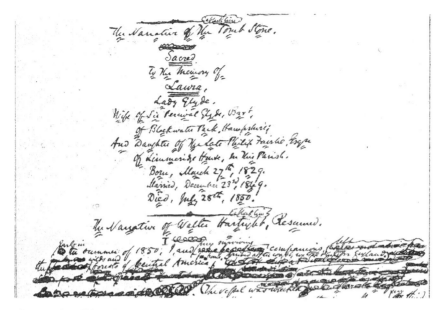

Figure 10. "The Narrative of The Tomb Stone." Manuscript. *The Woman in White*. Courtesy of The Pierpont Morgan Library (MA79).

me to the churchyard, and see the false inscription struck off the tombstone with their own eyes" (577). The epitaph, "The Narrative of the Tombstone," is its own piece of evidence. As the novel's "editor," Walter here exerts ultimate control over narrative. Reenacting Anne's tomb-cleaning, he demonstrates the power to erase and alter the fiction. The letters of the tombstone are then chiseled off; the false signature is erased: "Not a voice was heard; not a soul moved, till those three words, 'Laura, Lady Glyde,' had vanished from sight. Then, there was a great heave of relief among the crowd, as if they felt that the last fetters of the conspiracy had been struck off Laura herself" (577). Clearly the graphic tombstone that Collins provides makes the visualization of the erasure scene more violent and extraordinary. Similar to Pip who merges the epitaph with notions of the physical body, here Laura is a living representation of the engraved letters of death. As with other bodies in the novel (notably Fosco's corpse), Laura's body merges with text and must be "struck" in order to properly signify. Next, the false narrative is exposed and then an imposing revisionary narrative is laid over the inscription of origins. "It was late in the day before the whole inscription was erased. One line only was afterwards engraved in its place: 'Anne Catherick, July 25th, 1850' " (577). The reinscription of the narrative of the tombstone symbolizes the proper joining of Anne with Mrs. Fairlie in death, while the racter to Mr. Goodricke. He has known me for more than six years; and he will bear witness that I can be trusted to tell the truth.

            (Signed)   *Jane Gould.*

THE NARRATIVE OF THE TOMBSTONE.

Sacred
TO THE MEMORY OF
LAURA,
LADY GLYDE,
WIFE OF SIR PERCIVAL GLYDE, BART.,
OF BLACKWATER PARK, HAMPSHIRE;
AND
DAUGHTER OF THE LATE PHILIP FAIRLIE, ESQ.,
OF LIMMERIDGE HOUSE, IN THIS PARISH.
BORN, MARCH 27TH, 1829.
MARRIED, DECEMBER 23RD, 1849
DIED, JULY 28TH, 1850.

THE NARRATIVE OF WALTER HARTRIGHT, RESUMED.

I.

EARLY in the summer of 1850, I, and my surviving companions, left the wilds and forests of Central America for home. Arrived at the coast, we took ship there for England. The vessel was wrecked in the Gulf of Mexico; I was among the few saved from the sea. It was my third escape from peril of death. Death by disease, death by the Indians, death by drowning—all three had approached me; all three had passed me by.

The survivors of the wreck were rescued by an American vessel, bound for Liverpool. The ship reached her port on the thirteenth day of October, 1850. We landed late in the afternoon; and I arrived in London the same night.

These pages are not the record of my wanderings and my dangers away from home. The motives which led me from my country and my friends to a new world of adventure and peril are known. From that self-imposed exile I came back, as I had hoped, prayed, believed I should come back—a changed man. In the waters of a new life I had tempered my nature afresh. In the stern school of extremity and danger my will had learnt to be strong, my heart to be resolute, my mind to rely on itself. I had gone out to fly from my own future. I came back to face it, as a man should.

To face it with that inevitable suppression of myself which I knew it would demand

back to the old love. I write of her as Laura Fairlie still. It is hard to think of her, it is hard to speak of her, by her husband's name.

There are no more words of explanation to add, on my appearing for the second time in these pages. This final narrative, if I have the strength and the courage to write it, may now go on.

My first anxieties and first hopes, when the morning came, centred in my mother and my sister. I felt the necessity of preparing them for the joy and surprise of my return, after an absence, during which it had been impossible for them to receive any tidings of me for months past. Early in the morning, I sent a letter to the Hampstead Cottage; and followed it myself, in an hour's time.

When the first meeting was over, when our quiet and composure of other days began gradually to return to us, I saw something in my mother's face which told me that a secret oppression lay heavy on her heart. There was more than love—there was sorrow in the anxious eyes that looked on me so tenderly; there was pity in the kind hand that slowly and fondly strengthened its hold on mine. We had no concealments from each other. She knew how the hope of my life had been wrecked—she knew why I had left her. It was on my lips to ask as composedly as I could, if any letter had come for me from Miss Halcombe—if there was any news of her sister that I might hear. But, when I looked in my mother's face, I lost courage to put the question even in that guarded form. I could only say, doubtfully and restrainedly,

"You have something to tell me."

My sister, who had been sitting opposite to us, rose suddenly, without a word of explanation—rose, and left the room.

My mother moved closer to me on the sofa, and put her arms round my neck. Those fond arms trembled; the tears flowed fast over the faithful, loving face.

"Walter!" she whispered—"my own darling! my heart is heavy for you. Oh, my son! my son! try to remember that I am still left!"

My head sank on her bosom. She had said all, in saying those words.

II.

IT was the morning of the third day since my return—the morning of the sixteenth of October.

Figure 11. Graphic of epitaph. *The Woman in White*, serialized in *Household Words*, 1859–1860. Special Collections, Honnold/Mudd Library for The Claremont Colleges, Claremont, California.

subversive epitaph next to Mrs. Fairlie's inscription is a blank space waiting for Laura's true signification.

Though its ambiguity remains, the narrative now attempts to construct a credible version of the death story. The second half of the novel has worked to achieve this point—finally Laura is textually exhumed and Anne is properly and correctly buried. In the end the burial-plot is unraveled: bodies and corpses reflect their proper mortalities, and texts properly signify their referents. Yet the epitaph's textual vulnerability persists.[23] Elam explains: "The possibility of slippage remains, as does the narrative palimpsest on the tombstone: Anne's name inscribed over Laura's erased name" (61).[24] Indeed the trace of the erasure (reflecting the trace left earlier by Anne's cleaning), is now a trace of Laura's unwritten death. While Anne's name is chiseled over Laura's lying epitaph, the trace remains as a ghostly reminder of Laura's fate. As this scene exemplifies, language is unstable, under erasure, and consumable. Similar to the marriage register, the tombstone inscription incurs multiple versions: Mrs. Fairlie's, Laura's, Walter's copy, Laura's erased, and then Anne's. The tombstone, with its multiple narratives, is thus an emblem for the novel as a whole—an emblem for all textuality as a mourning of truth and presence.

V

This examination of narrativity and epitaph would be incomplete without the discussion of Wilkie Collins's own will and gravesite. When Collins died on September 23, 1889, he left clear and meticulous instructions about his funeral and burial. Kenneth Robinson notes: "His Will was drawn up with the precision and attention to detail that one would have expected. It is dated March 22nd, 1882" (324). Resembling Collins's attention to typographical detail in his fiction, particular consideration was paid to the tombstone and its inscription.

> I direct that all my just debts and funeral expenses shall be paid with all convenient speed after my decease. I desire to be buried in the Cemetery at Kensal Green and that over my grave there be placed a plain stone and no other monument and that there shall be placed on such stone cross the inscription which my executors will find written and placed in the same envelope occupied by this will and I desire that nothing shall be inscribed upon the said cross except the inscription which I have herein before directed.[25]

His will includes specific details regarding not only his gravesite, but the funeral expenses, mourning wear, and attendants.

And it is my will that exclusive of the expense of purchasing the customary grave and of setting up the plain stone cross and putting the inscription thereon my funeral expenses shall not exceed twenty five pounds and I direct that no scarves hat bands or feathers shall be worn or used at my funeral.

For an author of such notoriety and national acclaim (though at the time he was avidly read but "little esteemed or talked of" according to early biographers) he requested an unassuming headstone: "Over my grave a plain stone cross." The will resounds with Collins's own willfulness; there is an ironic pun on the phrase "it is my *will* that . . . my funeral expenses shall not exceed twenty five pounds," while the phrase "the plain cross" and his request that it should never be altered is stated three times. Propriety aside, perhaps this anxious statement reflects the acknowledgment in his fiction that tombstones are places of textual disruption and misreading; that somehow writing can be erased and reinscripted but that the layers of signification persist. His request for a large, white cross uncannily resembles the description of Hermanric's grave in *Antonina* on which is raised "a white marble cross" with a short Latin inscription, and Mrs. Fairlie's own "white marble cross."

Collins displayed his interest in epitaphs by not only graphically reproducing them in his novels, but by authoring his own. Collins's epitaph is engraved on a marble block below the cross, distinctly matching the placement of Mrs. Fairlie's inscription: "At the square block of marble below it [the cross]" (78). The tombstone is engraved with his name and dates and the inscription he had wanted (fig. 12).

In Memory of

WILKIE COLLINS

AUTHOR OF "THE WOMAN IN WHITE"
AND OTHER WORKS OF FICTION.

Born 8th January 1824
Died 23rd September 1889

The "inscription which my executors shall find included in this envelope" exemplifies his alignment in death with the immortal work for which he was most known. Indeed the epitaph is quite uncanny, for it emblematizes the fiction that so fetishizes the narrative function of the epitaph itself. Collins's epitaph is thereby a doubling of death and narrative. In *The King of Inventors: A Life of Wilkie Collins*, Catherine Peters observes: "The inscription he chose for his memorial, 'Author of The Woman in White and other works of fiction'—forbidding anything to be added to it—acknowledged where he felt the final significance of his life to lie. He wanted no religious or sentimental

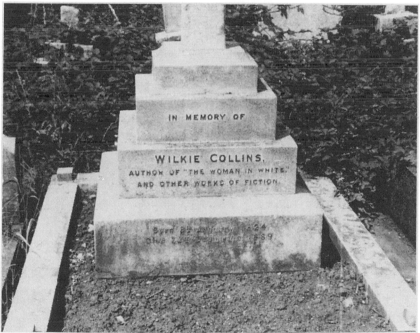

Figure 12. Wilkie Collins's gravesite, Kensal Green (Grave number/Square/ Row 31754/141/1). Before the recent restoration, ''In Memory Of'' was engraved in a script font. With kind permission of Andrew Gasson, Chairman, Wilkie Collins Society.

effusions, no mention of heaven or family'' (432). This choice in some way resembles Hugh Polwheal's tombstone in *The Dead Secret*, where Sarah Leeson's initials and dates will be inscribed upon her death according to Rosamund's belief that a ''short and simple inscription is the fittest and the best'' (361). Wordsworth designates the role of the epitaph for the heroic as one in which the contribution to the betterment of society should be noted: ''Of course ought the attention to be directed chiefly to those actions or that act'' (105). Appropriately the novel that is obsessed with writing death should be presented as the ''action'' for which Collins is to be memorialized. For Collins, his fictional burial-plot, *The Woman in White*, is to be considered his own true haunting legacy.

Significant to Collins's ''buried'' life is Caroline Elizabeth Graves. There has been much speculation regarding Caroline as the inspiration for *The Woman in White*, and many now dismiss that she was the ''shadowy'' woman in white he encountered on the streets of London in 1859.[26] The main source for the premise of the novel has since been identified by Hyder and is widely accepted (299).[27] Important for this discussion is that she can be seen to embody the fictional woman in white in important and disturbing ways. As Collins's mistress and muse for close to thirty years, Caroline Elizabeth Graves plays a considerable role in Collins's own burial-plot which is just as mysterious as one of his fictions. It is upon his death that his lifelong relationship with her (and the more recent with Martha Rudd) is revealed. In his will, which would become ''public'' knowledge, he leaves her his ''gold studs'' and the contents of her bedroom and his study. The income from his estate he put in trust, half going to Caroline and her daughter. For over five years Caroline Graves took care of his resting place at Kensal Green, London (eerily, the tender of Collins's grave is Mrs. ''Graves'').[28] It is somehow appropriate that the woman who possibly inspired the infamous scene at the opening of *The Woman in White* tends the grave of its creator, cleans the stone that marks her textual re-invention. Caroline's actions double those of Anne Catherick, not only in the infamous opening of the novel, but in Anne's fetishizing of Mrs. Fairlie's grave—both women are walking epitaphs, embodying ''the woman in white'' and *The Woman in White*.

Ironically, and in an uncanny reflection of the novel, upon Caroline Graves's death in 1895 (a reversal of the ''birth date'' of *The Woman in White* in 1859), no stone was erected, no inscription was engraved. She requested to be buried with Wilkie Collins, and as stated in his will, his epitaph was left without reinscription. ''When the grave was opened again in 1895, for Caroline's coffin, no word was added to mark it as her resting place'' (Peters 432). Collins's sealed instructions most likely contained Collins's wish to have Caroline (anonymously) buried with him. Hyder remarks, ''No other name is marked on that stone, but with Collins lies buried Caroline

Elizabeth Graves, who died in June, 1895, at 24 Newman Street, aged sixty-one, apparently the widow of a George Robert Graves'' (297).[29] Caroline Graves's grave is unmarked; it is a blank tombstone, infinitely awaiting inscription. Aptly, this woman in white is signified in death only by the novel she may have inspired. Even more disturbing is the fact that her surname (obviously missing from the inscription) signifies Collins's burial-plot(s)—the two bodies that lay below the white cross in Kensal Green. It is fitting that Collins's grave doubles Mrs. Fairlie's for both ''plots'' contain two corpses, suspend death, await the proper burial of an interred body, and include inscriptions that are only half-correct—both epitaphs fail to inscribe death. But while Collins's fiction concludes with the eventual ''righting'' and ''writing'' of death, Caroline Graves is infinitely represented by a blank space. Collins's intentional last words and testament are false and incomplete, for his own ''Narrative of the Tombstone'' demonstrates the uncanny workings of epitaph as it leaves us perpetually searching for its dead secret.

NOTES

I wish to thank Marc Redfield, Lillian Nayder, and William Baker for their thoughtful responses to early versions of this essay, and Steve Bamberger for his assistance with the illustrations.

1. Karen Mills Campbell, ''Poetry as Epitaph'' *Journal of Popular Culture* 14, 4 (1981) 659.
2. Cynthia Chase, ''Reading Epitaphs.'' *Deconstruction is/in America: A New Sense of the Political.* Ed. Anselm Haverkamp (New York: New York UP, 1995) 52.
3. *The Woman in White* was published serially in *All the Year Round* from Nov. 23, 1859–Aug. 22, 1860 while *Great Expectations* appeared Dec. 1, 1860–Aug. 3, 1861.
4. See studies such as those of Gilbert and Gubar, Diane Elam, and Tamar Heller. This paper is indebted to the work of Carolyn Dever whose work examines the feminist, Freudian, and deconstructive implications of the Victorian dead mother.
5. Tillotson further remarks that ''By 1870, 'dead, yet not dead' had become such a stereotype that it is difficult to imagine Dickens adopting it'' (xxv).
6. Wilkie Collins, *The Dead Secret* (Harper and Brothers 1873) 34. In his Introduction to the Oxford edition, Ira B. Nadel notes, ''For added, realism, Collins reproduces the inscription of the headstone, as he will do later in *The Woman in White*'' *The Dead Secret* (Oxford: Oxford UP, 1999. xiv). The Oxford edition does not reproduce the accurate spacing or font as printed in the serial version in *Household Words*.
7. Many thanks to Ira Nadel and Andrew Gasson for their help with confirming that the location of the manuscript for *The Dead Secret* is not known.

8. In the Introduction to Collins's *Mad Monkton and Other Stories* (Oxford: Oxford UP, 1994) Norman Page notes: "The chance meeting with a mysterious woman, always a potent stimulus to Collins's imagination, recurs most famously in *The Woman in White* (1860), though Collins had used it earlier, and crucially, in *Basil*" (xvii). The theme was also used in Collins's short story "The Ostler" (1855).

9. One of Dickens's sons recalled his father saying that the description was "one of the most dramatic descriptions he could recall." The other was the account of the march of the women to Versailles in Carlyle's *French Revolution*. See *The Recollections of Sir Henry Dickens* (London, 1934) 54. *The Woman in White* was published serially following Dickens's *A Tale of Two Cities* (1859). Both novels revolve around doubled figures that are substituted for each other. In the Introduction to Collins's *Mad Monkton and Other Stories* Norman Page remarks: " 'The Lady of Glenwith Grange' (1856) is a particularly good illustration of Collins's general tendency to anticipate in his short stories elements that would reappear more prominently in his—and sometimes not only his—longer fictions" (xix). Its double identity plot antedates the double identity plots of both *A Tale of Two Cities* and *The Woman in White*. See Laurie Langbauer's "Women in White, Men in Feminism" *Yale Journal of Criticism* 2,2 (1989) for a comparison of several literary "women in white."

10. Tamar Heller, in her feminist reading of the novel, also identifies Anne Catherick as the embodiment of "social invisibility that renders women blank pages to be inscribed by men."

11. This "cleansing" indeed has Christian connotations (baptism, spiritual cleansing, etc.) and also connects to Walter's own association with cleansing, water, and drowning. At the opening of the novel it is learned that he previously saved Professor Pesca (ironically meaning "fishing" in Italian) from drowning.

12. For a discussion of Anne's power in erasure see MacDonagh and Smith.

13. This date discrepancy is the minute evidence Walter must prove in order to legalize Anne's death and Laura's life. Ironically Collins himself had the travel and death dates wrong in the serial version of the novel. Reviewing the third edition in *The Times*, 30 October 1860, E.S. Dallas made the well-known objection about the impossibility of the novel's time scheme. See Sutherland, "Two Emergencies in the Writing of *The Woman in White*," for a detailed analysis of the death-date dilemma.

14. John Sutherland, "Wilkie Collins and the Origins of the Sensation Novel" *Dickens Studies Annual* 20, (1991): 255. Sutherland asks, "Why not just poison Laura? She is chronically delicate." The corpse-substitution plot was subsequently used by Collins in *The Haunted Hotel* (1879) and in his last completed work, *Blind Love* (1889) where Lord Harry substitutes a consumptive victim for himself in order to collect his own life insurance. Mary Elizabeth Braddon went on to further popularize the burial-plot in *Lady Audley's Secret* (1862). J.D. Coates remarks, "*Lady Audley's Secret* even uses what is, perhaps the most striking of Wilkie Collins's dramatic devices in *The Woman in White*, that of the false grave dug and the headstone put up during the life-time of the person supposedly buried

there." See "Techniques of Terror in *The Woman in White.*" *Durham University Journal* 73, 2 (1981): 181.

15. This is the partial inscription, visually demonstrating Walter's inability to read it in its entirety. The entire inscription is replicated later as its own chapter and "narrative" in the second part of the novel. Significant is the fact that Collins chooses to graphically reproduce the inscription in both the manuscript and serialized edition of the novel. Many thanks to Christine Nelson, Curator of Historical Documents at The Pierpont Morgan Library, New York for use of the manuscript (MA 79).

16. Collins earlier explored the "presumed dead but alive" theme in the play *The Red Vial* (1858) where Mrs. Wagner is presumed dead, but somehow kept alive. In *John Jago's Ghost* or "The Dead Alive" (1873–4) John Jago is presumed murdered yet returns to the surprise of the townspeople. And of course Mary Elizabeth Braddon utilizes the theme in *Lady Audley's Secret* (1862) in the figure of George Talboys who is assumed to be murdered by Lady Audley but manages to survive his attack.

17. Illegitimacy is a favorite theme in Collins's fiction, from *The Dead Secret* (1857) to *No Name* (1862). This may be due to the fact that he had three illegitimate children of his own with long time mistress Martha Rudd. In Collins's short story "The Lady of Glenwith" (1856) the alleged Baron Franval is actually an impostor and a criminal impersonating the real aristocrat, making him the prototype of Sir Percival and Count Fosco.

18. Collins will later use the forged marriage register in *Armadale* (1866) where the villainous Lydia Gwilt forges her marriage to Allan Armadale.

19. In his biography, Kenneth Robinson notes a particular visit by Collins in 1844: "In his idle wanderings through the Paris streets, some morbid impulse had again drawn him into the chilly corridors of the Morgue. 'A body of a young girl had just been fished out of the river. As her bosom was black and blue I suppose she had been beaten into a state of insensibility and then flung into the Seine.' Fifteen years later he chose this grim setting for our final glimpse of Count Fosco in *The Woman in White*" (40). Robinson also notes that Collins used another famous morgue for the setting of his play *The Red Vial* (1858). The sensational climax of the play is "the awakening of a supposed corpse in the Frankfurt dead-house. The sight of a naked arm thrust from the door of the mortuary-cell and clutching at the handle of an alarm-bell was more than even an Olympic audience could swallow" (120). See Hutter for a discussion of the morbid tourism of Dickens and Collins and the role of the Paris Morgue as *theatrum mundi*.

20. Collins's novels *Hide and Seek* (1854) and *The Dead Secret* (1857) are earlier plots that also include an illegitimate daughter.

21. In a certain manner Walter and Sir Percival are types of ironic "resurrectionists"—both steal or replace bodies (and identities) from graves.

22. See Sutherland's comments in the Oxford edition.

23. Jacques Derrida recognizes that the movement inside the crypt, the tearing away of a false front (monumental exterior) and the tearing down of a false dichotomy (outside/inside) would be endlessly repeated.

24. Though she rightly correlates loss of identity and lack of agency with the feminine, Elam doesn't acknowledge that powerful male characters also lose their identities and are relegated to the blank page.

25. The text of the will is courtesy of Paul Lewis and the Wilkie Collins Society website <http://www.wilkiecollins.org/>. The original lies in the London Public Record office and a copy can be found at The Pierpont Morgan Library.

26. Many disagree that it was Caroline Graves who inspired the novel, and therefore disregard the story in J.G. Millais's biography of his father that relays the encounter with a mysterious woman (supposedly Graves). In brief, Millais describes that his father, Wilkie, and Charles Collins were walking in London on a moonlit night sometime in the 1850s when they heard a "piercing scream coming from the garden of a villa close at hand. It was evidently the cry of a woman in distress; and while pausing to consider what they should do, the iron gate leading to the garden was dashed open, and from it came the figure of a young and very beautiful woman dressed in flowing white robes that shone in the moonlight. She seemed to float rather than run in their direction . . . '' (qtd in Robinson, 130). Most likely Collins met Graves sometime in 1859 (Collins composed *The Woman in White* from August 15, 1859 to July 26, 1860). See Robinson's *Wilkie Collins: A Biography* for further details regarding the relationship between Caroline Graves and Collins.

27. See Clyde Hyder's seminal article for his discussion of Mme. de Douhault's court case in Maurice Mejan's *Recueil des Causes Célèbre* and the similarities to the plot of Collins's novel.

28. Afterward, Martha Rudd, the mother of Collins's three illegitimate children, tended the grave. Hyder notes: "After Mrs. Graves's death Collins's grave was for a time under the care of Martha Rudd" (297). Interestingly, Robinson also recognizes "The Narrative of Wilkie Collins's Tombstone." He aptly remarks: "For some years after Caroline's death, the grave was tended by Martha Rudd until she too vanishes from the story" (326).

29. Hyder, 297.

WORKS CITED

Brooks, Peter. *Reading for the Plot: Design and Intention in Narrative.* New York: Knopf, 1984.

Collins, Wilkie. *Antonina.* NY: Harper and Brothers, 1850.

———. *Armadale.* NY: Harper and Brothers, 1866.

———. *Basil.* Oxford: Oxford UP, 2000.

———. *The Dead Secret.* New York: Harper and Brothers, 1873.

———. *Hide and Seek.* New York: Harper & Brothers, 1873.

————. *The Woman in White*. Oxford: Oxford UP, 1973.

Derrida, Jacques. "Fors" *Georgia Review* 31(1977). Trans. Barbara Johnson. 64–116.

Dever, Carolyn. *Death and the Mother from Dickens to Freud: Victorian Fiction and the Anxiety of Origins*. Cambridge: Cambridge UP, 1998.

Dickens, Charles. *Great Expectations*. Oxford: Oxford UP, 1991.

Elam, Diane. "White Narratology: Gender and Reference in Wilkie Collins's *The Woman in White.*" *Virginal Sexuality and Textuality in Victorian Literature*. Ed. Lloyd Davis Albany: State U of NYP, 1993. 49–63.

Gilbert, Sandra M. and Susan Gubar. *The Madwoman in the Attic: The Woman Writer and the Nineteenth-Century Literary Imagination*. New Haven: Yale UP, 1979.

Heller, Tamar. *Dead Secrets: Wilkie Collins and the Female Gothic*. New Haven: Yale UP, 1992.

Hutter, Albert D. "The Novelist as Resurrectionist: Dickens and the Dilemma of Death" *Dickens Studies Annual* 12 (1983): 1–39.

Hyder, Clyde. "Wilkie Collins and *The Woman in White*" *PMLA* 54 (1939): 297–303.

Kendrick, Walter M. "The Sensationalism of *The Woman in White.*" *Nineteenth-Century Fiction* 32,1 (1977): 18–35.

MacDonagh, Gwendolyn and Jonathan Smith. " 'Fill Up All the Gaps': Narrative and Illegitimacy in *The Woman in White.*" *Journal of Narrative Technique* 26, 3 (1996): 274–91.

Nadel, Ira B. Introduction. *The Dead Secret*. Oxford: Oxford UP, 1999. vii–xxv.

O'Neill, Philip. *Wilkie Collins: Women, Propriety and Property*. Totowa: Barnes & Noble, 1988.

Page, Norman. Introduction. *Mad Monkton and Other Stories*. Oxford: Oxford UP, 1994 vii–xxx.

Peters, Catherine. *The King of Inventors: A Life of Wilkie Collins*. Princeton: Princeton UP, 1991.

Robinson, Kenneth. *Wilkie Collins: A Biography*. New York: Macmillan, 1952.

Sutherland, John. Introduction. *Armadale*. London: Penguin, 1995. vii–xxvi.

————. "Two Emergencies in the Writing of *The Woman in White*," *Yearbook of English Studies* 7 (1977): 148–56.

————. "Wilkie Collins and the Origins of the Sensation Novel" *Dickens Studies Annual* 20, (1991): 243–58.

Tillotson, Kathleen. "The Lighter Reading of the Eighteen-Sixties." Introduction *The Woman in White*. Ed. Anthea Trodd. Boston: Houghton Mifflin, 1969. viii–xxvi.

Wordsworth, William. "Essay Upon Epitaphs—I" (1810). *Literary Criticism of William Wordsworth*. Ed. Paul M. Zall. Lincoln: U of Nebraska P, 1966.

Dickens in Latin America: Views from Montevideo

Beatriz Vegh

This section consists of the introduction and nine papers from the conference "Dickens in Latin America," held June 23 to 25, 2003, at the University of the Republic, Montevideo, Uruguay. Since this introduction offers brief comments on each of the essays, abstracts are not provided for the individual articles. Two papers explore how critical views expressed by Jorge Luis Borges may be applied to Dickens's fiction; two articles discuss the implications of the Uruguayan artist Rafael Barradas's innovative cubist illustrations (1921) for Hard Times; *two essays examine the influence of* Oliver Twist *on a book by Armonía Somers, a well-known Uruguayan novelist; two pieces consider Dickens and the theater or theatrical effects; and the closing essay comments on how the social problems prevalent today in Latin America affect responses to Dickens. From these papers, we can derive an awareness of the broad range of responses to Dickens in a culture very different from those in North America and Europe.*

Introduction

How may I offer a general sense of the present literary scene in Latin America in relation to Dickens's work, in order to introduce a series of essays focusing on this subject? Since each essay deals with a particular point related to this connection, let me mention here a few testimonial texts and documents that might shed light upon the complex lineaments shaping such a literary scene.

Everybody knows that Latin America is a big wor(l)d which has never referred at all (and doesn't currently refer at all) to any true unity, either of language (both Spanish and Portuguese are spoken in its territories) or of culture (its genealogy is marked by pluralities at every level: political, ethnic, religious). We know also that Dickens's times and Victorian times were for Latin America times of winning independence, of the making of nations and the constitution of states, a time of disorders and revolutions in which literature was very often politically dependent and lacked autonomy. On the other hand, that making of nations, at least in the case of former Spanish colonies such as Argentina and Uruguay—the Latin American Dickens readerships mostly represented in this set of essays—was to a large extent conceived and shaped against the metropolis, against Spain, against its literature, a literature that those Spaniards adhering to Western liberal ideals found excessively and unhealthily timorous, pushing them to be receptive to foreign literatures: "Let's cry and let's translate" was Spanish writer Mariano José de Larra's motto already in the 1830s.

Significantly, the Argentine Domingo Faustino Sarmiento (1811–1888) was going to make of Larra's claim a cultural and political commandment (Zanetti 156), largely followed by the native Latin American "intelligentsia," an intellectual and political minority who led the development of their countries in most of the Portuguese and Spanish former colonies in America. An eloquent document showing how this commandment worked in Southern South America and revealing, more specifically, the role that Dickens's novels played in this area, is the essay by Sarmiento himself commenting about a public reading by Dickens delivered in New York in 1868. Sarmiento had been an enthusiastic and analytic member of the audience at this reading a few months before being elected president of Argentina, an extremely influential president (from 1868 to 1874), as we are reminded in a recent study meaningfully titled *Sarmiento, Author of a Nation.* Sarmiento, in his essay (written for the magazine *Ambas Américas* [*Both Americas*]), underlines the skill with which Dickens the actor manages to mold a polyphony of voices into a show which creates various characters from his novels. Sarmiento enthusiastically translates into Spanish the passages of novels performed by Dickens and points out every detail of the reading as well as the deep significance to be found in Dickens's fiction: "Dickens is far more than what nature bestows on everybody, he is the truth we can approach" (Vegh 250).[1]

At the time, Latin American readerships shared Sarmiento's enthusiasm for Dickens and also for other Western fictional writers, mostly French authors like Balzac, Hugo, Dumas, Sue, and Lesage, but also Scott and the English Romantic poets, especially Byron.[2] And, gradually, as translations into Spanish began to circulate—very erratically, it must be said—these French and English novelists won readers belonging to more populous social classes. For example, *David Copperfield* was translated into Spanish (in Paris!) in 1871 for circulation in Spanish America.[3]

But, parallel to the Latin American native readership of British literature in Dickens's times, either in English or in more or less faithful Spanish translations, there was an important British readership—in numbers as well as in influence—since, as we know, English immigrants and settlers played a major and decisive role in the commercial, industrial, and cultural development of Latin America. This was so from times of independence, in the first decades of the nineteenth century, until early in the twentieth century. And those English-reading settlers (English but also Irish, Scotch, Welsh, and migrants from North America) read Dickens. A firsthand testimony of such reading comes to us from a British writer, W.H. Hudson, born on the Argentine pampas in 1846, having lived there up to his thirty-third year, and then writing extensively about his beloved pampas when he was already established in London. In one of his books of memoirs, Hudson recalls the figure of Mr. Trigg, an Englishman hired by his parents to live with the family when he was six or seven years old, so the children could "be taught their letters" as a substitute for the school they didn't attend. Mr. Trigg, writes Hudson, was "a schoolmaster who hated and despised teaching as much as children in the wild hated to be taught." But, "when the evenings were long, he would give a two hours' reading to the household. Dickens was then the most popular writer in the world, and he usually read Dickens, to the delight of his listeners" (27, 29).

Another testimony coming from British sources, and conveying a typical and expanded patriarchal and colonialist context, fictionally illustrates another readerly format of Dickens's English readerships in Latin America at the time. The locus of reading is now northern and jungly South America, and the role of listener to (rather than reader of) Dickens's novels is played by the illiterate Mr. Todd, an Evelyn Waugh character in *A Handful of Dust*. A fan of Dickens—a heritage handed down to him by his English Barbadian father—living isolated among Indians and foreign languages in Amazonian Brazil, Mr. Todd hoards and stores up his copies of Dickens's novels "in the eaves of the roof . . . in bundles tied up with rag, palm leaf and raw hide" to protect them from the ants that had already devoured some of his idolized novels. And to be able to enjoy Dickens's stories he makes a lost Englishman explorer his prisoner for life. Thus, his "visitor" will read to him, endlessly, Dickens's novels: " 'Let us read Little Dorritt again. There are passages in that book I can never hear without the temptation to weep" (209, 217) says Mr. Todd to his despairing and hopeless English "guest" in the last sentence of the story.

The essays gathered in this section attempt to explore other facets of this Dickensian literary scene in Latin America. Originally presented as papers in a "Dickens in Latin America" conference (June 23–25, 2003), organized by the School of Humanities and Educational Sciences, University of the Republic, Montevideo, Uruguay, they all deal with different ways of responding to Dickens's fiction in Spanish-speaking areas of Southern South America, especially in Argentina and Uruguay, in the mid- and late-twentieth century. They all explore how those Spanish audiences read, question, converse with, and thus interact with Dickens: with his imaginative and powerful strategies of novel-writing; with his social concerns, with his power of pictorial suggestion to modernist contexts, with his theatrical productions, and the anticipations of a Brechtian stance in some of his fictions.

From very different perspectives based on the authors' own readings of Dickens, two of the essays, those by Tomás de Mattos and Jean-Philippe Barnabé, develop some comments made by Jorge Luis Borges about Dickens during a class devoted entirely to him in 1966, at the University of Buenos Aires. develop some commentmade by Jorge Luis Borges about Dickens during a class devoted entirely to him in 1966, at the University of Buenos Aires.

In "A Borgesian Clue to Dickens's Characterization in *Pickwick Papers*," Tomás de Mattos, a novelist well-versed in nineteenth-century British and American fiction, presents his own analytical, vivid reading of *Pickwick Papers*, showing how, as maintained by Borges in contradicting G. K. Chesterton's view, Dickens's characters do change. Environment and events do modify them. And in his close reading of the novel and in his close examination of Mr. Jingle's and Mr. Pickwick's characters, de Mattos points out fictional procedures and novelistic strategies leading Dickens to shape characters who, far from remaining unchanged, are actually permeated by the kaleidoscopic situations they have gone through in "real" life and to which, changing accordingly, they react.

In "Borges as a Reader of Dickens," Jean-Philippe Barnabé focuses on Borges's extensive and singular comments about *The Mystery of Edwin Drood,* especially on those about the death of its author. When Dickens was midway in the writing of his novel, Borges observes, "God ordained his death." Out of this statement and a vast knowledge of Borges's work, Barnabé convincingly develops an intriguing and tight connection between both great writers, allowing a Borgesian way of reading *Drood.* And Barnabé reminds Dickensians that *The Mystery of Edwin Drood* was published in a Spanish translation in 1951 in Buenos Aires within a collection of detective stories selected by Borges and his close friend Bioy Casares.

In "A Cubo-Futurist Reading of Dickens: Rafael Barradas's 1921 Illustrations to *Hard Times*," the Uruguayan painter Miguel Battegazzore shows, from a pictorial perspective, the artistic path followed by Rafael Barradas in his production of twelve illustrations for a Spanish edition of *Hard Times*

(Madrid, 1921). Battegazzore analyzes how these very impressive illustrations were conceived and carried out in the wake of cubist strategies and futurist proposals. This essay shows also to what extent the use of certain pictorial motifs and the selection of certain colors create an insightful pictorial reading of Dickens and his novel. In Barradas's case, Battegazzore maintains, this creative and innovative pictorial reading is linked to aesthetic modernism as well as to an artistic romantic tradition shared by both the novelist and the painter and connected also to anarchist ideas largely spread in Spain at the time of Barradas's *Hard Times* illustrations.

My own essay, "Dickens and Barradas in Madrid, 1921: A Hospitable Meeting," investigates the complex interrelationship between Dickens's text of *Hard Times* and Barradas's illustrations. The paper proposes that these illustrations influence the ways in which readers may respond to the novel. For instance, Barradas's interesting use of the circus motif serves to strengthen the text's contrast between the beneficial, healthy openness of the circus world and the enclosed oppression associated with Coketown's educational system and domestic life.

Two articles, by María Cristina Dalmagro and by Alicia Torres, locate and explore the literary, cultural, and social affinities relating the novel *Un retrato para Dickens [A Portrait for Dickens]* (Montevideo, 1969), by Uruguayan writer Armonia Somers, to Dickens's *Oliver Twist*. Paying homage to the British writer, Somers creates in her novel an unnamed female Montevidean replica of the Dickensian Oliver as a paradigm of orphanhood, and both essays closely examine this connection. In "The Reversal of Innocence: Somers, Dickens and a Shared Oliver," Dalmagro does this by stressing in Somers's novel, and in other of her texts, issues such as marginality, loneliness, and the presence of evil—the demon Asmodeus in *A Portrait for Dickens*—as shared concerns with Dickens's writings. In "Dickens's Oliver and Somers's Orphan: A Traffic in Identities," Torres examines the narrative techniques used by both writers, the British and the Uruguayan, to handle, so illuminatingly in both novels, the complex problem of identity and identities through the fictional creations of their two orphans.

Considering the theatrical concerns that were always overpowering in Dickens's writing, Leticia Eyheragaray, in *"The Strange Gentleman:* Dickens on the Uruguayan Stage," gives a detailed account of a 1946 Montevideo performance, in Spanish translation, of Dickens's *The Strange Gentleman* in—appropriately—the Victoria Theatre. On the other hand, in "Spectacle and Estrangement in Dickens," Verónica D'Auria reflects on how the Brechtian modern theatrical values of distancing effect and estrangement are already used and put into practice in Dickens's narratives, with especial reference to *Great Expectations*.

Finally, in "Dickens in Latin America: Borrioboola-Gha Revisited" Lindsey Cordery considers the significance that reading Dickens today in an impoverished postcolonial Latin America might really have. Such a reading, Cordery proposes, reminds us that "the crossing sweeper" of *Bleak House* and his very hard times remain the daily paradigmatic and inescapable reality representing the inequality of our societies.

If we agree that Southern South American literatures (in Ricardo Piglia's terms referring to Argentine literature) "are constituted within a double vision, a relationship of difference and alliance with other practices and other languages" (130), these essays seek to shed light on such a double vision and, in doing so, to reenact and resignify at the same time, in one way or another, some of Dickens's major texts.

NOTES

1. See Beatriz Vegh's article, which includes an unabridged English translation by Trude Stern and Vegh of Sarmiento's essay on Dickens's 1868 public reading at Steinway Hall in New York.
2. For an excellent study of readerships in Latin America, see Susana Zanetti, especially ch. 3, "Leyendo en el siglo XIX," and ch. 4, "Modelos extranjeros y literatura nacional."
3. The three oldest Spanish translations of Dickens's books owned by the Buenos Aires National Library are *David Copperfield o El sobrino de mi tía.* Trans. Mariano Urrabieta. Paris: Lasalle Melan, Col. Correo de Ultramar, 1871; *El hijo de la parroquia (Oliver Twist).* Trans. Enrique Leopoldo de Verneuil. Barcelona: Maucci, Col. Artes y Letras, 1883; *Días penosos (Hard Times).* Trad. Lic. Barbadillo. Madrid: El Cosmos, 1884. From 1900 on, Dickens's more popular novels were widely circulating in Southern South America in Spanish translations published in Buenos Aires by La Nación Publishing House or in Madrid and Barcelona by various publishers.

WORKS CITED

Halperin, Tulio, et al. *Sarmiento, Author of a Nation.* Berkeley: U of California P, 1994.

Hudson, William Henry. *Far Away and Long Ago.* London: Dutton, 1918.

Piglia, Ricardo. "Sarmiento the Writer." *Sarmiento, Author of a Nation.* Ed. Tulio Halperín et al. Berkeley: U of California P, 1994. 127–144.

Vegh, Beatriz. "A Former President of Argentina Attends a Reading by Dickens in New York, in 1868." *Dickens Quarterly* 16:4 (December 1999): 243–55.

Waugh, Evelyn. *A Handful of Dust.* Harmondsworth, Middlesex: Penguin Books, 1966.

Zanetti, Susana. *La dorada garra de la lectura —Lectoras y lectores de novelas en America Latina.* Rosario: Beatriz Viterbo, 2002.

A Borgesian Clue to Dickens's Characterization in *Pickwick Papers*

Tomás de Mattos

Some time ago, in a book or essay that was not really focused on Dickens, with a title that I am unable to recall, I found a statement attributed to the novelist regarding the diverse relationships between literary characters and the author or reader. This comment maintained that, as occurs with real human beings, literary characters awaken in us a whole spectrum of feelings as we progress in our writing or reading. He believed that the first impression is decisive, but stressed that later events determine modifications that enlarge or diminish the personality being observed.

I think that this idea is especially applicable to Dickens's own work. Mr. Jingle in *Pickwick Papers* provides a good example: a wonderful character playing a strategic role because he is no less than the hero's main antagonist. Introduced as the timely savior in the first challenge faced by the Pickwickian explorers, who are wearing picturesque and tight garments, he soon voices his patter and shamelessly exhibits his manner of tackling the different pleasures of life, be it a bottle of wine that all the partygoers should enjoy, or someone else's jacket, showing unequivocal signs of an increasingly mischievous and predatory attitude. He quickly reveals himself as a cynic and seducer before an elderly lady and does not hesitate to abandon her for the sum of £120 that, weighed in the short term, is a necessary aid for the temporary satisfaction of his more urgent needs and which, in the long run, does not threaten his future with a commitment to her most unpalatable company. This improper image is maintained when, in chapters 15–16 and 23–25, he reappears twice. Nevertheless, when he and his endearing and unemployed colleague, the long-suffering but also transgressing Job Trotter, meet Pickwick once again in Fleet Prison, the simulating qualities Jingle has cultivated in his original occupation as a strolling actor contribute to hide, with pathetic dignity, his physical and spiritual pain. Dickens and Mr. Pickwick flood the reader's heart with great compassion towards this unhappy, unfortunate stroller, leading us to believe that the ungenerous winds of life have condemned him to this painful coastal navigation from one provincial port to another to earn his everyday living.

Nevertheless, both G. K. Chesterton and Jorge Luis Borges assert that Dickens's characters do not grow or change, but rather remain identical to themselves. For example, Borges states, "Dickens was not really interested in the plot, he was more concerned about the nature of his characters. The plot is just a mechanical means to enable the development of the action. *There isn't really any development of their personality . . . . The characters created by Dickens live in the perpetual ecstasy of being themselves''* (italics added).

Is there any real contradiction between this evidence of the mother-of-pearl shades manifested by Dickens's characters, clearly illustrated by the lovable Alfred Jingle, and this observation made by readers as perceptive as Chesterton and Borges?

I do not think so; moreover, it is Borges who gives us the hint that will serve to sort things out, when he introduces a truthful, subtle comment that I previously omitted in order to increase the impact caused by this seeming contradiction, and which I now restore: "There isn't any real development of their personality. *It is the environment and events that modify the characters as occurs in reality.* The characters created by Dickens live in the perpetual ecstasy of being themselves" (230; italics added).

Borges therefore does not deny the mutations suffered by the Dickensian characters. It could not be otherwise. But he highlights two particular ways of dealing with them: first, that the reasons for their mutations are exogenous and not endogenous; and second, that they are objective, and not perceived by the creatures that experience or enjoy them. Returning to the example of Mr. Jingle, I think that these two characteristics are totally applicable. Jingle is aware of his new fate: life has definitely beaten him. What lady will he seduce, what opulent table will he visit to satisfy his chronic hunger in Fleet Prison? He knows he is in a strait, but does not acknowledge the fact that his loss of freedom paradoxically releases him from that tormenting merry-go-round that led him to tie himself to fetters of tricks and mockery. An unpunished transgressor during the first half of the novel, and later confined to jail, a humiliating imprisonment, he always lives in "the perpetual ecstasy"—implacable purgatory in his case—"of being [him]self."

In the quotation from Borges in the paragraph preceding the last, there is a brief expression that I wish to extract and contextualize: "as occurs in reality.'' These words lead me to wonder if the great impact produced by Dickensian characters in the hearts of an immense mass of readers may be caused, precisely, by this very specific procedure of mimicking reality, by recreating the influence exerted by events on the personalities of his characters. Perhaps the less uncertain pathway to gain access to a certain *savoir vivre* depends basically on the possibility of throwing oneself into the waters of life, making the most of the method of trial and error, one's own and that of others, in real or imaginary adventures.

This is the reason why I link many of Dickens's novels to the German concept of the bildungsroman, the educational novel, a tale of initiation or learning, which was quite widespread at the time. Although much has been said about Dickens as a writer committed to social reform, I would add that I see him as especially eager to attack every mask of hypocrisy in *individual moral education.* Dickens's novels, insofar as they are true representations of different kinds of individual existence, do not so much question the social environment but rather, and perhaps in a greater degree, the ways in which we take care of our personal lives.

Many critics seem to use a double standard. On the one hand, they compliment Dickens for his intelligent economizing of resources in drawing portraits of his characters, who often are sketched with lines that are very few, but highly effective. On the other hand, and this view is more frequent in the essays that theorize about the general aspects of creation in his novels, the same critics at times practically transform this virtue into a fault by referring to Dickens's characters as ''flat'' or ''two-dimensional,'' shallow and lacking the psychological depths explored by Proust or Dostoievski.

If I were forced to choose a literary master, a teacher of life, it would be Dostoievski. Nevertheless, I do not believe I would be excessively subjective if I were to regard the so-called shallowness in Dickens's characters as an unavoidable outcome of his narrative choice—starting with the type of reader he chose as an accomplice or co-author of his work and ending with his position as an author vis-à-vis the stories he wrote.

What I have seen of his work makes me think of a narrator who carries his novels to the frontier with drama: there is an abundance of direct dialogue (in itself a very faithful manner of psychological portraiture because of the care shown in styling the way the words are expressed by each of his characters); there is also a tendency to concentrate the portrait in the description of external appearances; and there is often a noticeable hesitation in fully implementing the omniscient narrator's prerogatives, such as immediate access to thoughts and feelings of individual characters. This self-limitation is balanced by the exterior quality imposed on most of the narrative discourse, only overcome with the aid of a perceptive reader, practically placed in the role of spectator.

I also believe that the distinction between multi-dimensional and two-dimensional characters often coincides in Dickens with the line that separates protagonists and secondary characters. The latter are present in the plot for mainly two reasons: together, like the shrubs that create a thick hedge—the image is borrowed from Forster—they draw the social landscape, the scenery, always important in Dickens; at the same time, they act as external agents catalyzing reactions through their relationships with the protagonist.

In order to paint the protagonist, Dickens, an extremely sensitive author in the task of creating vast collective scenes, needs to include a wealth of secondary characters that typify or represent kinds of behavior or ideas reflecting the predominant existential options in the milieu. These are characters who interfere with fate and who receive Dickens's preferential attention. We admire the mastery with which he manages to transmit that special feeling of vitality to these sometimes very fleeting accessory characters with just a few brush-strokes He is a deeper and more powerful caricaturist than the wonderful artists that illustrated his work.

The protagonist, however, Mr. Samuel Pickwick, is one of the best examples of Dickens's skill in creating characters. But *Pickwick Papers* improves considerably when the protagonist's namesake and future servant, Samuel Weller, appears in chapter 10 shining innumerable pairs of the guests' shoes in the well-known White Hart Inn. Weller's popularity is undoubtedly well-earned. Surely, very few fictitious characters may compete with him in wit and lively humor. Having made this observation, I ask if Pickwick, Sam's master, is as well-sketched, if the joys and tribulations that he exults in or bears throughout the novel are not decisive to transform it into the highest hymn to benevolence. And if that is so, which of the two figures, the master or the servant, impresses us more deeply as living what Dostoievski, in the grim *Notes from the Underground,* glorifies with the name "an unsheltered life"?

I will not answer the question because it must be answered by each individual reader. I will only say that if Dickens himself had to respond, he might probably protect himself with similar reserve, although at the same time he might confess that Pickwick, and not Weller, was his protagonist and therefore the object of his greatest concern.

If we were to hand Sam Weller the book relating the adventures of his employer, and ask him how he feels about the figure of his master as described in the first chapters, he might perhaps resort to the image of a chickencoop and say that the Pickwick of the early chapters reminds him of an unhatched chick.

Pickwick's seeming rigidity in the first chapters might be accounted for by the fact that Dickens, a twenty-four-year-old who was just beginning to publish, had not yet been able to get a full grip of the story in his relation to his publishers, Chapman and Hall. He had managed to reverse the priority as to who decided the plot: he had snatched it from the illustrator and was now the first to imagine characters and events. He had modified something beyond the Club's name, no longer called Nimrod but Pickwick; he had transformed the very nature of the social link, no longer a grouping of unskillful sportsmen, but rather a group of fans and collaborators of an amateur scientific researcher. But he did not have the support of a reputation in the business, no fame to attract a significant number of readers. Much like Nathaniel Winkle, a young and clumsy sportsman, he seems a relic of the initial project, and therefore, perhaps in concession to the publisher, the atmosphere of the first chapters is spoilt by a creative desire seemingly intent on merely sketching a satirical entertainment. The person or persons responsible for the editorial control may have approved the modifications included by Dickens in the belief that he was extending the field for the darts he was throwing in his satire: if Winkle ensured the maintenance of the initial target, with an indiscriminate vocation for every existing sport in air, land, and water, then Pickwick, Snodgrass, and Tupman expanded it to other activities where they were exposed to very similar frustrations: the improvised scientific research, an artificial poetry plagued with platitudes, and an attraction towards unattainable young beauties.

The truth is that we will never know how the impossibility of gaining total control over the creation of the novel influenced those first chapters. Nevertheless, our first impression of Pickwick is not pleasant; he is treated mercilessly, kept at a distance, and he impresses the reader as ridiculous, rather foolish, and quite unlovable. The chicken still hides within the eggshell. Perhaps the author had not yet fully created him. But how Dickens did marvels with the old gentleman when he managed to discover him!

The magic is in the manner in which that wretched first impression serves as the very foundation for the whole meaning of the novel. If Mrs. Clarke, Sam Weller's stepmother, a devout Christian, under the stupid and hypocritical influence of her shepherd, the Reverend Mr. Stiggins, were to hear her stepson risk the image of an unhatched egg, she would emphatically agree and translate it into a religious language, more relevant and elevated in her view. She would say that later Mr. Pickwick is born again, although she would have undoubtedly disapproved of the scenes chosen by Dickens to lead the noble old man from that hollow and incipient benevolence to the most cordial and fertile brotherhood towards all those who shared his life and whom he sheltered, not excluding his adversaries, not even those towards whom he felt an apparently irreconcilable enmity; for she would have found these episodes profane and ungodly, too carnal and mundane.

In the light of what occurs in the later parts of the novel, Mr. Pickwick's infatuated stiffness in the first chapters seems deliberately constructed, and with very few precise and unequivocal strokes. Of course, we will never know if they were originally written with that intention, or if, subsequently, with a genius for improvisation, Dickens had made the most of what he had written before without knowing the direction it would ultimately take. One way or the other, we cannot hide our admiration for his talent and intuition.

I wish now to consider briefly a few examples of this expansive process of developing Pickwick as a person in the spacious extension of the novel. I will especially focus on the first phase of this transformation when, as Sam might say, the shell begins to crack.

What do we know of Mr. Pickwick's rather long life before deserving the author's attention, an event that would make him one of the more celebrated myths of England? Adding bits and pieces, and using the data available, we might assume he was a trader dedicated to an undefined field, living in London, with branches in other parts of the country, among them, clearly, Liverpool. Evidently, as an elderly man, he had retired with enough savings so as to lead a comfortable life, albeit insufficient to allow him to purchase a house of his own and, at the beginning, employ people in his service. We do not know if he had been—happily or unfortunately—married. The novel does not make him a married man, but we are not informed either if he was single or a widower, and no past love is mentioned either. It is therefore reasonable to suppose that he had no children, and that he was not previously united in matrimony with any lady. The greatest joys in his life seem to have been those provided by a good meal, as the size of his body makes clear, and a well-stocked library, although perhaps consisting of works that were rather boring and more scientific than literary. I would even dare to guess that Mr. Pickwick enjoyed, during these insipid years, the compensations provided by a good wine-cellar, although I presume a very respectable moderation on his part.

The trading business was surely unsatisfactory for him because he did not wait to die to abandon it, and just after retiring he enthusiastically devoted his time to scientific research, an activity which must have attracted him from his early years. A discreet man, he focused his curiosity on humble objectives, for the only reason that they had not yet drawn the attention of others. With a theoretical intelligence and a rather aged mastery of rhetoric, he was capable of awakening the admiration of a handful of acquaintances, and thus ensuring the availability of this slightly dim audience, whose members formed a club given his name without his expressing either approval or objection. He did not even oppose the enthusiastic Mr. Winkle when he designed a uniform for the members including a light blue coat and gold buttons bearing Mr.Pickwick's effigy, as if he were an emperor or a king.

Into this ignored past we have reconstructed with conjectures, we will now insert the data included in the first chapter. Our initial vision is that of a solemn and ridiculous figure with a bald head, scholarly spectacles, and an obese body, clothed in oppressive tights and dated garters, and poised in a trembling Windsor settee, his right hand concealed behind his coat tail while stirring the air with his left, in aid of his final impassioned speech before an audience of ten admirers and one opponent, who had been able to see and hear him quite comfortably before, when, without abandoning his seat, he read them his cumbersome essay called "Speculations on the Source of the Hampstead Ponds, with some Observations on the Theory of Tittlebats." One listener, Mr. Blotton, an angry servant of common sense, allows himself some criticism. Annoyed by that bothersome circumstance, a most worthy Pickwick cannot but attribute that impudence to the jealousy awakened by the compliments bestowed for the research he has just lectured on. Moving on, we may notice his awkwardness some days later while waiting for the carriage that will take him with his three favorite disciples to the nearest posthouse. The telescope in his overcoat pocket and his notebook eloquently speak of his indifference to anything apart from the eternal adventure of knowledge found in a distant and disengaged observation, carefully detailed in writing: an aide-memoire as a gift of his intelligence for future generations.

If Perker, the attorney, were to voice his opinion vis-à-vis the views we have just imagined that Sam Weller and Mrs. Clarke might have expressed, we may speculate that this little man with restless black eyes would have courteously dismissed them, repeating the words of both servant and Methodist with a questioning tone: unhatched chick? born again soul? Perhaps. But I would rather resort to the title of Mr. Pickwick's essay, and state that before venturing into the world he was a sad tittlebat whose only experience of the waters of life had been limited to the Hampstead Pond swamps.

Seen from this perspective, the innumerable winds and breezes blowing over his baroque life adventures, the sumptuous banquets and public breakfasts and the not always deplorable humiliations he endures and enjoys throughout the novel, acquire an unforeseen meaning and seem to drive him in a single direction, both starting point and destination; and the warm joys and cold tribulations only seem to function as necessary operations in the task of forging a very large, an immense, heart.

But the most beautiful and endearing aspect of this Dickensian novel, which rescues and raises it above its flaws and imperfections, and allows us to forgive all the aged fictions inside the fiction that nearly always and unnecessarily inhibit the admirable dynamism in the action and move us to call for Pickwick to return together with his friends, is the fact that this construction, this unprecedented release of an immense soul, is nearly always accompanied by smiles and laughter, and not invocations to the almighty, or breast beatings. All this occurs while he is led through a path hardly imaginable by the hollow morality that, much like rust, usually spoils human religiosity.

I am sure that none of the readers interested in *Posthumous Papers of the Pickwick Club* would reject the idea that each of the scenes belongs to a sequence of processes that ebb and flow according to the rhythms of life and silently direct the expansion of Mr. Samuel Pickwick in this very manifest development, accounting for the intimate bonds that link all the chapters. That is why, in chapter 10, when Sam Weller is made responsible for the novel's newly acquired momentum, a fact supported by the impressive increase of subscribers, I feel hurt because we are forgetting a decisive joint cause: by then Pickwick has already changed. His transformation has already begun, he has already started to win the readers' sympathy—although gradually and not immediately as his servant does later.

Before reaching the White Hart Inn, there is a memorable chapter, an example of Dickens's best writing. In my view this is a decisive sequence in the transformation of Pickwick's character: the first crack of the shell, in Sam Weller's imagined words; the first indications of Mr. Pickwick's new birth, as Mrs. Clarke might grudgingly admit; and, according to the wary and fair Mr. Perker, the first flood—of alcohol—to rescue the boring tittlebat from the stifling murky pond and lead him to the boundless and ineffable ocean waters of life.

I am speaking of the scene following the uneven cricket match that gathered the players and fans of two institutions confronted in the game around the generously served table of the Blue Lion Inn, the main inn of the most worthy Muggleton town, with plenty of good food and better drink. An ill-defined number of toasts follows the meal, and successively fills the cups with rosé wine or old port, leaving all the guests, including Mr. Pickwick, dazed and united in a Dionysian spirit that makes them sing together in solidarity "with great feeling and emphasis, the beautiful and pathetic national air":

> We won't go home 'till morning,
> We won't go home 'till morning,
> We won't go home 'till morning,
>   'Till daylight doth appear.   (7: 97)

The friends return to the houses where they are staying at well past midnight, but will not go to bed. The image Dickens uses to show us Mr. Pickwick is—we must admit—shameful, but wonderfully joyous. Inside the kitchen, he is one of the many newly arrived drunks: "Mr. Pickwick, with his hands in his pockets and his hat cocked completely over his left eye, was leaning against the dresser, shaking his head from side to side, and producing a constant succession of the blandest and most benevolent smiles without being moved thereunto by any discernible cause or pretence whatsoever."

A lady overcomes her disgust and invites them to bed, letting them know that two servants will lead them to their rooms. But when one of them, Mr.

Winkle, refuses, he is immediately seconded, in a louder manner, by Mr. Pickwick, who boasting a smile, vigorously states, "No living boy shall carry me."

Mr. Winkle gleefully observes how everybody stops short, and he murmurs a weak and drunken "Hurrah!" Mr. Pickwick seconds him once again, with a louder "Hurrah!" It is not enough for him to have cocked his hat so low that all his good manners seem to have disappeared; he now dashes it on the floor and, in extreme defiance of all sound judgment, fearlessly casts his spectacles into the middle of the kitchen floor (8: 101–02).

The uninhibited and joyful impulse that leads him to fling his hat and spectacles on the floor is a gesture of a newly acquired freedom. Mr. Pickwick's bald head is left in the open as naked as his soul. Free of his glasses, he now stands on his friends' kitchen floor, no longer a spectator, but actively engaged in life. If he had had his overcoat on, his telescope would have likewise exploded. The investigator of a distant and far-away nature is languishing; his pulse beats warmed by port: an old man belatedly determined to lead a true life.

As Dickens would have it, the release is not preached from the pulpit in a sermon we could hear from the Reverend Mr. Stiggins: it is as concrete as that overwhelming feeling of friendship that makes Pickwick beam with a wide array of never-ending smiles.

The man has spoken his mind and thus freed himself from the heavy prison of his narcissistic carapace of false decorum, a decorum that makes us measure our words and gestures unnecessarily, forcing us to look at ourselves from the outside and repress our impulses, subject to what others might think of us. The man, no longer inhibited, shows himself as he is and, more importantly, because he is genuine, closer to what his feelings force him to be.

But this man, who has taken so long to embrace life, is still handicapped, an atrophied spirit. If Sam Weller could have a say he would tell us: "Like the cook said, we can only tell that the turtle is the lizard's first cousin when we remove it from its carapace."

Dickens, with his inexhaustible imagination, will not tire of shaking the old protagonist day and night down the dusty roads and lodging him in the most diverse inns to be found in England in 1827 and 1828. During his initial adventures, Pickwick will sometimes turn back; as, for example, during the archaeological search that will increase his academic prestige, which no longer obsesses him, but which he still cares for and cherishes. He will still devote much time to drive the motor of his life adventures and, obeying his natural benevolence, he limits himself to accompany the initiatives of other characters: Mr. Wardle's anger, when he tries to save his sister from Mr. Jingle's mean and greedy clutches; the solemn invitation made by the complacent husband of Leo Hunter's wife (i.e., the very same, albeit insignificant,

Mr. Leo Hunter) to a pathetic and cathartic *fête champêtre,* that will estrange him from the amateur dedication to the arts and sciences; and, to cite a third example, the second hunting attempt. But in this phase, in these and other situations, we observe an increasing attitude of permanent availability to accept the lessons taught by life.

At the beginning I alluded to the second alcoholic prostration suffered by the dignified gentleman, for having exceeded himself under the shining midday sun and taken too much excellent cold punch. His shame will be greater because this drunkenness will not only expose him before the surprised eyes of the ladies in a friend's house, but to the mockery of a teasing crowd.

Once more in the company of his friends, Mr. Pickwick momentarily abandons himself to anger and announces "an action for false imprisonment" against those who decided to carry him in that condition to the Pound.

" 'No, you won't', said Mr. Wardle," his wonderful host. " 'I will, by . . . ,' " " 'Why not?', challenged Mr. Pickwick. 'Because,' said old Wardle . . . , 'because they might turn round on some of us, and say we had taken too much cold punch.' " Mr. Pickwick's face breaks into a smile, "the smile extended into a laugh; the laugh into a roar; the roar become general" (19: 260–61).

In this manner, and exposed to a more uncomfortable situation, he will now be able to overcome it because he counters with one of the more necessary resources for an appropriate life, the ability to laugh about himself, which releases him from one of the most terrible feelings: an undue and always unjustified self-pity.

We could mention additional episodes that show us how Mr. Pickwick gradually learns to drive the carriage of his own life with his own pulse, guiding the blind impulse of his horses in the direction he decides.

I believe that in this way we can defend Mr. Samuel Pickwick (without belittling Samuel Weller) as being the major and most significant character in this novel. Indeed, we may see him as one of Dickens's most effective literary creations, a character who has exerted a very great influence on readers of narrative in all nations since his origin. I believe that the only Pickwick we should have to defend is the old gentleman of the first part of the novel, numbed by the honorable inhibitions brought about by his attention to minor details of his image. And this defense should be planned to show that he already possessed the contagious joy of living, and that his inborn and unshakable courtesy, as well as a hard-headed loyalty to elementary principles of life in society and an unconditional solidarity, shines through—even during the three months which a blunted imagination, lacking the wings of Dickens's own imagination and vital experience, might have construed as extremely somber and forlorn. I am referring to the three months during which Pickwick was secluded in Fleet Prison, a period during which he deprived himself of freedom in order to avoid encouraging the greed of the two attorneys who duped a vengeful widow with their plan. By means of a free and dignified decision, he ends his imprisonment when very curious circumstances lead him to reconsider his decision. It is his interest in others that pushes Pickwick to allow his attorney to work out a way to free him. His intransigence would have indefinitely prolonged the seclusion of four other persons: the faithful Sam Weller, who had encouraged his own prosecution in order to continue serving Pickwick in prison: and three adversaries for whom he left aside all enmity and resentment—Mrs. Bardell, Mr. Jingle, and Mr. Trotter.

His inner integrity and vital wisdom acquired during the late years of life get Mr. Samuel Pickwick out of Fleet prison. He abandons it ready to become a most plausible deus ex machina when his loyal friends are besieged by trouble.

Dickens's intelligence in building the plot makes its outcome very true, especially if we analyze it as focusing our attention on Pickwick. And this it should be, for the novelist has worked hard over twenty installments to forge gradually his main character's heart.

NOTES

This essay was translated from the Spanish by Mrs. Inés Trabal, who also provided translations into English of internal quotations.

WORKS CITED

Borges, Jorge Luis. "Clase No. 17." In *Borges Profesor.* Ed. Martin Arias and Martin Hadis. Buenos Aires: Emecé, 2002. 228–35

Dickens, Charles. *The Pickwick Papers.* London: J.M. Dent, 1959.

Borges as a Reader of Dickens

Jean-Philippe Barnabé

Borges as a reader of Dickens. At first glance the reasons for examining this
relationship do not seem pressing. The "heterogeneous census of the authors
that I continuously re-read," sketched out in a postscript to the 1956 prologue
of *Ficciones*, selects from writers in the English language the names that
recur most frequently in Borges's admiration: De Quincey, Stevenson, Shaw,
and Chesterton. Going over his writings, we could add two or three more
(without doubt, Poe and Whitman), but in any case certainly not Charles
Dickens. In fact, until very recently, the only mention of any importance of
this writer, and a reference that Borges was obliged to make, given the
pedagogic nature of the book, seemed to be in his 1965 *Introducción a la
literatura inglesa* [*Introduction to English Literature*], where he describes
him as "a man of genius," and then "a great romantic novelist," who
"brought a gallery of immortal characters to the world" (62).

"Novelist," and on top of that "romantic": in both the noun and the
adjective here we can intuit the reasons why Dickens could hardly be allowed
into the Borgesian literary pantheon. If we just take the first term, we do not
need to reiterate that it is more than well known that Borges was reluctant
to accept the diluting of a story in a structure which unnecessarily expanded
it, gave it ramifications, and robbed it of sharpness and therefore of efficacy.
In 1941, in the prologue to *The Garden of Forking Paths*, he spoke of "the
laborious and impoverishing extravagance of composing vast books; of
stretching out over five hundred pages an idea whose perfect spoken exposi-
tion would take a few minutes" (*Ficciones* 12). The previous year, in his
famous prologue to Adolfo Bioy Casares's *Morel's Invention* (*Prólogos*
28–31), sheltering under the authority and the example of Stevenson, he had
already defended a poetics of narrative centered on the preeminence of a

"rigorous plot," something very often relegated to a secondary level in the great tradition of nineteenth-century social and psychological realism. At that time he wrote that "the psychological novel tends to be formless," and, in a sentence that is clearly condemnatory, he added that "such complete freedom ends up being the same as complete disorder."

It is not too hazardous to suppose that Borges thought this dangerous "formlessness" of the psychological (or "characteristic," as he calls it) novel could have found an excellent representation in Dickens's novels. At the beginning of the century, Chesterton, one of the first great analysts of the English writer, had already asserted that the idea of aesthetically necessary, that is to say justified and satisfactory, successive formal closures should not be applied to this work. As he wrote in his 1906 monograph, the different titles do not delimit autonomous novels but "simply lengths cut from the flowing and mixed substance called Dickens."[1]

We ought to understand, he added, that "the units of Dickens, the primary elements, are not the stories, but the characters who affect the stories, or, more often still, the characters who do not affect the stories" (*Charles Dickens* 66–67). This, he considered, makes Dickens not so much a novelist as a creator of characters of mythological stature and intangibility, that is to say, static characters who are immovable, unalterable, set apart from the external movement of the different events in which they find themselves involved, events whose logic (not to say whose interest) therefore passes, against all Borgesian principles, to a secondary plane.

When Peronism came to an end in 1955, Borges, as we know, regained his former weight in the Argentine intellectual scene. He was made director of the National Library, and the following year he assumed the chair of English literature at the University of Buenos Aires, a position he was to occupy for some twelve years. When he applied for this he said his only qualification, which was modest but at the same time conclusive, was that "he had been preparing for this all his life" (*Borges profesor* 16). It had seemed that no written testimony from this long period of teaching was available until, very recently, in the year 2000, *Borges profesor* was published. This is a book based on the meticulous transcription of a collection of well preserved magnetic tapes, and it offers us the carefully annotated reproduction of a complete reading cycle from the last quarter of 1966. And to our surprise one of the chapters of the book is the reproduction of a class about the Victorian era, and it is almost entirely given over to Dickens (228–35).

The style is conversational, there are digressions, it is almost disjointed, as was habitual in all the public "chats" of the *Oral Borges,* to borrow the title of a small volume of his lectures published in 1979. And, as is equally characteristic of his "critical" work, it is in a small biographical sketch, marked in this case by a declared sympathy for the public figure of the man ("'one of the great benefactors of mankind'"), that Borges weaves a few general considerations about the contributions of his work, in which it is possible to trace, without too much difficulty, and sometimes almost literally, Chesterton's opinions ("There is no real development in his characters"). These observations by Borges, whether his own or borrowed, are not always favorable ("But Dickens suffers from an excess of sentimentality," or "Many of his endings are artificial"), and they alternate with brief notes on some books, which go to show the breadth of his reading.

The list includes *David Copperfield, A Tale of Two Cities, Pickwick Papers, Martin Chuzzlewit,* and *Oliver Twist.* In the final part of the class, Borges suddenly brings in Wilkie Collins, whom he presents in implicit contrast to his friend as "a master in the art of weaving plots that are very complicated but never confusing," which, as we see immediately, is a way of introducing Dickens's last novel, *The Mystery of Edwin Drood.* The commentary on this book, which precedes the eulogistic and vibrant coda on which he afterwards concludes the class, is not in the least extensive, although it is considerably more thorough than those on the previous books. It is upon this commentary that I now propose to concentrate in the reflections below.

It is more than probable that what attracted Borges's attention to Dickens's last story was the "reading guide" which his venerated Chesterton had proposed in 1906. In his monograph about the novelist, Chesterton presents *Edwin Drood* as the effort of a writer who, in spite of a long and successful writing career, is increasingly conscious (and even somewhat "ashamed") of his shortcomings in the sphere of narrative structure, in the formal assembling of a story, to the extent that "the end finds him attempting things that are at the opposite pole to the frank formlessness of *Pickwick*" (144). According to Chesterton, in his last book Dickens tried more than simple amendments in this sense: *Edwin Drood,* as he summarizes a little later, "is an attempt to rely entirely on that power of construction. It not only has a plot, it is a plot" (177).

The fact is that for his students Borges unhesitatingly adopts the characterization of the book suggested by his intellectual guide, describing it as "a well-constructed detective novel." He identifies its source in harmony with the traditions of literary history: *Edwin Drood* proceeds almost directly from a desire to emulate the achievements of Wilkie Collins in the previous decade, that is to say *The Woman in White,* the Victorian "sensation novel" of 1860, and above all *The Moonstone* in 1868, which is more easily classifiable as a true detective novel and even, historically speaking, as the first. Borges sees it as the first detective *novel,* since throughout his life he in fact attributed the founding act of the genre to "The Murders in the Rue Morgue," Poe's masterly short story of 1841. In 1946, he included (and wrote a prologue for) *The Moonstone* in a collection called *El séptimo círculo,* which he was running

at that time with Bioy Casares in Emecé. Five years later *Edwin Drood*
(translated by Dora de Alvear) also appeared, in the 78th issue of the collection, and it was preceded by the prologue that Chesterton had written in 1909
for the edition of the book published by Dent's *Everyman's Library*.[2]

The promotion of these two detective novels fitted into the framework of
a fiery defense of the genre. The first manifestation of this defense was a text
in 1933[3] that listed some of its basic principles, which were obviously inspired
by the Father Brown stories whose author Borges held to be the most brilliant
modern follower of the original teachings of Poe. This "aesthetic campaign"
(Fernández Vega 27) continued with much determination and perseverance
all through the ensuing years from various platforms, beginning with the
numerous book reviews that appeared in the magazine *El Hogar* between
1936 and 1939, and going on almost until the end of Borges's life. In 1978,
in a lecture entitled "The Detective Story," he once again reformulated his
decisive argument in support of the genre, concluding that detective literature
"is safeguarding order in an era of disorder" (*Selected Non-Fictions* 499).
This can probably be understood not only on the strictly literary plane, in the
sense that the indispensable structural rigor of plots that center on the resolution of a mystery represent, at this time, the most effective (classic) antidote
to the arbitrary (romantic) "formlessness" of modern narrative, but also on
the philosophical plane, and perhaps even on the political plane.

Borges knew, however, that *Edwin Drood* could not be easily reduced to
the dimensions of a pure "detective novel." It seems evident to any thoughtful reader that although the structure of the novel is subjected quite firmly to
the setting up and the solving of the "mystery" alluded to in the title, something that was in fact quite ground-breaking for him, Dickens does not refrain
from enriching and adding to the vast gallery of picturesque, sympathetic,
ridiculous, or disagreeable characters of his previous works, and often loosens
the reins of the strict progression of the plot, inserting touches and even
whole sections of a frankly psychological tenor. And it could not have been
any other way, if, as Borges himself observed early on, developing the essential element in a detective story in a suitable way is a task that does not require
more than the moderate length of a short story, and if, when transposing this
element to a much greater scale, the author cannot reasonably do without an
elaborate psychological component. For these same reasons, beyond the rigor
of its plot, *The Moonstone* is also, as Borges tells his students, "an excellent
psychological novel." Or perhaps it could better be said the other way round:
a psychological novel which is an excellent detective story *as well*.[4]

At this point we should remember that *The Mystery of Edwin Drood* is
singular in Dickens's work not only in a literary sense but also in a way that
has to do with the circumstances under which it was written. Dickens conceived his "very curious and new idea," as he described it to his friend and

future biographer John Forster, around the middle of 1869. The contract with the publisher was signed in August, and it stipulated twelve monthly installments, somewhat less than the twenty that had been the norm for a number of his previous novels. The writing got under way in October, and regular publication began in April of the following year. It came as a complete surprise when, on the 9th of June, Dickens died of a fulminant stroke only a very few hours after having finished the manuscript of the sixth installment, and thus having reached the exact midpoint of the planned story. His "Half-Told Tale," to paraphrase Hawthorne's celebrated title, therefore leaves us in complete suspense about the enigma of the disappearance of Edwin one stormy Christmas Eve. At the end of chapter 23, completed that day, there is nothing that indicates for certain whether the young man is alive or dead, nor is there anything that unequivocally indicates who is guilty, although the narrator has taken pains, up until then at any rate, to see that the strongest suspicion should fall on the uncle, John Jasper, a gloomy and tormented opium addict. This uncertainty was to unleash a churning wave of conjectures, conflicting arguments, academic debates, and even hypothetical versions of the missing half of the book. By the end of the nineteenth century the irresistible seductiveness of this unfinished work had already engendered a veritable "Drood Literature," a profuse paraliterary tradition which, with few pauses, then continued throughout the entire twentieth century and after.[5]

What stands out about the short presentation of the novel that Borges makes to his class is that he leaves the plot itself to one side and chooses to dwell on the "dramatic" nature of the story of the writing of it, though in fact his comments do not go much beyond quoting some lines from Chesterton's original prologue almost word for word:

> In none of Dickens's novels, says Chesterton, did the plot matter. What was important was the characters, with their manias, their ways of dressing that were always the same and their special vocabulary. But in the end, Dickens resolves to write a novel in which the plot is important, and, almost at the exact moment when he is about to reveal who the murderer is, God ordains his death, and so we will never know the real secret, the hidden plot of Edwin Drood, says Chesterton, except when we meet Dickens in heaven. And then, says Chesterton, most probably Dickens will no longer remember, and he will be as puzzled as we are.   (234)

As we can see, this commentary is second-hand, and might not seem to matter much, but I think that in this focalization on Dickens's demise, a point of considerable importance emerges. The biographical anecdote, that Borges reformulates from Chesterton's words, turns out to be for him at least as attractive as the cut-off enigma which the novel leaves us with; it turns out to be a story in itself, a story that is perhaps more intriguing and suggestive than the other. Therefore, focusing on this passage, I would like to suggest the possibility of understanding the phrase "Borges as a reader of Dickens" in a way that is *not metonymical*, which is how we would spontaneously understand it. That is to say, to take it not so much as "Borges as a reader of *the works* of Dickens," but more literally as "Borges as a reader of the story *entitled* Charles Dickens." And, moreover, not so much Borges as a reader of a complete biography, but Borges, with the freedom and the assurance which was always characteristic of him in such things, as a selective reader of this peculiar and surprising *biographeme*, which is the sudden death of the writer in the act of unveiling a hidden truth, and at the same time in the act of managing to construct, in extremis, a kind of narrative structure hitherto unknown to him, or at any rate very different from anything he had done up until then.

The demonstration that this interpretation of my title might be something more than a mere play on words consists of two stages. The first is the observation that taking the life of a writer as a secondary text, as the source of a separate story, a stimulant for the imagination, is an eminently Borgesian idea, and there are many examples of this. One of these, ironically, has to do with Chesterton. In the article about him in *Other Inquisitions*, Borges sees in the Father Brown stories, in the oft-repeated pattern of finally giving an event that is apparently magical or supernatural a clear and very rational explanation, something like an "abbreviation" or a "symbol" or a "reflection" (82) of another story that is ultimately more enigmatic than the original. And this is the story of Chesterton *himself*, the story of a complex character in whom there was an intimate confrontation between professed Catholicism and "something [which] in the makeup of his personality leaned towards the nightmarish, something secret, and blind, and central" (84). In the 1966 course, Borges dwells on the biography of Coleridge, whom he presents (comparing him in this respect to Macedonio Fernández) as a man almost more brilliant for his conversation, for his delays and his great unfinished projects than for his writings. "To think of Coleridge," he tells his students, "is to think of a character in a novel" (179). It is similar with Browning, whose life also "arouses our interest because of its plot" (236). Later, in the lecture about "The Detective Story," he explains that Poe's stories "construct a character, a character who outlives all the characters [he] created" (*Selected Non-Fictions* 498), and suggests, on a general plane, that a writer may well stand higher in the image that we retain of him as a man, than do his writings.[6]

In support of all this we should also remember a fact that is well-known, but crucial from our perspective. Borges started out in the 1920s writing poetry and essays. His move into fiction came the following decade, first with the "possible biography" of Evaristo Carriego, which was published in 1930, and then through a very subtle game with this genre, a game which, as he would later acknowledge, owes a lot to what Marcel Schwob had devised in *Imaginary Lives*. I am referring to the amusing fictional biographies which came out in 1933 and 1934 in the *Revista Multicolor de los Sábados* [*Saturday Color Supplement*] of the newspaper *Crítica*, and which were collected in 1935 in Borges's *A Universal History of Infamy*. In the prologue to this he confesses to have maliciously overindulged, among other things, in "the paring down of a man's whole life to two or three scenes" (13), just as much later he was to pick out the scene of the sudden death of Dickens for his students. Immediately afterwards, he became the literary critic of *El Hogar*, where in the section on "capsule biographies" of writers he opened up a new field of literary experimentation. In these texts, one may well often find it quite difficult, at least on the stylistic level, to separate the intention to give information from another underlying purpose, that of transforming a biographical pre-text into a kind of laconic fictional story.

The second stage of my argument, which is perhaps more decisive, is to point out how productive this *biographeme* is for Borges, by mentioning some examples of its repeated use in his texts. Let us look at it again: "in the end, Dickens resolves to write a novel in which the plot is important, and, almost at the exact moment when he is about to reveal who the murderer is, God ordains his death, and so we will never know the real secret" (*Borges profesor* 234). [7] The idea of a secret that is on the point of being divulged, but is in fact lost forever, operates, as I have postulated, on two levels: not only in connection with what Dickens had in mind with the death (or not) of Edwin, and with the identity of his murderer, that is to say on the level of resolving the plot, but also less obviously, but no less suggestively, from Borges's point of view, on the level of *the other story*, that of a man who, after a long and successful literary career, is trying his hand at a new kind of novel and thus in some way discovering for himself a new identity as a writer.[8] Here we can note in parenthesis that Borges reads the story of Dickens as the exact reverse of the story of another writer, Jaromir Hladík, who, when condemned to death by the Nazis, asks God for the "secret miracle" alluded to in the title of the 1943 story, that is to say for the time necessary to be able to finish this time not a mystery story, but a drama in verse entitled *The Enemies*. In the fictional world, God hears Hladík's prayer and miraculously halts the progress of the surrounding universe for a year, until the precise moment at which the writer manages to get to the very last word of his work and is then shot. In real life, He was less generous to Dickens.

A careful reading of the *biographeme* shows that it is concentrated around the expression "is about to," which can only remind us of the beautiful and well-known final sentence of "The Wall and the Books," the first essay in *Other Inquisitions*: "Music, states of happiness, mythology, faces molded by

time, certain twilights and certain places, all these are trying to tell us something, or have told us something we should not have missed, or are about to
tell us something; that imminence of a revelation that is not yet produced is,
perhaps, the aesthetic reality (5)''.[9] As shown by the ebb and flow of speculation (about a disconcerting episode in Chinese history) that leads the essay
to this conclusion, the ''aesthetic reality'' alluded to here is the power that a
form has in itself to move us, relegating to a secondary level its possible
''content,'' a content that might perhaps be obscurely intuited, but never
properly enunciated, beyond approximate formulations, all equally plausible.
More generally, one could well say that the Borgesian subject, constantly
confronted with a complex world of forms, does no more than attempt partial
recognitions, transitory, more or less convincing (or useful) orderings, but
knowing, or understanding afterwards, that the phrase that would precisely
articulate the meaning of these forms will not be spoken. This is why, con-
densing an entire ethic, the moving ''Oración'' of *In Praise of Darkness*
declares: ''We do not know the designs of the universe, but we do know that
to reason with lucidity and to work with justice is to support those designs,
which will not be revealed to us'' (*Elogio* 144).

Of this thematic motif, that of the search and the imminent, but impossible,
revelation of an ultimate truth, whether it be the hidden order of the universe
or the real identity of an individual, we could doubtless say the same thing
that Borges said about the oft-repeated pattern in Chesterton, which is so far
from being a ''rhetorical artifice'' that it is an ''essential form'' in his own
work (82). Let us consider a story which displays this motif in the very title,
''Averroes's Search.'' In this, Borges imagines a few hours in the life of the
famous Andalusian Arab sage during which he tries to unravel the meaning
of two words in Aristotle's *Poetics* that do not have any possible representation in the Islamic ambit, ''tragedy'' and ''comedy.'' Averroes comes quite
close to his objective, since the theatrical game being played by some children
in the patio below him would seem to be able to enlighten him, but he
ultimately fails to attain it. The narrator concludes that the detail the sage is
seeking ''is not inaccessible to other men, but it is to him,'' just as he recognizes that when all is said and done it is also forbidden to him, as a contemporary writer, to reconstruct through his fragile fiction the true face of the
character so far removed from him in time. ''I sensed, on the last page,'' he
confesses, ''that my narrative was a symbol of the man I was while I wrote
it'' (*A Personal Anthology* 110). This brings us back in some way to the same
speculative interplay between the plot of the work and the story of the man
who imagines it that Borges the teacher was later to insinuate about Dickens's
writing of *Edwin Drood*. We could also think of stories like ''Pedro Salvadores,'' another of the prose pieces included among the poems in *In Praise
of Darkness*, which turns on the mysterious personality of a man who is

locked up for years in a cellar to escape from the underlings of the dictator Rosas. "Who, who, was Pedro Salvadores?" this other narrator, a close relative of the previous one, anxiously asks, and then admits with serene resignation that "like everything else, the fate of Pedro Salvadores seems to us to be the symbol of something we are about to understand" (*Elogio* 79). [10]

The same "essential form" is what underlies, once again right from the title, the text with which I will round off this brief recounting, *The Approach to al-Mu'tasim*, which first came out in 1936 among the essays in *The History of Eternity*. This is a key text, in that working freely from a book (in this case one that does not exist), it invents the "formal mould of the review" (González Perez 217) and forms the nexus between the fictional biographies of *A Universal History of Infamy* and the series of great short stories which Borges was to begin writing in 1939. The imaginary book reviewed here is the English-language novel *The Approach to al-Mu'tasim* by a certain Mir Bahadur Ali, that was supposedly published in Bombay in 1932. The first thing that the equally imaginary literary critic points out is that (exactly like Borges's own "symbolic" detective stories, or like *Edwin Drood*, a detective novel embedded in a psychological study) this one lends itself to a double reading, in the sense that its plot combines an intricate but attractive "detective-story mechanism" à la Wilkie Collins with an allegorical dimension, or, as he expresses it here, an "undercurrent of mysticism" (*The Aleph* 45). The protagonist, a law student, undertakes a long and troubled odyssey all over India, mingling "among the lowest class of people" (48) in search of a being with a divine nature called al-Mu'tasim. He is not absolutely sure this man exists, but he has a strong intuition and he believes him capable of redeeming so much wretchedness. The critic winds up his plot summary as follows:

> Finally, after many years, the student comes to a corridor "at whose end is a door and a cheap beaded curtain, and behind the curtain a shining light". The student claps his hands once and twice and asks for al-Mu'tasim. A man's voice, the unimaginable voice of al-Mu'tasim, prays him to enter. The student parts the curtain and steps forward. At this point the novel comes to its end.
> (49)

The author, then, cuts the story off with the mysterious indetermination of those steps. The revelation (of yearned-for divine purity) again seems imminent but does not materialize, and in this the novel seems like an extensive rewriting of Kafka's short and celebrated parable *Before the Law*, which Borges translated and more than once mentioned.[11]

The student's journey does not really come to its conclusion, any more than the characters involved with John Jasper find definite proof, in spite of their suspicions, that he really did murder his nephew, or than the reader ties up all the loose ends that the novel leaves hanging, or than Dickens's aim to write a novel in which plot was more important than in prior books (and thus, as Chesterton said, to give birth to "a new Dickens") is fulfilled. Borges reads all these imminences and all these failures simultaneously, and with intense delight.

In the first chapter of *Edwin Drood*, a man who is not yet identified as Jasper is lying on a bed in a sordid lodging house in a squalid London slum, lost in the phantasmagorical visions which he gets from a pipe of opium. At his side, Dickens notes, and in a similar state, lie a "haggard woman," a Chinaman, and a "Lascar," a term that at that time denoted a sailor from the Bombay area. Would it not be tempting perhaps to see in this fleeting character the unnamed protagonist of the novel by Mir Bahadur Ali, in one of the many stages of his long "approach," among low class people, to this "man called al-Mu'tasim" who he thinks would illuminate him with the sacred glow? After all, Jasper lives among churchmen, next to a Cathedral in which he is the organist. Let us remember also that some devoted exegetes, compiling and interpreting indications sown in the text, believed at one time that they had found the key to the mystery, discovering in Jasper nothing less than a secret ritual strangler, an adept of the Hindu sect of the *thugs*. But from another point of view, and playing even more freely with these fantastic reverses of time which Borges found so fascinating, might it not also be that when Dickens brought the anonymous sailor into his text, he was already dreaming of Mir Bahadur Ali's novel, and even of his future (and false) reviewer? In short, it is as if, when Dickens stood at the mysterious door he was on the point of opening, and before he obeyed God's severe command, he had revealed to us, between the lines, that he had already read and foreseen Borges, his future reader. [12]

NOTES

This essay was translated from the Spanish by Mr. Richard Manning, who also provided translations into English of internal quotations.

1. Of course, some Dickensians might reject the assertions by Chesterton that Dickens's narratives do not constitute independent novels and that the plots in these books are not really significant. Borges, however, seems to accept fully these ideas.
2. Like his other prologues, this was later included in the book *Appreciations and Criticisms of the Works of Charles Dickens* (218–28).
3. This text, "Leyes de la narración policial," recently published in *Textos recobrados (1931–1955)*, 36–39, was to be rewritten as "Los laberintos policiales y Chesterton," which appeared in *Sur*, in May 1935 ("The Labyrinths of the Detective Story and Chesterton," in *Selected Non-Fictions*, 112–14).

4. We read in *El Hogar* of 7 April 1939 that the detective novel "comes down to a kind of novel of characters or customs" (*Textos cautivos* 313). The mention of *The Moonstone* is in the issue of 3 September 1937 (165).

5. One of the most recent games played with the text is that by Carlo Fruttero and Franco Lucentini: *La Verità sul Caso D.*

6. At about the same time Roland Barthes, although he did not name Borges, translates the sense of the operation in more theoretical terms: "L'Auteur lui-même . . . peut, ou pourra un jour constituer un texte comme les autres . . . il suffira de le considérer lui-même comme un être de papier et sa vie comme une *bio-graphie* (au sens étymologique du terme) . . . l'entreprise critique (si l'on peut encore parler de critique) consistera alors à *retourner* la figure documentaire de l'auteur en figure romanesque" (217).

7. "God ordains his death" is a (not at all insignificant) Borgesian contribution to Chesterton's (for once) less religious version: "He drops down dead as he is in the act of denouncing the assassin" (*Appreciations* 219). Less religious perhaps, but on the other hand more dramatic, as already underlined in his 1906 monograph: "The tragic element of its truncation mingles somewhat with an element of tragedy in the thing itself" (*Charles Dickens* 179).

8. "A new Dickens was really being born when Dickens died" (*Charles Dickens* 145).

9. Once again, in Borges the dividing line between essay and fiction proves to be rather thin, as this sentence from his story "The End" suggests: "There is an hour of the afternoon when the plain is on the verge of saying something. It never says it, or perhaps it says it infinitely, or perhaps we do not understand it, or we understand it and it is untranslatable as music" (*A Personal Anthology* 169).

10. This same attempt to grasp a veiled and elusive truth is probably what is at the root of Borges's fascination with the detective story, and fuels his personal reworking of the genre in the three classic stories that make up his contribution ("The Garden of Forking Paths," 1941; "Death and the Compass," 1942; "Ibn Hakkan al-Bokhari, Dead in His Labyrinth," 1951), not forgetting so many other tales in which the plot centers on some form of search or investigation, such as "Tlön, Uqbar, Orbis Tertius," in which the two friends compare their research of Tlön to a tiring "minor detective work" (*Borges. A Reader* 114). In the first three above, it is clear that Borges goes far beyond the simple canonical problem of the identity of the murderer, that his stories play with a subtle superimposition of two stories, or of two levels of meaning, and that the uneasiness of his detectives can also be read in a metaphysical key (Brescia 156–61). With his usual (and ambiguous) modesty, Borges himself confirmed this when, talking about his own conception of the "detective story," he said: "I have taken it to a symbolic level, which I am not sure is appropriate" (*Selected Non-Fictions* 499).

11. For example, precisely in the same essay "On Chesterton" in *Other Inquisitions*, Borges asserts that the dark world Chesterton was drawn to, by the intimate "makeup of his personality," in spite of his efforts and his professions of faith, always led the English master to (re-)write Kafka's disturbing parable (84–85). The translation appears in *El Hogar* (*Textos cautivos*), 27 May 1938.

12. We bring the game to an end with a final turn of the screw. By coincidence (?), in the same issue of *El Hogar* in which his translation of "Before the Law" appeared, Borges includes a note (*Selected Non-Fictions* 185) about the republication of a book by an Englishman, Meadows Taylor, originally published in 1839 and entitled "The Confessions of a Thug." The (this time authentic) reviewer explains that "The subject is the *thugs*, a sect or corporation of hereditary stranglers who for eight centuries brought horror (with bare feet and fatal scarves) to the streets and shadows of India."

WORKS CITED

Arias, Martín and Martín Hadis (eds.). *Borges profesor*. Buenos Aires: Emecé, 2000.

Barthes, Roland. *S/Z*. Paris: Seuil, 1976.

Borges, Jorge Luis. *The Aleph and Other Stories 1933–1969*. Trans. Norman Thomas di Giovanni in collaboration with the author. London: Jonathan Cape, 1971.

———. *Borges. A Reader*. Eds. Emir Rodríguez Monegal and Alastair Read. New York: Dutton, 1981.

———. *Elogio de la sombra*. Buenos Aires: Emecé, 1969.

———. *Ficciones*. Madrid: Alianza Editorial, 1997.

———. *Introducción a la literatura inglesa*. 1965. Madrid: Alianza Editorial, 1999.

———. *Other Inquisitions. 1937–1952*. Translated by Ruth L.C. Simms. 1964. Austin: U of Texas P, 1984.

———. *A Personal Anthology*. Ed. Anthony Kerrigan. New York: Grove Press, 1967.

———. *Prólogos con un prólogo de prólogos*. Madrid: Alianza Editorial, 1998.

———. *Selected Non-Fictions*. Ed. Eliot Weinberger. New York: Viking Penguin, 1999.

———. *Textos cautivos. Ensayos y reseñas en "El Hogar" (1936–1939)*. Ed. Enrique Sacerio-Garí y Emir Rodríguez Monegal. Buenos Aires: Tusquets Editores, 1986.

———. *Textos recobrados (1931–1955)*. Buenos Aires: Emecé, 2001.

———. *A Universal History of Infamy*. Trans. Norman Thomas di Giovanni. New York: Dutton, 1972.

Brescia, Pablo A.J. "De policías y ladrones: Abenjacán, Borges y la teoría del cuento." *Variaciones Borges* 10 (2000): 145–66.

Chesterton, Gilbert Keith. *Appreciations and Criticisms of the Works of Charles Dickens*. London: Dent, 1911.

———. *Charles Dickens*. 1906. London: Methuen, 1960.

Fernández Vega, José. "Una campaña estética. Borges y la narrativa policial". *Variaciones Borges* 1 (1996): 27–66.

Fruttero, Carlo and Lucentini, Franco. *La Verità sul Caso D*. Torino: Giulio Einaudi, 1989. Trans. as *The D. Case. The Truth about the Mystery of Edwin Drood*. New York: Harcourt, Brace, 1992.

González Pérez, Aníbal. "Borges y las fronteras del cuento." *El cuento hispanoamericano*. Ed. Enrique Pupo-Walker. Madrid: Editorial Castalia, 1995. 211–34.

A Cubo-Futurist Reading of Dickens: Rafael Barradas's 1921 Illustrations for Hard Times

Miguel Angel Battegazzore

[Illustrations for this article appear at the end of Beatriz Vegh's "Dickens and Barradas in 1921: A Hospitable Meeting", which refers to the same images.—Editors]

In order to be able to place Rafael Barradas's illustrations for a 1921 Spanish translation of *Hard Times*[1] in their context, it is necessary to take into account the artistic language the artist was employing at that time, and this was closely linked to Cubist practice.

From all the options derived from the Modernist movement in painting, the Uruguayan Barradas, along with his countryman Joaquín Torres García, chose that which was most related to writers and poets because it proposed the paradigm of writing itself as a creative route to a new formula in painting. According to Ernst Gombrich, the theorist of this particular kind of painting and its enthusiastic spokesperson was the dealer and collector Daniel-Henri Kahnweiler, who, in his published book on Juan Gris, took the work of Gris as the most characteristic example of the genre.

The Uruguayan painters Barradas and Torres García, who knew each other in 1916 and 1917 in Barcelona and Madrid, shared Kahnweiler's admiration for the work of Juan Gris, and readily subscribed to Kahnweiler's idea that Cubism had inaugurated a new path for painters that made painting an equivalent to writing. They both agreed on the fact that painting had to be constructed like a piece of writing on a flat surface, in order to establish a break in the identification between visual reality and meaning which had been and still was the basis of Impressionism or of the academic Naturalism that was most accepted in the artistic milieu in which Barradas worked in Madrid. And it is this artistic stance which Barradas was to put successfully into practice in his 1921 illustrations for *Hard Times*.

The best documentation of this aesthetic posture that Torres García and Barradas shared can be found in a painting by Barradas dated 1919, that is to say two years before he did his illustrations for Dickens's novel. A painting entitled *Still Life with Joaquín Torres García's Letter* (National Museum of Visual Arts, Montevideo), it follows the orthodox Cubist practice and uses a collage technique with labels, playing cards, and matchboxes. But what undoubtedly makes this work a manifesto that yields insight into the artist's concern to establish an innovative painting technique based on writing procedures is the central role in the painting that Barradas gives to a letter he received from Torres García. It and its envelope are glued in place in the center of this 1919 composition. Better evidence of Barradas's identification between painting and writing could not be imagined.

Thus, even though in pictorial Modernism the signs had visual reality as their starting point, these painters stepped back from that visual reality and offered a schematic equivalent to it, something Kahnweiler, in his book on Juan Gris, analogically associated with Chinese writing. In this, he showed how this kind of writing evolved from pictograms to the present ideographic signs. Thus Chinese calligraphy, which as we know does not discriminate between painting and writing, became an alternative mythology for Cubism, comparable to the Japanese stamp in Impressionism.

This innovative conception of pictorial art was partly derived from the close contact modernist painters had with writers and poets. In an inverse way, Apollinaire, for example, practiced a sort of visual writing and composed ideograms and typographic poems which were collected in his book *Calligrammes*. And we know that such ideogramatic and typographic artistic praxis was shared by Italian Futurist painters.

Significantly, all these calligraphic characteristics are found in a painting by Barradas also dated 1919, entitled *Casas de vecindad [Tenement Housing]* (National Museum of Visual Arts, Montevideo). It represents a typical popular *corrada*, a collective building organized around an indoor patio. Close examination of this painting may help us in the "reading" of the *Hard Times* illustrations because in it Barradas started working with his innovative modernist mechanisms of communication with the viewer. These were precisely those new mechanisms of communication which the critic Arnold Gehlen was wittily to characterize as "intentional commonplaces" (144; my translation). The painting does not have any naturalistic context; instead, there are numbers and notices indicating the continuation of floors, ideographic signs, arrows, hands, all signs indicating direction just as they appear in typographic text in real life. In this way, the viewer obtains a visual equivalent to a dynamic of going up the stairs in a building.

Kahnweiler also drew attention to the constructive character of the new Cubist writing practice, since the viewer is called upon by the artist to assume a participatory responsibility, and one that is not just limited to the retina, as was the case in Impressionism and Post-Impressionism. According to this new practice, not only data given by the senses but also data from memory and personal experience that also have to be structured and taken into account allow the viewer to interpret and recompose the fragmentally configured object represented in the painting either in movement or from different points of view.

When it came to the task of drawing for Dickens's novel, this structural conception of pictorial language enabled Barradas to handle the *Hard Times* illustrations with great freedom and with independence from his traditional-minded predecessors. We should point out here that even though Barradas used to practice artistic caricature and possessed rare physiognomic intuition, in his illustrations for *Hard Times* he set aside this traditional and predominant style.

Barradas, then, produced these illustrations within a Cubo-Futurist practice, the same as he was using in his paintings at that time, through the procedure of the "intentional commonplace," that is, by repeating chimneys, roofs, circus tents, desks, flowers, stars and so on in his illustrations to the novel, not descriptively, but as a leitmotif made of signs. These leitmotifs invite *Hard Times* readers to get inside the novel, to set aside all their a priori conceptions, and to project themselves into Dickens's text. And the wise chromatic economy, so successfully employed by Barradas in these illustrations, greatly contributes to creating this powerful effect of projection. This chromatic economy seems to fit in perfectly not only with the methods and techniques of graphic reproduction at that time (the 1920s) but also with the new role played by color in the Modernist artistic language practice, as in Robert Delaunay's Orphism and Italian Futurism.

In the *Hard Times* illustrations, color is used openly, as in a xylographic carving, in clear, neat bidimensional planes, and in this way, it is freed from its descriptive function and able to play a more emblematic role. Three color values, red, yellow, and green, are enough for the twelve illustrations. These values alternate with the black graphics on the white page, which serve as a common denominator between the illustrations and the typographic pages facing them.

The color distribution in the twelve *Hard Times* full-page illustrations is marked by the prominent role played by the red and black pairing in six of these illustrations, the green and black pairing in four others, and the yellow and black pairing in two.

The color red occurs in Dickens's text in the descriptions of brick chimneys and roofs in Coketown, and it contrasts with the black soot, as in the following passage from the novel: "It was a town of red brick, or of brick that would have been red if the smoke and ashes had allowed it; but as matters stood, it was a town of unnatural red and black like the painted face of a savage. It was a town of machinery and tall chimneys, out of which interminable serpents of smoke trailed themselves for ever and ever, and never got uncoiled" (1:5:22). In Barradas's illustrations the color red is enhanced by a sort of shorthand of nervous, insistent black strokes that, in their rhythmic counterpoint to the red vermilion planes, characterize Barradas's so-called Vibrationist pictorial language.

Given the open character of the Modernist practice, the dialectic of red/black as brick/smoke can by association naturally draw in others, such as the dialectic of fire/coal (related to work in hydroelectric dams and factories and to industrialization in general). Or the dialectic of red-life/black-death as related to the emblem of the anarchist movement that was still so important in Spain at the time Barradas was doing these drawings. And Dickens's text seems to confirm this open and conflicting red/black dialectic when he says (as quoted above) that Coketown "was a town of unnatural red and black city, like the painted face of a savage" (1:5:22).

On the other hand, along with the ubiquity which color acquires in these illustrations, the red/black relationship is not descriptively limited to Coketown but also shapes Sissy's picture in front of the circus (fig. 1), and the way a musical leitmotif follows the picture of Bitzer at school and the picture of Thomas at home (figs. 3 and 6).[2]

The color yellow plays a leading role in these illustrations. In the image of the circus, the flag waving against the wind contrasts with the gloomy chimneys of Coketown (figs. 7 and 8).

If we consider the 1837 illustrations for *Pickwick Papers* by Phiz, in which, according to J. Hillis Miller's analysis, the sun's rays on the senior Weller's belly are shown (107), a somewhat parallel reading of Barradas's use of yellow in the *Hard Times* illustrations could be made. According to this, we could project solar connotations, connotations of a cosmic harmony, and also of those feelings that have to do with freedom and the inalienable value given by humanity to this. All these values are shared by Barradas, by García Lorca in his poetic language, and by the painter Torres García's artistic language (even though the latter does not rely on the emotional), and we know that they are widely employed in Dickens's work.

On the other hand, the choice of the color green is reserved for those illustrations whose scenes are associated with what we would call affective patterns, and in *Hard Times* these are often linked to nature and childhood. The fact that there is a sketch for one of Barradas's *Hard Times* illustrations painted in blue (sketch of fig. 9, National Museum of Visual Arts, Montevideo) might show this charge of emotive meaning that reminds us of the tone of Picasso's blue period, which shares this same sensitivity with Barradas's work. It is evident that Barradas thought of the color blue before choosing green for the final print, after having intuited that the color green better matched the hopeful nature of Dickens's text, which in its final lines projects nostalgia for virgin nature free of pollution.

This contrast of black signs with green planes gets more dramatic when it is used for the ominous figure of the teacher in front of the children in the classroom (fig. 5) or the ghostly image of the missing clown who is shown marked by a black star (fig. 2), and it acquires greater balance when it is used for Gradgrind with Sissy and Louisa seen from the back (fig. 9).

But the secret of the exceptional effect achieved by Barradas in his *Hard Times* illustrations lies in the leading role played by the white color of the paper, by its empty blankness. It is this blankness that circulates like a ground bass among illustrations and typographic pages, and it makes them compatible for the viewer. In effect, it is precisely this white that sustains and structures the calligraphic graphics. It is precisely this blankness that constitutes the space onto which Dickens's readers will project.

We should point out here that Barradas very probably would not have reached such a level of dematerialization in his descriptive shapes in these illustrations without the severe discipline of syncretic removal which the practice of caricature had given him.

Modernist illustration established a new dialectic, audaciously allowing the visual and the literary texts to work in parallel on the reader and viewer, in the way that a two-voice canon does. The illustration "enlightens" the literary text, which at the same time induces meaning into the images. The view that text and image are irreconcilable or subordinated one to the other is clearly rejected by the Modernist Barradas as a false opposition. The new concept of scriptorial painting now helped those visual and literary spaces that formerly had been conflictive to be perceived as complementary.

The leading role that Barradas assigns to color in his *Hard Times* illustrations is evident. The color is almost overflowing orthodox Cubist practice with its sparing chromatic handling, reminiscent of Delaunay's Orphism and Italian Futurism. Both Orphism and Italian Futurism helped Barradas broaden his own language and reach, in his *Hard Times* illustrations, what he significantly baptized as Clownism or a Clownist pictorial manner. And the predominance of color in this plastic language of his in the 1920s clearly shows emotional sensitivity.

On the other hand, Barradas's illustrations allude to aspects of a social reality caused by the advance in industrialization, a phenomenon which was unknown on the Iberian Peninsula. Spain and Portugal retained a medieval sensitivity, and agrarian economic conditions still predominated. The imagery of the 1920s in Spain, the time when Barradas lived there and which he shared with his friends the artist Torres García and the poet García Lorca, was the result of a conjunction of mystical medieval religious sensitivity with the last modulations of Romanticism. It was from this atmosphere that Picasso escaped when he moved to Paris, and his friend, the filmmaker Buñuel, was later to go the same way.

It is precisely on that common ground inherited by the twentieth century from the iconography of late Romanticism that the emotional sensitivity of Barradas and Dickens came together. The adoption by Barradas of the Cubo-Futurist practice for illustrating Dickens evidently meant a break with that agrarian, medieval, and late Romantic Hispanic sensitivity that was already anachronistic in the context of the rest of Europe, which was becoming immersed in modernity. But if we look closely into Barradas's illustrations for Dickens, and are not blinded by the Modernist language, iconographic motifs which have a sensitivity still indebted to Romantic iconography will very soon emerge. Let us focus on the circus motif (fig. 8). The axis of this composition is the tree, which emerges from the blank whiteness of the paper dividing it into two sides. On the right is the circus tent, and it is nowhere, in "neither town nor country," placed on "neutral ground," as the text says (1:3:11). On the other hand, to the left, a fence suggests private property. The carriage in yellow in the other circus illustration (fig. 7) may allude to a nomadic dwelling.

In the novel *Hard Times*, the circus is an equestrian circus, and even though in his illustrations Barradas projects onto it all those Modernist connotations from Seurat (*The Circus*, 1890–1891, Musée d'Orsay, Paris) to Picasso (scenery to Satie's *Parade*), when he draws the horse he places it outside the tent, right outside it, grazing freely. He doesn't show it performing some practiced trick or carrying a weightless rider on its back. The circus horse ambiguously complies with Dickens's text, but it still responds to the Romantic iconography in which a horse represents freedom. This attachment to Romantic sensitivity is confirmed in the illustrations for Dickens by the use of one of Barradas's most characteristic features: that of showing characters from the back (figs. 5, 9 and 12), which occurs frequently in Romantic painting.

One of the illustrations (fig. 12) shows Louisa Gradgrind at home, presumably in her room. Although in Dickens's text she is very often at the fireplace, in Barradas's plate she is shown from the back, in front of a window, looking at a distant view through the pane. Rather than fulfilling a descriptive role, this view turns into a construction in the sense that Kahnweiler conceived of construction in the framework of cubist practice. This is what enabled Barradas to turn the window into a projection screen and show the deep inner pain the female character is suffering, and also to set up the opposition between the anarchist tent of the wandering circus with its flag flying high and Coketown with its regimented school and factories with red and sooty facades and chimneys. In this illustration for *Hard Times* we find Romantic iconography once again, here with reference to the most representative pictorial image ever produced in the whole Romantic period: *Woman at the Window* by Caspar David Friedrich (1822, National Gallery, Berlin). Significantly, the image of Louisa indoors at the window has as its opposing illustration that of Sissy outdoors among circus tents (figs. 1 and 8).

Barradas's last illustration for *Hard Times*, which converges iconographically with Friedrich's well-known and emblematic Romantic painting, shows us one of Dickens's main characters in the novel metaphorically locked in her bedroom like a bird in its cage, behind the bars and longing for freedom. These iconographic affinities (and many more can be found) enable us to see how, in his illustrations, Barradas manages to amplify the potential for suggestion in the text of the novel through an innovative Cubo-Futurist practice that proposes a modulation of Dickens's text, pointing out a dimension of sensitivity and Romantic emotiveness in it.

NOTES

1. Beatriz Vegh published an introductory article on Barradas's 1921 illustration for *Hard Times* in *Dickens Quarterly*. This essay includes black-and-white reproductions of the twelve illustrations and of the three vignettes, one for each section of the novel (fig. 13).
2. The first twelve figures presenting black-and-white reproductions of Barradas's color illustrations are numbered in the order in which they appear in the 1921 Spanish translation published in Madrid by Estrella. The page numbers are in parentheses: Fig. 1, Sissy Jupe in front of the circus (16); fig. 2, Jupe (64); fig. 3, Bitzer in the classroom (112); fig. 4, The classroom (168); fig. 5, A class (169); fig. 6, Thomas studying in his room (209); fig. 7, The circus with carriage (247); fig. 8, The circus with Sissy leaning on a tree (248); figure 9, Gradgrind with Louisa and Sissy (273); fig. 10, Coketown I (311); fig. 11, Coketown II (312); fig. 12, Louisa at the window (337); fig. 13: black-and-white vignettes for the three books into which *Hard Times* is divided.

WORKS CITED

Dickens, Charles. *Hard Times*. Oxford: Oxford UP, 1997.

———. *Tiempos difíciles*. Ill. by Rafael Barradas. Tr. by J. Camino Nessi. Madrid: Estrella, 1921.

Gehlen, Arnold. *Imágenes de época. Sociología y estilística de la pintura moderna.* Barcelona: Península, 1994.

Gombrich, Ernst. "Platón con traje moderno". In *Temas de nuestro tiempó. Propuestas del siglo XX acerca del saber y el arte.* Madrid: Debate, 1997. 131–41.

Kahnweiler, Daniel-Henri. *Juan Gris. Sa vie, son oeuvre, ses écrits.* Paris, Gallimard, 1946. *Juan Gris, His Life and Work.* Trans. Douglas Cooper. London: Lund Humphries, 1947.

Miller, J. Hillis. "Dickens and Phiz." In *Illuminations.* Cambridge: Harvard UP, 1992. 96–111.

Vegh, Beatriz. "*Hard Times* Gone Modernist: The 1921 Rafael Barradas Illustrations for *Tiempos difíciles.*" *Dickens Quarterly* 15:1 (March 1998): 3–27.

Dickens and Barradas in Madrid, 1921:
A Hospitable Meeting

Beatriz Vegh

[Illustrations appear at the end of the article.—Editors]

A publication from the Spanish-speaking world that has, I believe, significance for Dickens studies is the Spanish translation of *Hard Times* issued in Madrid in 1921 under the title *Tiempos difíciles*. It was part of a collection by the Estrella publishing house, which was managed by the Spanish promoter of culture Gregorio Martínez Sierra. The collection included ten other works of world literature, all of them with illustrations by Rafael Pérez Barradas (or simply Barradas, as he was known in artistic circles). The originals of some of Barradas's illustrations for *Tiempos difíciles* are in the National Museum of Visual Arts in Montevideo, Uruguay, and were put on exhibition during a recent conference called "Dickens in Latin America," held June 23–25, 2003. Some of these illustrations seem particularly valuable in helping us to consider the complex interrelationship between the verbal and the graphic in literary texts.[1]

Barradas "accompanies" Dickens's text in *Tiempos difíciles* with twelve illustrations and three borders (or vignettes). These illustrations and borders have great visual impact, and they differ markedly in conception and execution from the iconographic tradition of prior artists, especially Hablot K. Browne ("Phiz"), who prepared illustrations for many of Dickens's works. *Hard Times* was first published in 1854 without a single illustration either in the serialized version in Dickens's weekly *Household Words* or in the book version that also came out in 1854. But in 1870, the year in which Dickens died, there was a new edition that was illustrated with twenty plates by Harry

French, all of which were done in the realistic tradition of Browne and other artists. A comparison of these plates by Harry French with the Barradas illustrations for the 1921 Spanish edition is eloquent testimony to the difference in graphic expression between the two styles, and to the novelty of Barradas's work.

We know that the term and the concept of "accompaniment" define the trans-textual relation and function which Gérard Genette calls paratext, and in this case this would be the role that Barradas's graphic illustrations play with respect to the text of *Hard Times*. Thus, the paratext (title, prologue, postscript, and notes, or, as in this case, illustrations) stands in respect to the text that it accompanies in a border area, a threshold, or to use the expression which Gérard Genette borrows from Borges, a "hallway" (a *zaguán* in Spanish), which Genette translates into French as *vestibule*, to describe what is poetically paratextual. That is to say, the paratext announces or presents the text—in the sense of making it present—strengthening it and guaranteeing its presence in the world, its reception and its consumption in the form of a book—although this doesn't guarantee that it will be read (7–8).

Considering Barradas's illustrations as a graphic discourse that provides an accompaniment to Dickens's novel, as a vestibule, a threshold, and a paratextual borderland, and seeking to describe from this perspective the interplay of relations between the two components, the literary from Dickens and the graphic from Barradas, we find that this term "paratext" also includes or refers to the figure of hospitality—cultural and artistic—from the semantic diversity which its ambivalent prefix "para" assumes. In fact, within this semantic diversity and its antithetical connotations—proximity and distance, similarity and difference, the internal and the external—the prefix "para" also includes the duality guest/host (Genette 7, n. 2). This authorizes us to describe and analyze the binomial of text and paratext, novel and illustration, in terms of the relation of hospitality which would articulate and connect these two discursively dissimilar elements that are verbal language on the one hand and graphic expression on the other. In this way the relation of hospitality would rule the meeting and the negotiation between the English Dickens of 1854 and the Latin American Barradas of 1921, or vice versa, since the relation of hospitality can be, and often is, inverted.

Let us see, then, how this relation between guest and host can be materialized for the reader in some of the Barradas's illustrations for *Hard Times*.

In illustration number 8 (fig. 8), in the sequence in which the illustrations appear in the Spanish edition, the plastic artist presents us with a young girl seated at the foot of a stylized and emblematic tree in the company of a dog and a horse, and in the same space a modest but glamorous circus tent with its fluttering flag has been set up. In the background there are some chimneys that represent an industrial reality. This illustration, then, in a very concise way and with an economy of details and plastic seduction in its drawing and its colors (yellow/white/black), suggests to the viewer, as a major motif, a circus ambit which is at the same time a rural one.

We know that the circus, as a paradigm of fantasy, as artistic *topos*, as a sign and cipher of what is individual and socially libertarian or anarchic, was a common subject in Barradas's time for the avant-garde of European plastic arts, from Seurat to Picasso. Also, in that same era and from this same paradigmatic signification, the circus was evoked in musical compositions like those by Eric Satie for the theatrical productions of Shakespeare's *A Midsummer Night's Dream* at the Medrano circus in Paris in 1915. The circus show was also lived as a total popular experience by artists like Maiakovski in Moscow around 1914, a time when the Russian poet had a strong personal and artistic friendship with Victor Lazarenko, who was an actor-clown in theater productions in Moscow.

So, to return to Dickens's novel, Barradas's depiction of the circus, from the historical-cultural and artistic contextual references of the illustration that we have just mentioned, while it illustrates and accompanies the literary text, would refer more to the order of what is borderline and a hallway (to return to Borges's term in Genette's definition of paratext) and would not be strictly or immediately related to the *Hard Times* text. The viewer, interested by those references that have to do with the era in which the illustrator lived and with the intellectual and artistic ambit which corresponds to Barradas and not to Dickens, or simply pleased with the visual composition, may or may not move on to a second stage, for he or she may or may not go from what is graphic and chromatic to what is verbal and its connotations, and may or may not move from the plastic paratext to the literary text, from Barradas's colored modernist vestibule to Dickens's Victorian room of characters printed on the page in black and white.

On the other hand, in the text of the novel, throughout the three parts, the dozens of chapters and hundreds of pages, this circus girl, an avant-garde figure of naturalness and colorful fantasy in the illustration, turns out to be called Cecilia or Sissy. She is the daughter of Jupe, the circus clown in the industrial town of Coketown where, among much else that is going on, a workers' strike has set union members and anti-union forces against each other, where there is a Benthamite-type school in which the circus girl is subjected to a Utilitarian, rational, and limiting education, where there is also Josiah Bounderby, a pompous mill-owner and banker who falsely claims to be a self-made man, Louisa Gradgrind, who marries Bounderby as a favor to her brother Tom, and her father, Thomas Gradgrind, a Utilitarian who is the Member of Parliament for Coketown, the patron of the Coketown school, and a friend of Bounderby's. In the aforementioned illustration, which does not explicitly evoke any specific scene in the novel but which does distil the subject of the work, Barradas seems to modulate the text, destabilizing what is linear, detailed, and minutely rendered (Borges would say "copious") in the incidents and plot of the novel.

To what extent, then, do these two aesthetic discourses, the plastic modernist of Barradas and the textual Victorian of Dickens, settle into their respective contexts in the relation between guest and host?

Whatever the perspective from which one reflects on hospitality, there are two elements which seem to be essential when it comes to defining it: in all relations of hospitality the codes are respected but at the same time modulated both on the part of the host and on that of the guest, and these roles are often inverted, as was observed above. And it is always in a coming and going with respect to the codes, in a modulation and negotiation on the part of both protagonists, in an interweaving of permanence and changes that is always demanding and complex, that all activities and all the politics of hospitality are played out. In the specific instance that concerns us, this respect for and at the same time modulation of codes can be identified both for Dickens's host text and for Barradas's guest illustrations. Or vice versa, since, in moving from the world of the book to the world of reading, it will be the user (the buyer or possessor) of the 1921 Madrid edition of *Hard Times* who will take the decision whether to prefer the plastic or the verbal, to favor Barradas or Dickens, and to make the plastic artist or the writer the hospitable host of the other.

Let us favor the illustrator and let us consider Barradas as the reader/artist of Dickens and the host of the visitor-text *Hard Times*. This text was one of the nine or ten literary guests which Barradas in his artistic hospitality received in the context of the collection published in Madrid by Estrella.[2] And in his role as host, in many among his *Hard Times* illustrations, Barradas celebrates the circus again and again. From the graphic expression of this celebration, these illustrations reflect the marked anti-Utilitarian perspective which the circus and its ambit present in Dickens's novel, a perspective which, as we know, constitutes an essential element in the reading code throughout the text. They refer (figs. 1, 2, 7, and 12, and the vignette for book 3 in fig. 13), as the novel does at different points in its story, to the circus ambit, and thus they represent (in the various meanings of this word) the authorial narrator of *Hard Times*. In effect, as we know, already by 1854 Dickens had sought time and again to make real and to promote, in his fictional narrative and in the work of imagining that all narrative brings into play, spaces for lucid reflection when faced with the generalized imposition in a Victorian world of the suffocating economic thought and policies of Utilitarianism. Thus it is clearly with a tone of humorous questioning that Dickens christens Gradgrind's two little children with the names Adam Smith and Malthus. In this way Dickens ironically verbalizes and gives a caricature of the questioning which Barradas picks up on and gives another dimension to in his illustrations.

Barradas also does a series of illustrations around a motif that he created from his reading of Dickens: the prison bars in the window (of the school, of Louisa's room in her "home"). These illustrations are in contrast to the circus pictures with their ambit of healthy and beneficial openness, and they eloquently show what enclosedness and oppression can come to in the educational ambit and also in the domestic and family sphere, when desire and imagination are ignored. In this way, as a graphic host respecting the code of his literary guest, Barradas adheres to the posture proposed in the narrative of the novel which constantly plays with the opposition between imagination and fact, between the fantasy of Sleary's circus—the circus of the girl Sissy and her father Jupe the clown—with its acrobats and its performing dog, and the oppressive atmosphere in both the Coketown school and Louisa's home. And Jupe the clown will appear more than once in Barradas's work, beyond his appearance in an illustration (fig. 2) to the 1921 Madrid edition of *Hard Times*. Actually, a colored copy of the black-and-white picture of Jupe printed for the border of book 1 in *Hard Times* is currently exhibited at the Fine Arts Museum of Maldonado (Uruguay), as Barradas's undated portrait of an anonymous clown.

The narrator's posture of questioning the industrial reality of his time, which is translated into the emblematic creation of Coketown in the novel, is welcomed in a hospitable way by Barradas in his disturbing factory compositions with their reds and blacks (figs. 10 and 11). In one of these illustrations there is a plastic representation of Dickens's simile—a clearly ethnocentric one—comparing Coketown with the painted face of a savage. The passage in *Hard Times* is as follows:

> It was a town of red brick, or of brick that would have been red if the smoke and ashes had allowed it; but as matters stood it was a town of unnatural red and black **like the painted face of a savage**. It was a town of machinery and tall chimneys, out of which interminable serpents of smoke trailed themselves for ever and ever, and never got uncoiled. It had a black canal in it, and a river that ran purple with ill-smelling dye, and vast piles of building full of windows where there was a rattling and a trembling all day long, and where the piston of the steam-engine worked monotonously up and down like the head of an elephant in a state of melancholy madness.   (I, ch. 5: 22, my emphasis).

At the same time Barradas's illustrations for *Hard Times* counterpoint and modify the Victorian graphic expression of the disturbing industrial reality which in the novel is a response to the socio-economic situation of a mid-nineteenth-century England that is already industrialized. In these illustrations, however, we may find a reference also to the pre-industrial Spain that Barradas lived in when he produced this work for Estrella in 1921.

Other changes and counterpoints are introduced and made concrete by the Uruguayan host into the visiting Englishman's code—very specifically on the level of plastic expression. Barradas makes great play with the circus motif, with domestic and educational imprisonment, and with the disturbing industrial atmosphere of *Hard Times*, but he does not do this with a realistic-naturalistic graphic style in the tradition of Dickens illustrations that follow the steps of the text of the story in a linear and detailed way. Quite the contrary, his innovative plastic modernism of the 1920s is an example of Cubo-Futurism, which was one of the most creative "-isms" in international plastic arts in the early decades of the twentieth century.[3] In this way Barradas's illustrations negotiate with Dickens's text, reactivating it and giving it new dimensions from his, Barradas's, new aesthetic paradigms. Barradas thereby participates in a dialogue between Dickens and the modernism in the visual arts of the early years of the twentieth century, a dialogue that in the cinema of the time also took place between the North American filmmaker David Wark Griffith and Dickens concerning *The Cricket on the Hearth* (Eisenstein 200–201).

There has been much discussion in recent years about the figure of hospitality from many different points of view, especially from socio-cultural (immigrational, legal, juridical) or ethical-philosophical perspectives.[4] We may think that in the field of poetics of the text this figure could also serve as a useful concept and element in stages of description and analysis. This is especially so when dealing with productions both literary and plastic, as is the case here. To approach these collaborative productions from the figure of hospitality may turn out to be auspicious, for this element and this relation make successful communication real through the diversity or heterogeneity of efficiently concerted and conciliated discourses.

In Spain, in the Baroque period in the seventeenth century, musical compositions that "tempted," that is to say, attempted, to create something new out of a musical text that already existed were called *tientos,* that is, attempts or variations: attempts to converse with the Other. In the same way perhaps we can say that Barradas's illustrations "tempt," that is to say attempt and generate, fifteen hospitable and successful variations on different motifs of *Tiempos difíciles*, Dickens's host novel.

NOTES

1. For an introductory approach to these illustrations to *Hard Times* see my article "*Hard Times* Gone Modernist: The 1921 Barradas Illustrations for *Tiempos difíciles,*" which includes black and white reproductions of the twelve color illustrations and the three black-and-white borders by Barradas.
2. The books illustrated by Barradas for this series by Estrella are: *Pablo y Virginia* by B. de St Pierre, in 1919; *Nido de Nobles* by Ivan Turgenev, *Ella y él* by

George Sand, *La Feria de Neuilly* by Gregorio Martínez Sierra, *La Estrella de Sevilla* by Lope de Vega, *En el Fondo* by Maxim Gorki, *La dama de las camelias* by Alexandre Dumas (fils), *Museo de Beguinas* by J. Rodenbach, and *Tam-Tam* by Tomás Borrás, all in 1920; *Lorenzaccio* by Alfred de Musset, and *Tiempos difíciles* by Charles Dickens in 1921.

3. The term "Cubo-Futurism" to designate this period in Barradas's work is used by Miguel Battegazzore in his analysis of Barradas's illustrations for *Hard Times* (see the preceding essay in this volume of *DSA*).

4. Among other publications on this subject, see: *Autour de Jacques Derrida—De l'hospitalité,* ed. Mohammed Seffahi, and also Jacques Derrida, *De l'hospitalité—Anne Duformantelle invite Jacques Derrida à répondre.*

WORKS CITED

Derrida, Jacques. *De l'hospitalité.—Anne Duformantelle invite Jacques Derrida à répondre.* Paris: Calmann-Lévy, 1997.

Dickens, Charles. *Hard Times.* Oxford: Oxford UP, 1997.

———. *Tiempos difíciles.* Trans. by J. Camilo Nessi. Madrid: Ediciones Estrella, 1921.

Eisenstein, Sergei. "Dickens, Griffith and the Film Today." In *Film Forum and the Film Sense.* Ed. and trans. by Jay Leyda. New York: Meridian Books, 1957. 195–255.

Genette, Gérard. *Seuils.* Paris: Seuil, 1987.

Seffahi, Mohammed, ed. *Autour de Jacques Derrida—De l'hospitalité—Manifeste.* Genouillex: la passe du vent, 2001.

Vegh, Beatriz. "*Hard Times* Gone Modernist: The 1921 Barradas Illustrations for *Tiempos difíciles.*" *Dickens Quarterly* 15: 1 (March 1998): 3–27.

Fig. 1. Sissy Jupe in front of the circus.

Fig. 2. Jupe.

Fig. 3. Bitzer in the classroom.

Fig. 4. The classroom.

5

6

Fig. 5. A Class.   Fig. 6. Thomas studying in his room.

7

8

Fig. 7. The circus with carriage.   Fig. 8. The circus with Sissy leaning on a tree.

9

10

Fig. 9. Gradgrind with
Louisa and Sissy.

Fig. 10. Coketown I.

11

12

Fig. 11. Coketown II.

Fig. 12. Louisa at a window.

Libro Primero   La Siembra

Libro Segundo   La Siega

Libro Tercero   La Cosecha

Fig. 13. Black-and-white vignettes for the three books into which *Hard Times* is divided. By permission of The Dickens Society.

The Reversal of Innocence: Somers, Dickens, and a "Shared Oliver"

María Cristina Dalmagro

> There is no bigger cruelty than that of the rever-
> sal of innocence when its subtle pattern has been
> disfigured by violent circumstances.
> Armonía Etchepare, *Educación de la adolescencia*
> [my translation]

There are several noticeable similarities that allow us to identify the presence of Dickens in the short novel *Un retrato para Dickens* [*A Portrait for Dickens*] (1969) by the Uruguayan writer Armonía Somers. Apart from the obvious sign in the title and explicit elements in the girl's story, there are further aspects that stand out both as clear connections and as notable differences. The homage that Somers pays (in the form of a type of parody) to Dickens, master of the realistic novel, is directed toward meanings that also combine the symbolic with the experiential.[1]

Some connections, however, can be analyzed, not only in strictly literary terms, but also in their articulation with a facet of the writer that has not been examined by critics. This aspect can, I believe, illuminate areas of her literary creation from another perspective, one based on her personal reality and her pedagogical activities and investigations. Somers herself, who for 32 years worked in a primary school as a teacher of children ranging in age from 6 to 12, tried to differentiate her roles as a teacher and as literary artist by using her real name, Armonía Etchepare, for her writing about pedagogy but employing the pseudonym Armonía Somers for her fiction.

One text, the source of the epigraph of this article, operates as a link. It is a pedagogic-literary essay published in Mexico in 1956 entitled *Educación de la adolescencia. El adolescente de novela y su valor de testimonio [The Education of adolescents. The Adolescent in the Novel and His Testimony]* in which we can observe some concerns and themes that allow us to understand the experiential, theoretical, and aesthetic perspectives from which Somers reads Dickens. Thus, the homage (as parody) that she renders in *A Portrait for Dickens* to the master of the realistic novel has multiple manifestations.

We can assert that what is depicted by Dickens in the novel *Oliver Twist*, is updated by Somers in her novel from the perspective of a contemporary Montevideo, where hunger, misery, and hardships of all types aggravate the conflicts that surround abandoned children. What is more, the narrative form taken by these issues reveals her reflections over the course of almost a decade. Dickens's narrative underlies a story from the Apocrypha that combines texts of different genealogies and hierarchies (the Biblical story of Tobias, son of Tobit, *The Baker's Manual,* and the story of the parrot that is the reincarnation of the Jewish demon Asmodeus) while retaining as its central concern the eternal presence of evil in the world.

In this article I will sketch some links among those three texts: the essay *Educación de la adolescencia [The Education of Adolescents]* (1956), the novel *A Portrait for Dickens* (1969), and Dickens's *Oliver Twist.* One of these links has as its starting point a concept of novel that Armonía Somers proposes in her essay (signed Armonía Etchepare), with references to a theoretical grounding in *Sociología de la novela [Sociology of the Novel]* by Roger Caillois. Echoing Caillois, she asserts that a novel "portrays society as a whole and that its only topic of interest is the condition of man" (Caillois 56). It is, therefore, attributed to a realistic line that descends directly from nineteenth-century narrative and also shares features with cinema. A novel is, then, a document, a testimony, a source of data, and it can help assess reality (although this view does not coincide with the concept of "documentary" narrative as described in current theories). This explains the significant presence of Dickens's narrative as an aesthetic and theoretical substratum in some of Somers's stories.

Further points of contact can be found in Etchepare's interest in the problems of antisocial attitudes held by children and adolescents. The re-education and security systems hold a privileged position in Etchepare's essay, especially in chapter VII, in the section entitled "Misconduct and Antisocial Attitudes." The examples arise from sources of different types and origins, such as films, novels, official documents, and journalism, and are offered from the perspective of Eduard Spranger and Alfred Adler, who focus their interest on corrective pedagogy and recovery, as well as on the importance of the study of causes.

Armonía Somers also underscores the testimonial value of cinema, since she is convinced of the effectiveness of mass media in the construction of a collective social conscience to such an extent that she considers the social impact of films to be even more significant than that of scientific studies. The following quotation from her essay supports this: "this exposure of the adolescent's social crossroads has been, perhaps, almost as useful in rooting the topic in the collective mind in the last twenty-five years as the same quarter of a century's worth of congresses and essays" (111).

The examples start with the Russian movie *El camino hacia la vida* [*The Road to Life*] (1931) by Nicolai Ekk, a film that deals with destitute children and adolescents. Reference is also made to *Los bajos fondos* [*Down Under*] (France), *Punto muerto* [*Dead Point*] (USA), *Somos todos asesinos* [*We Are All Murderers*] (France), *Bajo el sol de Roma* [*Under the Roman Sun*] and *Lustrabotas* [*The Shoeshine*] (Italy), *Los olvidados* [*The Forgotten Ones*] (Mexico), and *Semillas de maldad* [*The Bad Seed*] (USA), all dealing with the topics of bereaved childhood, marginalized adolescence, and the consequences of society's lack of responsibility regarding juvenile delinquency. The child/adolescent in these movies, as well as the main characters in *A Portrait for Dickens* and *Oliver Twist*, all have features in common: abandoned by their families and lacking systematic education, they suffer all sorts of abuses and limitations. They work from an early age to help their family economically, live in crowded conditions, and, in many cases, commit crimes because of circumstances beyond their control.

Criticism directed against institutions of detention for the young and at society's responsibility for the persistence of these problems are the thematic signposts of all the movies mentioned above. *Los olvidados* [*The Forgotten Ones*], by Luis Buñuel, filmed in Mexico in the early fifties, exposes the problems of gangs, orphanages, child labor, and the methods used in reformatories. The revelation of the injustice, the violence against the weak, and the numerous privations that prompt the behavior of youngsters is central to a film that begins with this explanation: "this is a movie based on real facts, it is not optimistic and leaves the solution of the problem to the progressive forces of reality." An interesting point in relation to Armonía Somers's (or Armonía Etchepare's) pedagogic postulate is the fact that, in the film, the director of the reformatory blames the boy's mother and, indirectly, society, for the child's misconduct. There is an obvious connection between the problematics of impoverished childhood in Dickens's novels and in those of Somers.

A similar thematic sequence can be seen in *The Shoeshine*, by Vittorio de Sica, an exponent, together with Federico Fellini and Rosellini, of Italian neo-realism, as well as in another novel, *Cell 2455* (Caryl Chessman) that deals with "juvenile antisocial attitudes within a historical setting in the 50s" (*The Education of Adolescents* 103) and offers a pointed critique of orphanages where violence gives rise to hatred towards society. The same is true of the French movie *We Are All Murderers*, by André Cayatte, which is set during World War II and in which the main character, a mistreated boy of eleven or twelve, is taken to an orphanage. The criticism of the condition of the children in those institutions and of the authorities is very relevant, and the resemblance to *Oliver Twist*, the intertext of *A Portrait for Dickens*, is most evident.

It is important to highlight the ideological background that is depicted in the cited films and novels in correlation with the theoretical framework mentioned above and with the documentary sources that focus on social motivations. In general, the selected works are true denunciations in this respect. In *We Are All Murderers, The Shoeshine, The Forgotten Ones,* and also in *A Portrait for Dickens*, the perspective on all the conflicts relates specifically to the context (the social setting, generally unknown and alcoholic parents, prostituted mothers, siblings of different parentage, lack of education, child labor, abuse, etc.).

However, in addition to films and novels, in *The Education of Adolescents* Armonía Etchepare makes use of official documents and articles published in the press at that time. One of them, also signed by her, "La delincuencia infantil en el Uruguay" ["Juvenile Delinquency in Uruguay"] (1958),[2] is the rewriting, with the addition of a personal interpretation, of the "Statement by Mr. Hector Ruiz Prinzo, Director of Legal Affairs in the Commissioners' Office" (January 30, 1954), accompanied by data from the House of Representatives of the Legislature (1955), annual statistic reports of the Montevideo Police Headquarters concerning juvenile delinquency, and the report by the Statistical and Census Office Department and the Office of Legal Affairs of the Montevideo Police.[3]

In Etchepare's article there is a discussion of the same problem as that described in her essay and in her novel, but from a different perspective and in a different discourse. The possible causes of juvenile delinquency are shown, with a special emphasis on marginalized childhood, on parentless children, and on the importance of a supportive and loving family. The inefficiency and slowness of institutions are criticized, together with the absence of pertinent measures by politicians.

In the statement by the Director of Legal Affairs before the Montevideo Police Commissioners, the analysis of juvenile delinquency and the presentation of statistical data are followed by a description of the role of the police officer, together with its importance to the child's future when the policeman is the magistrate's collaborator in the investigation of lifestyles, environment, work habits, or literacy. He is the one in charge of discovering to what extent the families have been able to offer their children education, affection, or support, and is presented here through an image that is quite different from the stereotype of the despotic or violent authority figure of the fictional narratives and press reports. The police receive a positive evaluation for their function in the reeducation process. This depiction coincides with that of the policeman in *A Portrait for Dickens*. In both texts, fictional and journalistic, the image of the authority figure is far from the generally negative one present in the collective subconscious.

I propose that *A Portrait* relates to Dickens's text through a type of parody called "homage." Among the procedures that are used to construct it, we can highlight several paratextual elements: the direct reference in the title to "Dickens," both the explicit addressee of the portrait/narration and the starting point for the intertextual reading; the reproduction of the photograph/portrait of a girl/boy placed before the text; and, lastly, the dedication: "To the model. To the photographer."[4] What model does Somers refer to? To the girl that served as a model for the picture reproduced, or to Dickens's narrative, or to the character Oliver Twist, or to the young female protagonist? We can infer that the homage is to all of them.

In addition to these early indications, other aspects mark the confluence of both texts. Approximately in the middle of the novel, an incidental character is depicted, the "photographer" (the same one as in the dedication), who has to photograph the child-protagonist for a competition at the factory where she works. After looking at her attentively, he recognizes and reconstructs Oliver's image in her, while dressing her up to achieve a closer resemblance: "he returned with a man's hat that he planted on my head, without asking permission, and a wide black ribbon that he tied in a bow below the collar of my blouse . . . he placed who knows what copy of his anarchies in my crossed hands and went back to his observation post" (89–90).

When he is finished, he says: "What a picture for a book by Dickens. I would never have thought that Oliver Twist himself would come into my house." And the girl, unaware of what was happening around her says: "I looked at the book he had placed in my hands and *I felt as if my heart had found its roots. . . .* Is this who I am?" (90; italics added).

In his answer, the photographer formulates his theory on the direct correlation between fictional character and real person: "I would say yes. It is a personal theory that never fails. I know that any day I could meet the characters that escaped from the geniuses' minds after they had brought them to life. And it always happens" (90).

The identification is revealed in the statement. The portrait, the same as the picture on the cover, has been freed by means of a metonymic reconstruction of each one of its distinctive components, and it coincides with Oliver's image as described by Dickens. The process that takes place in connection with the picture is twofold: on the one hand, on a paratextual level, Somers, bearing its origin in mind (a present from a friend of hers), explains its interpretation in an interview.[5] On the other hand, on the textual level, that picture becomes a signifier that allows its association with a literary character.

Thus, the description of the photographic composition adds meaning to the picture on the cover of the book. The examination of each one of the objects that complement the character is yet another strategy to give to that picture new meanings, the result of an association of ideas that connotes multiple identifications: it is, at the same time, the girl in the picture given to the author; it is Oliver Twist; it is the girl that narrates her memory of the moment when they took a picture of her and how she felt projected outside herself by it; it is the interpretation by the anarchist photographer who believes in the possibility of real life for the characters in a novel; it is the explanation and the recreation that the author herself makes of the picture and of Dickens's text in his honor, but it is also the combination of her concerns as a teacher. The "historical" reading of the picture[6] facilitates the combination of literary, cultural, and personal elements that allow the transfer to a specific time and place (marginalized children and rehabilitation institutions in Uruguay) in order to carry out a profound critique of particular situations that share a common context, that of human suffering.

Another link among the three texts under discussion is, precisely, that of the ambiguous identity of the girl/boy of the reconstructed portrait. Etchepare also deals in her essay with the topic of sexual ambiguity in adolescents. In the chapter "Confusión" ["Confusion"] she analyses this issue through *Nuevas ideas sobre el problema de la intersexualidad y sobre la cronología de los sexos* [*New Ideas About the Problem of Intersexuality and about Sexual Chronology*], by Gregorio Marañón, and *El problema de la homosexualidad* [*The Problem of Homosexuality*] by Adler. According to her reading of both Marañón and Adler, both authors consider the state of confusion as normal, beyond possible discussions about homosexuality and its varied clinical, ethical, historical, or legal factors. Marañón asserts the impurity of the sexes and the bisexual substratum, which he calls an "inter-sexual transitory state" that is present at critical ages, when it clashes with punitive, ethical, and social structures.

It is pertinent to relate this aspect to the character of the girl of *A Portrait for Dickens,* because there are numerous connections. A ten-year-old girl is portrayed without a definite sexual image. She reveals this when she is disguised as a boy (as Oliver) for a picture: "Since I had nothing else to wear, I put on one of my brothers' jackets. Though I kept aloof from what might be happening with my *contradictory appearance of half a boy*" in addition she asserts: "Me, so young, and under the autosuggestion of a portrait out of sex . . . " (91; italics added). A photographer constructs this image, but it is also facilitated by her family, since she wears clothes that belong to her brother (and we know that clothes are a form of role assignment, in many cases); and it also results from her poverty, if we remember that the money that her mother had saved for her only dress had been eaten by rats.

This androgynous image pervades the text until her violent awakening to sexual life and her forced entrance into maturity as a consequence of a rape. Her observation of scenes of lesbianism in the factory where she works, her stepbrothers' jokes about her sexual organs, and the obscene advances of her supervisor at the factory are all factors that accelerate her sexual awakening. Ten years before Armonía Somers published *A Portrait,* Armonía Etchepare discussed in her essay the issue of poor children being rushed into maturity, a problem also present in her novel, where she also grouped poor adolescents according to various heterogeneous cultural experiences. In this essay, she included a proletarian adolescent (the girl in *A Portrait*), a black, an Indian, and the so-called "*wild societies* whose lifestyle drags the kid into hazardous situations." (*The Education* 41) (italics added). Her reflections made her consider as the dominant feature of these topics the way that adolescents are forced and conditioned by social circumstances, to enter, often violently, into maturity, without going through the period of adaptation that is characteristic of adolescence.

Evaluating all the elements and characteristics observed before, we can assert that, if Dickens's work was influenced, according to his critics, by his youthful experience, his early journalistic job covering Parliament and a social sensibility that enabled him to gather documentation and show the human realities beyond the systems and the laws, what is fundamental in the work of Armonía Somers is not just the presence of Dickens, but also her parallel activity as a teacher and as a pedagogic investigator, which colors her work, exactly as she claims when she says, "Here is where the strongest link could be found between educating, as in leading by the hand, and exploring dark consciences in another dimension" (Penco 3), as we have witnessed through the established connections.

In order to investigate more deeply the degree of Dickens's presence in Somers' s work, we must also review the intertextual relationships at different levels, that is, the plot, character portrayal, the resolution of conflicts, and, especially, narrative techniques and choice of words.

Despite obvious differences, both texts depict the same atmosphere and similar social backgrounds: criticism is directed at orphanages that lack the bare essentials; both coincide in the portrayal of poverty (delinquency, violence, prostitution, lack of systematic education) and in the construction of the character in charge of the institutions for children. Both Mr. Bumble in *Oliver Twist* and the "inspector" in *A Portrait for Dickens* are authoritarian, have many negative features, and are absolutely frightening, when in fact they should be affectionate and supportive of "the poor orphan."

Other similarities include the representation of innocence in the character of an orphan boy (a stereotype of those who suffer social injustice) and the punishment of innocent children. They also coincide in the use of irony, although in *A Portrait* it is intensified to the point of becoming black humor. Some of the narrative techniques are also similar, both in the prevalence of metonymy and attention to detail, and in the register and dominance of a point of view as the point of departure for representation.

On the basis of these similarities, the narratives are built on different aesthetic patterns that correspond to the genre changes that occurred in the course of a century. In Dickens, the story follows a lineal development with a prevalence of realistic conventions; it also makes use of a personal perspective and an omniscient narrator, with stable character roles and obvious connections among different lines of the story. Armonía Somers pays homage to him since she admires the richness in the depiction of his characters and places, although she does not adhere to his aesthetic codes. In Dickens, the character's interior world is not ambiguous, since the narration adheres to the realistic purpose of transmitting information while avoiding as much as possible any interferences that might hinder communication. Another difference is reception, since Dickens is a popular writer who is accessible to a large audience. When George Wing wonders why Dickens is so popular, he answers, rather innocently, after reviewing the answers of several critics, Chesterton among them, "because he is healthy, pure . . . because in his work, evil is evil and good is good" (46). That is to say, he offers a Manichaean perspective that is alien to Somers.

A Portrait for Dickens, on the other hand, surprises us from the beginning with a complex plot made up of inserted fragments, just as we have described it. If the reader expected to be told a story "in Dickens's style," he or she is bound to feel confused and disappointed. The "parrot" as narrator of an entire section of "documents" (the final chapter of the novel), subverts all the possibilities to hold on to reality and to all the realistic versions of the different narrative lines of the text.

Considering other aspects in this comparison, we can justify our assertion. In Dickens's novel we learn about Oliver's mother, her identity, the causes of the abandonment, and her family history. There is also a vision of a much more happy future that reverses the past experience of poverty and marginality. Let us think about the comforting end of the novel: "Mr. Brownlow adopted Oliver as his son. Removing with him and the old housekeeper to within a mile of the parsonage-house, where his dear friends resided, he gratified the only remaining wish of Oliver's warm and earnest heart, and thus linked together a little society, whose conditions approached as nearly to one of perfect happiness as can ever be known in this changing world" (53, 476). The character, constructed from the omniscient narrator's point of view, helps fulfill the author's stated intention in the foreword to the third edition of his novel: "I wished to show, in little Oliver, the principle of Good surviving through every adverse circumstance, and triumphing at last" (33).

In connection with this, Rosemary Jackson observes in *Fantasy* that in *Oliver Twist*, as well as in *The Old Curiosity Shop* (1841) or *Dombey and Son* (1848):

> [Dickens] uses a Gothic rhetoric to refer to certain parts of society considered dreadful by a safe bourgeoisie. Thieves, criminals, single mothers, prostitutes, the insane, the poor, the working classes, are all represented according to the Gothic convention as something hideous, melodramatic, "devilish," "the other." (136; my translation).

That is why Dickens's works are defined by Jackson as "fantastic realism," for they are full of contradictions regarding the use of fantastic elements, since the novels are used both to denounce poverty and abandonment and to "place all energy and vividness in that underworld" (Jackson 136; my translation).

In Dickens, the situation of poverty and abandonment is corrected and Oliver has found a safe home. But here we find the key point in Somers's reading of Dickens: She asks if the plight of orphan children who suffer injustice and mistreatment at the institutions that should comfort them could be reverted. Somers also asks if mistreatment of children is a particular situation during a particular historical era (mid-nineteenth-century England), the time of the Poor Laws, of the workhouses, and of substantial change in urban society, or is it a problem that is repeated with similar features in different societies and at different historical moments? These themes concern both writers but their aesthetic approaches are considerably different.

In *A Portrait* the reader's understanding of the girl's character originates from two incomplete versions: the main character's first-person narration and that of the parrot. Nothing is known about the girl's past, and her situation doesn't change, since at the end she is found orphaned again and faces an uncertain future.

One character in *Oliver Twist*, Fagin, the dominant figure in the "underworld," is associated with a terminology usually reserved for a demon: Nancy, the prostitute, calls him "demon"; Sikes, another thief, suggests that Fagin comes directly from Hell, as he seems to confirm with his whole appearance (red hair, villainous look, and repulsive face). But the essential difference between *Oliver Twist* and *A Portrait* resides in the fact that for Dickens the devilish atmosphere and the belief in a wicked world do not permeate the whole novel.

The techniques of legibility and verisimilitude that characterize Dickens's intertext are disassembled in *A Portrait*, since the realistic principles are contaminated by an ambiguous discourse composed of disjointed, disconnected fragments. Now, bearing in mind the way Somers reads Dickens's text, in opposition to the legibility that that very text establishes, we ask: what is, then, the nature of Somers's homage and subversion?

It is pertinent to note that Armonía Somers makes reference to three historical landmarks in the different intertexts present in the novel: to the Biblical
story (both to the apocryphal book of Tobit that precedes the Gospels, and to
the book of Revelation that follows them), to the nineteenth-century England
depicted in Dickens's novel, and to her own contemporary setting in the
Montevideo of the twentieth century, where her preoccupation with juvenile
delinquency and children's marginality was the subject of great reflection, as
evidenced in her pedagogic writings and essays. I do believe that, with all
these elements, connections, and analyses at hand, it is accurate to think that
Somers reads Dickens as another milestone in the story of evil in the world
and of the suffering of innocent children, a story that is the history of mankind.
There is a symbolic and eschatological universe that allows her to expand the
possibilities for the representation of the real that are available in Dickens's
narrative world: she can complicate the realistic point of view without abandoning certain messages typical of denunciatory realist narratives. Here lie
both Somers's originality and her difference, her homage and her subversion.

NOTES

1. All translations from Spanish in this essay are my own. In *A Portrait for Dickens*,
   the plot is complex. The beginning of the narration is the textual reproduction of
   the biblical story of Tobias, from the Hebrew Bible, interrupted by fragments
   of the *Manual del Pastelero y Confitero Universal* [*Baker's and Confectioner's
   Manual*], a real book from the early part of the twentieth century. Interspersed
   among the fragments of both texts there is a first-person narration (fifteen sequences) by an orphan girl who remembers her life since her mother adopted her
   (with a black stepbrother) from an orphanage, until the moment in which she is
   taken to a police station after a suicide attempt following her mother's death and
   her rape by one of her stepbrothers. This story describes countless calamities
   that affect the girl's life: child labor and exploitation, sexual harassment by her
   supervisor, her adoptive father's alcoholism, aggression on the part of her stepbrothers, prostitution, crime, and misery in all its forms. She retells her story to
   the policeman, who creates a favorable atmosphere for the confession by feeding
   her with milk and cake, her greatest wish. There is also a final section called
   "Los rollos de Asmodeo" ["Asmodeus' rolls"] (twenty sequences), in which
   the narrative voice is that of a demon-parrot, a last reincarnation of the Jewish
   demon Asmodeus, that lives with the girl in the same tenement. In its story the
   parrot gathers and reinterprets all the stories. Except for the girl's summary, each
   of the other three sections bears the title "Documents."
2. Sources: personal files. Unpublished material.
3. There is a reference to the Children's Code, as stated in Montevideo in 1934, and
   to its high international esteem. There is also an allusion to the gap between the

legislation and its actual enforcement, a disparity which accounts for the need to tackle the problem seriously by means of political measures that would solve these conflicts.

4. In the second and last edition (*Un retrato para Dickens*. Barcelona: Península, 1990), the photo appears on the cover and in color.

5. Regarding the portrait displayed on the cover, Somers claims in an interview that the adult model gave it to her as a present and then adds: "It is a photograph of a very special girl. . . . When the old photographer placed the man's hat on her, the free-thinker's bow, and a bunch of paper rolls in her hand, he fulfilled his aim, which was the aesthetic interpretation of a being. When I discovered the human suffering behind that portrait, based on some fragmented stories, I contributed to its recreation." (Interview with Elvio Gandolfo.)

6. Roland Barthes discusses the topic of the photographic image in the chapter "La imagen" in *Lo obvio y lo obtuso*.

WORKS CITED

Barthes, Roland. *Lo obvio y lo obtuso*. Madrid: Paidós, 1995.

Caillois, Roger. *Sociología de la novela*. Buenos Aires: Sur, 1942.

Dickens, Charles. *Oliver Twist*. Harmondsworth: Penguin, 1966.

Espada, Roberto de. "*Un retrato para Dickens*, de Armonía Somers". En: *Ya*, Sección Literarias, Montevideo, 29 June 1970.

Etchepare de Henestrosa, Armonía. *Educación de la adolescencia. El adolescente de novela y su valor de testimonio*. Montevideo, 1956. (typed version). [Published in México D.F.: Guerrero, 1957].

Gandolfo, Elvio. "Un país pequeño, una gran novelista. Para conocer a Armonía Somers". ["A Small Country, a Great Novelist. To Know Armonía Somers"] *Clarín, Cultura y Nación*, Buenos Aires, Thursday 9 January 1986.

Genette, Gérard. *Palimpsestos. La literatura en segundo grado*. Madrid: Taurus, 1989.

Hamon, Philippe. "Un discours contraint." In *Littérature et réalité*. Ed. Philippe Hamon. Paris: Seuil, 1982. 119–81.

Jackson, Rosemary. *Fantasy. Literatura y subversión*. Buenos Aires: Catálogos Editora, 1986.

Kermode, Frank. *El sentido del final*. Barcelona: Gedisa, 1983.

Rufinelli, Jorge. "Historia de ángeles y demonios. *Un retrato para Dickens*. "In *Marcha*, Montevideo, 30 November 1970.

Somers, Armonía. "Respuestas a Wilfredo Penco." In *Revistas Noticias*, Montevideo, 1980.

————. *Un retrato para Dickens*. Montevideo: Arca, 1969.

Visca, Sergio Antonio. "Un enigmático dibujo (Sobre *Un retrato para Dickens*)." In *El País*, Montevideo, 11 January 1970.

Wilson, Edmund. "Los dos scrooges." In *La herida y el arco*. México D.F.: Fondo de Cultura Económica, 1983.

Wing, George. *Dickens*. Edinburgh: Oliver and Boyd, 1969.

Dickens's Oliver and Somers's Orphan:
A Traffic in Identities

Alicia Torres

Armonía Somers was once asked what she thought of the idea that every person has a novel inside him or her, and she answered with a comment that Scott Fitzgerald might have made, "Give me a name and I will give you a tragedy."[1] On the front cover of the book by Armonía Somers that I will discuss in this essay appear both the author's own name[2] and another that is part of the title of the novel, and in which the tragedy is reflected as in a mirror. That name is Dickens, and it is a paradigm that functions as a sign or a clue.[3] In the full title, *Un Retrato para Dickens*[4] [*A Portrait for Dickens*], the name opens the way for this story by the Uruguayan writer, one of those tales of helpless childhood which the English novelist was so fond of: the little orphan girl who is plucked from an orphanage and taken away to a boarding house.[5]

This girl, who is one of the narrators of the novel, is not given a name, and this makes for a degree of vagueness in the way the character is received, and this in turn is diffused in the Dickensian paradigm. In the realist tradition, a name legitimizes a character and puts him or her in a context for the reader. But, in this novel, since the girl is not named or described, her individuality is generated in paratexts, like the title of the story and the enigmatic photograph in the book.[6]

I was stimulated by what I read (inferred) in some of Nelly Richard's work,[7] and I am interested in exploring the common space which underlies the two novels, a space that is the locus of a number of systems of "loans." It is like an area of "exchanges, appropriations and counter-appropriations" of scattered phrases selected from the repertoire and the tradition of neglect

Dickens Studies Annual, Volume 36, Copyright © 2005 by AMS Press, Inc. All rights reserved.

in childhood in which Dickens is Somers's distinguished predecessor. The girl does not betray the name she has inherited because the name of Oliver Twist encompasses all poor orphans. But, when we adopt a central point of view, we have to ask whether this distant copy is or is not (and why it is or is not) a watered-down double, a pale imitation of an original that enjoys the advantage of being a metropolitan reference point. From what perspective did Somers read Dickens? How should we read these mechanisms of dubbing and simulation? How do we re-define the copy? When we go beyond the ambiguities of the substitute photograph and the shared name (Dickens? Oliver?), we are led to another image, that of the signs of neglect in society which these child characters construct as a stage that is criss-crossed with the marginalizing cracks of orphanhood and destitution. These works of fiction, beneath their shared disguise of a narrative of defeat, represent various different dramas about victims who are oppressed by their societies, one of them in the North and the other in the South.[8]

In the Beginning Was the Name

In a paper in 1993, Beatriz Vegh referred to that orphan girl as "a double . . . , a female variation on Oliver Twist." What is more interesting is that, in the same paper the little orphan girl is "christened" with the name *Oliveria*, and this is repeated on three occasions (225–35). It so happened that while I was working on my own essay, I was using the second edition of *Un retrato para Dickens*. Since I did not have the first edition with me at the time, and since I did not wish to trust my memory too much, I thought for a moment that perhaps Vegh had been working with the first edition, and Somers had revised that text and decided to take out the little girl's name for the second edition, which would be the definitive one. But the fact that a possible name had been explicitly given seemed to me, in a certain way, to be inexplicable. It aroused my curiosity. I consulted Beatriz Vegh, and she sent me an e-mail with a theoretical argument that was most interesting. She said, "I suppose that my [invention of] Oliveria was a spontaneous response in reading. It is probably questionable from more than one point of view . . . , it surely has to do with the two instances where the name 'Oliver' is actually written, with all its letters, in the passage about the photographer's studio."[9] As we know, the reader, in this case the female reader, cooperates with the author in constructing the character, and even contributes by herself what is "missing" in the text. This is the mobilizing function of paratexts, like the title and the photograph, which are Dickensian in each of the images, and to whose model and photographer Somers dedicates her novel.

When Nicasio Perera speaks of characters in Somers's work that are strange "especially because of their names," he points out that "the name which creates strangeness'' serves as a base for constructing otherness ''in the character-effect,'' and therefore ''for the functioning of aesthetic distancing'' in the Brechtian sense, to make us discover, he says, ''the other that there is inside ourselves, or the same self that there is in the other'' (32).

As many critics have noted, the subject of the nature of society and the slant of critical realism which run through *Un retrato para Dickens* seem to set this novel apart from Somers's customary style, which usually features many strange names, like the unforgettable Sembrando Flores [Sowing Flowers]. But it is also true that the author is determined to deny a name to the protagonist of *Un retrato*, thus confusing this character specifically and explicitly with Dickens's Oliver. On other occasions the author anticipates the complicity of the reader; indeed, we have a marvelous example of this in what Beatriz Vegh did when reading the book. Therefore, I do not think that in this particular instance it is either *strangeness* or *aesthetic distancing* that makes us discover the *other* (Oliver) in the *other one* (Oliveria), or both of them as paradigmatic victims of the relentless aggression of social circumstances that mold and mark their lives. Quite the contrary. Both are orphans and both are helpless; the little boy and the little girl have both been involved in the same struggle for survival for as long as they can remember, suffering their irredeemable loneliness from the very beginning.[10]

I searched in the two books for some instances in the writing of a more explicit manifestation of names being absent, or being played with, or being bestowed capriciously. The first example I came across was at the police station where the little girl in *Un retrato para Dickens* recalls the woman ''who decided to be [her] mother without having given birth to [her],'' and took her out of the orphanage ''forgetting [her] identification tag'' (14). Another example is the incident when the director of the orphanage asks for ''her full name'' and smiles when he hears it, as if it reminded him of something related to ''a certain weeping bundle wrapped in newspapers which has to be given a name somehow'' (52).[11] There is also the time when the little girl asks her foster mother what her name is, and the mother replies that that is not important because ''when you have nothing to leave behind when you die you can even live without a name'' (77). I switched from *Un retrato para Dickens* to *Oliver Twist*, to the scene at the home at the very moment that the main protagonist of the story is born, and nobody believed that ''the child would survive to bear any name at all.''[12] But when the newborn baby manifests an obstinate will to live, Mr. Bumble quickly gives him a name, and so ''he was badged and ticketed, and fell into his place at once—a parish child—the orphan of a workhouse—the humble half-starved drudge—to be cuffed and buffeted through the world—despised by all, and pitied by none'' (47). When, some years later, Mrs. Mann asks the beadle how it is possible that Oliver has a name when it is not known who his parents were, Bumble brags about his clever idea, "We name our foundlings in alphabetical order . . . This was a . . . T,—Twist, I named him . . . I have got names ready made to the end of the alphabet" (52). The grotesque parade of surrogate names that survive the imposture nourishes an anti-patriarchal logic that names do not have any real sense at all. I asked myself what importance the authenticity of a name could have for Scott Fitzgerald, when the person's illegitimacy is the very nature of this tragedy. Nelly Richard asserts that "the theology of names is a mockery to be deconstructed" (67). It is interesting to observe that the name "Oliver" does not legitimize the child character as the real owner of his identity, but it does disguise him with something "alien." In fact, his name-emblem is second-hand, a commodity to be traded, a patronymic lent by bureaucratic hypocrisy and by a scornful peddler in names.

   In this rhetoric of (de)identification that can vary from one situation to another, the little girl is constructed inside and outside herself. She cannot fully draw a picture of herself if she does not interweave her nature with that of this European mirror, which, even though it is cracked, still reflects her. Oliver is the fraternal other, the twin, and she is a variation on the postmodern clone, a double who has been born not of him but at his side, in a duality that comes together as an act of resistance against the neglect and poverty that go beyond geography and stories. Rather than suppressing her, the absence of a name has (pre)disposed her, almost naturally over a long century, to become part of a regimented Dickensian code that expresses the desolation of an era as few other codes have done.[13] But it goes beyond this: disgracefully and shamefully it reaches our South American peoples, for it connects with the boys and girls of flesh and bone who, even in these opening years of the twenty-first century, are still starving to death in Third World countries. In our own country.

"Is This Who I Am?"

The traffic in identities that has been interwoven between these two neglected fictional children reaches its climax in the text at the point where the photographer gives his model the book which tells the story of Oliver, saying, "It cannot be that they should live apart after they had met each other" (87). Even before this, he had prepared her for the picture, saying, "What a picture for a book by Dickens" (87) while dressing her up in "a man's hat and a wide black ribbon . . . tied in a bow below the collar of her blouse" (86). In the telling of the story, the girl has been refused a name and has not merited even a perfunctory physical description, and this ceremony could be interpreted as the (re-) foundation of her identity starting as a photographer's model, which takes us into terrain which is no less ambiguous and borderline. She herself speaks of "her contradictory appearance of half boy" (86), a shifting cartography where her sexual identity is inverted and subverted before her own eyes and in the eyes of other people. "I looked at the book he had placed in my hands and I felt as if my heart had found its roots . . . Is this who I am?" (87) she asks (herself). The changing of a grammatical mark of gender does not seem any more bizarre to her than the discovery of a virtual starting point of her existence, or the situation that she is inheriting from an original who is in turn a paradigm of a social marginality that both foundlings share, lending her a name which is and is not her own.

The transvestite girl is given this Dickensian *disguise* by the anarchist reader in a ritual the child herself contributes to in all innocence: since she does not have an overcoat she covers herself with "one of her brothers' jackets" and becomes one with Oliver, re-staging herself through the biographical fiction of the English orphan which is reflected in her image. "Is this who I am?" she asks, questioning the echo of her confusion. Her new identity raises the vindicating flag of a reference which is supposedly real but which, like her, is only appearance, an imaginary support which on this occasion is (re-) created by the libertarian portrait-maker who takes the photograph and who says, "I would never have thought that Oliver Twist himself would come into my house." It is also created by the girl's most childish fantasies, like her dreams of flying, or the illusion of the sponge-cake which can be made with a magical recipe,[14] products all of a mind given to creating substitute situations when faced with real situations that are disappointing.[15] To avoid having to confront the certainties of her hapless existence, or sometimes as a result of confronting them too much, the girl is attracted by another image, the mirror-like image of Oliver. This is constructed by and for the orphans of the world, and it has a name or emblem in which they are all included, so that it has the virtue of representing her. Nevertheless, the fact that this usurpation of identities is transitory does not mean a betrayal of the inherited name: "I felt as if I had been projected out of myself, and that was all there was to it." The little girl quickly distances herself from what has happened, laying aside "all the borrowed garments." The portrait that captures the image of deception becomes a substitute simulacrum that only serves to prolong this lapse into juggling, and again shows up the traffic in identities.

When the girl's belly is paining her after a rape, and faced with the sudden death of her "mother," she thinks, "Mummy and her tummy. I never came out of a tummy. Therefore, does that mean I was never born? . . . And what do you do . . . when you find out you were never born?" (98). The voice that narrates Oliver's misfortunes tells us that, between the almost simultaneous birth of the baby and the death of his mother, which left him completely alone in the world, the nurse wrapped him in a blanket, and that was when

"He might have been the child of a nobleman or of a beggar, it would have been hard for the haughtiest stranger to have fixed his station in society'' (47).

Both Oliver and the little girl are denied their social class, their identities are made problematic by the imposition of a series of masks, they are cheated of their names as the primary matrix of identity,[16] and the myth of individuality is questioned in them.[17] They globalize poverty and helplessness, and they raise questions about society's pitiless calculation, hypocrisy, and indifference.

Dickens was a chronicler of his time, and he said more than once that he wished "to attempt a something which was needed, and which would be a service to society.''[18] Somers, who according to most critics wrote in a way that was far from social realism, knows better than most how to write from the pain and anguish of human beings. Harold Bloom maintains that Dickens does not have a real heir in the English language (329) but Somers's work is at the antipodes of this truncated line of succession. Along with Bloom, I also wonder how it might be possible again to practice "an art in which fairy tales are narrated as if they were sagas of social realism'' (329). No. Somers's work is of a different kind, from a different literature and from a different continent. Perhaps it is here that the greatest difference between the discursive universes of the two writers can be found, in the here and now of a work of art, in its unique existence in the place where it is, because, as Benjamin says, it is precisely in that "unique existence, and not in any other thing, that the whole course of the story which has been subject to it occurred'' (20).

I am not referring to the anxiety of her influences when Somers borrows an image and a name; the importance of her text cannot be put down to a debt or to imitation. Dickens and his novel have only served as a model in the organization of the Uruguayan writer's work. Like the girl in her story, Somers very quickly lays aside the "borrowed garments.'' What interests me as something of critical value, and as something from this Uruguay where I am now writing, is not so much the source as the differences from the source.[19] In the source I see mainly an explicit and deserved homage which Somers transfigures because in her writing there is no place for the appropriation of something that is out of fashion. There is a tension in appearing to be what one is not, neither a boy, nor Oliver, nor original, and this (re-) defines the distant copy which in no way detracts from the prestige of the source. This Oliveria is neither counterfeit nor second-hand, for she has a meaning in herself and in her dialogue that stands on equal terms with the metropolitan Oliver. The question initially raised by the title and by the original will be reformulated by the modern reader in line with his or her own ideological leanings, and he or she will probably conclude, or at least I conclude, that the point at which the two novels and the two characters (in spite of their differences or perhaps because of them) come closest to each other is in the fact that they have both been constructed from the pain and the pity aroused by the social helplessness of children marginalized by societies both in the North and in the South. The reason for this, as Somers's parrot claims the puppeteer said, is that "we are all puppets; the thing is that God's fingers that pull the strings of some of us have grown stiff, while with others he is a great artist" (117).

NOTES

1. Conversation with Miguel Angel Campodónico, read on 29 November 1985 at the National Library, and later included in the *Revista de la Biblioteca Nacional*, no. 24, 1986—in Campodónico 231. All translations from Spanish in the essay are my own.
2. Somers was born in 1914 as Armonía Liropeya Etchepare Locino. When she published her first novel in 1950, she adopted the pseudonym by which she is known as a writer. She later explained, "Armonía Somers had two genetic branches. One was the craving for liberty and to be free from having to commit to a parallel profession (that of school teacher). Though now I have found out . . . that in those legendary times of *La mujer desnuda*, [*The Naked Woman*] her first novel, 1950, I would try something more than taking a new name. Maybe the change of identity that this involves had existential roots that were deeper than they seemed . . . who knows if that new name for me . . . might not be like the shiny new skin of a snake that has left the old skin behind . . . " (Delgado Aparaín 32). She also observed, "I chose 'Somers' hastily, for the edition of the magazine that was going to include my novel. I liked it because it is the root of the word 'summer' in both English and German, and I love the summer (. . .) perhaps because I was conceived in the summer" (Copani 24). On another occasion she confessed that the change of name "was probably a protest that . . . I made against the fact that I had been born without first being asked for my permission, and had the audacity to go on surviving in a world like this, which [I] do not like" (Risso 254). The question of the family surname and the problematic identity of Armonía Somers are examined by Larre Borges, 311–46.
3. See Foucault, 42–45.
4. I use the second and last edition, Somers 1990. Henceforth, I will give the page numbers in parentheses.
5. The daughter of an anarchist father who was always involved in "social struggle, libraries, instructing people" (Risso 248), and a Catholic mother, who wrote for a magazine in Canelones, and who had had experience of free theater before meeting the man who was to be her husband. Armonía found that her fondness for reading emerged in early childhood, but "for want of children's stories, I went straight for the only thing that was available, a great library on social background" (Gandolfo 1986).

6. When asked in an interview about the origin of this photograph, Armonía Somers said, ''It is the photo of a very special girl, a photo that I was given by the subject herself when she was an adult. The old photographer played his part when he dressed her up in the man's hat and the freethinker's ribbon and put a roll of papers in her hand, the plastic interpretation of being. When I found out from some fragmentary stories about the human suffering behind that picture, I did my part, the re-creation'' (Gandolfo 1988).

7. Especially, ''Contorsión de géneros y doblaje sexual: la parodia travesti'' 64–75.

8. On the subject of the North, it is interesting to recall some of Hobsbawn's remarks about the Poor Law of 1834. This historian says that ''Few statutes have been more inhuman'' and ''It made any welfare worse than the lowest salary.'' This law, which punished the poor for their poverty, remained the basis of the English welfare system up until the eve of the First World War, and, as Hobsbawm goes on to say, ''Charlie Chaplin's experiences in childhood show that it was still the same as it had been when Dickens' s *Oliver Twist* expressed people's horror at it in the 1830s'' (Hobsbawm 1998).

9. E-mail dated 4 December 2002.

10. The depersonalization suffered by children when they are denied a name is shown in other of Dickens's works. It is painful to see the identification made by Mr. Gradgrind when he questions Sissy in her class at school. He insists on calling her ''girl number twenty'' since, according to him, ''Sissy is not a name'' (*Hard Times* 4).

11. Although in Armonía Somers's lifetime the identity of the girl in the picture that was used to illustrate the two editions of the book was never made clear, Larre Borges traces the history of this photograph in her research and concludes the model might have been Mercedes Lloroso, who was a cleaner at the pedagogical museum where Somers used to work and a friend of the writer. This woman's life might well have been the inspiration for the novel. ''Mercedes, sources say, came from an orphanage, and she had been named Lloroso because as a baby she cried a lot'' (328). (''Lloroso'' is the Spanish word for ''weeping'').

12. *Oliver Twist* (45). Henceforth I will give the page numbers.

13. Eric Hobsbawm points out that that age was dominated by ''a pietistic, rigid, pharisaic, anti-intellectual Protestantism, which was obsessed with puritan morality to the point that hypocrisy was automatically a companion'' (1997, 24).

14. The sponge-cake/talisman is a world of symbols that, triggered by immense desire and need, is embodied in the thought of the little girl as cornerstones of her inner world that make possible an alternative, that of escape. See Alicia Torres, ''Un retrato para Dickens o el dolor de estar vivo.''

15. In *Hard Times*, the teacher at the school tells the pupils, ''You are not to see anywhere, what you don't see in fact; you are not to have anywhere, what you don't have in fact . . . but *you mustn't fancy* . . . That's it! *You are never to fancy*'' (italics added).

16. In the orphanage, when the newborn baby girl is handed over to her future foster mother, this woman fears that it could be another boy and the first thing she does is examine the child, ''She opened the blanket at a certain place,'' to see the sex, and this becomes not only the first but the only possible identification. ''She

wanted this baby she had been given without being told that it was to be a girl, and my little female sex that was only a few hours old must have communicated so strongly with her insides that she ran home quite forgetting the identification tag'' (14).

17. The professional language in the report made by the official when the orphan is rescued from the sea, after she had attempted suicide by throwing herself in (''By that time I was the miserable and nameless *thing* that had been fished out of the dock'') speaks of *''the aforementioned,''* a name that alarms the girl, ''I did not have that strange name, but it was all the same to me'' (13) (italics added).

18. In the preface to the third edition, *Oliver Twist* (35).

19. See Silviano Santiago 66.

WORKS CITED

Benjamin, Walter. ''La obra de arte en la época de su reproductibilidad técnica.'' In *Discursos Interrumpidos I*. Madrid: Taurus, 1973. 17–57.

Bloom, Harold. ''La novela canónica: *Casa desolada,* de Dickens, y *Middlemarch* de George Eliot.'' *El canon occidental*. Barcelona: Anagrama, 1995.

Campodónico, Miguel Ángel. ''Homenaje a Armonía Somers: diálogo con Miguel Ángel Campodónico.'' *Armonía Somers. Papeles Críticos*. Ed. Rómulo Cosse. Montevideo: Linardi y Risso, 1990. 225–245.

Copani, María. ''Armonía Somers y el fervor por lo oculto: el oficio de buscar mandrágora.'' Interview. *Clarín. Cultura y Nación*. Buenos Aires: May 26, 1988. 24.

Delgado Aparaín, Mario. ''Interview.'' *Búsqueda* 500, Montevideo: August 31, 1989. 32.

Dickens, Charles. *Hard Times*. London: Dent, 1957.

———. *Oliver Twist*. Harmondsworth: Penguin, 1966.

Foucault, Michel. ''La prosa del mundo.'' *Las palabras y las cosas*. México D.F.: Siglo XXI, 1968. 26–52.

Gandolfo, Elvio E. ''Para cercar lo indecible.'' Interview. *La Razón*. Buenos Aires: November 7, 1986. 36.

———. ''En busca de la mandrágora.'' Interview. *La Vanguardia*. Barcelona: February 16, 1988. 25.

Hobsbawm, Eric J. *La era de la revolución. 1789–1848*. 1962; Buenos Aires: Crítica, 1997.

———. *Industria e imperio*. 1968; Buenos Aires: Ariel, 1998.

Larre Borges, Ana Inés. "Armonía Somers. La mujer secreta." *Mujeres uruguayas. El lado femenino de nuestra historia.* Montevideo: Alfaguara-Fundación Bank Boston, 2001. 311–46.

Perera San Martín, Nicasio. "Armonía Somers. Una trayectoria ejemplar." *Armonía Somers. Papeles Críticos.* Montevideo: Linardi y Risso, 1990.

Richard, Nelly. "Contorsión de géneros y doblaje sexual: la parodia travesti." *Masculino/Femenino. Prácticas de la diferencia y cultura democrática.* Santiago de Chile: Francisco Zegers Editor, 1989. 64–75.

Risso, Alvaro J. "Un retrato para Armonía". *Armonía Somers. Papeles Críticos.* Montevideo: Linardi y Risso, 1990. 247–96.

Santiago, Silviano. "El entrelugar del discurso latinoamericano." *Absurdo Brasil.* Ed. Adriana Amante and Florencia Garramuño. Buenos Aires: Biblos, 2000. 61–79.

Somers, Armonía. *Un retrato para Dickens.* Montevideo: Arca, 1969.

———. *Un retrato para Dickens.* Barcelona: Península, 1990.

Torres, Alicia. "Un retrato para Dickens o el dolor de estar vivo." Dossier Armonía Somers. *Fundación* 2–3. Montevideo: July 1995. 59–61.

Vegh, Beatriz. "La rumia y el caramillo: figuras relacionales en la narrativa de Armonía Somers." *Deslindes. Revista de la Biblioteca Nacional* 2–3. Montevideo: May 1993. 225–35.

The Strange Gentleman: Dickens on the Uruguayan Stage

Leticia Eyheragaray

Throughout his adult life, Dickens showed an intense interest in the theater. As a young man, he arranged to have an audition as an actor before the director of Covent Garden, and although illness forced the cancellation of this appointment (Johnson, *Theatrical Reader* 11), and his success as a writer precluded rescheduling of the audition, he wrote several dramatic pieces. Later in his career, of course, he gained distinction as an amateur actor and stage manager, and then won great acclaim as a performer reading his own fiction.

Recently, research carried out by a team led by Professor Roger Mirza, of the Facultad de Humanidades at the Universidad de la República, Montevideo, focused on the contemporary Uruguayan professional theatrical system and compiled complete data regarding the premieres and revivals that took place in Montevideo between the years 1945 and 1984.[1] Among these thousands of productions our team discovered that Dickens is represented by only one play, *The Strange Gentleman,* staged in Uruguay for the first time on May 9, 1946. But this discovery seems truly significant, for there exist only four plays written by Dickens, only three of which were staged. Of these, just one, *The Strange Gentleman,* was considered successful. I wonder if the spectators in May 1946 at the Victoria Hall in Montevideo appreciated what a rare opportunity they were being given to witness a performance of this early piece by Dickens. Although this work provided his major fulfillment as a dramatist, he subsequently, after his amazing success as a writer of fiction, disregarded *The Strange Gentleman,* claiming it had been done "without the least consideration or regard to reputation" (*Letters* 598) and that he would leave it behind "with so light a pace that no one heard him moving off, and never once turning back his head" (R.H. Horne, in Dickens, *Letters* 598).

Before creating *The Strange Gentleman*, Dickens had agreed to write a libretto for a comic opera by the composer John Hullah, a work originally entitled *The Gondolier* and set in Venice, but eventually transformed by Dickens into a bucolic drama called *The Village Coquettes* (Johnson, *Theatrical Reader* 12). At this time, however, he met the tenor John Braham, who would open the new St. James's Theatre, and Dickens, at the request of the comic actor John Pritt Harley, began writing a farce based on "The Great Winglebury Duel," one of the pieces in *Sketches by Boz* (Johnson, *Charles Dickens* 127). This play, which Dickens called *The Strange Gentleman*, was first performed on September 29, 1836, with Harley in the principal role, and would continue running for more than sixty nights (Johnson, *Charles Dickens* 152), later sharing the program with Dickens's other creation, *The Village Coquettes,* which was first staged the same year on December 6 (Johnson, *Charles Dickens* 153).

Even though *The Strange Gentleman* was well received by the audience, this may have been more attributable to external factors than to the play itself. While Harley—a famous actor at the time—was said to be "a riot as the 'strange gentleman' " (Johnson, *Theatrical Reader* 12), there was also "the red-and-gold magnificence of the St. James Theatre" (Johnson, *Charles Dickens* 127) which had recently opened; and, finally, Dickens's rising popularity due to *The Pickwick Papers* that during that summer had "caught fire [and] skyrocketed to spectacular and hilarious fame" (Johnson, *Theatrical Reader* 12).

Dickens's second play, *The Village Coquettes*, did not evoke comparable interest, hardly reaching twenty performances, and a similar disappointment occurred a few months later with his new play entitled *Is She His Wife? or Something Singular,* first produced on March 6, 1837 (Johnson, *Charles Dickens* 191).

Dickens then broke away from the St. James's Theatre, since he was occupied with his monthly publications of *Pickwick Papers* and then of *Oliver Twist.* However, he would write another play in 1838, *The Lamplighter,* a one-act farce that he offered to William Charles Macready, the famous actor, who rejected the work as not suitable for his company at the Covent Garden Theatre (Johnson, *Charles Dickens* 223). Macready thought that although the dialogue was very good, the plot failed (Collins 29), and so Dickens ended up turning this, his fourth and last play, into a story (Forster 106). From then on, the author devoted himself primarily to the literary commitments that established him as a novelist, but he would never entirely abandon his inclination to write for the theater, collaborating with Mark Lemon on the farce *Mr.*

Nightingale's Diary in 1851 and with Wilkie Collins on the melodrama *The Lighthouse* in 1855 (Collins 95).

Perhaps anticipating the unfavorable criticism that *The Village Coquettes* would receive, Dickens explained in a preface that "the libretto of an opera must be, to a certain extent, a mere vehicle for the music, and that it is scarcely fair or reasonable to judge it by those strict rules of criticism which would be justly applicable to a five-act tragedy, or a finished comedy" (Fawcett 24). Years later he would maintain that he only wrote the libretto because the music created by Hullah pleased him, but that ever since then he had felt "most sincerely repentant" (Fawcett 25).

Regarding *The Strange Gentleman,* Dickens would claim that it was written as a "sort of practical joke" for Harley, and he would acknowledge that he "wouldn't repeat them [his two early dramatic works] for a thousand pounds apiece, and devoutly wished them to be forgotten" (*Letters* 598). Hence, two years after his death, when *The Strange Gentleman* was revived at the Charing Cross Theatre, some of his relatives requested that it should be withdrawn, and W. H. Nation, the theater lessee, agreed to their request (Fawcett 25).

We should not forget, however, that before Dickens referred disparagingly to his early efforts at drama, he experienced a certain success, regardless of how brief, as a result of his first play, *The Strange Gentleman,* "a comic burletta in two acts." Set at the "St. James's Arms" inn, the play has a simple central idea: the protagonist, originally played by John Pritt Harley, is a comic hero who flees a duel to which he has been challenged, refuses to give his name, and is subsequently mistaken for somebody else, a supposed lunatic. Diverse confusions and cross-purposes develop around him—involving two couples and a woman awaiting her fiancé—until he is led to believe he is staying at an inn full of maniacs. However, everything gets solved in an expeditious ending, and the protagonist, relieved at having lost an unwanted fiancée, who had urged him to fight a duel, will leave with Julia Dobbs, who was waiting for a future husband—the supposed lunatic—who will never arrive. Fanny Wilson is reconciled with Charles Tomkins. Fanny's sister Mary, after the economic difficulties that troubled her prospective mate, John Johnson, have been solved, leaves with him. The play, which runs for approximately eighty minutes, ends with these three couples heading for the town of Gretna, where they are to be married. The last lines belong to Walker Trott—finally revealed as the true name of the protagonist—who addresses the public and asks if they could be indulgent in considering his mistakes and the trouble he caused and agree to receive *The Strange Gentleman* again the next day.

The work, a vaudeville piece with countless misunderstandings of dialogue and situation, was announced as a "musical farce" only due to regulations applied to the minor theaters at the time. Because Covent Garden, Drury

Lane, and the Haymarket were the only theaters authorized to present "serious" plays, the other playhouses could only offer "musical performances of a dramatic nature" (Fawcett 22), and hence some kind of music had to be introduced in the plays. This is why there is a duet performed by the sisters Wilson in the first act.

According to Fawcett, it is a "strange concoction indeed" in which the machinery of the farce fails at times—the protagonist, for instance, has an explanatory monologue of over five hundred words and another one of two hundred, and the play includes a greatly excessive number of "asides" (21).

The critical reception of the time was mixed. A review in the *News and Sunday Herald* observes,

> The well-earned reputation of Mr. Charles Dickens . . . induced us to regard the first dramatic production of "Boz" with more than ordinary interest, and we are truly happy to record the triumphant success of *The Strange Gentleman* as a pleasant and *really* humorous a piece . . . a wide field is open, and Mr. Dickens will be alike regardless of his own interest and the public's gratification if he neglects to maintain that position to which his maiden effort so justly entitles him.   (Dexter, on net)

However, the *Champion* states that the play "was lively, certainly: but the humour throughout was not worthy of the great reputation he [Dickens] had acquired" (Dexter). A notice in the *Satirist* argued,

> There is certainly no want of point or cleverness in the piece, yet strange to say it did not as a whole, "tell" with the audience. It is in truth clogged with matter which may be very good, and probably *is* so, in the very sketch, on which the drama is founded, but which somehow destroys the effect in many instances, of the dialogue. The position of the parties assembled at "The St. James's Arms", is astonishingly improbable; the situations are too forced, the perplexities too prolonged, to keep up a genuine interest among an audience.
> (Dexter, on net)

Despite the unfavorable comments, apparently audiences agreed to continue "receiving" the play, and it was staged at the Park Theatre in New York (September 15, 1837), at the Chestnut Street Theatre in Philadelphia (January 29, 1838), and at the Olympic on Broadway in New York (December 16, 1839). After being removed from the Charing Cross Theatre in 1873, it was staged a few times by branches of the Dickens Fellowship in Toronto, in 1930, and in St. Pancras, in 1933, by English companies in Portsmouth and in Cantonbury in 1970, and by a group at London's Birkbeck College in 1984 (Sabatini).

As I observed previously, however, in Montevideo the play's premiere was on May 9, 1946, in a performance by the professional juvenile group Teatro

Libre at the Victoria Hall theater[2]. In this instance the play was delivered in Spanish, and although it is possible that a member of the company had translated the text, it is perhaps more probable that the actors utilized a translation from the original published in Buenos Aires in 1943. This work, by the Spanish dramatist Francisco Madrid, is paired with *The Lamplighter,* in a volume published by the Editorial Poseidón for its "Pandora" collection. This was, apparently, the first translation into Spanish of these comedies, and it seems surprising considering the limited popularity Dickens obtained as a dramatist—particularly with his last play, which was never staged.

From this perspective, this translation is undoubtedly valuable; however, when comparing the text with the original, we find that the performance of the translator seems at times questionable. He himself, in a prologue, offers the following remarks about his work:

> It is difficult to translate plays from the comic theater, for they lean, many times, only on the joke, the pun, the quibble . . . such is the trouble for the translator with a humourous play. If he translates in a literal way, the reader will find phrases that will seem mere nonsense or senseless vulgarities. If he performs the job a bit freely, searching in his own language for jokes or puns that could substitute the ones from the original, it may be said that he falsifies or mocks the text. Nonetheless, to our judgment, it is better [to follow] this formula than the previous one.   (11, my translation)

Evidently, what he states is reasonable, and by applying this formula he often successfully achieves in various cases the conversion of expressions which, if translated literally, would lose all sense.

In a few instances, however, we may find errors of translation that affect the comprehension of the plot. The protagonist, when handing over the two letters which will decide his luck to the "boots," states, "Well, that's to be left at the Royal Hotel. This, *this,* is an anonymous one; and I want it to he delivered at the Mayor's house." This is translated, "Perfecto. Esta debe ser entregada en el Hotel Real. Es un anónimo. Se trata de que llegue a manos del alcalde" ("Perfect. This must be delivered at the Royal Hotel, it's anonymous. It must get to the Mayor"), creating confusion.

Something similar happens when Charles observes to Fanny, "I am delighted to have escaped you, ma'am," and we read, "Estoy encantado, al contrario, estoy encantado de haberte podido esperar, señorita" ("I am delighted, on the contrary, I am delighted to have been able to wait for you, miss") and abruptly goes away from her.

In addition, at one point Overton remarks, "Then I must have misunderstood her, and you must have misunderstood her too," a line that is translated, "Entonces no habré comprendido lo que me dijo. Tampoco usted me ha entendido, al parecer" ("Then I must have misunderstood what she said.

You have not understood me either, it seems''). Moreover, these are only some of the examples of confusing translation that may be found throughout the text of Francisco Madrid.

On the other hand, there are cases in which the translator facilitates the interpretation of some line, through explanatory "attachments" which bring the text closer to the reality of a reader probably unfamiliar with certain Dickensian referents. In the denouement, for instance, when the three couples decide to leave, the protagonist says, "on to Gretna, directly." The translator adds a clause: "On to Gretna, where people get married the fastest."

Despite these modifications, as well as the previously mentioned flaws, Francisco Madrid's Spanish version of *The Strange Gentleman*, if read without comparing it to the original English text, is a play in which the essence of this early dramatic creation by Dickens remains practically unaltered. It was perhaps from this perspective that the audience welcomed the performance in Montevideo, with the great expectations which would accompany any work from this famous author, and this one in particular since it was regarded as a novelty.

In fact, this is how the newspaper *El Diario* justified its staging, in a story written the day before the performance: " 'Teatro libre de Montevideo' has chosen this comedy, juvenile, merry, unimportant, if you may, but of an indisputable theatrical value, for it is an absolute novelty on the scene." (May 8, 1946: 5, my translation). Perhaps because the playwright was Dickens, the farce was praised even before the performance. "The notable cleverness of Charles Dickens appears throughout the play, which has moments of sharp comicality and entertains and interests during its whole development," observed *El Diario*, on May 8 (my translation). Both *La Mañana* and *El Pais* would later state that it was a "delicious and fecund comedy of misunderstandings by *Carlos* Dickens . . . in which the cleverness of the novelist pours onto the stage in his pure and simple way" (*La Mañana*, May 12, 1946: 10; *El Pais*, May 9, 1946: 11, my translation).

Even though Rafael Bertrán's staging was not considered entirely satisfactory, the efforts of the juvenile company were appreciated, and the faults were attributed primarily to the difficulty of performing this play. So we read in *La Mañana*,

> it cannot be denied that it is a refined play, ingenious . . . this is why we say that such a production meant a serious commitment for this new group . . for it must be "played" a bit in the tone of Molière and a bit in that of Musset . . . it cannot be strange then that . . . some fixable defects had been noticed . . . which disappear among many achievements.   (May 12, 1946: 10, my translation)

Although critical commentary after the premiere was limited, the fact that the production was reported in most of the newspapers of the time suggests that there was a high degree of public interest and that the implicit value of such a performance was accepted.

Despite the fact that in London in 1836 this play was overshadowed by Dickens's enormously popular monthly publications of fiction, and despite Dickens's own later statement that he regretted having written the piece, *The Strange Gentleman,* when produced in Montevideo over a century later, evidently received a surprisingly positive reception. But this positive response should not surprise us, for Dickens had achieved such fame and popularity that the public in Montevideo was unwilling to ignore any of his artistic creations. Thus, in 1946 the Uruguayan scene had the privilege to witness a gentleman pass, a strange gentleman perhaps, but certainly a welcome one, named Charles Dickens.

NOTES

1. Ongoing investigation, the first volume of which has been printed only for departmental use; soon to be published by Banda Oriental editors, Montevideo, Uruguay.
2. Even though the newspapers at the time are not clear about how many performances this play reached, it evidently ran for at least three nights.

WORKS CITED

Collins, Phillip, ed., *Dickens, Interviews and Recollections*, Vol. I, Hong Kong: Macmillan, 1981.

Dexter, Walter. "A Stage Aside: Dickens's Early Dramatic Productions: I. *The Strange Gentleman,* September, 1836." *Dickensian* 33 (1937) in http://home.earthlink.net/~bsabatini/Inimitable-Boz/etexts/Strange Gentleman.html

Dickens, Charles, *The Pilgrim Edition of The Letters of Charles Dickens.* House, Madeleine, Graham Storey, Kathleen Tillotson, eds. Vol. III, 1842–1843, Oxford: Clarendon Press, 1974.

Dickens, Charles. *The Strange Gentleman* (1836) in http://home.earthlink.net/~bsabatini/Inimitable-Boz/etexts/Strange Gentleman.html

Fawcett, Frank D. *Dickens the Dramatist.* London: W. H. Allen, 1952.

Forster, John, *The Life of Charles Dickens*, Vol. I, London: J.M. Dent & Sons, 1966.

Johnson, Edgar, *Charles Dickens, His Tragedy and Triumph*, Vol. I, London: Victor Gollancz, 1953.

Johnson, Edgar, and Eleanor Johnson. *The Dickens Theatrical Reader*. London: Victor Gollancz, 1964.

Madrid, Francisco. *El extraño caballero y El farolero*. Buenos Aires: Editorial Poseidón, 1943.

Mirza, Roger, *Cronología de estrenos teatrales en Montevideo: 1945–1972*. Montevideo: ediciones de la FHUCE, Universidad de la República, 2003.

Sabatini, Beppe. Prologue to *The Strange Gentleman* in http://home.earthlink.net/ ~bsabatini/Inimitable-Boz/etexts/Strange Gentleman.html

Newspapers:

El Diario, Montevideo, 8 de Mayo de 1946.

El Pais, Montevideo, 9 de Mayo de 1946.

La Mañana, Montevideo, 12 de Mayo de 1946.

Spectacle and Estrangement in Dickens

Verónica D'Auria

David Lodge, who adapted a version of *Martin Chuzzlewit* for television, stated that if Dickens had lived in Shakespeare's time he would have been a playwright (1996, 202). Similarly, we could say that if he were living today he might have been a film director. From what position today do we read, do we perceive, the Dickensian novels?

The first answer, linked with the globalization of our environment, is that we perceive them as part of the "spectacle" culture. We are speaking of a passive show where, instead of allowing the whole person to take part in the celebration, the media exclude all manner of active participation (Salabert 107). The individual, who was first subject to authority and later given the rights and responsibilities of a citizen, is now regarded as a consumer who has undergone an infantilizing development (Salabert 113). There is an abyss separating him or her from reality; the cathartic aspects are diluted in a spectacle and lead to flight, and the spectacle itself is so absorbing that things themselves cease to be in their alterity (Salabert 160). Indeed, for this newly infantile spectator all acts become a spectacle: terrorism, accidents, extreme poverty.

Already in *Le Père Goriot* Balzac mentioned the white hands of the reader who sat comfortably in a soft sofa contemplating the misfortune of others as a form of entertainment (50). In order to lead readers to perceive the real, it must be presented as a spectacle mediated by stories. Both documentaries and newsreels are presented as narrative sequences; if this were not the case, we would find it impossible to construe the data from reality, which would in time become implausible (Salabert 130). As Uruguayans, in a clearly deteriorating society, we perceive Dickens as part of this global spectacle culture, but we are also surrounded by and form part of the spectacle of misery.

Dickens's stories are not only a true spectacle in themselves, but they are also part of our cultural heritage: they form part of the narrations that enable us to interpret in our social imagination the spectacle of poverty and human misery.

In other words, for us the suffering often described by Dickens is not a picturesque image of an industrial past that has been already overcome, as could be the case for some first world readers. In our street children here, we can also recognize Oliver Twist when he was working for Fagin. When we see this spectacle of degradation we are also reminded of the Scrooges, the Bounderbys, and the irredeemable Marleys, whom we consider responsible for this situation of marginalization and social injustice. Nevertheless, a naive reading of Dickens or of reality itself could lead us to make the same mistake as that attributed to a character in David Lodge's novel *Nice Work*, Robyn Penrose, a university teacher specializing in the Victorian social novel. In Robyn, we find satirized the intellectual who thinks that modern factories are satanic mills, and that middle management plays the role of the villain while the workers are the victims, even though she at the same time ignores the exploitation she herself suffers as a university teacher.

George Orwell, who himself provides another example of oversimplification when he refers to all art as a form of propaganda (145), describes Dickens in his famous essay on the author as an honest writer who always sided with the helpless and oppressed, those who are made outcasts by the dominating social system—for example, aristocrats in *A Tale of Two Cities*, or Catholics in *Barnaby Rudge* (156).

We could conceive of the Dickensian spectacle as a melodrama or a Victorian fairy tale (especially after *Oliver Twist* and *David Copperfield*), where the hero at one time a victim manages to thrive socially thanks to the aid of a donor or supplier, to use the terms employed by Vladimir Propp. Although these categories have been questioned by E. Souriau and A. Greimas (see Ducrot 263), the terms seem useful in understanding some of the fairy-tale types or characters in Victorian novels. In Dickens's narratives, the hero's benefactor belongs to another social level or possesses great fortune, which the hero of course lacks, but the patron is committed to the hero's well-being and contributes towards his social integration and happiness. It is clearly possible to read Dickens's work as a successful struggle between charitable forces on one side and villains, the embodiment of all social evils, on the other, all included in what we could call Victorian kitsch, a kitsch vaguely described by Orwell as a "rococo" of Dickens (149). Even this reductionist position allows us to observe very important elements such as the author's attempt to enhance the feminine aspects of Coketown in *Hard Times* and bring this monotonous and grotesque, excessively artificial and masculine world closer to nature. The flowers on the wallpaper are harshly criticized in this society as the product of a female fantasy that does not contribute to the development of an industrial civilization. Cecilia Jupe's nickname, Sissy, recalling the noun "sissy" (an effeminate person), is likewise strongly rejected by her patron, Mr. Gradgrind, as if it were ultimately improper and inappropriate for this society.

This very same Victorian kitsch, however, permits Dickens to include in his narratives the exploration of tenderness among the male characters, an element frequently absent in the stories that have shaped us, where the relationships among males always seem to include elements of rivalry, hatred, or competitiveness. We are mostly referring to the friendship that occurs between an imperfect father-figure and the hero-victim. These relationships do not always form part of the central narration, but contribute to make the hero's life and sufferings more tolerable. Thus, the relationship between Pip and Joe Gargery in *Great Expectations* is one of the most important relationships for the protagonist, in spite of the fact that Joe is only another battered person. Wemmick, who becomes Pip's friend, also manages to impress us with the nutrient filial care he provides for his old and deaf father; and David Copperfield, who had no acceptable father-figures, enjoys his limited relationship with the eccentric and deranged Mr. Dick.

It is also possible to read another Dickens, who, apart from the melodramatic elements (helpful for serial pubication, and contributing to the massive sale of his books), uses other resources which, paraphrasing Brecht, we could consider as "estranging" or "distancing" effects in this kitsch narration of victimization and hypocritical villains, with many miraculous social recoveries introduced by the author as a deus ex machina. Although the terms used by Brecht are applied to the spectacle offered in drama, here we are proposing Dickens's stories as spectacles, and we may therefore consider it possible to apply these categories. Brecht criticized what he called "the theatre of illusion" that succeeded in maintaining poverty at a distance and lifted the burden of existence from the spectators (Ewen 202; Esslin 106). In a certain sense, Victorian melodrama had this numbing function; but Dickens managed to go beyond the pathetic and the reader's immediate identification with the experiences of his characters through these estranging effects.

In *Great Expectations*, considered by many critics to be one of his most effective and complex novels, there is a reversal of the wonderful story where the victim-hero attains the fortune he sought. The author manages to distance the narrative from this formula and transforms this narration by using doubles, self-parody, and the exchange of traditional roles. In this case the victim-hero is identified through an object (a file or an iron leg-shackle, both perhaps with a male identification value) with his aggressor, who in time becomes his donor or supplier by investing an important fortune in him (Connor 119–22). This help, however, does not enable the hero to reach happiness or overcome his social condition, but rather leads to his fall, for the supplier is also fleeing from the Victorian jails. In this sad fairy tale the princess is unattainable, as her name, Estella or star, indicates, and only returns to him as a battered woman who, like him, has lost all those great expectations. In this way, even the happier version of the ending is ambivalent. In this narration the providers are not generous or philanthropic ladies and gentlemen, but are much rather trying to shape other destinies, compensatory for their own shortcomings, and end by spoiling the lives of their protégés—Miss Havisham with Estella, and Magwitch with Pip.

The victim-hero, moreover, is not presented as a helpless child stoically bearing abuse and miraculously escaping his miserable condition. The sister (a real aggressor) is punished in the way that the stepmothers of children's stories are, by Orlick, a character that could be construed as Pip's double. Like Pip, he works together with Joe Gargery in the forge, and is also linked to him by the same leg-iron. When Orlick later tries to kill Pip, he accuses the hero, in spite of having no evidence, and says it is Pip who has encouraged him to attack Mrs. Joe. Undoubtedly, there is a displacement of desire, and Orlick has only carried out Pip's hidden wish for revenge on Mrs. Joe for all the violent corporal punishment and verbal abuse he has suffered. (Connor 125).

The early links between the victim-hero and Magwitch, the aggressor-provider, are complex, for the latter terrorizes the child in the cemetery. Magwitch later referring to his childhood, states, "I first became aware of myself, down in Essex, a thieving turnips for my living. Summun had run away from me—a man—a tinker—and he'd took the fire with him, and left me very cold" (316). Perhaps Pip did not become a delinquent because another man, Joe, another battered person like him, gave him his friendship and affection, both of which he rejected to become a gentleman. His rise in society, as opposed to that of Oliver and David Copperfield, does not lead to social integration, but instead brings him closer to an uprooted existence.

And it is in this novel, in two very minor scenes, that Dickens uses self-parody in a very effective way. When Pip, wishing to become a gentleman, seeks Mr. Trabb, the tailor and haberdasher, to change his clothing, an insolent young man working for Trabb sweeps over Pip in a mocking manner. Similarly, when the hero returns to his place of origin, after having lived among gentlemen and interacting with them, this same young man uses a blue bag as a cloak and lifting his shirt collar tells all his friends he sees in the street, "Dont know yah!" mocking the hero's behavior during the process of his social rise.

If Dickens was simply a Victorian moralist, his fiction was not as straightforward as Orwell claimed. In his letters to Angela Burdett-Coutts, Dickens, when discussing philanthropic tasks such as the reeducation of prostitutes before sending them to Australia, often sounds more like Mr. Bounderby or Mr. Bumble than like an adult David or Oliver, who was sorry for and capable of understanding the misery of others. A certain disciplining undertone may be heard, the wish to control the bodies of these women, to control what he believes to be perverse. In similar fashion, in the debate about the social question, his own speech is framed within a discourse that tries to tame the violence of the chartists who walked through the streets of London with the effigies of the heads of their class enemies (Rooke 29). Dickens, like other reformist intellectuals, attempted and managed to avoid having these images replaced by real heads, as occurred with Charles I, a fact which so much obsessed Mr. Dick in *David Copperfield*.

Nevertheless, Dickens at times goes beyond his customary role regarding the social question, for he is very skilled when he deals with social problems in aesthetic terms. Thus David remembers the very beautiful eyes of Em'ly, a girl he admired during his childhood, who may end as a prostitute. A battered boy may also become a batterer, or may become extremely neurotic, or may develop into a gentle, decent person (like Joe Gargery in *Great Expectations*). There are some very plain stories where social ascent is a sinister search, and philanthropy the least generous activity, where social justice is either too late or insufficient, and where the objects sought are ultimately unattainable. It is a somber and sad situation, but the cracks allow a glimpse of tenderness, the very same tenderness that occurs in some human relationships.

Steven Connor refers to a narcissistic domesticity as a Dickensian manner of evading the problems posed in this novel (143). The domestic affections described and fully realized are only part of the backdrop in this case. If this is the solution proposed, and although domestic affections and the acceptance of otherness are not a major part of the narrations of the great social utopias, these features are nevertheless quite significant. We are speaking of solutions and not of evasion, something shared with other narrators such as those created by George Eliot in *Middlemarch*, Charlotte Brontë in *Jane Eyre*, or even Mary Shelley in *Frankenstein*, where domestic happiness transcends the merely narcissistic, and becomes the basis for the acceptance of the other.

In *Great Expectations*, Dickens illustrates domestic happiness by depicting such nourishing and caring relationships as those involving Wemmick and his father, Wemmick and Miss Skiffins, whom he later marries, and Biddy and Joe. In contrast to the hero's unsatisfactory relationship with Estella, with all the unhappiness and lack of fulfillment it brings, this happiness transcends the individual sphere and becomes part of a greater, collective dream, as it does in the aforementioned works by women novelists for whom domesticity and reciprocity were tantamount to the great utopias conceived by men.

WORKS CITED

Balzac, Honoré de. *Le Père Goriot*. Paris: Gallimard—Pléiade (vol. III), 1976.

Connor, Steven. *Charles Dickens*. Oxford: Blackwell, 1985.

Dickens, Charles. *Great Expectations*. Godfrey Cave, ed. London: Penguin, 1964.

Ducrot, Oswald, and Tzvetan Todorov. *Diccionario Enciclopédico de las Ciencias del Lenguaje*. Mexico D.F.: Siglo XXI, 1984.

Esslin, Martin. *Brecht: A Choice of Evils*. London: Eyre and Spottiswoode, 1963.

Ewen, Frederic. *Bertold Brecht: His Life, His Art, and His Times*. London: Calder and Boyars, 1970.

Greimas, Algirdas J. *La semántica estructural: investigación metodológica*. Madrid, Gredos, 1971.

Lodge, David. *Nice Work*. New York: Viking, 1989.

———. *The Practice of Writing*. London: Secker and Warburg, 1996.

Orwell, George. *Selected Writings*. Oxford: Heinemann, 1989.

Propp, Vladimir. *Morfologia del Cuento*. Madrid: Fundamentos, 1985.

Rooke, Patrick. *The Age of Dickens*. London: Wayland, 1970.

Salabert, Pere. *De la Creatividad y el Neo-Kitsch: Meditaciones Postmodernas*. Montevideo: Vintén Editor, 1993.

Soriau, Etienne. *Les 200.000 situations dramatiques*. París, Flammarion, 1950.

Dickens in Latin America:
Borrioboola-Gha Revisited

Lindsey Cordery

When we read the later works of Dickens in Latin America today, we cannot ignore the striking resemblance between the social conditions described in his novels written 150 years ago, and conditions in today's Latin American countries. The distance that separates the first world from the third is vast: many of the social issues that Dickens denounced in his great mid-nineteenth century novels are still unresolved in Latin America in the twenty-first century. Dickens was a man of his time, when the British Empire was at its peak. He was aware, as we clearly see in the novels of this period, of the tremendous contradiction that in Britain, the richest country on earth, multitudes known as "the poor" barely managed to exist, in wretched conditions. Disraeli's denomination of this situation as the "Two Nations" in England, that of the Rich and that of the Poor, is apt. Over one hundred years later, in our twenty-first century world and in global terms, we are facing the same situation: two worlds that co-exist, the world of the Poor and the world of the Rich, just like Disraeli's two nations. Bearing in mind this context of globalization, I should like to suggest that in Latin America today one cannot read Dickens without an awareness of the nineteenth century British imperialist project, relating, in turn, this project to present—day imperialist projects at work in Latin America. This "against the grain" reading of a cultural icon like Dickens, a resisting, questioning reading of Dickens, a reading as a Latin American, from a Latin American rather than a European perspective, is, I believe, central to the issue of defining a Latin American, as different from a European, culture. European literature and culture in general are a part of

Latin American culture; however, many times we read, still today, as willing Ariels submissive to benevolently tyrannical Prosperos.

Between 1848 and 1861, Dickens published *Dombey and Son, David Copperfield, Bleak House, Hard Times, Little Dorrit, A Tale of Two Cities,* and *Great Expectations.* Edward Said has declared that the European mainstream novel of the nineteenth century "is a cultural form consolidating but also refining and articulating the authority of the status quo" (85–87). Following Said, Elleke Boehmer describes how "Empire enters the nineteenth century novel chiefly as a commodity, in images of riches and trade . . . [it] carried either the fascination or the fear of the forbidden. The Other could signify anything from irresistible delight to social unacceptability and instability, to moral pollution, nightmare and syphilis . . . [as, for example the case in *Jane Eyre* of] Bertha's madness [which] stems from the tormented sexuality of her Caribbean past" (25–27). Although Dickens's works question and probe deeply into the unjust social and administrative systems of his time, his "body of humanistic ideas co-existed . . . comfortably with imperialism," and his "narratives sanction a spatial moral order" (Said 96, 94).

In 1853, the year *Bleak House* was completed, the British Empire was reaching its zenith. Two years earlier, in 1851, Prince Albert had inaugurated the Great Exhibition at the Crystal Palace in London. The building was a huge glass and steel structure that had been built especially to harbor every kind of product from Britain and from the Empire. The show of the variety and exoticism of the products exhibited converted the Great Exhibition into a symbol for London, the capital of the world. This was a world where the greatness and the stability of the Empire were indubitable in spite of the many wars waged to sustain or expand it; however, in Britain, the heart of the Empire, social unrest was growing. The Chartist Movement was becoming increasingly important and virulent as the gulf between the "two nations" within Britain was becoming impossible to ignore. The "condition of England question"—the situation of the poor and the duty the wealthy classes had toward the poor—was incisively analyzed by Thomas Carlyle, one of the most charismatic personalities of his time. Carlyle's influence on his era, and on writers like Thackeray and, in particular, Dickens, was notable. Of a poor Calvinist family himself, Carlyle extolled in his numerous writings the moral duties of more affluent Englishmen towards the needy. Dickens's admiration for Carlyle and the friendship between them are documented in a rich correspondence (see Oddie 19–33 for comments on the correspondence and personal relationship; Carlyle's influence on *Hard Times* and *A Tale Of Two Cities,* has been studied in depth. Oddie, 41–85).

For Carlyle, the poor and the needy were incapable of thinking for themselves, or of organizing; therefore the moral duty of every Victorian gentleman was to do both for them. The poor, Carlyle affirmed, believed in their right to be guided by wiser men along the paths that these would assign them. In his "Chartism" Carlyle clearly describes what we might see as the Victorian construction of the Other: extremely ignorant, he cannot express clearly what his needs are; he needs someone to speak for him, resolve for him, and think for him; otherwise, the consequences could be dire: "Leave *them* to do? the thing they will *do, if so left*, is too frightful to think of!" (quoted by Oddie 116, my italics). This "Other" then, was to be the recipient of Victorian philanthropy, an essential aspect of middle-class evangelical Protestantism in the nineteenth century.

In *Bleak House*, Dickens depicts the terrible and pathetic worlds of some inhabitants of Disraeli's second nation, those poor described by Carlyle, recipients of philanthropy, the miserable inhabitants of London in the grim slum of Tom-all-Alone's, and in particular, the movingly-portrayed Jo the crossing sweeper, versions of whom are found throughout Latin America today. Crucially in this novel, the forgotten and the marginalized are secretly linked, sometimes through sordid ties, to the highest social classes. Dickens weaves a complex web where everything is related, all the characters and the events being part of the great cold, sad house, the Bleak House that England is, despite its glorious Empire. This view of England as one whole achieves a dramatic rendering of poverty and misery in the novel which could be descriptions of parts of twenty-first-century Latin America. If we go back to the idea I mentioned earlier, that of two worlds today instead of Disraeli's two nations, then our globalized world would indeed find a just representation in an image like Dickens's "Bleak House"—a whole Bleak World where hidden links and secret agreements are intertwined to form the ugly side of globalization.

Dickens's commitment to social justice is clearly expressed in *Bleak House*. Philanthropic works alleviate poverty and social injustice, but charity, according to Dickens, must begin at home. In *Bleak House* Dickens presents a controversial character: Mrs. Jellyby and her "telescopic philanthropy". Mrs. Jellyby is a lady of forty or fifty years of age whose life is dedicated to philanthropic projects for the colonies, and she pays no attention whatsoever to her household tasks as a wife and mother. Instead of looking after her home, she is dedicated to the Borrioboola-Gha project, telling us that " The African project at present employs my whole time . . . I am happy to say it is advancing. We hope . . . to have from a hundred and fifty to two hundred healthy families cultivating coffee and educating the natives of Borrioboola-Gha on the left bank of the Niger" (IV, 36).

In the character of Mrs. Jellyby, Dickens presents a caricature of what he sees as misdirected philanthropy. It would be far more important, he suggests, for Mrs. Jellyby to set her own house in order before looking after foreign homes or causes. As a character, she was much discussed by readers of the time. Many were in favor of this clearly humorous presentation of this woman

who, with her ridiculous telescopic philanthropy, disregards her home; others
saw in her an attack against the benevolent missionary institutions who were
shouldering what Kipling would call "the white man's burden": the responsibility of taking care of the natives, those "others" that the Victorian Empire
saw as its duty to educate, evangelize, heal, and in many cases punish if this
benevolence was resisted—the Victorians dealt zealously with their "poor"
at home and with their "natives" abroad.

An evangelical conscience then, of the Victorian middleclass pointed out
a clear duty: that of "saving" the natives of the colonies through projects
such as the Borrioboola-Gha project. What this ridiculing name, similar to
others used to designate the "natives" and the places they lived shows, is
the humorous and obviously derogatory category they were assigned (like
Sambo, Quashee, or Boggly Wallah, for example).

Theories of racial and cultural supremacy were beyond dispute at the time.
Both Dickens and Carlyle were convinced that philanthropy should be aimed
at the British workman and not at the "dark-skinned" or "black" races.
With the passing of time, Dickens became increasingly intolerant. As a young
man he toured the United States and was moved by the way slaves were
treated; however, in 1853 he wrote an article for *Household Words* titled
"The Noble Savage," which has many similarities with an essay Carlyle
wrote, "Occasional Discourse on the Nigger Question." The "nigger," according to Dickens, is dirty and wild, a savage animal; vain and bothersome,
he is the antithesis of civilization and progress. Both Dickens and Carlyle
believed that the black people in the West Indies had stopped working after
emancipation (in 1833), and that it was the negative impact of emancipation
that led to the downfall of West Indian economy. Because the black people
refused to work as they should and refused to recognize white men as their
superiors, their spiritual condition, Carlyle and Dickens believed, was worse
than when they were slaves. Black people should be treated with justice,
Carlyle said, but if they refused to work, the benevolent whip should be used,
to improve their spiritual well-being. (see Oddie 136–42).

Dickens's and Carlyle's view regarding black people was shared by the
vast majority of the Victorian middle class, and was intensified as a result of
the Indian Mutiny in 1857 and the rebellion in Jamaica in 1865. Both were
fiercely repressed, and whole populations were punished. When Dickens,
before these events, presents Borrioboola-Gha, with its comical-sounding,
derogatory name, as a project, it serves to make Mrs. Jellyby's efforts appear
absurd and wrong. In Victorian novels, including Dickens's, the remoter
corners of the Empire had another function, besides being recipients of philanthropy: they were sources of commerce and wealth. In *Dombey and Son*, for
instance, this is made very clear from the start: "The Earth was made for
Dombey & Son to trade in . . . Rivers and seas were formed to float their

ships . . . Stars and planets circled their orbits, to preserve inviolate a system of which they were the centre . . . " (I, 50). This, clearly, is the ideology of any form of imperialism.

In the same novel, Walter Gay leaves for Barbados in order to seek his fortune, promising to send back turtles, limes, and ginger. The West Indies appear in *Barnaby Rudge*, in the tale "A Schoolboy's Story," in *The Pickwick Papers,* and in several stories and articles in *Household Words,* as a place where fortunes can be made and exotic products obtained. Alternatively, remote outposts of the Empire were places where people could resolve, purge, or receive punishment for their transgressions, be they moral (sexual) or social. Micawber and Little Em'ly in *David Copperfield*, for example, readily come to mind.

In mainstream novels, such as those I have mentioned by Dickens, the Empire project constructs the "Other" simply by taking for granted the moral integrity and the superiority and power of Europe, with the corresponding view of an amoral, intellectually inferior, weak "native." In presenting this view through works of literature, writers were not only exercising political or economic power; they were also seeking control of the imagination. Through works of fiction, as in actual fact, the Europeans imposed their order on, and appropriated, far-off, complex, strange places. So, "[t]he objective of colonial discourse," as Homi Bhabha says, "is to construe the colonized as a population of degenerate types on the basis of racial origin, in order to justify conquest and establish systems of administration and instruction" (70).

This colonialist discourse is not explicit in nineteenth-century novels, but in *Mansfield Park*, for example, the family wealth comes from a sugar cane plantation in Antigua; in *Jane Eyre,* the madwoman Bertha Mason comes from the Caribbean. It is only towards the end of the twentieth century that post-colonialist readings will make the connections explicit. Significantly, the largest number of novels produced in Europe in the second half of the nine-teenth century came from Britain; we might say that the consolidation of British imperialism, in cultural and imaginary terms, was carried out through the novels of the period.

In the colonies, then, the inhabitants learned to view the world and them-selves from the British optic. When the British colonies in the Caribbean obtained their independence around 1960, and in the process that led to inde-pendence (and after), they discovered that they had to seek cultural models that were different from the British in order to construct an identity of their own, one that would exalt and celebrate their African origin.

Kamau Brathwaite observes that, before independence, the educational system recognized and kept the language of the conqueror, of the planter, of the officer, of the Anglican priest (Ashcroft, Griffiths and Tiffin 310). In the Caribbean, Shakespeare, George Eliot, Jane Austen, Charles Dickens, that is,

the literature and the literary models of their British education had little to
do with Caribbean geography or history. The people knew the kings and
queens of England and the stories of the English novelists better than their
own. Children of the Caribbean would draw pictures of snow and of fair-
haired children and write underneath "Snow is falling on the sugar-cane
fields," so that snow on the sugar-cane fields became an emblem of cultural
confusion and the imposition of British culture, with its Dickensian white
Christmases among black people in the tropics. (Ashcroft, Griffiths and Tiffin
310, 311).

In 1933, in the Trinidadian *The Beacon*, Albert Gomes wrote a kind of
manifesto that attempted to describe what a West Indian literature would
be like:

> It is important . . . that we break away as far as possible from the English
> tradition; and the fact that some of us are still slaves to Scott and Dickens is
> merely because we lack the necessary artistic individuality and sensibility in
> order to see how incongruous the tradition is . . . the sooner we throw off the
> veneer of culture . . . the better for our artistic aims . . . we are still slaves to
> English culture and tradition.   (Qtd. in Donnell and Welsh 113)

Around 1930 or 1940 there appeared in the English Caribbean what might
be termed a West Indian aesthetic linked to a cultural identity project. Today
the literature of the English Caribbean, like that of all Latin America, has
appropriated and modified imperialist narratives. New stories are written and
the stories belonging to the colonial past re-written. It is by reading against
the grain, subversively, and appropriating narratives (such as *The Tempest* in
multiple versions in Latin America), that people creatively and critically
appropriate a culture, legitimately their own, forging a clearly defined identity,
where past and present are integrated.

A hundred and fifty years ago the world was full of Borrioboola-Ghas, and
projects which, in various ways, consolidated the status quo of Empire. In
the postcolonialist globalized world we live in today, the projects to grow
coffee and educate the natives of the left bank of the Niger, or south of the
Rio Grande, are surely still with us. We might then ask, Why do we read
Dickens in Latin America today, and answer easily: Dickens is a great writer,
a creative artist of genius, whose powerful treatments of universal themes of
kindness and cruelty, greed and generosity, and the need for parental love,
are still current today. These are some of the reasons why we read Dickens,
but in Latin America, another question must be considered: not why we read
Dickens, but *how* we read Dickens in Latin America today, and in answering
it, I believe that we cannot disregard contexts: the context of the Victorian
Empire and the present context of globalization.

WORKS CITED

Ashcroft, Bill, Gareth Griffiths and Helen Tiffin. *The Post-colonial Studies Reader*. London: Routledge 2001.

Bhabha, Homi. *The Location of Culture*. London: Routledge, 1994.

Boehmer, Elleker. *Colonial and Postcolonial Literature*. Oxford: Oxford UP, 1995.

Dickens, Charles. *Bleak House*. London: J. M. Dent, 1994.

———. *Dombey and Son*. London: Penguin, 1988.

Donnell, Alison, and Sarah Lawson Welsh. *The Routledge Reader in Caribbean Literature*. London: Routledge, 1996.

Oddie, William. *Dickens and Carlyle. The Question of Influence*. London: Centenary, 1972.

Said, Edward. *Culture and Imperialism*. London: Chatto and Windus, 1993.

INDEX

(Page numbers in *italics* represent illustrations)